Summary of Contents

Build Your Own Web Site The Right Way Using HTML & CSS

by Ian Lloyd

Build Your Own Web Site The Right Way Using HTML & CSS

by Ian Lloyd

Copyright © 2006 SitePoint Pty. Ltd.

Expert Reviewer: Marc A Garrett
Managing Editor: Simon Mackie
Technical Editor: Matthew Magain
Technical Director: Kevin Yank
Printing History:
  First Edition: April 2006

Editor: Georgina Laidlaw
Index Editor: Bill Johncocks
Cover Design: Jess Mason
Cover Layout: Alex Walker
Latest Update: February 2007

Published by SitePoint Pty. Ltd.

424 Smith Street Collingwood
VIC Australia 3066.
Web: www.sitepoint.com
Email: business@sitepoint.com

ISBN 978-0-9752402-9-8
Printed and bound in the United States of America

About the Author

Ian Lloyd is a web designer and developer who believes passionately in the importance of web standards. He is a member of the Web Standards Project (http://webstandards.org/) and has spoken at several high profile web conferences, including South By Southwest (SXSW) in Austin, Texas and @media in London. Unlike many of his peers, Ian does not run his own company—or work for Yahoo!—but remains a "salary man", working for Nationwide Building Society in the UK (where he constantly harps on about web standards, accessibility and usability to anyone with a sympathetic ear!).

Ian lives in Swindon, UK, a town that is known only for two things:

❏ the famous "magic roundabout"—a mega roundabout that comprises five individual but joined roundabouts

❏ for being that place from the television show *The Office* (thus making it second in dullness only to Slough)

That said, Ian does his best to get out of Swindon in his treasured air-cooled VW camper van (http://vwkombi.com/) when he's not glued to the laptop for one reason or another.

Ian is married to Manda, who really doesn't get the Volkswagen fascination but puts up with it regardless.

About The Expert Reviewer

Marc A. Garrett was born in Japan and raised in Stone Mountain, Georgia. After receiving a Bachelor of Arts at the University of Georgia, he earned a Juris Doctor at the American University Washington College of Law. He has co-authored two computer books, published by Macromedia Press and Apress; served as technical editor for several titles from O'Reilly and New Riders; and has written for Digital Web Magazine. Mr. Garrett specializes in web-based applications written in ColdFusion, PHP, and ASP.NET.

About The Technical Editor

Before joining the SitePoint team as a technical editor, Matthew Magain worked as a software developer for IBM and also spent several years teaching English in Japan. He is the organizer for Melbourne's Web Standards Group (http://webstandardsgroup.org/), and enjoys swimming, listening to classical jazz and drinking Coopers Pale Ale, though not all at the same time. Matthew lives with his wife Kimberley and their daughter Sophia.

About SitePoint

SitePoint specializes in publishing fun, practical and easy-to-understand content for web professionals. Visit http://www.sitepoint.com/ to access our books, newsletters, articles and community forums.

For Manda, my "better half".
This book would not have been
possible without your continued
support. All my love, Lloydi.

Table of Contents

Build Your Own Web Site The Right Way Using HTML & CSS

Preface

Congratulations on buying this book. Oh, wait a minute—perhaps you haven't yet. Perhaps you've just picked up the book in your local bookshop, and are trying to decide whether it's right for you. Why should this be the book that makes it into your shopping basket? The answer can be found in the title of the book: it's all about getting things right the first time, not learning bad habits—bad habits that you have to *un*-learn at a later date—for the purposes of getting a quick result.

Let's take a step back for a moment, and look at another skill that many people learn at some point in their lives: learning to drive. Apologies if that particular experience is *also* new to you, but stick with me. For many people, first driving lessons can be very confusing—you've got to figure out which pedals to press, in what order, and manage to get out of the driving school car park without hitting the other students. Meanwhile, other more experienced people just get into their cars, start the engine, and drive from A to B without even really thinking about what they're doing. These drivers may have picked up a few bad habits along the way, but if they learned with a proper driving instructor, the chances are that they were taught properly from the beginning, following a strict set of rules and guidelines to ensure they stay safe.

The driving instructor tells you to check your mirrors diligently, observe speed limits, and avoid cutting corners (literally as well as metaphorically!). Imagine, though, if the instructor told you not to worry about the speed limit signs, to "put your foot down" because the road is clear, or told you that the one-way sign "wasn't all that important at that time of night." It'd be a miracle if you passed your driving test, and the chances are that those bad habits would stay with you (so long as you could manage to keep your license).

Learning to build web pages can be a bit like that.

I've been designing and building web sites for around eight years now, but I can clearly remember the joy of creating my first site. Admittedly, in hindsight, it was a pretty nasty-looking web site, but it achieved the goal at the time—I had published something, and I was able to create it with the bare minimum of tools. It gave me an enormous sense of achievement, and made me want to learn more and create even better web sites.

At the time, there weren't that many books that really seemed to what I wanted, but I lapped up everything I could find, learning some tricks from books, and getting other ideas from visiting web sites. But then I discovered that I'd been doing it all wrong. The books I had learned from had given me what later turned out to be poor advice, and the web sites I'd visited had themselves learnt from the same sources and made use of similar bad techniques. So, what had gone wrong?

In the early days of the web, when people first started properly to embrace the technology, to publish homepages, and to develop online corporate presences for their companies, they all realized fairly quickly that the medium was quite limiting. Necessity is the mother of invention, though. People began to coax out of their web pages tricks and displays that were never intended by the technologies they used, and the browsers helped them along the way by adding features that offered even more opportunities for this kind of behavior.

Numerous books have been written on the topics of web design and programming, as have many free tutorials that you can read on the 'Net. Many of them were written during those heady years, and were based on what seemed like best practices back then, but their authors were constrained by browsers that often rendered the same well-designed pages in vastly different ways. This meant that the tutorials' authors needed to resort to abusing various features of those browsers, such as using data tables to lay out pages. This certainly got many people building their first web pages, but it ensured that bad habits were ingrained at an early stage, and many people are still using these bad practices years later.

Web developers the world over have learnt bad habits (myself included) and must now try to un-learn them all. There's no longer a need for these practices—they often produce pages that are inflexible, slow to download, and difficult to maintain, but like the badly taught driver who insists on flouting the rules because it's worked for him so far, many developers find those outdated habits difficult to break.

I saw the light many years ago, and have tried to educate as many people as possible since. But for the eager beginner, those same old books are still peddling the same bad old ideas. This just *has* to stop. And it stops now.

You're not going to learn any bad habits in this book. Not one.

In this book, you'll learn the right way to do things. If there's a wrong way to do things—a way that cuts corners to save time but encourages bad techniques—we won't even tell you about it. Not even as a "by the way, you might try this..." You won't need to avert your eyes—we'll take care of that for you!

What is a Browser?

If you use Microsoft Windows, the browser is probably what you know as the "little blue e on the desktop" (shown in Figure 1), but is commonly called Internet Explorer. The majority of people don't stray beyond using this program for the purposes of viewing web pages—for many, Internet Explorer *is* the Internet.

Figure 1. Internet Explorer—the "little blue e on the desktop"

Internet Explorer (or **IE**, as we'll refer to it from now on) is the most commonly used browser, largely because Microsoft included it as part of the Windows operating system as far back as Windows 95 (this was later to come back and haunt Microsoft—it became the catalyst for a massive anti-trust trial which ruled that the company had stifled competition by bundling IE with the operating system to the exclusion of all others).

However, there are other browsers that you can use instead of IE. Currently riding an ever-increasing wave of popularity is Firefox,[1] a small, speedy program that has a number of attractive features that aren't available in IE (at the time of writing), and handles the features of some web pages better than IE can. It's also available for Windows, Mac OS X, and Linux, while the latest versions of IE are only available for Windows. The screen shots you'll see in this book were taken using Firefox on Windows XP, unless stated otherwise. We recommend that you download a copy of Firefox for the purposes of working through the exercises in this book.

Alternatively, you might like to try another browser that supports web standards well—check out BrowseHappy[2] for some more ideas.

Not interested in a different browser? Well, you can use IE, as indeed the majority of web users still do. In fact, you can be sure that everything you read here will work in all recent browsers without any real hiccups.

---

[1] http://www.mozilla.com/firefox/
[2] http://browsehappy.com/

Who Should Read this Book?

Does this sound like you?

❑ an absolute beginner—at least as far as creating web pages goes

❑ confident with using a computer, but not necessarily a "power user"

❑ someone who uses the Web a lot, enjoys other people's web sites, and would like to create your own

Perhaps you have a hobby that you want to tell the world about, or you want to start a web site for a community that you belong to (be that a knitting circle or remote-control car racing club)

❑ quickly put off by the techno-babble that computer people tend to speak

When you have conversations with your more tech-savvy relatives about a problem you're having with your computer—perhaps you've been struck down by a computer virus—do you find a lot of the jargon goes over your head?

❑ perhaps a little daunted about learning this new skill, but keen to learn (with some friendly hand-holding)

If any of the above descriptions strikes a chord with you, then this is the book to put in your shopping cart—we'll ease you in gently, and have you building web pages like a pro in no time!

Don't worry if you don't understand the terminology that your 15-year-old nephew (or cousin!) keeps spouting when you ask him about building web sites. I've assumed no prior knowledge of any of these terms, and I'll be guiding you all the way through the process of creating a web site from scratch. By the end of this book, you'll know how to build the site, how to secure hosting, how to promote the site, and how to keep it running once it's live.

The best part is this: what you learn in this book, you'll never have to un-learn. You'll be learning how to build sites the right way from the get-go.

What you'll Learn from this Book

By the time that you finish reading this book, and trying out the exercises contained within, you'll be able to build a complete web site—the right way—without incurring any costs for expensive software or web hosting.

Using an example web site, I'll guide you through the process of developing web pages from scratch. From these humble beginnings, great things will evolve! By the end of the book, you'll be able to create a web site that includes the following features:

❏ easy-to-use navigation

❏ a professional-looking site header

❏ a regularly updated news/events section

❏ a "Contact Us" page

❏ tables—the presentation of data in neatly organized grids

❏ attractive forms

❏ a simple image gallery

❏ a search engine that covers our site, as well as related sites

❏ simple statistics that you can use to see who's using your site, how they found your site (e.g. from search engines), and so on

You'll also learn how to manage your web site effectively, without it becoming a chore or getting too technical. I'll show you how you can:

❏ Get your own dot-com (or dot-net or dot-org) web address.

❏ Find somewhere to host your web site.

❏ Upload your files to your web site.

❏ Get feedback from visitors while avoiding spam emails.

How you'll Learn to Build your Web Site

This book will take you through each new topic using a step-by-step approach. It provides a mixture of examples and practical exercises that will soon have you feeling confident enough to try a little **HTML** for yourself.

HTML, Markup, CSS... Welcome to your First Bits of Jargon!

From here on in, you're going to see these phrases more and more. But what do they mean?

HTML   HTML stands for HyperText Markup Language. It's the primary language that's used to create web pages, so you'll come to know it very well through the course of this book. We'll be using the latest version of HTML, which is called XHTML.

markup   Imagine, if you will, that you're a newspaper editor. You've been passed a news story, but the text—from the heading through to the conclusion—is all the same size, and the headings, paragraphs, quotes, and other features of the text are not clearly indicated. It's just one big block of text. For starters, you'd probably want to emphasize the headline, maybe by displaying it in bold or italic text (or in all caps with an exclamation mark if you were working for a tabloid). As an editor, you'd probably grab a pen and start scribbling annotations on the print-out—an "h" here to signify a heading, "p"s here, there, and everywhere to show where paragraphs start and end, and "q"s to denote quotations.

This is essentially what markup is—a set of simple tags that suggest the structure of a document (this section is a heading, paragraph, a quote, etc.). We'll cover the various tags that HTML uses in detail a little later.

Markup isn't Computer Code

Markup is not the same thing as "code." Often, people incorrectly refer to markup as code, but code goes beyond the basic abilities of markup. With code, you can create programs, and do more dynamic things with your web page, while markup simply deals with the page's structure. So, if you want to impress your friends and relatives, refer to markup rather than code. See, we told you we'd teach you good habits!

CSS   CSS stands for Cascading Style Sheets. We'll be using a combination of HTML and CSS to create web sites. CSS is a language that lets you control how your web pages look, but we'll get into that in more detail later. For now, it's important that you know what the abbreviation stands for.

Building the Example Site

Each example that's presented in this book will be backed up with a sample of the markup you need to write, and a screen shot that shows how the results should look.

Each example is complete: nothing's missing. You'll see the picture build gradually, so you won't be left trying to guess how the example web site got to the point it's at. The files we'll use in all the examples are provided in a separate code archive (described in more detail in a moment).

What you Can Expect from the Example Web Site

- ❑ a fun web site project that will be built up through the chapters

- ❑ a complete web site that demonstrates all the features you're likely to need in your own web site

- ❑ all the XHTML and CSS used to progress the site through each chapter—in a single download

You can pick up the project at any point, so you don't need to worry about mistakes you might have made in previous chapters' exercises!

What this Book Won't Tell You

While it might be tempting to cram everything into one book and claim that the reader will learn everything in 24 hours, the honest truth is that this is not necessarily the right approach for everyone.

This book won't try to force-feed you everything there is to know about creating web pages; instead, it focuses on the most useful aspects that you'll find yourself using over and over again.

This book does not cover:

❑ JavaScript

❑ other programming languages, such as ASP or PHP

❑ advanced CSS techniques

❑ search engine optimization techniques

By the time you've finished this book and have had a chance to tackle your own web site, you might want to take the next steps to increasing your site-building knowledge. We'll be recommending next steps where appropriate throughout the book, and suggesting other resources that you might like to check out.

So, this is where the introductory piffle ends and the process of learning begins—learning how to build web sites the *right* way. So step this way, ladies and gentlemen...

What's in this Book?

Chapter 1: *Setting Up Shop*
In this chapter, we'll make sure that you have all the tools you're going to need to build your web site. I'll explain where you can get the right tools—all of them for free! By the end of the chapter, you'll be ready to get cracking on your first web site.

Chapter 2: *Your First Web Pages*
In this chapter, we'll learn what makes a web page. We'll explore XHTML, understand the basic requirements of every web page, and investigate the common elements that you'll see on many web pages. Then, you'll start to create pages yourself. In fact, by the end of this chapter, you'll have the beginnings of your first web site.

Chapter 3: *Adding Some Style*
In this chapter, we'll start to add a bit of polish to the web pages we created in Chapter 2. You'll learn what CSS is, and why it's a good thing, before putting it into action for yourself. As the chapter progresses, you'll see the

project web site start to take shape as we apply background and foreground colors, change the appearance of text, and make web links that have been visited look different from those that haven't.

Chapter 4: *Shaping Up with CSS*

This chapter builds on the previous chapter's introduction to the color and text-styling abilities of CSS to reveal what CSS can do for border styles and page layouts in general. First, we'll review the full range of border effects that you can apply to elements such as headings and paragraphs. We'll experiment with dotted borders, and big, bold borders, as well as some slightly more subtle effects. In the second half of the chapter, we'll learn how it's possible to use CSS to position the elements of a web page—including blocks of navigation—anywhere on the screen.

Chapter 5: *Picture this! Using Images on your Web Site*

As the chapter title suggests, this one's all about images. We'll discover the difference between inline images and background images, and look into the issue of making images accessible for blind or visually impaired people (blind people surf too!). We'll also learn how to adjust pictures to suit your web site using the software that we downloaded in Chapter 1. Then we get practical, putting all this knowledge together to create a photo gallery for the project site.

Chapter 6: *Tables: Tools for Organizing Data*

In this chapter, we'll learn when tables should be used and, perhaps more importantly, when they should *not* be used. Once we've got the basics out of the way, I'll show how you can breathe life into an otherwise dull-looking table—again, using CSS—to make it much more visually appealing.

Chapter 7: *Forms: Interacting with your Audience*

In Chapter 7, we learn all about forms—what they're used for, what's required to build a form, and what you can do with the data you collect through your form. I'll teach you what the different form elements—such as text inputs, checkboxes, and so on—do, and show you how to use CSS to make a form look more attractive. Finally—and this is something that other books may not explain—I'll show you how you can use a free web service to have the data that's entered into your form emailed to you.

Chapter 8: *Getting your Web Site Online*

It's all well and good to build a web site for fun, but you need a way for people to see it—that's what this chapter is all about. We'll learn about hosting plans, discuss the pros and cons of using free services, and look at the tools that you'll need in order to transfer your files from your computer at home to a web server for the world to see.

Chapter 9: *Adding a Blog to your Web Site*

Blogging's one of the best ways to keep your web site's content fresh and ever-changing. In this chapter, you'll learn what a blog is (that's always a good start), and how you can set one up for yourself. We'll also spend some time making sure it looks consistent with the rest of your web site.

Chapter 10: *Pimp my Site: Cool Stuff you can Add for Free*

You've heard of the MTV program *Pimp My Ride*, right? No? Well, every week, the guys on this show take an everyday car and transform it—with some well-placed and carefully executed cosmetic touches—into a real head-turner of a vehicle. And that's this chapter's aim for your web site! You'll discover that there are all kinds of tools, plugins, and add-ons that you can build into to your web site to make it even more useful for you and your visitors. Among the tools on offer we'll find site search facilities, statistics programs, and online discussion forums.

Chapter 11: *Where to Now? What you Can Learn Next*

In this final chapter, we summarize the skills that you've learned in this book, then consider your options for learning more. I'll recommend web sites that I feel can take you to that next level, and books that really should be on your bookshelf (or rather, open on your desk next to your computer!), in an effort to ensure that you continue to learn the good stuff once you've put this book down.

Appendix A: *XHTML Reference*

This appendix lists all of the XHTML elements that are available for use in your web pages. It's not intended to replace the official W3C reference, but it does provide detailed information about each element and how it can be used. The appendix also includes an example of how each element can be applied within markup, so you should find it to be a handy reference not just as you work through this book, but in the web projects you tackle in future.

The Book's Web Site

Located at http://www.sitepoint.com/books/html1/, the web site supporting this book will give you access to the following facilities:

The Code Archive

As you progress through the text, you'll note a number of references to the code archive. This is a downloadable ZIP archive that contains complete code for all the examples presented in the book. It also includes a copy of the Bubble Under web site, which we use as an example throughout the book.

Updates and Errata

No book is perfect, and I expect that watchful readers will be able to spot at least one or two mistakes before the end of this one. The Errata page, at http://www.sitepoint.com/books/html1/errata.php on the book's web site, will always have the latest information about known typographical and code errors, and necessary updates for new browser releases and versions of web standards.

The SitePoint Forums

If you'd like to communicate with me or anyone else on the SitePoint publishing team about this book, you should join theSitePoint Forums.[3] In fact, you should join that community even if you *don't* want to talk to us, because there are a lot of fun and experienced web designers and developers hanging out there. It's a good way to learn new stuff, get questions answered (unless you really enjoy being on the phone with some company's tech support line for a couple of hours at a time), and just have fun.

The SitePoint Newsletters

In addition to books like this one, SitePoint offers free email newsletters.

The SitePoint Tech Times covers the latest news, product releases, trends, tips, and techniques for all technical aspects of web development. The long-running *SitePoint Tribune* is a biweekly digest of the business and moneymaking aspects of the web. Whether you're a freelance developer looking for tips to score that dream contract, or a marketing major striving to keep abreast of changes to the major search engines, this is the newsletter for you. *The SitePoint Design View* is a monthly compilation of the best in web design. From new CSS layout methods to subtle

---

[3] http://www.sitepoint.com/forums/

Photoshop techniques, SitePoint's chief designer shares his years of experience in its pages.

Browse the archives or sign up to any of SitePoint's free newsletters at http://www.sitepoint.com/newsletter/.

Your Feedback

If you can't find your answer through the forums, or you wish to contact me for any other reason, the best place to write is books@sitepoint.com. We have a well-manned email support system set up to track your inquiries, and if our support staff are unable to answer your question, they send it straight to me. Suggestions for improvement as well as notices of any mistakes you may find are especially welcome.

Acknowledgements

While writing a book sometimes seems like quite a solitary process, the truth is that there are a lot of people who indirectly guide—or have guided—the hands that type the words on these pages. None of this would have been possible had I not been pointed in the direction of influential and persuasive web sites like webmonkey.com, whose CSS tutorial first made me see the light, and individuals such as Jeffrey Zeldman, Molly Holzschlag, and Eric Meyer, whose pioneering work has benefited me (and many others) greatly. However, if I were to list the names of all the people who have inspired me in way, shape, or form in the last few years, this acknowledgments section would end up looking more like an index! You folks know who you are, keep up the good work!

I would like to acknowledge the work undertaken by the Web Standards Project (of which I am also a member, albeit a pretty inactive one for the last couple of years!), and give a little shout-out to my fellow "Britpackers"—wear those Union Jack pants with pride, folks!

Thanks to all those at SitePoint who have helped me in the crafting of this book, particularly to Simon Mackie, my main point of contact and sounding board, and my expert reviewer, Marc Garrett—your comments were always on target. Thanks to Matthew Magain, who tech edited the book—I hope I didn't leave you much to correct or find fault with! And then of course there's Georgina Laidlaw, who ensured that any peculiarly British turns of phrases were removed, despite my best efforts to sneak a few in.

Finally, thanks to Manda for putting up with me when deadlines loomed and I all but shut myself off from civilization to get the chapters in on time. Social life? Oh that! I remember… At those times it seemed like it would never end, but finally we can both see the fruits of my labour. Now, if only it were something she'd actually want to read!

Conventions Used in this Book

You'll notice that we've used certain typographic and layout styles throughout this book to signify different types of information. Look out for the following:

Markup Samples

Any markup—be that HTML or CSS—will be displayed using a fixed-width font like so:

File: **webpage.html (excerpt)**

```
<h1>A perfect summer's day</h1>
<p>It was a lovely day for a walk in the park. The birds were
    singing and the kids were all back at school.</p>
```

Menus

When you need to select something from a menu, it'll be written as File > Save; this means "select the Save option from the File menu."

Tips, Notes, and Warnings

Hey, you!

Tips will give you helpful little pointers.

Ahem, Excuse me…

Notes are useful asides that are related—but not critical—to the topic at hand. Think of them as extra tidbits of information.

Make Sure you Always…

…pay attention to these important points.

Watch Out!

Warnings will highlight any gotchas that are likely to trip you up along the way.

1

Setting Up Shop

Before you dive in and start to build your web site, we need to take a little time to get your computer set up and ready for the work that lies ahead. That's what this chapter is all about: ensuring that you have all the tools you need installed and ready to go.

Tooling Up

If you were to look at the hundreds of computing books for sale in your local bookstore, you could be forgiven for thinking that you'd need to invest in a lot of different programs to build a web site. However, the reality is that most of the tools you need are probably sitting there on your computer, tucked away somewhere you wouldn't think to look for them. And if ever you don't have the tool for the job, there's almost certain to be one or more free programs available that can handle the task.

We've made the assumption that you're already on the Internet—your web site wouldn't be of much use without it! And, though it's not essential, it will also be handy if you have a broadband internet connection. Don't worry if you don't have broadband: it won't affect any of the tasks we'll undertake in this book. It will, however, mean that some of the suggested downloads may take a while to load onto your computer, but you probably knew that already.

Planning, Schmanning

At this point, it might be tempting to look at your motives for building a web site. Do you have a project plan? What objectives do you have for the site?

While you probably have some objectives, and some idea of how long you want to spend creating your site, we're going to gloss over the nitty-gritty of project planning to some extent. This is not to say that project planning isn't an important aspect to consider, but we're going to assume that because you've picked up a book entitled *Build Your Own Web Site The Right Way*, you probably want to just get right into the building part.

As this is your first web site, and will be a fairly simple one, we can overlook some of the more detailed aspects of site planning. Later, once you've learned—and moved beyond—the basics of building a site, you might feel ready to tackle a larger, more technically challenging site. When that time comes, proper planning will be a far more important aspect of the job. But now, let's gear up to build our first, simple site.

The Basic Tools you Need

As I mentioned earlier, many of the tools you'll need to build your first web site are already on your computer. So, what tools *do* you need?

☐ The primary—and most basic—tool that you'll need is a **text editor**. You'll use this to write your web pages.

☐ Once you've written a web page, you can see how it looks in a **web browser**.

☐ Finally, when you're happy with your new web page, you can put it on the Internet using an **FTP client**. Using FTP can be a little complicated, but thankfully you won't need to do it too often. We'll discuss FTP clients in detail in Chapter 8.

You've already got most of these programs on your computer, so let's go find them.

Windows Basic Tools

Your Text Editor: Notepad

The first tool we'll consider is the text editor. Windows comes with a very simple text editor called Notepad. Many professional web designers who use complicated software packages first started out many years ago using Notepad; indeed, many professionals who have expensive pieces of software that should be time-savers still resort to using Notepad for many tasks. Why? Well, because it's so simple, little can go wrong with it. Bells and whistles are definitely not on the menu here.

You can find Notepad in the Start menu: go to Start > All Programs > Accessories.

 Tip

Shortcut to Notepad

To save yourself navigating to this location each and every time you want to open Notepad, create a shortcut on your desktop. With the Start menu open to display Notepad's location, hold down the **Ctrl** key, click and hold down the mouse button, then drag the Notepad icon to your desktop. When you release the mouse button, a shortcut to the application will appear on your desktop, as in Figure 1.1.

Figure 1.1. Creating a shortcut to Notepad

Notepad

Notepad is the simplest of simple applications. See Figure 1.2 for a depiction of its fancy interface (that was sarcasm, by the way).

Figure 1.2. Notepad: a contender for the world's ugliest program?

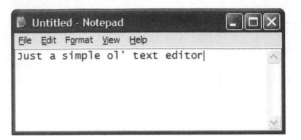

Your Web Browser: Internet Explorer

Once you've created a web page using Notepad, you'll need a way to view the results of your handiwork. You'll remember that, in the preface to this book, we mentioned Internet Explorer. Well, that's your viewer! As Figure 1.3 shows, Internet Explorer sits right there in the Programs folder, and also lurks on your desktop.

Figure 1.3. Internet Explorer: there's no hiding this baby away!

Mac OS X Basic Tools

Like Windows, the Mac operating system (specifically OS X; we won't be looking at previous versions of the Mac OS) has a number of tools that you can use straight out of the box. These tools are virtually equivalent to the Windows programs mentioned above.

Your Text Editor: TextEdit

While Windows has Notepad, the Mac has TextEdit, which can be found in the Applications folder, as Figure 1.4 illustrates.

Figure 1.4. TextEdit comes as part of Mac OS X's default installation

Unlike Notepad, TextEdit works as what we call a "rich text editor" by default, which means we can work with fonts, make text bold and italic, and so on. However, we want to work with TextEdit as a plain text editor, so you'll need to fiddle with some of TextEdit's preferences. Start TextEdit, then select TextEdit > Preferences from the menu to bring up the Preferences screen. Select Plain text within New Document Attributes, then close the Preferences screen. The next time you create a new file in TextEdit, it will be a plain text document.

Your Web Browser: Safari

Internet Explorer is also available for Mac, but was abandoned by Microsoft when Apple began to make its own web browser, Safari, so it's considerably outdated. You can usually find Safari in the dock, but you can also access it through the Applications folder, as Figure 1.5 illustrates.

Figure 1.5. Internet Explorer and Safari are available via Mac's Applications folder

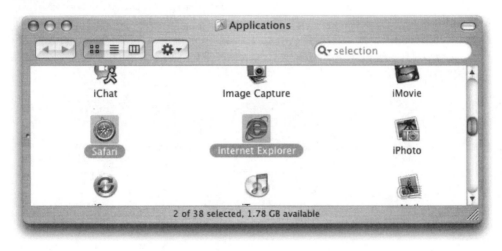

Stick it in the Dock

Tip

Just as you can drag shortcuts to programs onto the Windows desktop, you can add programs to the dock in Mac OS X (the dock is the bar of icons at the bottom of your screen). To add a program to the dock, just drag it from the Applications folder onto the dock, and presto! The application is now easily accessible whenever you need it.

Beyond the Basic Tools

You can certainly make a good start using the tools mentioned above. However, once you're dealing with a handful of web pages and other resources, you may want to go beyond these basic tools. We'll show you how to use some slightly more advanced applications later in the book.

Countless other text editors and web browsers are available for download, and many of them are free. Obviously, we don't have time to describe each and every one of them, so I've settled on a few options that have worked for me in the past, and which you might like to download and have at your disposal.

Windows Tools

NoteTab

NoteTab's tabbed interface lets you have many different files open simultaneously without cluttering up your screen, as Figure 1.6 illustrates. Files that you've opened are remembered even after you close the program and open it again later (very useful when you're working on a batch of files over many days, for instance). You can download the free NoteTab, or its Light version, from http://www.notetab.com/.

Figure 1.6. NoteTab Light's tabbed interface

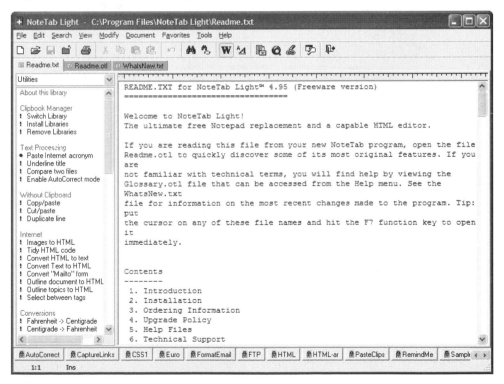

Firefox

Firefox is a popular alternative to Internet Explorer, and, as we proceed through this book, it will be our browser of choice for a number of reasons. As with NoteTab, Firefox offers a nice tabbed interface that keeps your computer free from window clutter. You can download Firefox from http://www.mozilla.com/firefox/; the browser is depicted in Figure 1.7.

Figure 1.7. Firefox—this critter is worth hunting down

Mac OS X Tools

It is true that there are fewer free programs available for the Mac operating system than there are for Windows. However, there are a few programs that you might like to consider as you move beyond the basics.

TextWrangler

TextWrangler is a free, simple text editor made by BareBones Software. As with NoteTab for Windows, TextWrangler can tidy up your workspace by allowing several text files to be open for editing at the same time (the documents are listed in a pull-out "drawer" to one side of the interface, rather than in tabs). You can download TextWrangler, which is shown in Figure 1.8, from the BareBones Software web site.[1]

Figure 1.8. TextWrangler, a free text editor from BareBones Software

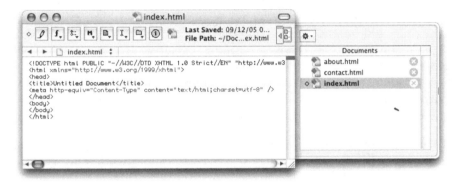

Firefox

Firefox is gaining popularity not just among Windows users, but among Mac users too! A web page viewed in Firefox should display the same regardless of whether the browser is installed on a PC running Windows XP, on a Mac running OS X, or on Linux (an operating system favored by people who really, *really* hate Microsoft products with a vengeance). The predictability of Firefox is a welcome change from the bad old days of endless browser competition, and is one very good reason why we will primarily use Firefox in the examples included in this book.

---

[1] http://www.barebones.com/products/textwrangler/

Not Just Text, Text, Text

You can build an entire web site using just the tools mentioned above, but it won't be the sexiest site on the Web. The missing element here is images: so far, the programs we've mentioned are used to manipulate plain text or view web pages. If your web site is going to be visually appealing, you'll need to be able to create and manipulate images, either from scratch, using photos you've taken, or using images that you have the legal right to use on your web site.

Unfortunately, when it comes to image editing software, that old saying—"You get what you pay for"—is alive and well. A professional image editing program, like Photoshop or Fireworks, costs hundreds of dollars. While these programs offer some excellent capabilities, we cannot really recommend that you go out and pay for them unless you are *absolutely sure* that they're right for you. If you already have a copy of one of these, or a similar image editing program, by all means use it and experiment with it. Programs like Paint Shop Pro or Photoshop Elements (a cut-down version of Photoshop) are more reasonably priced. However, for the purposes of this book, we'll look only at tools that are free to download, and offer enough functionality to give you an idea of what's possible.

Keep an eye open for free image editors that are included on disks attached to the covers of internet, computing, and design magazines. Software vendors often give away older versions of their software in the hopes that users might be tempted to upgrade to a new version at a later date. Look out for Paint Shop Pro, or any image editor that supports "layers." While we'll keep our image editing fairly simple throughout this book, it's certainly worth keeping an eye open for free (and full-featured) image editing software, as these offers will not always be available.

Taking the Big Boys for a Spin

Tip

The most commonly used image editing packages are available for trial download. They are large downloads (hundreds of megabytes) and will probably need to be downloaded overnight, even on a broadband connection.

These trial versions are typically available for 30 days' use; after that time, you can decide whether you want to pay for the full software, or stop using the program. However, those 30 days might just be enough time for you to use the software while you work through this book.

Adobe Photoshop	A trial of the latest version of Photoshop is available for download.[2] If you'd rather try the lighter Photoshop Elements, trial versions are available for Windows[3] and Mac.[4]
Macromedia Fireworks	You can download a trial version of Fireworks from the Macromedia web site.[5]
Paint Shop Pro	Paint Shop Pro is available for Windows only. To download a trial version, visit the Paint Shop Pro site,[6] and click the "Try" link on the right.

Windows Tools

A standard Windows install is not exactly blessed with image editing software (although you might be lucky enough to have bought a PC, scanner, or digital camera that came bundled with some image editing software; scout around in your Start > All Programs menu to see what you can uncover). As a general rule, you'll have to look elsewhere for useful image manipulation software.

Picasa

Though the Windows default image editing and management tools are distinctly lackluster, the good news is that there's an excellent program just begging to be downloaded and used, and it's brought to you by those good people at Google. The program is called Picasa, and it's extremely well equipped to handle most of the tasks that you're likely to encounter as you manage imagery for your web site. Download a copy from the Picasa web site,[7] and soon enough you'll be using this program to crop, rotate, add special effects to, and catalogue the images stored on your computer. Figure 1.9 gives you an idea of the program's interface.

---

[2] http://www.adobe.com/products/photoshop/tryout.html
[3] http://www.adobe.com/products/photoshopelwin/
[4] http://www.adobe.com/products/photoshopelmac/
[5] http://www.macromedia.com/go/tryfireworks/
[6] http://www.corel.com/paintshoppro/
[7] http://www.google.com/picasa/

Figure 1.9. Picasa, Google's free, fully-featured photo and image editing and management tool

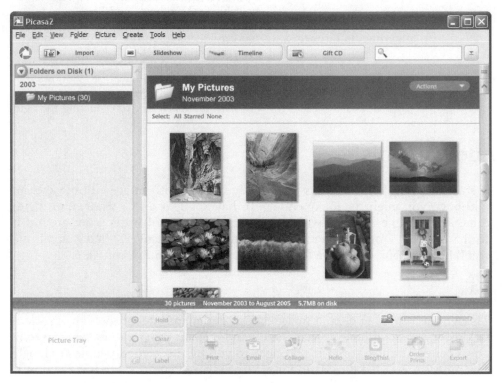

Mac OS X Tools

The Mac has a reputation for being favored by designers and creative types, and the platform makes many tools available to the budding artist. However, they usually come at a price, and often that price is higher than those of the Windows equivalents! So, what free software can we use on the Mac, assuming that we want something more permanent than a 30-day trial version of Photoshop or Fireworks?

GraphicConverter

GraphicConverter has much greater capabilities than its name suggests. It's bundled with most newer Macs, and is also available for download[8] (you'll be encouraged to pay a modest registration fee for the software, but you can try it out for free). Sure, this is primarily a tool for converting graphic files, but it can also be used for simple editing tasks. Using GraphicConverter, which is illustrated in Figure 1.10, you'll be able to crop, resize, rotate, and add text to any image.

Figure 1.10. GraphicConverter does a lot more than simply convert graphics!

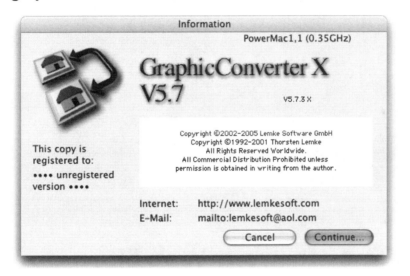

iPhoto

Also included with Mac OS X is a program that probably needs no introduction to the experienced Mac user: iPhoto. This excellent program is not intended as a fully-featured image editor; it's really designed for managing and viewing large numbers of photos stored on a computer. It's great for organizing photo albums, but with recent updates, iPhoto has been given some editing facilities that have promoted it beyond a mere cataloguing tool. Unfortunately, the latest version of iPhoto is not available as a free download, and must be purchased as part of Apple's iLife suite of programs.

---

[8] http://www.graphicconverter.net/

iPhoto, pictured in Figure 1.11, can be found in the Applications folder, or in the dock.

Figure 1.11. The iPhoto 5 image adjustment tools

Creating a Spot for your Web Site

So far, we've looked at some of the tools that you'll need to create your web site. We've looked at programs that are readily available, and where you can find them on your computer. And for cases in which the free tools that came with your computer are not up to the job, we've suggested other programs that you can download and use. The next task we must tick off our to-do list before we go any further is creating a space for your web site on the hard drive.

Windows

The easiest and most logical place to keep your web site files is in a dedicated folder within the *My Documents* folder. There should be a *My Documents* folder on your desktop, but don't worry if it's not there: it's easy to get it to appear there (see the tip below for details). Double-click on My Documents, then create a new folder called Web by selecting File > New > Folder.

Displaying the "My Documents" Folder

Lost your "My Documents" folder? It's easily done: in an effort to clean up your desktop, you may have removed the icon by accident. You can return the folder to your desktop as follows:

❑ From the Start Menu, select Control Panel.

❑ Select Appearance and Themes, then select Display (if you don't see Appearance and Themes, but do see Display, double click on that). A Display Properties window will appear.

❑ Select the Desktop tab along the top, then click the Customize Desktop… button at the bottom.

❑ You'll be presented with the Desktop Items dialog, which will include a set of Desktop icons checkboxes that allow you to select the icons you'd like to see on your desktop. Check the My Documents checkbox, then click OK on both open dialogs.

❑ Your My Documents folder should now be back on the desktop, as shown in Figure 1.12.

Figure 1.12. The My Documents folder displaying on the desktop in XP

My Computer

My Network
Places

My Documents

Mac OS X

In Mac OS X, there's already a handy place for you to store your web site files: the Sites folder shown in Figure 1.13. Open your home directory (from Finder, select Go > Home), and there it is!

Figure 1.13. The Sites folder displaying in the Mac OS X home directory

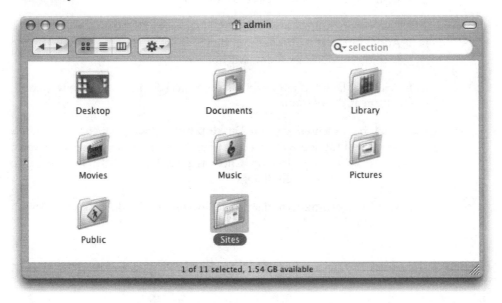

It's easy to add the Sites folder to your sidebar (which you can see in Figure 1.14) for quick access: just drag the folder to the sidebar in the same way you add items to the dock.

Figure 1.14. The Sites folder appearing in the sidebar

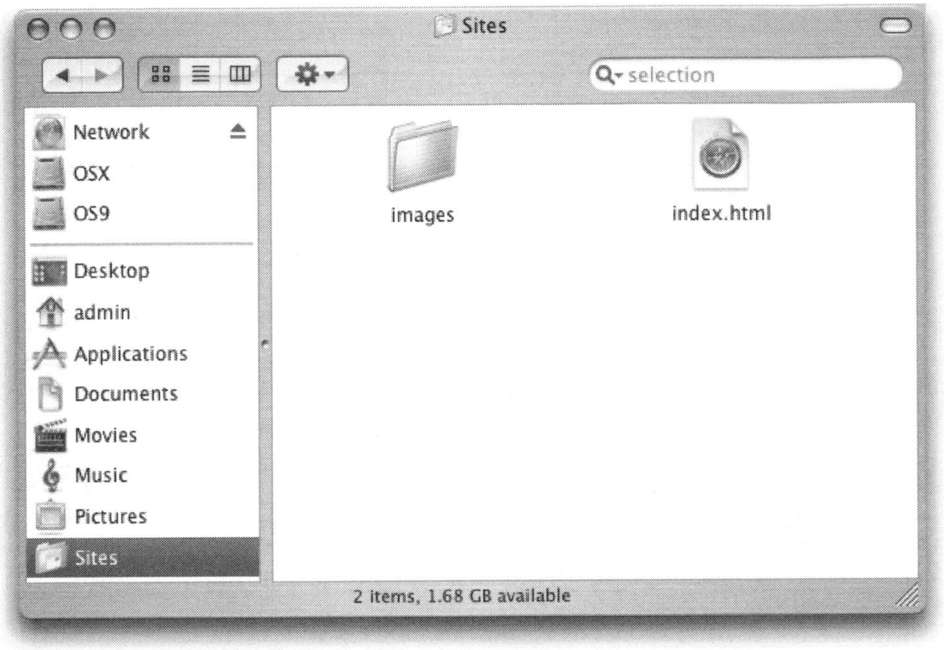

Getting Help

Books may be a wonderful way to learn: you're sitting there with a computer running, a cup of coffee keeping your mind ticking over (you've got one there, right? A coffee, that is, not a mind), and a bookmark signifying your progress to date. Great. But what if you don't understand something in the book? What do you do next? Shouting at the book won't help (well, it may be therapeutic, but you won't get a response)!

Hopefully, you won't find yourself asking too many questions as you work through this book, but if you're the curious type—or a quick learner—you might want to go beyond what we're going to teach you here.

Whether you're getting stuck on something, or you want to learn more, your first stop should be the SitePoint Forums.[9] It will only take a few moments to register, and once you've done so, you can log in and ask questions in a range of different

---

[9] http://www.sitepoint.com/forums/

forums. Whether you have questions about writing your web site, you need marketing tips, or you're facing a few tricky graphic design issues, the hundreds of experts who contribute to and moderate these pages every day will be happy to help out.

Register at SitePoint's forums today; then, when we recommend further reading or research, you'll be good to go. Oh, and did we mention that all this friendly, helpful advice is 100% free of charge? I thought that might encourage you!

Summary

Believe it or not, we've now got everything we need to build our own web site—and all without spending a cent! Not only do we have the basic tools—our text editor (Notepad or TextEdit) and our web browser (Internet Explorer or Safari)—but we've also looked at some alternatives to these.

We've reviewed some simple and freely available image editing programs that can help us spruce up our sites: Picasa for Windows, and GraphicConverter and iPhoto for Mac. Finally, we mentioned some more capable—and more expensive—options, such as Photoshop and Paint Shop Pro.

Now we've got the tools, let's learn how to use them!

2

Your First Web Pages

A wise man once said that a journey of a thousand miles begins with a single step. In this chapter, you'll take that first metaphorical step on your journey towards web site enlightenment: you'll create your first web page. By the end of the chapter, you'll have duplicated that first page to form the beginnings of a multi-page web site.

Nice to Meet you, XHTML

In the preface to this book, we touched briefly on what XHTML is. In this chapter, we'll learn the basics of XHTML, periodically previewing our progress in a browser, and steadily building up our knowledge of various XHTML **elements**. Elements are the basic building blocks of XHTML; they tell the web browser what a particular item in the page is: a paragraph, a heading, a quotation, and so on. Elements contain all the information that the browser requires, as we'll soon see.

Anatomy of a Web Page

In the preface, we said that learning XHTML was like taking a driving lesson. To take that analogy a step further, you can imagine a web page as being the car in which you're learning to drive. There are some things that are essential to the process of driving; others are mere fashion items. For instance, the interior might have two seats, or it may have four or six; it might have black leather trim, fluffy dice, or faux leopard-skin door panels. But, while you may dearly love those door panels, they're not essential to driving.

You can't drive the car unless you have a steering wheel to hold onto, four wheels (at a minimum!), and a place to sit. The car must also have some kind of chassis to which the bodywork can be bolted. An engine is needed to power the car, as is bodywork to which your (nonessential, but spiffy) trim can be attached. Anything less, and all you have is a collection of attractive—but useless!—spare parts.

Like the car, your web page also needs to have a chassis: a basic structure upon which everything else can be built. But what does this hypothetical "chassis" look like? The best way to find out is to get down on our hands and knees (again, figuratively speaking) and take a close look under the hood.

Viewing the Source

One of the great things about learning to build web pages is that you and I have the ability to view the source code of other people's web pages. You can learn a lot by simply taking a peek at how someone else's web page was built ... but how do you do it?

Although every browser uses slightly different terminology, the variations in the ways different browsers let us view web page code are so small that the process doesn't need to be spelled out for every browser. Here's the technique you'd use to view a web page's source in IE:

❑ Bring up a page in your browser. (I'd suggest the Web Standards Project's homepage.[1] The Web Standards Project (WaSP) is a group that promotes the benefits of building your web site correctly, so you can be pretty sure they've got it right!)

❑ Position your cursor somewhere on the page (other than over an image), and right-click (Ctrl-click on a Mac). You should be presented with the context menu shown in Figure 2.1.

---

[1] http://webstandards.org/

Figure 2.1. Selecting the View Source command after right-clicking on a web page

☐ Select View Source, and a new window will appear, displaying all of the page's underlying markup.

At this point, we're not going to analyze the markup that you're looking at, but this is one of those tricks that's really useful to know from the beginning. A note of warning, though: most web pages don't use best-practice techniques, so avoid looking at a page's source unless the web site in question is mentioned in this book as being a good example.

Basic Requirements of a Web Page

As we've already discussed, in any web page, there are some basic must-have items (all of which you could pick out if you scanned through the markup that appeared when you tried to "view source" a moment ago):

☐ a doctype

☐ an <html> tag

☐ a <head> tag

☐ a <title> tag

☐ a <body> tag

These requirements make up the basic skeleton of a web page. It's the chassis of your car with some unpainted bodywork, but no wheels or seats. A car enthusiast would call it a "project"—a solid foundation that needs a little extra work to turn it in to something usable. The same goes for a web page. Here's what these requirements look like when they're combined in a basic web page:

```
<!DOCTYPE html PUBLIC "-//W3C//DTD XHTML 1.0 Strict//EN"
    "http://www.w3.org/TR/xhtml1/DTD/xhtml1-strict.dtd">
<html xmlns="http://www.w3.org/1999/xhtml">
  <head>
    <title>Untitled Document</title>
    <meta http-equiv="Content-Type"
        content="text/html; charset=utf-8" />
  </head>
  <body>
  </body>
</html>
```

The markup above is the most basic web page you'll see here. It contains practically no content of any value (at least, as far as someone who looks at it in a browser is concerned), but it's crucial that you understand what this markup means. Let's delve a little deeper.

The Doctype

```
<!DOCTYPE html PUBLIC "-//W3C//DTD XHTML 1.0 Strict//EN"
    "http://www.w3.org/TR/xhtml1/DTD/xhtml1-strict.dtd">
```

This is known as the **doctype** (short for Document Type Declaration). It must *absolutely* be the first item on a web page, appearing even before any spacing or carriage returns.

Have you ever taken a document you wrote in Microsoft Word 2003 on one computer, and tried to open it on another computer that ran Word 97? Frustratingly, without some pre-emptive massaging when the file is saved in the first place, this just doesn't work. It fails because Word 2003 includes features that Bill Gates and his team hadn't even dreamed of in 1997, and Microsoft needed to create a new version of its file format to cater to these new features. Just as Microsoft has many different versions of Word, so too are there different versions of HTML, the latest of which is XHTML. Mercifully, the different versions of HTML have been designed so that this language doesn't suffer the same incompatibility gremlins as Word, but it's still important to identify the version of HTML that you're using. This is where the doctype comes in. The doctype's job is to specify which version of HTML the browser should expect to see. The browser uses this information to decide how it should render items on the screen.

The doctype above states that we're using XHTML 1.0 Strict, and includes a **URL** to which the browser can refer: this URL points to the **W3C**'s specification for XHTML 1.0 Strict. Got all that? Okay: jargon break! There are too many abbreviations for this paragraph!

Jargon Busting 101

URL

URL stands for Uniform Resource Locator. It's what some (admittedly more geeky) people refer to when they talk about a web site's address. URL is definitely a useful term to learn, though, because it's becoming more and more common.

W3C

W3C is an abbreviation of the name World Wide Web Consortium, a group of smart people spread across the globe who, collectively, come up with proposals for the ways in which computing and markup languages that are used on the Web should be written. The W3C defines the rules, suggests usage, then publishes the agreed documentation for reference by interested parties, be they web site creators like your good self (once you're done with this book, that is), or software developers who are building the programs that need to understand these languages (such as browsers or authoring software).

The W3C documents are the starting point, and indeed everything in this book is based on the original documents. But, trust me: you don't want to look at any W3C documents for a long time yet. They're just plain scary for us mere mortals without Computer Science degrees. Just stick with this book for time being—I'll guide you through!

The `html` Element

So, the doctype has told the browser to expect a certain version of HTML. What comes next? Some HTML!

An XHTML document is built using elements. Remember, elements are the bricks that create the structures that hold a web page together. But what exactly *is* an element? What does an element look like, and what is its purpose?

- An XHTML element starts and ends with **tags**—the **opening tag** and the **closing tag**.[2]

- A tag consists of an opening angled bracket (<), some text, and a closing bracket (>).

- Inside a tag, there is a **tag name**; there may also be one or more **attributes**.

Let's take a look at the first element in the page: the html element. Figure 2.2 shows what we have.

Figure 2.2. Constituents of a typical XHTML element

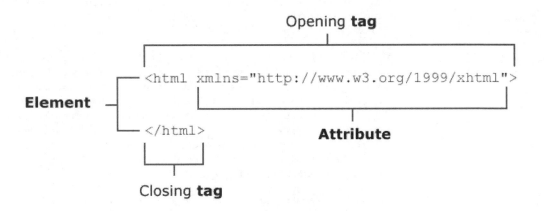

Figure 2.2 depicts the opening tag, which marks the start of the element:

```
<html xmlns="http://www.w3.org/1999/xhtml">
```

Below it, we see the closing tag, which marks its end (and occurs right at the end of the document):

```
</html>
```

Here's that line again, with the tag name in bold:

```
<html xmlns="http://www.w3.org/1999/xhtml">
```

---

[2] Like any good rule, there are exceptions to this: empty elements, such as meta, use special empty tags. We'll take a look at empty tags soon.

And there is one **attribute** in the opening tag:

```
<html xmlns="http://www.w3.org/1999/xhtml">
```

What's an Attribute?

HTML elements can have a range of different **attributes**; the available attributes vary depending on which element you're dealing with. Each attribute is made up of a **name** and a **value**, and these are always written as *name*=*"value"*. Some attributes are optional, while others are compulsory, but together they give the browser important information that the element wouldn't offer otherwise. For example, the image element (which we'll learn about soon) has a compulsory "image source" attribute, the value of which gives the filename of the image. Attributes appear in the opening tag of any given element. We'll see more attributes crop up as we work our way through this project, and, at least initially, I'll be making sure to point them out, so that you're familiar with them.

Back to the purpose of the html element. This is the outermost "container" of our web page; everything else is kept within that outer container—there are no exceptions! Let's peel off that outer layer and take a peek at the contents inside.

There are two major sections inside the html element: the head and the body. It's not going to be difficult to remember the order in which those items should appear, unless you happen to enjoy doing headstands.

The head Element

The head element contains information *about* the page, but no information that will be displayed on the page itself. For example, it contains the title element, which tells the browser what to display in its title bar:

```
<!DOCTYPE html PUBLIC "-//W3C//DTD XHTML 1.0 Strict//EN"
    "http://www.w3.org/TR/xhtml1/DTD/xhtml1-strict.dtd">
<html xmlns="http://www.w3.org/1999/xhtml">
  <head>
    <title>Untitled Document</title>
    <meta http-equiv="Content-Type"
        content="text/html; charset=utf-8" />
  </head>
  <body>
  </body>
</html>
```

The `title` Element

The opening `<title>` and closing `</title>` tags are wrapped around the words "Untitled Document" in the markup above. Note that the `<title>` signifies the start, while the closing `</title>` signifies the end of the title. That's how closing tags work: they have forward slashes just after the angle bracket.

The "Untitled Document" title is typical of what HTML authoring software provides as a starting point when you choose to create a new web page; it's up to you to change those words. However, if you're creating a web page from scratch in a text editor (like Notepad), you will, I hope, remember to type something a little more useful. But just what is this `title`? Time for a screenshot: check out Figure 2.3.

Figure 2.3. "Untitled Document"—not a very helpful title

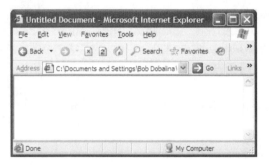

It really would pay dividends to put something useful in there, and not just for the sake of those people who visit our web page. The content of the `title` element is also used for a number of other purposes:

❑ It's the name that appears in the Windows Taskbar for any open document, as shown in Figure 2.4. It also appears in the dock on a Mac, as Figure 2.5 illustrates. When you have a few windows open, you'll appreciate those people who have made an effort to enter a descriptive `title`!

Figure 2.4. The `title` appearing in the Windows Taskbar

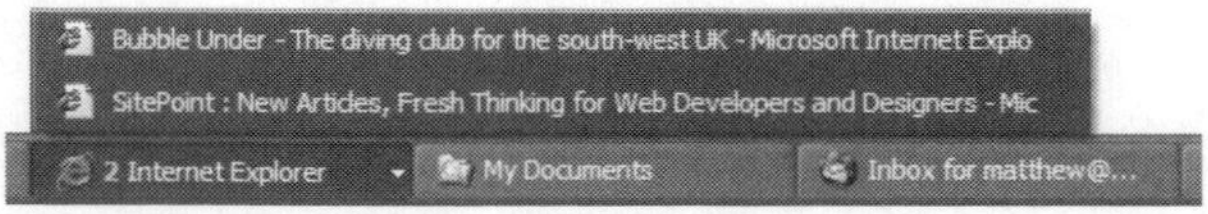

Figure 2.5. The `title` displaying in the Mac dock

❑ If users decide to add the page to their bookmarks (or favorites), the `title` will be used to name the bookmark, as Figure 2.6 illustrates.

Figure 2.6. An untitled document saved to IE's favorites

❑ Your `title` element is used heavily by search engines to ascertain what your page contains, and what information about it should be displayed in the search results. Just for fun, and to see how many people forget to type in a useful `title`, try searching for the phrase "Untitled Document" in the search engine of your choice.

meta Elements

Inside the `head` element in our simple example, we can see a `meta` element, which is shown in bold below:

```
<!DOCTYPE html PUBLIC "-//W3C//DTD XHTML 1.0 Strict//EN"
    "http://www.w3.org/TR/xhtml1/DTD/xhtml1-strict.dtd">
<html xmlns="http://www.w3.org/1999/xhtml">
  <head>
    <title>Untitled Document</title>
    <meta http-equiv="Content-Type"
        content="text/html; charset=utf-8" />
  </head>
```

```
  <body>
  </body>
</html>
```

`meta` elements can be used in a web page for many different reasons. Some are used to provide additional information that's not displayed on-screen to the browser or to search engines; for instance, the name of the page's author, or a copyright notice, might be included in `meta` elements. In the example above, the `meta` tag tells the browser which **character set** to use (specifically, UTF-8, which includes the characters needed for web pages in just about any language).

There are many different uses for `meta` elements, but most of them will make no discernible difference to the way your page looks, and as such, won't be of much interest to you.

Self-closing Elements

The `meta` element is an example of a **self-closing element** (or an **empty element**). Unlike `title`, the `meta` element needn't contain anything, so we could write it as follows:

```
<meta http-equiv="Content-Type"
    content="text/html; charset=utf-8"></meta>
```

XHTML contains a number of empty elements, and the boffins who put together XHTML decided that writing all those closing tags would get annoying pretty quickly, so they decided to use self-closing tags: tags that end with `/>`. So our `meta` example becomes:

```
<meta http-equiv="Content-Type"
    content="text/html; charset=utf-8" />
```

The Memory Game: Remembering Difficult Markup

If you're thinking that the doctype and `meta` elements are difficult to remember, and you're wondering how on earth people commit them to memory, don't worry: most people don't! Even the most hardened and world-weary coders would have difficulty remembering these elements exactly, so most do the same thing—they copy from a source they know to be correct (most likely from their last project or piece of work). You'll probably do the same as you work with project files for this book.

Fully-fledged web development programs, such as Dreamweaver, will normally take care of these difficult parts of coding.

Other head Elements

Other items, such as CSS markup and JavaScript code, can appear in the head element, but we'll discuss these as we need them.

The body Element

Finally, we get to the place where it all happens! The body element of the page contains almost everything that you see on the screen, including headings, paragraphs, images, any navigation that's required, and footers that sit at the bottom of the web page.

```
<!DOCTYPE html PUBLIC "-//W3C//DTD XHTML 1.0 Strict//EN"
    "http://www.w3.org/TR/xhtml1/DTD/xhtml1-strict.dtd">
<html xmlns="http://www.w3.org/1999/xhtml">
  <head>
    <title>Untitled Document</title>
    <meta http-equiv="Content-Type"
        content="text/html; charset=utf-8" />
  </head>
  <body>
  </body>
</html>
```

The Most Basic Web Page in the World

Actually, that heading's a bit of a misnomer: we've already showed you the most basic page (the one without any content). However, to start to appreciate how everything fits together, you really need to see a simple page with some actual content on it. Let's have a go at it, shall we?

Open your text editor and type the following into a new, empty document (or grab the file from the code archive if you don't feel like typing it out—I understand completely!).

File: **basic.html**

```
<!DOCTYPE html PUBLIC "-//W3C//DTD XHTML 1.0 Strict//EN"
    "http://www.w3.org/TR/xhtml1/DTD/xhtml1-strict.dtd">
<html xmlns="http://www.w3.org/1999/xhtml">
  <head>
    <title>The Most Basic Web Page in the World</title>
    <meta http-equiv="Content-Type"
```

```
        content="text/html; charset=utf-8" />
  </head>
  <body>
    <h1>The Most Basic Web Page in the World</h1>
    <p>This is a very simple web page to get you started.
        Hopefully you will get to see how the markup that drives
        the page relates to the end result that you can see on
        screen.</p>
    <p>This is another paragraph, by the way. Just to show how it
        works.</p>
  </body>
</html>
```

Once you've typed it out, save it as `basic.html`.

If you're using Notepad, select File > Save As... from the menu and find the Web folder you created inside My Documents. Enter the filename as **index.html**, select UTF-8 from the Encoding drop-down list, and click Save.

If you're using TextEdit on a Mac, first make sure that you're in plain text mode, then select File > Save As... from the menu. Find the Sites folder, enter **index.html**, select Unicode (UTF-8) from the Plain Text Encoding drop-down list, and click Save. TextEdit will warn you that you're saving a plain text file with an extension other than `.txt`, and offer to append `.txt` to the end of your filename. We want to save this file with an `.html` extension, so click the Don't Append button, and your file will be saved.

The Importance of UTF-8

If you neglect to select UTF-8 when saving your files, it's likely that you won't notice much of a difference. However, when someone else comes along to view your web site (say, a Korean friend of yours), they'll probably end up with a screen of garbage. Why? Because their computer is set up to read Korean text, and yours is set up to create English text. UTF-8 can handle just about any language there is (including some quite obscure ones!) and most computers can read it, so UTF-8 is always a safe bet.

Next, using Windows Explorer or Finder, locate the file that you just saved, and double-click to open it in your browser. Figure 2.7 shows how the page displays.

Figure 2.7. Displaying a basic page

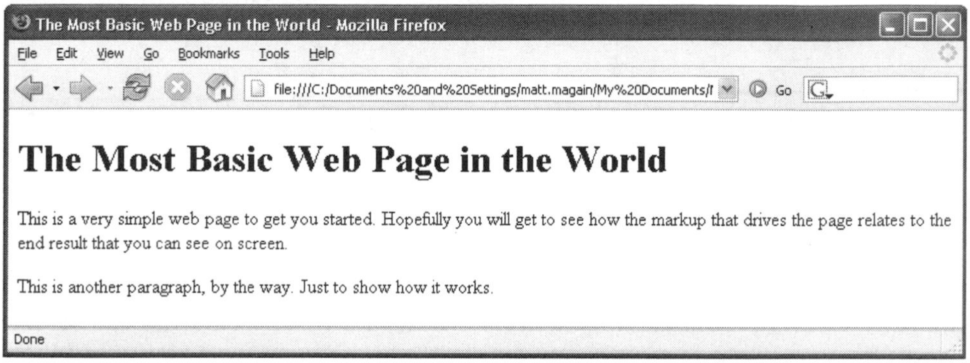

The Most Basic Web Page in the World - Mozilla Firefox

File Edit View Go Bookmarks Tools Help

file:///C:/Documents%20and%20Settings/matt.magain/My%20Documents/t ▾   Go

The Most Basic Web Page in the World

This is a very simple web page to get you started. Hopefully you will get to see how the markup that drives the page relates to the end result that you can see on screen.

This is another paragraph, by the way. Just to show how it works.

Done

Analyzing the Web Page

We've introduced two new elements to our simple page: a heading element, and a couple of paragraph elements, denoted by the <h1> tag and <p> tags, respectively.

Figure 2.8. Comparing the source markup with the view presented in the browser

Do you see how the markup you've typed out relates to what you can see in the browser? Figure 2.8 shows a direct comparison of the document displays.

The opening `<h1>` and closing `</h1>` tags are wrapped around the words "The Most Basic Web Page in the World," making that the main heading for the page. In the same way, the `p` elements contain the text in the two paragraphs.

There's another point to note: the tags are all lowercase. All of our attribute names will be in lowercase, too. Many older HTML documents include tags and attributes in uppercase, but this isn't allowed in XHTML.

Headings and Document Hierarchy

In the example above, we use an `h1` element to show a major heading. If we wanted to include a subheading beneath this heading, we would use the `h2` element. There are no prizes for guessing that a subheading under an `h2` would use an `h3` element, and so on, until we get to `h6`. The lower the heading level, the lesser its importance and, as a rule, the smaller (or less prominent) the font.

With headings, an important (and commonsense) practice is to ensure that they do not jump out of sequence. In other words, you should start from level one, and work your way down through the levels in numerical order. You can jump back up from a lower-level heading to a higher one, provided that the content under the higher-level heading to which you've jumped does not refer to concepts that are addressed under the lower-level heading. It may be useful to visualize your headings as a list:

- First Major Heading

    - First Subheading

    - Second Subheading

        - A Sub-subheading

- Another Major Heading

    - Another Subheading

Here's the XHTML view of the example shown above:

```
<h1>First Major Heading</h1>
<h2>First Subheading</h2>
<h2>Second Subheading</h2>
<h3>A Sub-subheading</h3>
```

```
<h1>Another Major Heading</h1>
<h2>Another Subheading</h2>
```

Paragraphs

Of course, no one wants to read a document that contains only headings—you need to put some text in there. The element we use to deal with blocks of text is the p element. It's not difficult to remember: p is for paragraph! That's just as well, because you'll almost certainly find yourself using this element more than any other. And that's the beauty of XHTML: most elements that you use frequently are either very obvious, or easy to remember once you're introduced to them.

For People who Love Lists

Let's imagine that you want a list on your web page. To include an **ordered list** of items, we use the ol element. An **unordered list**—called "bullet points" by the average person—makes use of the ul element. In both types of list, individual points or list items are specified using the li element. So we use ol for an ordered list, ul for an unordered list, and li for a list item. Easy!

To see this markup in action, type the following into a new text document, save it as lists.html, and view it in the browser by double-clicking on the saved file's icon.

File: **lists.html**

```
<!DOCTYPE html PUBLIC "-//W3C//DTD XHTML 1.0 Strict//EN"
    "http://www.w3.org/TR/xhtml1/DTD/xhtml1-strict.dtd">
<html xmlns="http://www.w3.org/1999/xhtml">
  <head>
    <title>Lists - an introduction</title>
    <meta http-equiv="Content-Type"
       content="text/html; charset=utf-8" />
  </head>
  <body>
    <h1>Lists - an introduction </h1>
    <p>Here's a paragraph. A lovely, concise little paragraph.</p>
    <p>Here comes another one, followed by a subheading.</p>
    <h2>A subheading here</h2>
    <p>And now for a list or two:</p>
    <ul>
      <li>This is a bulleted list</li>
      <li>No order applied</li>
```

```
      <li>Just a bunch of points we want to make</li>
   </ul>
   <p>And here's an ordered list:</p>
   <ol>
     <li>This is the first item</li>
     <li>Followed by this one</li>
     <li>And one more for luck</li>
   </ol>
  </body>
</html>
```

How does it look to you? Did you type it all out? Remember, if it seems like a lot of hassle to type out the examples, you can find all the markup in the code archive, as I explained in the preface. However, bear in mind that simply copying and pasting markup, then saving and running it, doesn't really give you a feel for what's happening—it really will pay to learn by doing. Even if you make mistakes, it's still a better way to learn (you'll be happy when you can spot your own errors and fix them for yourself). When displayed in a browser, the above markup should look like the page shown in Figure 2.9.

There are many, many different elements that you can use on your web page, and we'll meet more of them as our web site development progresses. As well as the more obvious elements that you'll come across, there are others that are not immediately obvious: what would you use div, span, or a elements for? Any guesses? Don't worry, all will be revealed in good time.

Figure 2.9. Using unordered and ordered lists to organize information

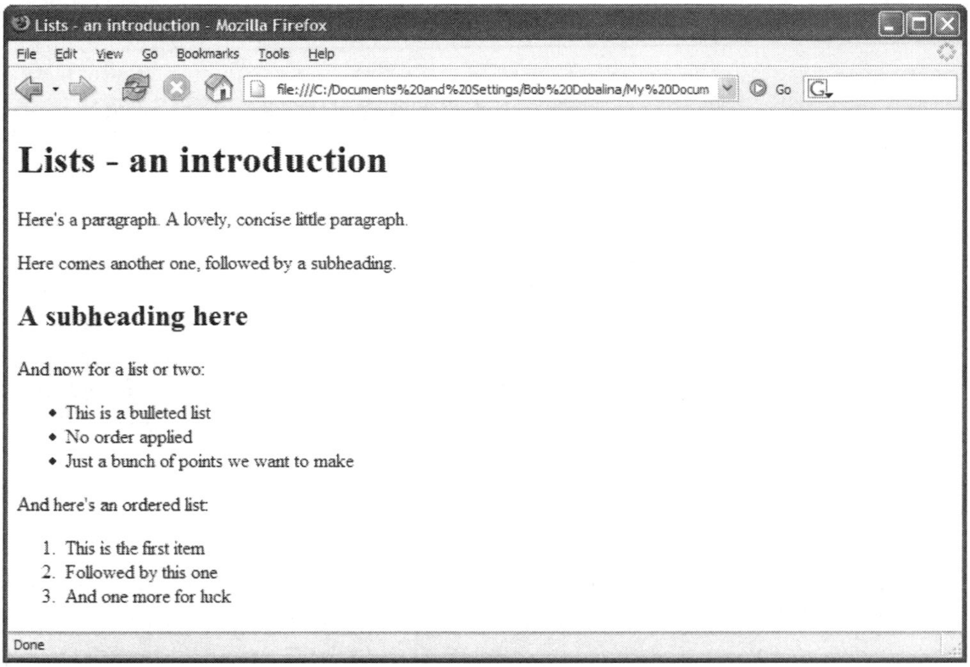

Commenting your Web Pages

Back in the garage, you're doing a little work on your project car and, as you prepare to replace the existing tires with a new set of low-profile whitewalls, you notice that your hubcaps aren't bolted on: you'd stuck them to the car with super glue. There must have been a good reason for doing that, but you can't remember what it was. The trouble is, if you had a reason to attach the hubcaps that way before, surely you should do it the same way again. Wouldn't it be great if you'd left yourself a note when you first did it, explaining why you used super glue instead of bolts? Then again, your car wouldn't look very nice with notes stuck all over it. What a quandary!

When you're creating a web site, you may find yourself in a similar situation. You might build a site, then not touch it again for six months. Then, when you revisit the work, you might find yourself going through the all-too-familiar head-scratching routine. Fortunately, there *is* a solution!

XHTML—like most programming and markup languages—allows you to use **comments**. Comments are perfect for making notes about something you've done and, though they're included within your code, comments do not affect the on-screen display. Here's an example of a comment:

File: **comments.html**

```
<!DOCTYPE html PUBLIC "-//W3C//DTD XHTML 1.0 Strict//EN"
    "http://www.w3.org/TR/xhtml1/DTD/xhtml1-strict.dtd">
<html xmlns="http://www.w3.org/1999/xhtml">
  <head>
    <title>Comment example</title>
    <meta http-equiv="Content-Type"
        content="text/html; charset=utf-8" />
  </head>
  <body>
    <p>I really, <em>really</em> like this XHTML stuff.</p>
    <!-- Added emphasis using the em element. Handy one, that! -->
  </body>
</html>
```

Figure 2.10 shows the page viewed on-screen.

Figure 2.10. The comment remains hidden in the on-screen display

Comments must start with <!--, after which you're free to type whatever you like as a "note to self." Well, you're free to type *almost* anything: you cannot type double dashes. Why not? Because that's a signal that the comment is about to end—the --> part.

Oh, and did you spot how we snuck another new element in there? The emphasis element, denoted with the <em> and </em> tags, is used wherever … well, do I *really* need to tell you? Actually, that last question was kind of rhetorical. It was there to make a point: did you notice that the word "really" appeared in italics?

Read that part to yourself now, and listen to the way it "sounds" in your head. Now you know when to use the em element!

Using Comments to Hide Markup from Browsers Temporarily

There is no limit to the amount of information you can put into a comment, and this is why comments are often used to hide a section of a web page temporarily. Commenting may be preferable to deleting content, particularly if you want to put that information back into the web page at a later date (if it's in a comment, you won't have to re-type it). This is often called "commenting out" markup. Here's an example:

File: **commentout.html**

```
<!DOCTYPE html PUBLIC "-//W3C//DTD XHTML 1.0 Strict//EN"
    "http://www.w3.org/TR/xhtml1/DTD/xhtml1-strict.dtd">
<html xmlns="http://www.w3.org/1999/xhtml">
  <head>
    <title>Commenting out XHTML</title>
    <meta http-equiv="Content-Type"
        content="text/html; charset=utf-8" />
  </head>
  <body>
    <h1>Current Stock</h1>
    <p>The following items are available for order:</p>
    <ul>
      <li>Dark Smoke Window Tinting</li>
      <li>Bronze Window Tinting</li>
      <!-- <li>Spray mount</li>
      <li>Craft knife (pack of 5)</li> -->
    </ul>
  </body>
</html>
```

Figure 2.11 shows how the page displays in Firefox.

Figure 2.11. The final, commented list items are not displayed

Remember, you write a comment like this: `<!--Your comment here` followed by the comment closer, two dashes and a right-angled bracket`-->`.

Symbols

Occasionally, you may need to include the greater-than (>) or less-than (<) symbols in the text of your web pages. The problem is that these symbols are also used to denote tags in XHTML. So, what can we do? Thankfully, we can use special little codes called **entities** in our text instead of these symbols. The entity for the greater-than symbol is `&gt;`; we can substitute it for the greater-than symbol in our text, as shown in the following simple example. The result of this markup is shown in Figure 2.12.

File: **entity.html**

```
<!DOCTYPE html PUBLIC "-//W3C//DTD XHTML 1.0 Strict//EN"
    "http://www.w3.org/TR/xhtml1/DTD/xhtml1-strict.dtd">
<html xmlns="http://www.w3.org/1999/xhtml">
  <head>
    <title>Stock Note</title>
    <meta http-equiv="Content-Type"
        content="text/html; charset=utf-8" />
  </head>
  <body>
    <p>Our current stock of craft knives &gt; our stock of spray
        mounts, but we still need to get both of them in as soon
        as possible!</p>
  </body>
</html>
```

Figure 2.12. The > entity is displayed as > in the browser

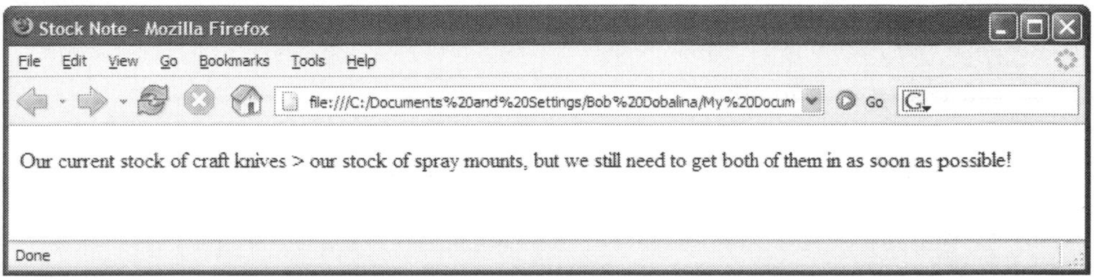

Many different entities are available for a wide range of symbols, most of which don't appear on your keyboard. They all start with an ampersand (&) and end with a semicolon. Some of the most common are shown in Table 2.1.

Table 2.1. Some common entities

Entity	Symbol
>	>
<	<
&	&
£	£
©	©
™	™

Diving into our Web Site

So far, we've looked at some very basic web pages as a way to ease you into the process of writing your own XHTML markup. Perhaps you've typed them up and tried them out, or maybe you've pulled the pages from the code archive and run them in your browser. Perhaps you've even tried experimenting for yourself—it's good to have a play around. None of the examples shown so far are keepers, though. You won't need to use any of these pages, but you will be using the ideas that we've introduced in them as you start to develop the fictitious project we'll complete in the course of this book: a web site for a local diving club.

The diving club comprises a group of local enthusiasts, and the web site will provide a way for club members to:

- ❑ share photos from previous dive trips

- ❑ stay informed about upcoming dive trips

- ❑ provide information about ad-hoc meet-ups

- ❑ read other members' dive reports and write-ups

- ❑ announce club news

The site also has the following goals:

- ❑ to help attract new members

- ❑ to provide links to other diving-related web sites

- ❑ to provide a convenient way to search for general diving-related information

The site's audience may not be enormous, but the regular visitors and club members are very keen to be involved. It's a fun site that people will want to come back to again and again, and it's a good project to work on. But it doesn't exist yet! You're going to start building it right now. Let's start with our first page: the site's home page.

The Homepage: the Starting Point for all Web Sites

At the very beginning of this chapter, we looked at a basic web page with nothing in it (the car chassis, with no bodywork or interior, remember?). You saved the file as `basic.html`. Open that file in your text editor now, and strip out the following:

- ❑ the text contained within the opening `<title>` and closing `</title>` tags

- ❑ all the content between the opening `<body>` and closing `</body>` tags

Save the file as `index.html`.

Here's the markup you should have in front of you now:

File: **index.html**

```
<!DOCTYPE html PUBLIC "-//W3C//DTD XHTML 1.0 Strict//EN"
    "http://www.w3.org/TR/xhtml1/DTD/xhtml1-strict.dtd">
<html xmlns="http://www.w3.org/1999/xhtml">
  <head>
    <title></title>
    <meta http-equiv="Content-Type"
        content="text/html; charset=utf-8" />
  </head>
  <body>
  </body>
</html>
```

Let's start building this web site, shall we?

Setting a Title

Remembering what we've learned so far, let's make a few changes to this document. Have a go at the following:

❏ Change the title of the page to read "Bubble Under – The diving club for the south-west UK."

❏ Add a heading to the page—a level one heading (hint, hint)—that reads "BubbleUnder.com."

❏ Immediately after the heading, add a paragraph that reads, "Diving club for the south-west UK — let's make a splash!" (This is your basic, marketing-type tag line, folks!)

Once you make these changes, your markup should look something like this (the changes are shown in bold):

File: **index.html**

```
<!DOCTYPE html PUBLIC "-//W3C//DTD XHTML 1.0 Strict//EN"
    "http://www.w3.org/TR/xhtml1/DTD/xhtml1-strict.dtd">
<html xmlns="http://www.w3.org/1999/xhtml">
  <head>
    <title>Bubble Under - The diving club for the south-west
        UK</title>
    <meta http-equiv="Content-Type"
        content="text/html; charset=utf-8" />
  </head>
  <body>
```

```
    <h1>BubbleUnder.com</h1>
    <p>Diving club for the south-west UK - let's make a
        splash!</p>
  </body>
</html>
```

Save the page, then double-click on the file to open it in your chosen browser. Figure 2.13 shows what it should look like.

Figure 2.13. Displaying our work on the homepage

Welcoming New Visitors

Now, let's expand upon our tag line a little. We'll add a welcoming subheading—a second level heading—to the page, along with an introductory paragraph:

File: **index.html** (excerpt)

```
<body>
  <h1>BubbleUnder.com</h1>
  <p>Diving club for the south-west UK - let's make a splash!</p>
  <h2>Welcome to our super-dooper Scuba site</h2>
  <p>Glad you could drop in and share some air with us! You've
      passed your underwater navigation skills and successfully
      found your way to the start point - or in this case, our
      home page.</p>
</body>
```

Apologies to anyone who doesn't get my hilarious puns on diving terminology. Come to think of it, apologies to those who do … they're truly cringe-worthy!

Hey! Where'd it All Go?

You'll notice that we didn't repeat the markup for the entire page in the above example. Why? Because paper costs money, trees are beautiful, and you didn't buy this book for weight-training purposes. In short, we won't repeat all the markup all the time; instead, we'll focus on the parts that have changed, or have been added to. And remember: if you think you've missed something, don't worry. You can find all of the examples in the book's code archive.

Once you've added the subheading and the paragraph that follows it, save your page once more, then take another look at it in your browser (either hit the refresh/reload button in your browser, or double-click on the file icon in the location at which you saved it). You should be looking at something like the display shown in Figure 2.14.

Figure 2.14. The homepage taking shape

So, the homepage reads a lot like many other homepages at this stage: it has some basic introductory text to welcome visitors, but not much more. But what exactly is the site about? Or, to be more precise, what will it be about once it's built?

What's it All About?

Notice that, despite our inclusion of a couple of headings and a couple of paragraphs, there is little to suggest what this site is about. All visitors know so far is that the site's about diving. Let's add some more explanatory text to the page, along with some contact information:

❑ Beneath the content you already have on the page, add another heading: this time, make it a level three heading that reads, "About Us" (remember to include both the opening and closing tags for the heading element).

❑ Next, add the following text. Note that there is more than one paragraph.

> Bubble Under is a group of diving enthusiasts based in the south-west UK who meet up for diving trips in the summer months when the weather is good and the bacon rolls are flowing. We arrange weekends away as small groups to cut the costs of accommodation and travel, and to ensure that everyone gets a trustworthy dive buddy.

> Although we're based in the south-west, we don't stay on our own turf: past diving weekends have included trips up to Scapa Flow in Scotland and to Malta's numerous wreck sites.

> When we're not diving, we often meet up in a local pub to talk about our recent adventures (any excuse, eh?).

Save yourself Some Trouble

If you don't feel like typing out all this content, you can paraphrase, or copy it from the code archive. I've deliberately chosen to put a realistic amount of content on the page, so that you can see the effect of several paragraphs on our display.

❑ Next, add a Contact Us section, again, signified by a level three heading.

❑ Finally, add some simple contact details as follows:

> To find out more, contact Club Secretary Bob Dobalina on 01793 641207 or email bob@bubbleunder.com.

So, just to recap, we suggested using different heading levels to signify the importance of the different sections and paragraphs within the document. With that in mind, you should have something like the markup below in the body of your document:

File: **index.html** (excerpt)

```
<h1>BubbleUnder.com</h1>
<p>Diving club for the south-west UK - let's make a splash!</p>
```

```
<h2>Welcome to our super-dooper Scuba site</h2>
<p>Glad you could drop in and share some air with us! You've
    passed your underwater navigation skills and successfully
    found your way to the start point - or in this case, our home
    page.</p>
<h3>About Us</h3>
<p>Bubble Under is a group of diving enthusiasts based in the
    south-west UK who meet up for diving trips in the summer
    months when the weather is good and the bacon rolls are
    flowing. We arrange weekends away as small groups to cut the
    costs of accommodation and travel and to ensure that everyone
    gets a trustworthy dive buddy.</p>
<p>Although we're based in the south-west, we don't stay on our
    own turf: past diving weekends away have included trips up to
    Scapa Flow in Scotland and to Malta's numerous wreck
    sites.</p>
<p>When we're not diving, we often meet up in a local pub
    to talk about our recent adventures (any excuse, eh?).</p>
<h3>Contact Us</h3>
<p>To find out more, contact Club Secretary Bob Dobalina on
    01793 641207 or email bob@bubbleunder.com.</p>
```

Clickable Email Links

It's all well and good to put an email address on the page, but it's hardly perfect. To use this address, a site visitor would need to copy and paste the address into an email message. Surely there's a simpler way? There certainly is:

```
<p>To find out more, contact Club Secretary Bob Dobalina
    on 01793 641207 or <a
    href="mailto:bob@bubbleunder.com">email
    bob@bubbleunder.com</a>.</p>
```

This clickable email link uses the a element, which is used to create links on web pages (this will be explained later in this chapter). The `mailto:` prefix tells the browser that the link needs to be treated as an email address (that is, the email program should be opened for this link). The content that follows the `mailto:` section should be a valid email address in the format *user-name@domain*.

Add this to the web page now, save it, then refresh the view in your browser. Try clicking on the underlined text: it should open your email program automatically, and display an email form in which the To: address is already completed.

Figure 2.15. Viewing `index.html`

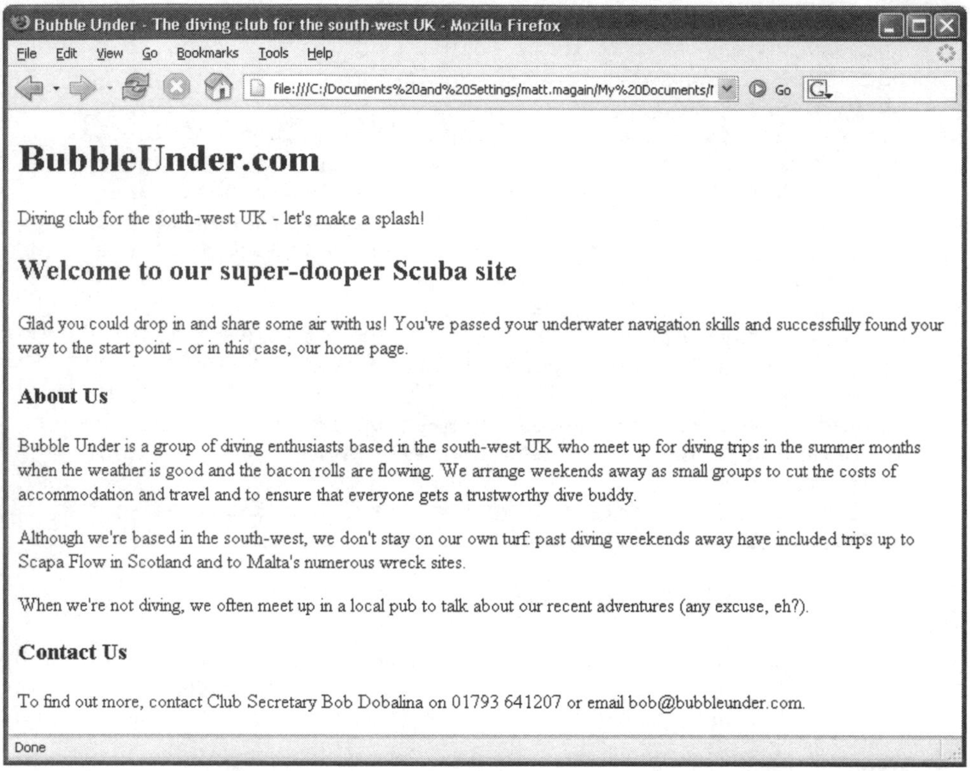

It's still not very exciting, is it? Trust me, we'll get there! The important thing to focus on at this stage is what the content of your site should comprise, and how it might be structured. We haven't gone into great detail about document structure yet, other than to discuss the use of different levels of headings, but we'll be looking at this in more detail later in this chapter. In the next chapter, we'll see how you can begin to **style** your document—that is, change the font, color, letter spacing and more—but for now, let's concentrate on the content and structure.

The page so far seems a little boring, doesn't it? Let's sharpen it up a little. We can only keep looking at a page of black and white for so long—let's insert an image into the document. Here's how the `img` element is applied within the context of the page's markup:

File: **index.html (excerpt)**

```
<h2>Welcome to our super-dooper Scuba site</h2>
<p><img src="divers-circle.jpg" width="200" height="162"
    alt="A circle of divers practice their skills" /></p>
<p>Glad you could drop in and share some air with us! You've
    passed your underwater navigation skills and successfully
    found your way to the start point - or in this case, our home
    page.</p>
```

Whoa, hold up there. Let's talk about all this img stuff (don't worry, it's pretty simple). The img element is used to insert an image into our web page, and the attributes src, alt, width, and height describe the image that we're inserting. src is just the name of the image file. In this case, it's divers-circle.jpg, which you can grab from the code archive. alt is some alternative text that can be displayed in place of the image if, for some reason, it can't be displayed. This is useful for visitors to your site who may be blind (they have web browsers, too!), search engines, and users of slow Internet connections. width and height should be pretty obvious: they give the width and height of the image, measured in pixels. Don't worry if you don't know what a pixel is; we'll look into images in more detail a bit later.

Figure 2.16. Divers pausing in a circle

Go and grab `divers-circle.jpg` from the code archive, and put it into your web site's folder. The image is shown in Figure 2.16.

Open `index.html` in your text editor and add the following markup just after the level two heading (h2):

File: **index.html (excerpt)**

```
<p><img src="divers-circle.jpg" width="200" height="162"
    alt="A circle of divers practice their skills" /></p>
```

Save the changes, then view the homepage in your browser. It should look like the display shown in Figure 2.17.

Figure 2.17. Displaying an image on the homepage

Adding Structure

Paragraphs? No problem. Headings? You've got them under your belt. In fact, you're now familiar with the basic structure of a web page. The small selection of tags that we've discussed so far are fairly easy to remember, as their purposes are obvious (remember: p = paragraph). But what the heck is a div?

A div is used to divide up a web page and, in doing so, to provide a definite structure that can be used to great effect when combined with CSS.

The strange thing about a div is that, normally, it has no effect on the styling of the text it contains, except for the fact that it adds a break before and after the contained text. Consider the following markup:

```
<p>This is a paragraph.</p>
<p>So is this.</p>
```

If you were to change those paragraph tags to divs, there would be very little obvious change in the page's appearance when you viewed it in a browser (as Figure 2.18 shows).

```
<p>This is a paragraph.</p>
<div>This looks like a paragraph, but it's actually a div.</div>
<p>This is another paragraph.</p>
<div>This is another div.</div>
```

Figure 2.18. Paragraphs displaying similarly to divs

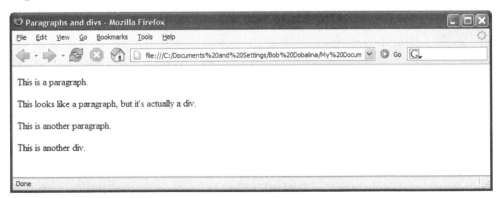

"But they look exactly the same! What's the difference between using a div and a p?", you may protest. Well, the purpose of a div is to divide up a web page into distinct sections, adding structural meaning, whereas p should be used to create a paragraph of text.

Use Elements as Intended

IMPORTANT Never use an XHTML element for a purpose for which it was not intended. This really is a golden rule!

Rather than leaving the paragraph tags as they are, you might decide to have something like this:

```
<div>
  <p>This is a paragraph inside a div.</p>
  <p>So is this.</p>
</div>
```

You can have as many paragraphs as you like inside that div element, but note that you cannot place div elements inside paragraphs. Think of a div as a container that's used to group related items together, and you can't go wrong.

If we look at our homepage in the browser, it's possible to identify areas that have certain purposes. These are listed below, and depicted in Figure 2.19. We have:

❏ a header area that contains:

   ❏ the site name

   ❏ a tag line

❏ an area of body content

Figure 2.19 shows how the different segments of content can be carved up into distinct areas based on the purposes of those segments.

Take the homepage we've been working on (`index.html`) and, in your text editor of choice, add `<div>` and `</div>` tags around the sections suggested in Figure 2.19. While you're adding those `div`s, add an `id` attribute to each, appropriately allocating the names `header`, `sitebranding`, `tagline`, and `bodycontent`. Remember that attribute names should be written in lowercase, and their values should be contained within quotation marks.

Figure 2.19. Noting distinct sections in the basic web page

No Sharing ids!

Tip

id attributes are used in XHTML to identify elements, so no two elements should share the same **id** value. You can use these **id**s later, when you're dealing with elements via CSS or JavaScript.

h1, header, and head

Tip

An **id** attribute set to **header** should not be confused with headings on the page (**h1**, **h2**, and so on); nor is it the same as the **head** of your HTML page. The **id=** attribute could just as easily have been named **topstuff** or **pageheader**. It doesn't matter, so long as the attribute name describes the *purpose* of that page section to a fellow human being (or to yourself 12 months after you devised it, and have forgotten what you were thinking at the time!).

To get you started, I've done a little work on the first part of the page. In the snippet below, that section has been changed to a **div** with an **id** attribute:

File: **index.html (excerpt)**

```
<div id="header">
  <h1>BubbleUnder.com</h1>
  <p>Diving club for the south-west UK - let's make a splash!</p>
</div> <!-- end of header div -->
```

Now, try doing the same: apply `divs` to the parts of the content that we've identified as "site branding" and "tag line."

Nesting Explained

We already know that `divs` can contain paragraphs, but a `div` can also contain a number of other `divs`. This is called **nesting**. It's not tricky, it's just a matter of putting one div inside the other, and making sure you get your closing tags right.

```
<div id="outer">
  <div id="nested1">
    <p>A paragraph inside the first nested div.</p>
  </div>
  <div id="nested2">
    <p>A paragraph inside the second nested div.</p>
  </div>
</div>
```

As Figure 2.19 shows, some nesting is taking place: the "site branding" and "tag line" `divs` are nested inside the "header" `div`.

The Sectioned Page: all Divided Up

All things being well, your XHTML should now look like this:

File: **index.html**

```
<!DOCTYPE html PUBLIC "-//W3C//DTD XHTML 1.0 Strict//EN"
    "http://www.w3.org/TR/xhtml1/DTD/xhtml1-strict.dtd">
<html xmlns="http://www.w3.org/1999/xhtml">
  <head>
    <title>Bubble Under - The diving club for the south-west
        UK</title>
    <meta http-equiv="Content-Type"
        content="text/html; charset=utf-8" />
  </head>
  <body>
    <div id="header">
      <div id="sitebranding">
        <h1>BubbleUnder.com</h1>
      </div>
      <div id="tagline">
        <p>Diving club for the south-west UK - let's make
            a splash!</p>
```

```
    </div>
  </div> <!-- end of header div -->
  <div id="bodycontent">
    <h2>Welcome to our super-dooper Scuba site</h2>
    <p><img src="divers-circle.jpg" width="200" height="162"
        alt="A circle of divers practice their skills" /></p>
    <p>Glad you could drop in and share some air with us! You've
        passed your underwater navigation skills and
        successfully found your way to the start point - or in
        this case, our home page.</p>
    <h3>About Us</h3>
    <p>Bubble Under is a group of diving enthusiasts based in
        the south-west UK who meet up for diving trips in the
        summer months when the weather is good and the bacon
        rolls are flowing. We arrange weekends away as small
        groups to cut the costs of accommodation and travel and
        to ensure that everyone gets a trustworthy dive
        buddy.</p>
    <p>Although we're based in the south-west, we don't stay on
        our own turf: past diving weekends away have included
        trips up to Scapa Flow in Scotland and to Malta's
        numerous wreck sites.</p>
    <p>When we're not diving, we often meet up in a local pub
        to talk about our recent adventures (any excuse,
        eh?).</p>
    <h3>Contact Us</h3>
    <p>To find out more, contact Club Secretary Bob Dobalina on
        01793 641207 or
        <a href="mailto:bob@bubbleunder.com">email
        bob@bubbleunder.com</a>.</p>
  </div> <!-- end of bodycontent div -->
  </body>
</html>
```

 Tip

Indenting your Markup

It's a good idea to "indent" your markup when nesting elements on a web page, as is demonstrated with the items inside the div section above. Indenting your code can help resolve problems later, as you can more clearly see which items sit inside other items. Note that indenting is only really useful for the person—perhaps you!—who's looking at the source markup. It does not affect how the browser interprets or displays the web page.[3]

---

[3] The one exception to this is the **pre** element. Pre is short for pre-formatted, and any text marked up with this element appears on the screen exactly as it appears in the source; in other words, carriage

Notice that, in the markup above, comments appear after some of the closing `div` tags. These comments are optional, but again, commenting is a good habit to get into as it helps you fix problems later. Often, it's not possible to view your opening and closing `<div>` tags in the same window, as they're wrapped around large blocks of XHTML. If you have several nested `<div>` tags, you might see something like this at the end of your markup:

```
    </div>
  </div>
</div>
```

In such cases, you might find it difficult to work out which `div` is being closed off at each point. It may not yet be apparent why this is important or useful, but once we start using CSS to style our pages, errors in the XHTML can have an impact. Adding some comments here and there can really help you debug later.

```
    </div> <!-- end of inner div -->
  </div> <!-- end of nested div -->
</div> <!-- end of outer div -->
```

How does the web page look? Well, we're not going to include a screen shot this time, because adding those `div` elements should make no visual difference at all. The changes we just made are structural ones that we'll build on later.

Show a Little Restraint

Don't go overboard adding `div`s. Some people can get carried away as they section off the page, with `<div>` tags appearing all over the place. Overly enthusiastic use of the `div` can result in a condition that has become known as "div-itis." Be careful not to litter your markup with superfluous `<div>` tags just because you can.

Splitting Up the Page

We've been making good progress on our fictitious site … but is a web site really a web site when it contains only one page? Just as the question, "Can you have a sentence with just one word?" can be answered with a one-word sentence ("Yes"), so too can the question about our one-page web site. But it's not really ideal, is it? You didn't buy this book to learn how to create one page, did you?

---

returns, spaces, and any tabs that you've included will be honored. The `pre` element is usually used to show code examples.

Let's take a look at how we can split the page we've been working on into separate entities, and how these pages relate to each other.

First, let's just ensure that your page is in good shape before we go forward. The page should reflect the markup shown in the last large block presented in the previous section (after we added the `<div>` tags). If not, go to the code archive and grab the version that contains the `divs` (`/chapter2/web-site_files/05_with_divs/index.html`). Save it as `index.html` in your web site's folder (if you see a prompt that asks whether you want to overwrite the existing file, click Yes).

Got that file ready? Let's break it into three pages. First, make two copies of the file:

❑ Click on the `index.html` icon in Windows Explorer or Finder.

❑ To copy the file, select Edit > Copy.

❑ To paste a copy in the same location, select Edit > Paste.

❑ Repeat the process once more.

You should now have three HTML files in the folder that holds your web site files. The `index.html` file should stay as it is for the time being, but take a moment to rename the other two (select each file in turn, choosing File > Rename, if you're using Windows; Mac users, simply select the file by clicking on it, then hit **Return** to edit the filename).

❑ Rename one file as `contact.html` (all lowercase).

❑ Rename the other one as `about.html` (all lowercase).

Where's my File Extension?

If your filename appears as just `index` in Windows Explorer, your system is currently set up to hide extensions for files that Windows recognizes. To make the extensions visible, follow these simple steps:

1. Launch Windows Explorer.

2. For Windows ME/2000/XP, select Tools > Folder Options... (on Windows 98, this is View > Folder Options...).

3. Select the View tab.

4.   In the Advanced Settings group, make sure that Hide extensions for known file types does not have a tick next to it.

We have three identical copies of our XHTML page. Now, we need to edit the content of these pages so that each page includes only the content that's relevant to that page.

To open an existing file in Notepad, select File > Open..., and in the window that appears, change Files of type to All Files. Now, when you go to your Web folder, you'll see that all the files in that folder are available for opening.

Opening a file in TextEdit is a similar process. Select File > Open... to open a file, but make sure that Ignore rich text commands is checked.

In your text editor, open each page in turn, and edit them as follows (remembering to save your changes to each before you open the next file):

index.html   Delete the "About Us" and "Contact Us" sections (both the headings and the paragraphs that follow them), ensuring that the rest of the markup remains untouched. Be careful not to delete the `<div>` and `</div>` tags that enclose the body content.

about.html   Delete the introductory spiel (the level two heading and associated paragraphs, including the image) and remove the "Contact Us" section (including the heading and paragraphs).

contact.html   You should be getting the hang of this now (if you're not sure you've got it right, keep reading: we'll show the altered markup in a moment). This time, we're removing the introductory spiel and the "About Us" section.

Now, each of the three files contains the content that suits its respective filename, but a further change is required for the two newly created files. Open about.html in your text editor and make the following amendments:

❑   Change the contents of the `title` element to read "About BubbleUnder.com: who we are; what this site is for."

❑   Change the level three heading `<h3>About Us</h3>` to a level two heading. In the process of editing our original homepage, we've lost one of our heading levels. Previously, the "About Us" and "Contact Us" headings were marked up as level three headings that sat under the level two "Welcome" heading.

It's not good practice to skip heading levels—an h2 following h1 is preferable to an h3 following an h1.

Next, open contact.html in your text editor and make the following changes:

☐ Amend the contents of the title element to read, "Contact Us at Bubble Under."

☐ Change the level three heading to a level two heading, as you did for about.html.

If everything has gone to plan, you should have three files named index.html, about.html, and contact.html.

The markup for each should be as follows:

File: **index.html**

```
<!DOCTYPE html PUBLIC "-//W3C//DTD XHTML 1.0 Strict//EN"
    "http://www.w3.org/TR/xhtml1/DTD/xhtml1-strict.dtd">
<html xmlns="http://www.w3.org/1999/xhtml">
  <head>
    <title>Bubble Under - The diving club for the south-west
        UK</title>
    <meta http-equiv="Content-Type"
        content="text/html; charset=utf-8" />
  </head>
  <body>
    <div id="header">
      <div id="sitebranding">
        <h1>BubbleUnder.com</h1>
      </div>
      <div id="tagline">
        <p>Diving club for the south-west UK - let's make a
            splash!</p>
      </div>
    </div> <!-- end of header div -->
    <div id="bodycontent">
      <h2>Welcome to our super-dooper Scuba site</h2>
      <p><img src="divers-circle.jpg"
          alt="A circle of divers practice their skills"
          width="200" height="162" /></p>
      <p>Glad you could drop in and share some air with us! You've
          passed your underwater navigation skills and
          successfully found your way to the start point - or in
          this case, our home page.</p>
```

```
    </div> <!-- end of bodycontent div -->
  </body>
</html>
```

```
<!DOCTYPE html PUBLIC "-//W3C//DTD XHTML 1.0 Strict//EN"
    "http://www.w3.org/TR/xhtml1/DTD/xhtml1-strict.dtd">
<html xmlns="http://www.w3.org/1999/xhtml">
  <head>
    <title>About Bubble Under: who we are, what this site is
        for</title>
    <meta http-equiv="Content-Type"
        content="text/html; charset=utf-8" />
  </head>
  <body>
    <div id="header">
      <div id="sitebranding">
        <h1>BubbleUnder.com</h1>
      </div>
      <div id="tagline">
        <p>Diving club for the south-west UK - let's make a
            splash!</p>
      </div>
    </div> <!-- end of header div -->
    <div id="bodycontent">
      <h2>About Us</h2>
      <p>Bubble Under is a group of diving enthusiasts based in
          the south-west UK who meet up for diving trips in the
          summer months when the weather is good and the bacon
          rolls are flowing. We arrange weekends away as small
          groups to cut the costs of accommodation and travel and
          to ensure that everyone gets a trustworthy dive
          buddy.</p>
      <p>Although we're based in the south-west, we don't stay on
          our own turf: past diving weekends away have included
          trips up to Scapa Flow in Scotland and to Malta's
          numerous wreck sites.</p>
      <p>When we're not diving, we often meet up in a local pub
          to talk about our recent adventures (any excuse,
          eh?).</p>
    </div> <!-- end of bodycontent div -->
  </body>
</html>
```

File: **contact.html**

```
<!DOCTYPE html PUBLIC "-//W3C//DTD XHTML 1.0 Strict//EN"
    "http://www.w3.org/TR/xhtml1/DTD/xhtml1-strict.dtd">
<html xmlns="http://www.w3.org/1999/xhtml">
  <head>
    <title>Contact Us at Bubble Under</title>
    <meta http-equiv="Content-Type"
        content="text/html; charset=utf-8" />
  </head>
  <body>
    <div id="header">
      <div id="sitebranding">
        <h1>BubbleUnder.com</h1>
      </div>
      <div id="tagline">
        <p>Diving club for the south-west UK - let's make a
            splash!</p>
      </div>
    </div> <!-- end of header div -->
    <div id="bodycontent">
      <h2>Contact Us</h2>
      <p>To find out more, contact Club Secretary Bob Dobalina on
          01793 641207 or <a
          href="mailto:bob@bubbleunder.com">email
          bob@bubbleunder.com</a>.</p>
    </div> <!-- end of bodycontent div -->
  </body>
</html>
```

Linking Between our New Pages

We've successfully created a three-page web site, but there's a small problem: there are no links between the pages! Try for yourself: open index.html and take a look at the display. How will you get from one page to another?

To enable site visitors to move around, we need to add navigation. Navigation relies on **anchors**, which are more commonly referred to as links. The XHTML for an anchor, or link, is as follows:

```
<a href="filename.html">Link text here</a>
```

The a element might not be intuitive (it stands for "anchor"), but you'll get to know this one very quickly: it's what the Web is built on! There are almost as many links in use on the Web as there are Elvis impersonators in Las Vegas. *Almost.*

❑ The a element contains the **link text** that will be clicked (which, by default, appears on the screen as blue, underlined text).

❑ The href attribute refers to the URL to which you're linking (be that a file stored locally on your computer, or a page on a live web site). Unfortunately, again, href is not immediately memorable (it stands for "hypertext reference"), but you'll use it so often that you'll soon remember it.

Don't Click Here!

The link text—the words inside the anchor element, which appear underlined on the screen—should be a neat summary of that link's purpose (to "email bob@bubbleunder.com," for example). All too often, you'll see people asking you to "Click here to submit an image," or "Click here to notify us of your change of address." Never use "Click here" links—it really is bad linking practice and is discouraged for usability and accessibility reasons.[4]

Let's create a simple navigation menu that you can drop into your pages. Our navigation is just a list of three links. Here's the markup:

```
<ul>
  <li><a href="index.html">Home</a></li>
  <li><a href="about.html">About Us</a></li>
  <li><a href="contact.html">Contact Us</a></li>
</ul>
```

We'll place all of this inside a div, so we can quickly and easily see what this block of XHTML represents.

```
<div id="navigation">
  <ul>
    <li><a href="index.html">Home</a></li>
    <li><a href="about.html">About Us</a></li>
    <li><a href="contact.html">Contact Us</a></li>
  </ul>
</div> <!-- end of navigation div -->
```

Now, we just need to paste this markup into an appropriate place on each of our pages. A good position would be just after the header has finished, before the

---

[4] *Why 'Click here' is bad linking practice* [http://www.cs.tut.fi/~jkorpela/www/click.html], Jukka Korpela.

main body content starts. In the code below, the navigation block appears in position on the homepage:

File: **index.html**

```
<!DOCTYPE html PUBLIC "-//W3C//DTD XHTML 1.0 Strict//EN"
    "http://www.w3.org/TR/xhtml1/DTD/xhtml1-strict.dtd">
<html xmlns="http://www.w3.org/1999/xhtml">
  <head>
    <title>Bubble Under - The diving club for the south-west
        UK</title>
    <meta http-equiv="Content-Type" content="text/html;
        charset=utf-8" />
  </head>
  <body>
    <div id="header">
      <div id="sitebranding">
        <h1>BubbleUnder.com</h1>
      </div>
      <div id="tagline">
        <p>Diving club for the south-west UK - let's make a
            splash!</p>
      </div>
    </div> <!-- end of header div -->
    <div id="navigation">
      <ul>
        <li><a href="index.html">Home</a></li>
        <li><a href="about.html">About Us</a></li>
        <li><a href="contact.html">Contact Us</a></li>
      </ul>
    </div> <!-- end of navigation div -->
    <div id="bodycontent">
      <h2>Welcome to our super-dooper Scuba site</h2>
      <p><img src="divers-circle.jpg" width="200" height="162"
          alt="A circle of divers practice their skills" /></p>
      <p>Glad you could drop in and share some air with us!
          You've passed your underwater navigation skills and
          successfully found your way to the start point - or in
          this case, our home page.</p>
    </div> <!-- end of bodycontent div -->
  </body>
</html>
```

You should now be looking at a page like the one shown in Figure 2.20.

Figure 2.20. Displaying simple navigation on the page

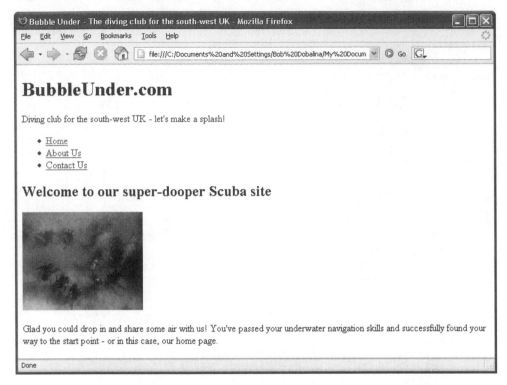

Add the links to `contact.html` and `about.html`, then try clicking on the links that you've just added. It should be possible to flick between all three pages, as shown in Figure 2.21.

This is a landmark: you're now the creator of a working, navigable web site! Don't crack open the bubbly just yet, though: first, let's discuss a few more XHTML elements that you can add to your pages.

Figure 2.21. Navigating the web site

The blockquote (Who Said That?)

We're going to add a sound-bite—well, a written quote, to be precise—to the About Us page. Here's the line:

> "Happiness is a dip in the ocean followed by a pint or two of Old Speckled Hen. You can quote me on that!"

We'll add the quote after the final paragraph in `about.html`; here's the markup you'll need:

```
<blockquote>
  <p>"Happiness is a dip in the ocean followed by a pint or two of
      Old Speckled Hen. You can quote me on that!"</p>
</blockquote>
```

Or is it? Who's doing the talking? Well, it's our dear (though fictional) Club Secretary, Bob Dobalina.

File: **about.html (excerpt)**

```
<p>Or as our man Bob Dobalina would put it:</p>
<blockquote>
  <p>"Happiness is a dip in the ocean followed by a pint or two of
     Old Speckled Hen. You can quote me on that!"</p>
</blockquote>
```

The quotation can contain as many paragraphs as you like, as long as each one starts and ends correctly, and the opening <blockquote> tag is closed off properly.

Displaying `blockquote`s

In most browsers, your use of `blockquote` will see the quoted text indented in the page display. This effect can be overridden if it's not to your taste, but that's something we'll cover in a later chapter. On the flip side, you should *never* use the `blockquote` element for the purposes of indenting text. This is very poor form. Only use `blockquote` for its intended purpose: to present a quotation. There are other, better ways to create visual indentations.

Figure 2.22 shows how the `blockquote` above will appear on the page.

Figure 2.22. Displaying a quotation on the page

The `cite` Element

If the quote to which you've referred is written elsewhere—in a magazine, for instance, or a book, or even your own web site—you can add some information to communicate the quote's source. One way is to use the `cite` element. A citation, by default, will style the text in italics. Here's how the markup would look for a citation:

```
<p>I remember reading <cite>Salem's Lot</cite> by Stephen King as
    a child, and being very scared of the dark for days after.</p>
```

So what do we do if something is both a quotation *and* a citation? I'm glad you asked! The `blockquote` element has a `cite` attribute for this very purpose:

```
<blockquote cite="http://www.petermoore.net/sftb/chapter1.htm">
  <p>It didn't take long for a daily routine to form: when they
        left for work in the morning I'd still be in bed. And when
        they came home they'd find me sitting on the sofa, drinking
        beer and watching TV soaps.</p>
</blockquote>
```

We're not using the `cite` element (or the `cite` attribute) in the diving web site, but you may find them useful in your own web site projects.

strong and em

We mentioned the `em` element earlier in this chapter. It's a fairly straightforward element to remember. If you can imagine yourself adding some kind of inflection as you say a word, then emphasis is probably what you need. If you're looking to strike a slightly more forceful tone, then you should consider "going in `strong`."

By default, adding `em` will style text in italics, while using `strong` makes the text bold. You can combine the two if you want, but usually, one or the other will suffice. The examples below should help you understand what these elements are used for. Figure 2.23 shows how they appear in the browser.

```
<p>Although Jimmy was told to <strong>never</strong> put his hands
    on the exhaust pipe, he <em>still</em> couldn't help
    himself.</p>
```

Figure 2.23. Displaying different emphasis styles in the browser

> **Silly Jimmy - Mozilla Firefox**
>
> File   Edit   View   Go   Bookmarks   Tools   Help
>
> file:///C:/Documents%20and%20Settings/Bob%20Dobalina/My%20Docum ▾   Go
>
> Although Jimmy was told to **never** put his hands on the exhaust pipe, he *still* couldn't help himself.
>
> Done

Taking a Break

The chapter's almost at an end, so why take a break? Well, this is just an excuse for a headline pun! We have one more element to look at: the break element.

The break element (br) basically replicates what happens when you hit the carriage return on an old typewriter. To create a paragraph on an old typewriter, you'd hit **Enter** twice to give the necessary spacing. In XHTML, the fact that you're marking up a paragraph with <p> and </p> tags means the spacing is worked out for you automatically. However, if you just want to signify the start of a new line, rather than a new paragraph, the element you need is br, as demonstrated in this limerick:[5]

```
<p>The limerick packs laughs anatomical,<br />
Into space that is quite economical.<br />
But the good ones I've seen,<br />
So seldom are clean,<br />
And the clean ones so seldom are comical.</p>
```

IMPORTANT

Avoid Multiple Breaks

It's all too easy to resort to using multiple breaks in a web page to achieve a visual effect. If you find yourself doing this, something's wrong: you almost certainly need to look for a more suitable technique (we'll look at how this visual affect should be achieved later). Be careful in your use of br.

Note that br is an empty element, just like meta and img, so it's written as <br />.

---

[5] http://en.wikipedia.org/wiki/Limerick_(poetry)

Summary

Wow—what a great start we've made! In this chapter, you've built a single web page gradually into three linked pages. You've become familiar with the most commonly used XHTML tags, as well as some of the less common ones that you can apply to your web pages. But, somehow, despite all your efforts, the web pages are still looking a little on the bland side. We're going to fix that very soon: in the next chapter, we'll start to add some splashes of color, and make the site look a little more like a fun diving site and less like a boring old Word document.

3

Adding Some Style

In Chapter 1 and Chapter 2, we stepped through the process of setting up your computer so that we could develop web sites, and pulled together the beginnings of a web site with which you could impress your friends and family! The trouble is, when you came to show off your fledgling site to your nearest and dearest, they *weren't* impressed!

"That's nice dear," said your better half, then carried on doing the dishes. Even Rover (normally your biggest fan), was singularly unimpressed, and decided it would be better to curl up in a warm corner until you stopped waving the laptop in his face. What have you done wrong?

The answer is: nothing. It's true that the web site *may* look a little bland at present, but the underlying structure on which it's built is rock-solid. To return to our automotive analogy, you now have a perfect chassis and some decent bodywork, and, while your car's not making people turn their heads just yet, it's only a matter of time. Just let them see what you can do with this rolling shell!

In this chapter, we'll begin the process of adding that lick of paint to your otherwise plain site. The tool for the job is **Cascading Style Sheets—CSS** to those in the know (or with limited typing abilities). Let's take a look at what CSS can do for you.

What is CSS?

As this chapter revolves almost exclusively around CSS, it's probably a good idea to begin with a basic discussion of what CSS is, and why you should use it. As we've already mentioned, CSS stands for Cascading Style Sheets, but that's too much of a mouthful for most people—we'll stick with the abbreviation!

CSS is a language that allows you to change elements such as text size, color, bolding, background colors, border styles, and colors—even the position of elements on the page. Let's take a look at some CSS in action; we'll start by learning about **inline styles**.

Inline Styles

If you're familiar with Microsoft Word (or a similar word processing package), you may well have created your fair share of flyers, advertisements, or personal newsletters (as well as the more mundane letters to the local authorities and so on). In doing so, you've probably used text formatting options to color certain parts of your text. It's as simple as highlighting the words you want to change, then clicking on a color in a drop-down palette. The same effect can be achieved in XHTML using a little bit of inline CSS. This is what it looks like:

```
<p style="color: red;">The quick brown fox jumps over the lazy
    dog.</p>
```

In the example above, we use a `style` attribute inside the opening `<p>` tag. Applying a style to a specific XHTML element in this way is known as using an "inline style."

The `style` attribute can contain one or more **declarations** between its quotation marks. A declaration is made up of two parts: a **property**, and a **value** for that property. In the example above, the declaration is `color: red` (`color` being the property and `red` being its value).

If you wanted to, you could add another declaration to the example above. For instance, as well as having the text display in red, you might want it to appear in a bold typeface. The property that controls this effect is `font-weight`; it can have a range of different values, but mostly you'll use `normal` or `bold`. As you might expect, you'd use the following markup to make the paragraph red and bold:

```
<p style="color: red; font-weight: bold;">The quick brown fox
    jumps over the lazy dog.</p>
```

Notice that a semicolon separates the two declarations. You could carry on adding styles in this way, but beware: this approach can get messy! There are cleverer ways to apply styling, as we'll see very soon.

Adding Inline Styles

Open about.html in your text editor, and add an inline style. We want to make the text in the first paragraph after the "About Us" heading bold and blue. Refer to the previous example as you create the style.

Does the markup for your paragraph look like this?

```
<p style="color: blue; font-weight: bold;">Bubble Under is a group
    of diving enthusiasts based in the south-west UK who meet up
    for diving trips in the summer months when the weather is good
    and the bacon rolls are flowing. We arrange weekends away as
    small groups to cut the costs of accommodation and travel and
    to ensure that everyone gets a trustworthy dive buddy.</p>
```

If the markup *does* look like that shown here, save about.html and take a look at it in your browser. It should appear like the page shown in Figure 3.1.

Figure 3.1. Content displaying with blue and bold styles

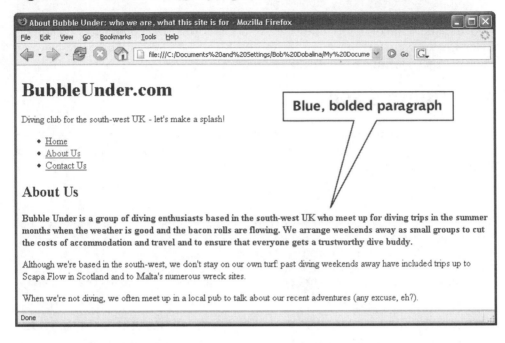

The span Element

You can easily color a whole paragraph like this, but more often than not, you'll want to pick out just a couple of specific words to highlight within a paragraph. You can do this using a `span` element, which can be wrapped around any content you like. Unlike `p`, which means paragraph, or `blockquote`, which signifies a quotation, `span` has no "meaning." A `span` is little more than a tool for highlighting the start and end of something to which you want to apply a style.[1] Instead of making that whole paragraph blue, we might want just the first two words, "Bubble Under," to be blue and bold. Here's how we can use the `span` element to achieve this:

```
<p><span style="color: blue; font-weight: bold;">Bubble
    Under</span> is a group of diving enthusiasts based in the
    south-west UK who meet up for diving trips in the summer
    months when the weather is good and the bacon rolls are
```

---

[1] Applying a `span` also gives you the ability to do some other clever things to your web page with scripting, but for our purposes, its scope is limited to the things it allows you to do with CSS.

```
flowing. We arrange weekends away as small groups to cut the
costs of accommodation and travel and to ensure that everyone
gets a trustworthy dive buddy.</p>
```

When we view that markup in a browser, we see the display shown in Figure 3.2.

Figure 3.2. Using the span element to pick out specific words for styling

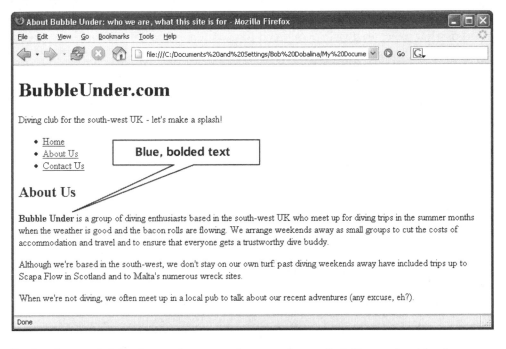

Let's take a quick look at other ways that we can apply inline styles (don't worry, this isn't part of our project site; feel free to experiment).

```
<p style="font-style: italic">The quick brown fox jumps over the
    lazy dog.</p>
```

Not surprisingly, that CSS declaration will italicize all the text in the paragraph. Here's another example, in which span is used to highlight specific words:

```
<p>The quick brown fox <span style="font-style: italic;
    font-weight: bold">jumps</span> over the lazy dog.</p>
```

Embedded Styles

Inline styles are a simple, quick way to apply some "makeup" to specific sections of a document, but this is not the best method of styling a page. Wouldn't it be better if you could set styles in just one place, rather than having to type them out every time you wanted to use them?

Embedded style sheets are a logical step up. An embedded style allows you to add to the start of a web page a section that sets out all the styles that will be used on that page. To do this, you need to use the `style` element inside the `head`:

```
<head>
  <title>Bubble Under - The diving club for the south-west
      UK</title>
  <meta http-equiv="Content-Type"
      content="text/html; charset=utf-8" />
  <style type="text/css">
    p {
      font-weight: bold;
    }
  </style>
</head>
```

In the markup shown above, we've moved the inline style into an embedded style sheet. The embedded style sheet starts with a `<style type="text/css">` tag and, predictably, ends with a `</style>` tag. The actual style declarations are enclosed in a set of **curly braces**: { and }. The p that appears before the first curly brace tells the browser what the style rules are for; in this case, we're making the text inside every p element bold. The p is called the **selector**, and it's a great tool for quickly and easily changing the appearance of lots of elements on your page. The selector, curly braces, and declarations combine to make up what's called a **rule**.

In this case, our style sheet contains one rule: "Please style all the paragraphs on this page so that the text appears in a bold font."

If we wanted to, we could add more declarations to our rule. For instance, if we wanted to make the text bold and blue, we'd add the declaration `color: blue` to our rule:

```
<style type="text/css">
  p {
    font-weight: bold;
```

```
      color: blue;
  }
</style>
```

Jargon Break

Okay, okay. There's been an awful lot of jargon so far. Let's recap: Figure 3.3 brings the theory into focus.

Figure 3.3. The anatomy of a rule

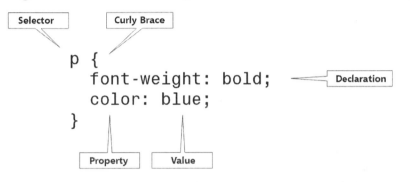

Why Embedded Styles are Better than Inline Styles

In the example provided in Figure 3.3, text in all paragraphs will display in bold, blue type. This is useful because it saves you having to type `<p style="font-weight: bold; color: blue">` every time you start a new paragraph—a clear benefit over inline styles. If you wanted to change the color of all paragraph text to red, you need only to change it in the style sheet at the top of the page. That's efficiency for you!

```
<style type="text/css">
  p {
    font-weight: bold;
    color: red;
  }
</style>
```

For this reason, an embedded style sheet is a marked improvement over inline styles. But what if you have a web site that comprises many pages? If you want to make your changes across the whole site, using embedded style sheets in the way I demonstrated above is still not quite the perfect solution. Why not? Because, to make a site-wide change, you'd have to edit the embedded style sheet on every single page of that site. The best solution is to use an **external style sheet**.

External Style Sheets

Why External Style Sheets are Better than Embedded Styles

An external style sheet provides a location in which you can place styles that can be applied on all of your web pages. This is where the true power of CSS lies, and it's for this reason that we haven't spent too much time applying inline styles or embedded styles to our diving club project site.

The Bad Old Days

In the past, or The Bad Old Days, as we'll call them, people would create web sites on a page-by-page basis, and style them on a page-by-page basis using all manner of nasty elements of which I dare not even speak! Sometimes, these sites grew beyond the webmaster's wildest imagination. "Fantastic," thought Mr or Mrs Webmaster. "My web site now has over 200 pages! Soon I'll be bigger than Microsoft." A few months later, the webmaster decided to redesign the web site and realized, with considerable horror, that he or she would have to alter each and every single web page in order to redesign the site in a consistent manner. Every page needed 20 or more different tweaks, and each tweak had to be applied consistently to every page of the site. Inevitably, some pages were missed, and eventually the redesign plan got unceremoniously dropped. In short, the ugly web site remained ugly for a whole lot longer before dying a nasty death through sheer negligence (indeed, there are many such "legacy" documents littered around the Web today). This need not be the case, though.

CSS gives you the power to set styling rules in one place. When you want to make changes to your web site, you make changes in that one place, and your whole web site changes automatically to reflect those new styles.

Happy Days! CSS Support is Here!

The good news is that the large majority of web browsers in use today offer excellent support for CSS (though this has not always been the case, which is why some people have been slow to adopt CSS-based design). Some browsers can choke on a few of the more advanced CSS techniques, but, by and large, you can style your web pages with CSS and be confident that what you see on your screen is the same view that 99.5% of your intended audience will see.

Creating an External CSS File

If you are to make use of all the benefits that an external style sheet can provide, you'll first need to create a CSS file that can be shared among all the pages of your web site. Open your text editor and enter the following:

File: **style1.css**

```
/*
CSS for Bubble Under site
*/

p {
  font-weight: bold;
  color: blue;
}
```

Save the file in the same folder as your HTML files, naming it `style1.css`; you can save a CSS file in the same way you saved your HTML files.

Note that the first few lines we typed into our CSS file will not actually do anything. Like HTML, CSS allows you to add comments. It's a shame that the tags for HTML comments are different from those for CSS comments, but they do exactly the same thing: they allow you to make notes about your work without affecting the on-screen display. In CSS, a comment starts with a `/*` and ends with a `*/`; the browser ignores anything in between. Above, we used the comment simply to make a note about the purpose of the file, namely that it is the CSS for the Bubble Under site. We've also added a rule to turn the type in all our paragraphs bold and blue.

Linking CSS to a Web Page

Before your CSS can have any effect, you need to link it to the web page, or pages, to which you want the styles to apply. To do this, you need to add a `link` element to the head of each and every web page that will be styled with CSS. Our site contains just three pages at the moment, so this will be nice and easy. The link element simply "links" a file to the page on which the element appears; in this case, the linked file is a style sheet.

Below, the new line appears in the context of the homepage:

File: **index.html** (excerpt)

```
<head>
  <title>Bubble Under - The diving club for the south-west
      UK</title>
  <meta http-equiv="Content-Type"
      content="text/html; charset=utf-8" />
  <link href="style1.css" rel="stylesheet" type="text/css" />
</head>
```

Let's take a look at what the markup means.

The href attribute tells the web browser where the style sheet file (style1.css) can be found, in the same way that the href attribute is used in an anchor to point to the destination file (e.g. <a href="home.htm">Home</a>).

The rel="stylesheet" and type="text/css" parts of the link tag tell the browser what kind of file is being linked to, and how the browser should handle the content. You should always include these important attributes when linking to a .css file.

Empty Element Alert!

The link element is another of those special empty elements we discussed in Chapter 2: it has no start or end tags. link is a complete element in its own right, and ends with the space and forward slash required by XHTML.

Now that we know how to link our pages to our CSS file, let's try it out on our project site:

❑ Open each of your web pages—index.html, about.html, and contact.html—in your text editor. Add the following line just before the closing </head> tag in each of those files.

```
<link href="style1.css" rel="stylesheet" type="text/css" />
```

❑ Be sure to save each page. Then, try opening each one in your web browser.

All of your paragraphs should now display in bold, blue text. If so, congratulations—you've now linked one style sheet to three separate pages. If you change the color specified in your `.css` file from blue to red, you should see that change reflected across your pages the next time you open them.

Now, using blue, bold text might be a good way to make sure your style sheets are correctly linked, but it's not necessarily the design effect we want to use. Remove the p rule from your style sheet, but leave the comment, and let's start building our style sheet for real.

Starting to Build our Style Sheet

The style sheet is ready to be used: it's saved in the right location, and all of your web pages (all three—count 'em!) are linked to it correctly. All we need to do, then, is set some styles!

One of the first changes that people often make to a web site's default styling is to alter the font (or typeface) that's used. On Windows, most browsers will opt for Times New Roman—the font that has been used in all the screen shots we've seen so far. For many people, though, it's a little bit dull, probably because this font is used more than any other. It's very easy to change fonts using CSS's font-family property. The best place to use this is within the body element, as shown below.

File: **style1.css**

```
/*
CSS for Bubble Under site
*/

body {
  font-family: Verdana;
}
```

Here, I've chosen to use the Verdana font. It's applied to the body element because body contains every element that you will see on the web page. The nature of the way in which CSS is applied means that every element contained in the body element will take on the same font (unless another font is specified for a given element or elements within body—but more on that a little later).

Great: Verdana it is! But … what if some people who view your site don't have Verdana installed on their computers? Hmm, that's a tricky one. The short answer is that the browser will make its best guess about which font it should use instead, but we don't have to make the browser do *all* the guesswork. The `font-family` property allows us to enter multiple fonts in the order in which we'd prefer them to be used. So, we could type something like this:

```
body {
  font-family: Verdana, Helvetica, Arial, sans-serif;
}
```

This translates as: "Please style everything in the body of my web page so that the text appears as Verdana. Failing that, please try using Helvetica and, failing that, Arial. If none of the above are installed, just use whatever sans-serif font is available."

We'll use this selection of fonts in our diving site, so let's open the style sheet file and play around with some CSS.

❑ Type the above CSS into `style1.css`.

❑ Save the file, then open the homepage (`index.html`) in your browser.

If everything went to plan, your web page (all three of them, actually) should display slightly differently than they did before. Figure 3.4 shows the appearance of our newly-styled homepage.

Sans-serif Fonts: Better for On-screen Viewing

A serif font is one that has all those fancy extensions and flourishes at the ends of each letter. These "flourishes," which are shown in Figure 3.5, are known as **serifs**. They're great for reading printed material, as they give a little shape to the words, making them easier to read.

However, on the screen, serif fonts can become a little messy, especially when they're used for smaller type—there simply aren't enough pixels on the screen to do these little flourishes justice. For this reason, you'll notice that many web sites use **sans-serif** fonts (French words that literally mean "without serif") when the font size is set quite small.

Note that when you refer to a sans-serif font in CSS, you must hyphenate the two words, i.e. `sans-serif`.

Figure 3.4. A font change in the style sheet affects the body of our web pages

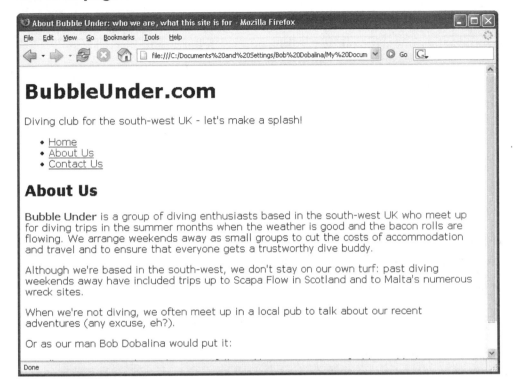

Figure 3.5. Highlighting the serifs of a serif font (Georgia)

Stylish Headings

The first element that we'll style is our level 1 headings, denoted by the h1 element. Let's add some rules to our CSS file to see what's possible when it comes to those headings. In your text editor, add the following to style1.css:

```
h1 {
  font-family: "Trebuchet MS", Arial, Helvetica, sans-serif;
}
```

Save the CSS file and refresh your view of the homepage in your browser. Can you see what's changed? All the first-level headings now display in the Trebuchet MS font, while everything else displays in Verdana.

The font we've chosen is another sans-serif font, but it's different enough to provide plenty of contrast with the paragraphs, as Figure 3.6 illustrates.

Figure 3.6. h1 headings displaying in one font (Trebuchet MS) while other text displays in another (Verdana)

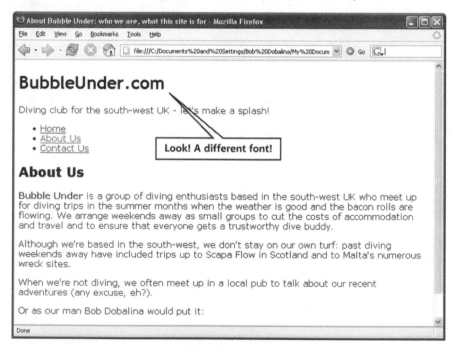

Some Font Names Deserve Quotes

In the example above, "Trebuchet MS" appeared in quotation marks. You don't need to bother wrapping quote marks around font names, unless the font comprises several words, such as "Courier New" or "Times New Roman." A single-word font name, such as Arial or Verdana, does not need to be wrapped in double quotes.

Have a quick look around all three pages of the web site and you'll see that your new styles have been applied to all your web pages. Let's go a step (or two) further.

What's Going On? Nothing's Changed!

If you try refreshing your browser's view of a page and nothing appears to change, first check that you saved the changes you made to the CSS file. If you have saved the altered file, check that you typed the CSS exactly as described. If you did, you may be experiencing a **caching** problem with your browser.

Web browsers "cache" some content. What this means is that, to save having to download files each and every time you visit a given web page, your browser uses versions of the files that it saved to the hard drive previously. This reduces the time it takes to display a web page that has been loaded once before. Unfortunately, your cache can get out of date, and when that happens, the page you visit (i.e. you enter the URL, and the browser pulls the page stored in its cache) might not display the most recent data.

This happens most frequently with images, but it can also occur with CSS files. The good news is that you have control over your browser's cache settings and the amount of space the cache takes up on your hard disk before previously cached content gets replaced with newer data. You can poke around your browser's settings for words like "Cache" or "Temporary Internet Files" to change these settings; however, most users opt to leave their caches to the default settings.

If you're positive that you've made the necessary changes to your CSS file (and saved them) correctly, you may need to "force-reload" the CSS file in your browser.

To stop the caching problem and force the browser to get the most up-to-date version of your CSS file, simply hold down the **Shift** key and click on the Refresh (or reload) icon on your browser's toolbar.

A Mixture of New Styles

Let's change the look of the site a little more: we'll add more styles to the body, and change the look of the navigation. Copy the CSS below into your `style1.css` file (or copy it from the book's code archive):

File: **style1.css**

```
/*
CSS for Bubble Under site
*/

body {
  font-family: Verdana, Helvetica, Arial, sans-serif;
  background-color: #e2edff;
  line-height: 125%;
  padding: 15px;
}

h1 {
  font-family: "Trebuchet MS", Helvetica, Arial, sans-serif;
  font-size: x-large;
}

li {
  font-size: small;
}

h2 {
  color: blue;
  font-size: medium;
  font-weight: normal;
}

p {
  font-size: small;
  color: navy;
}
```

Save the CSS file, then click Reload in your browser. Hopefully, you'll be looking at a page like the one shown in Figure 3.7.

Figure 3.7. Applying subtle changes to the CSS that affects font display

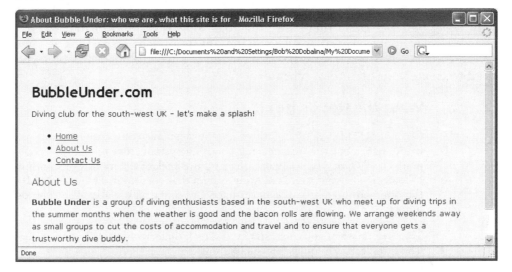

A New Look in a Flash!

We've introduced quite a few new style declarations here. Let's examine a few of them in the order in which they appear in the CSS file.

File: **style1.css (excerpt)**

```
body {
  font-family: Verdana, Helvetica, Arial, sans-serif;
  background-color: #e2edff;
  padding: 15px;
  line-height: 125%;
}
```

The background-color property can be applied to most elements on a web page, and there are many different ways in which you can specify the color itself. One is to use recognized color names[2] such as navy, blue, red, yellow, and so on. These are easy to remember and spell, but you are limited somewhat by the range. Another way of referencing colors is to use a **hexadecimal** color specification. Yes, you're right: that *does* sound a little scary. I mean, just look at it:

---

[2] http://www.w3schools.com/html/html_colornames.asp

```
background-color: #e2edff;
```

It's hardly intuitive, is it? This obscure-looking reference translates to a light shade of blue. You could not, as a beginner, begin to guess that this would be a light blue, but thankfully there are numerous tools on the Web that let you choose a color from a chart, then give you the code to match. Take a look at some of these tools,[3] and you'll soon be able to find the hexadecimal numbers you need to create your ideal color schemes.

What the Heck's Hex?

Colors in HTML are often written as a hexadecimal color specification. You might remember the hexadecimal counting system from your high school math class. Or maybe you were asleep up the back of the room. Never mind. Hexadecimal is that weird counting system that goes up to 16 instead of 10; the one you thought you'd never have any practical use for. Well, you do now!

That's right: when you count in hexadecimal, there are not ten, but **16 digits**. The hexadecimal sequence looks like this:

```
0, 1, 2, 3, 4, 5, 6, 7, 8, 9, A, B, C, D, E, F, 10, 11,
12, 13...
```

Eh? What's happening here? Well, as you can see, after we get to 9, instead of going straight to 10 (as we do when counting in decimal) we go through A, B, C, D, E, and F before we finally hit 10. That gives us six extra digits to use when we count! Sound confusing? Well, it is. But as it so happens, computers can count in hexadecimal far better than humans can.

The key here is that all of those numbers that we know and love in the decimal system, like 2,748, 15,000,000 and 42, can be represented in hexadecimal. Look, Table 3.1 proves it!

Table 3.1. Decimal to hexadecimal conversion

Decimal	Hexadecimal
7	7
15	F
2,748	ABC
15,000,000	E4E1C0
42	2A

---

[3] A good selection of links to color scheme tools is available at http://www.clagnut.com/blog/260/.

When a color is expressed as a hexadecimal number, such as `ff0000`, that number actually comprises three values that are joined together. The values represent the proportions of red (the `ff` part), green (the first two zeros), and blue (the second two zeros) that are mixed to create the specified color. Those three primary colors can be combined to display any color on the screen, similar to the way a television set uses different intensities of red, green, and blue to create a single dot on its screen. In this example, `ff` is the value for red, while the green and blue values are zero. It may not surprise you, then, to learn that `#ff0000` will give you the color red.

The `padding` property is used to provide space between the outside edge of the element in question and the content that sits inside it. Because we're referring to the `body` element, you can think of the outside edge as being the top, bottom, and sides of the browser's viewport (that being the part of the browser where the web page is viewable, not including any of the browser's tool bars, menus, or scroll bars). We'll take a look at `padding` in more detail in Chapter 4.

The value we've given to this property specifies how much space must exist between the edge of the viewport and the content. In this case, we've specified `15px`, or 15 pixels. We mentioned pixels before, when we specified the size of an image, but what is a pixel? Basically, one pixel is one of the tiny dots that make up what you see on the computer screen. The screen itself is made up of hundreds of thousands of these pixels, so a 15-pixel border isn't going to take up too much space on your screen!

The `line-height` property is an interesting one. By increasing that value (we used 125% in our example), you can increase the space between lines of text—something that can greatly increase legibility. Try tweaking this value, save your CSS file, and see how the new value affects the text on your web page.

Now, to the paragraph styles:

File: **style1.css (excerpt)**

```
p {
  font-size: small;
  color: navy;
}
```

We've already shown that it's possible to change the color of text in a paragraph; now, we're going to settle on the sensible (and appropriate!) color of navy.

Let's see what's changed with the list item style:

File: **style1.css (excerpt)**

```
li {
  font-size: small;
}
```

The size of the list items has changed ever so slightly through our application of the `font-size` property. Here, we've decided to set the font size using the `small` keyword, but we could just as easily have used the percentage or pixel methods we've already seen—there are many ways to skin a cat with CSS! Font size keywords range from `xx-small` to `xx-large` and offer a quick way to style text. Unfortunately, different browsers implement font size keywords slightly differently, and unfortunately you can't be guaranteed that an `xx-large` font will render at the same size in all browsers. However, unless you're extremely worried about precise sizing, these keywords make a good starting point.[4]

Next, we introduced a new rule, this time for the `h1` element (the main heading on our web pages, which displays the site name) and, once again, used a `font-size` property to specify the size of the text (extra large is the answer!).

File: **style1.css (excerpt)**

```
h1 {
  font-family: "Trebuchet MS", Helvetica, Arial, sans-serif;
  font-size: x-large;
}
```

The `h2` element also gets a minor makeover:

File: **style1.css (excerpt)**

```
h2 {
  color: blue;
  font-size: medium;
  font-weight: normal;
}
```

Browsers usually display headings in bold type, but we can have them display in standard type by giving the `font-weight` property a value of `normal`.

---

[4] For more reasons than we have space to discuss, text sizing in CSS is a topic that causes heated debate in some circles. As you become familiar with CSS, you may want to learn more about the other text-sizing techniques that it offers. A good place to start would be SitePoint's CSS discussion forum at http://www.sitepoint.com/launch/cssforum/.

A Beginner's Palette of Styling Options

We've looked at some examples of styles that can be applied to your web pages through CSS, but the examples we've seen have been a mixed bag (deliberately so). There are so many more from which you can pick and choose—too many possibilities, in fact, for us to be able to list them all here. However, this section lists some of the basic properties and values with which you might like to experiment. Feel free to try any of these in your CSS file. Note that we'll be adding to this list in subsequent chapters; it's by no means exhaustive!

color
background-color

As we've seen, both of these properties can take color keywords (e.g. `red`, `blue`, `green`, or `yellow`) or hexadecimal color specifications such as `#ff0000`.

font-family

This property takes a list of fonts, containing any fonts you choose in order of preference. Be sure to provide options that users are likely to have on their computers (e.g. Arial, Verdana, etc.). This list should end with one of the "generic" CSS fonts such as `serif` or `sans-serif`, which any browser that supports CSS will recognize.

font-size

This property can be any one of the following:

font size keywords

- ❑ `xx-small`
- ❑ `x-small`
- ❑ `small`
- ❑ `medium`
- ❑ `large`
- ❑ `x-large`
- ❑ `xx-large`

a relative unit
such as a percentage (e.g. `140%`)

fixed font sizes

❏ pixels (e.g. `20px`)

❏ points (e.g. `12pt`, as you may be used to using in Microsoft Word)

Fixed font sizes are not always a great idea, as they cannot easily be scaled up or down to suit the reader's needs. Relative font sizes are definitely the preferred option.

font-weight   `bold` or `normal`

font-style   `normal` or `italic`

text-decoration   `none`, `underline`, `overline`, or `line-through`

 Tip

Backing it Up!

Before you experiment with the CSS properties above, it might be an idea to make a backup of your CSS file, just in case you run into difficulties. Remember that you can download all the examples used in this chapter from the code archive if you accidentally mangle your CSS file. If this happens, don't worry! It's all part of the learning process, and you can be sure that no animals will be harmed in the process. Only a handful of poor CSS selectors will be mistreated. Shed no tears!

Recap: the Style Story so Far

Let's allow ourselves a moment to reflect. Our site now boasts a CSS file with a selection of attractive styles. We're in the enviable position of being able to change the site at a whim by altering just that one CSS file. Let's try styling some more of the elements on our web pages.

Changing the Emphasis

❏ Open `about.html` in your text editor.

❏ Find the paragraph about meeting up in a local pub and add an emphasis element as shown here:

File: **about.html** (excerpt)

```
<p>And when we're not diving, we often meet up in a local pub
   to talk about our recent adventures (<em>any</em> excuse,
   eh?).</p>
```

☐ Save the page, then view it in your web browser; it should appear as shown in Figure 3.8. As you can see, emphasis elements appear in italics by default. We're going to use CSS to change that default style.

Figure 3.8. Using emphasis to set type to italics by default

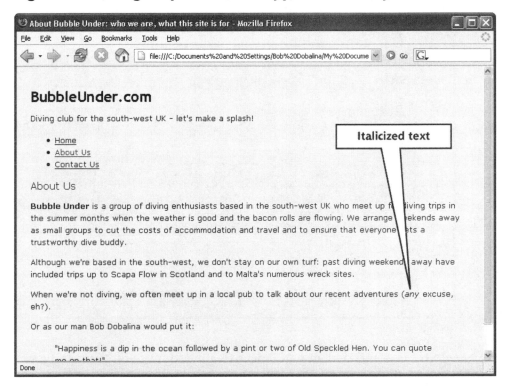

☐ Open `style1.css` (if you haven't already opened it for editing) and add the following rule below the others:

File: **style1.css** (excerpt)

```
em {
  font-style: normal;
```

```
text-transform: uppercase;
}
```

❏ Save the CSS file, then refresh your browser's view of the About Us page. Does your page look like Figure 3.9?

Figure 3.9. The emphasis appearing as capitalized text instead of italics

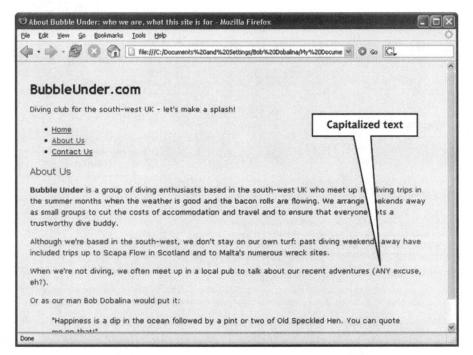

Now, whenever you add an **em** element to any web page of your site (assuming that page is linked to `style1.css`), the emphasized text will appear in capital letters, not italics. But this raises an interesting point: when should you override a browser's default style for one of your own choosing? Presumably, the default styles that browsers use were selected carefully; how can you be sure that your redefinition of the styles is a good idea? Weren't italics a suitable style for emphasis? They probably were. As Spiderman's creators say, "With great power comes great responsibility," so be sure to exercise caution. Just because you *can* change a default style does not always mean you *should*.

Perhaps a compromise is in order. Let's change the emphasis so that it's still italic, but also appears in uppercase letters. All we need to do is remove the `font-style` declaration; the `em` element will then revert to its default italicized appearance, as depicted in Figure 3.10.

File: **style1.css (excerpt)**

```css
em {
  text-transform: uppercase;
}
```

Figure 3.10. Emphasis displaying as uppercase italics

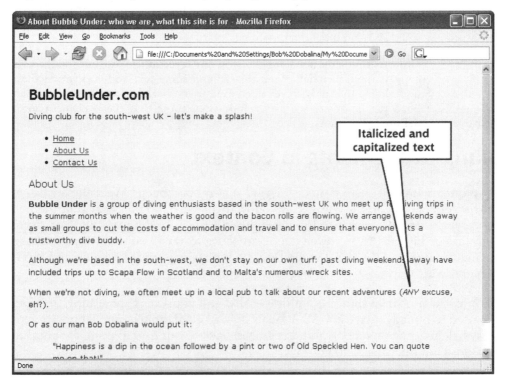

Emphasis vs Italics

You might well be asking yourself, "If I want an italic font, can't I use an italic element?" In fact, HTML provides an `i` element for just this purpose, but its use isn't recommended. Why not? Well, marking something up as `i` says nothing about its meaning; `i` only communicates how it should be presented on the screen. Such elements are referred to as **presentational**

HTML elements, and they should be avoided. Likewise, the **b** element (for bold), another old HTML element, should not be used. The preferred option is to use **strong** or, if you just want to display headings in bold, to use CSS.

Why is this important? It mightn't seem important to you, as you look at the italicized text in your web browser. But imagine you were a blind user of software that read web pages aloud to you, instead of displaying them on the screen. Such a program (called a **screen reader**) would read text marked up with an **em** element with slight emphasis, and text marked up with **strong** in a slow, powerful voice … but what would it do with text marked up with **i** or **b**? Well, these elements say nothing about the meaning of the text, so it would ignore them. The same is true of many programs that analyze web pages, such as web indexing programs run by Yahoo! and Google—**em** and **strong** tags tell these programs that the words inside them are important, whereas **i** and **b** tell them nothing.

One other presentational tag that you might see others use, but should *never* copy, is the **u** element. Wrap this around some text and you get needless underlining that only serves to confuse users (because in web pages, underlined text normally signifies a link—something that the **u** element most definitely does not).

Looking at Elements in Context

Pop quiz: which of these items is bigger? A pen or a sheep? Well, the answer is either, depending on the context. If you were a farmer, you'd swear that the pen is bigger. After all, you spend many hours a week rounding up herds of sheep into a nice big pen. If, however, you're an office worker, you'd opt for the sheep being the larger of the two—you'd find it a lot easier to pick up a pen and flip it around your fingers.

Context can change things quite drastically, and context is something that can be used to our advantage in CSS. We can style an element in a number of different ways, depending on its position. Let's head back to our example site for another lesson. Don't be sheepish, now!

Currently, we have styled paragraphs so that they appear in a navy blue, sans-serif font (Verdana, specifically), as does almost everything else on the page:

File: **style1.css (excerpt)**

```
body {
  font-family: Verdana, Helvetica, Arial, sans-serif;
}
```

```
p {
  font-size: small;
  color: navy;
}
```

This is all well and good, but there's one paragraph on our site that's a little different than the others in terms of its purpose. Can you spot which one it is? It's our first paragraph, the one in the tag line. Here's the XHTML for that section:

File: **index.html** (excerpt)

```
<div id="tagline">
  <p>Diving club for the south-west UK - let's make a splash!</p>
</div>
```

It's different because it's not really part of the document content and, as such, it might benefit from some different styling. The fact that this particular paragraph is contained within a specific div element—which has an id attribute of tagline—is something that we can put to great use. Because it's contained within its own div, we can set a rule for this paragraph and this paragraph only.

❏ Open the CSS file for editing, and add the following after the first paragraph rule:

File: **style1.css** (excerpt)

```
#tagline p {
  font-style: italic;
  font-family: Georgia, Times, serif;
}
```

❏ Save the file, then refresh the About Us page (or any of the three, for that matter) in your browser. Your page should now look something like the one shown in Figure 3.11.

Figure 3.11. The tag line appearing in italics

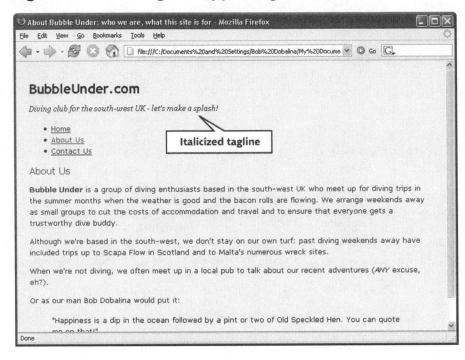

What's happening here? Perhaps a CSS-to-English translation is required. This CSS rule means, "For any paragraph element that occurs inside an element that has an `id` of `tagline`, set the text to italics and the font to Georgia, Times, or some other serif font if you don't have either of those."

Getting a Positive ID

The # notation in the CSS refers to an element with a specific `id` attribute—in this case, `tagline`. We'll learn more about selecting `id`s and manipulating them in subsequent chapters.

Contextual Selectors

`#tagline p` is known as a **contextual selector**. Here are some other examples (with their English translations):

❑
```
#navigation a {
    text-decoration: none;
}
```

Translation: for any link found inside the navigation area (an element with an id of navigation), remove any decoration on that text; in other words, remove the underline (any other links on the page will remain underlined).

❑
```
#footer p {
    line-height: 150%;
}
```

Translation: set the vertical height between lines of text contained in paragraphs inside the footer area (e.g. a div element with an id of footer) to 150%. This would override the browser default of 100%, or other line-height values that might be set, for example, on the body.

❑
```
h1 strong {
    color: red;
}
```

Translation: for any text inside a level one heading that's marked up as strong, set the color to red (any other instance of strong on the page will not be set to red).

❑
```
h2 a {
    text-decoration: none;
}
```

Translation: don't underline the text of any link inside a level two heading (the default setting underlines all links, so any other links on the page will remain underlined).

Grouping Styles

If you want to apply the same style to different elements on a web page, you don't have to repeat yourself. For example, let's say that you want to set heading levels one through three in yellow text with a black background. Perhaps you'd do this:

```
h1 {
  color: yellow;
  background-color: black;
}
```

```
h2 {
  color: yellow;
  background-color: black;
}

h3 {
  color: yellow;
  background-color: black;
}
```

That's very messy, and once you have a lot of styles on the page, it gets even more difficult to maintain. Wouldn't it be great if you could reduce some of that work? You can! Here's how:

```
h1, h2, h3 {
  color: yellow;
  background-color: black;
}
```

Translation: if the element is a level one heading, a level two heading, or a level three heading, set the text to yellow and the background to black.

Tip   **Comma = "Or"**

Think of the commas in the selector above as the word "or."

Let's try grouping some styles in our project site. We don't have any h3 headings yet, but they're coming:

❏ Edit your CSS file (style1.css) by adding the following to the bottom of it:

File: **style1.css (excerpt)**

```
h1, h2, h3 {
  font-family: "Trebuchet MS", Helvetica, Arial, sans-serif;
  background-color: navy;
  color: white;
}
```

❏ Save the file, then refresh the "About Us" page in your browser (assuming it's still open from your last exercise). You should be looking at a page like the one shown in Figure 3.12.

Figure 3.12. Displaying the changed heading styles

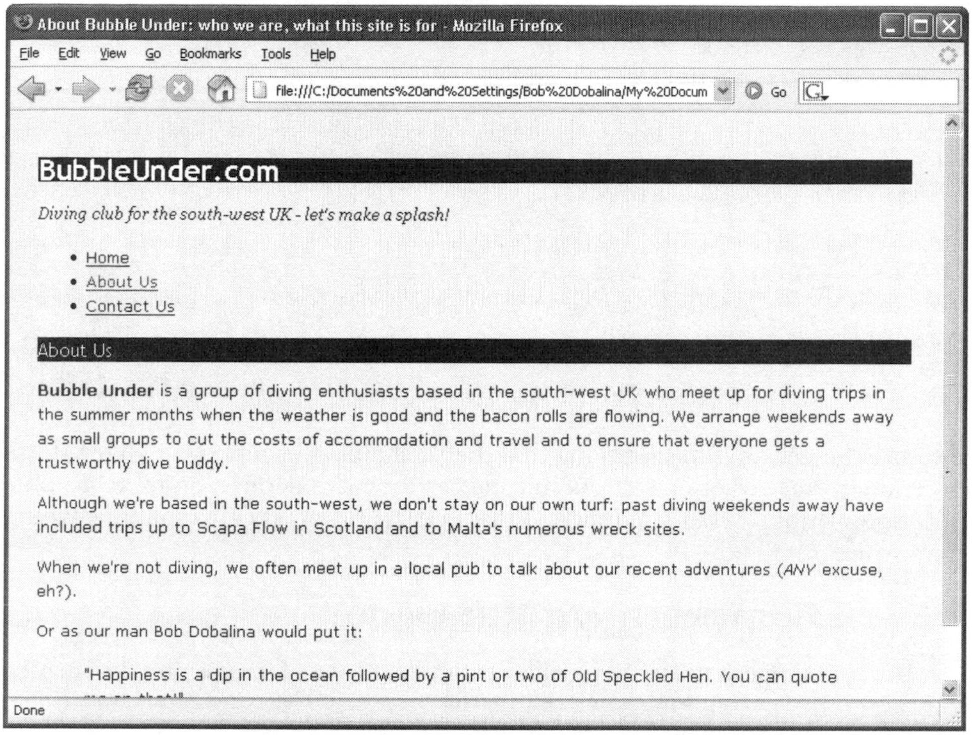

That CSS really does kill several birds with one stone (and I said no animals would be harmed! Apologies to ornithologists). Now, not only do you have the convenience of being able to style many pages from one central location (your CSS file), but you have the added convenience of being able to style many elements in one go. Your CSS file becomes easier to manage and—a nice little side-benefit—smaller, and therefore quicker to download.

But something interesting is happening in our CSS file: it appears that we may have a conflict in our rules. Or have we?

Which Rule Wins?

When we added the grouped declaration for the headings, we changed some styles that we'd set previously. A look at the source shows that the level two heading, h2, has been set to be blue *and* white in different places in our style sheet:

File: **style1.css (excerpt)**

```css
h2 {
  color: blue;
  font-size: medium;
  font-weight: normal;
}

em {
  text-transform: uppercase;
}

h1, h2, h3 {
  font-family: "Trebuchet MS", Helvetica, Arial, sans-serif;
  background-color: navy;
  color: white;
}
```

Because the declaration specifying that the h2 should be white comes later, it has overridden the earlier one. It doesn't matter if you've defined an h2 to be blue 100 times through your style sheet; if the last definition says it should be white, then white it will be!

Filenames for your Style Sheets

Tip

Although we've been working with `style1.css` for some time, you may be wondering why we named the file this way. The name is deliberate. You might want to add another style to your web site at a later date, and numbering is a basic way to keep track of the styles you can apply to a site.

You might be thinking, "Why not name it something like `marine.css` because it uses marine colors, references to under-sea animals, and so on?" That's a fair question, but the important thing to note about CSS is that you can always change the styles later, and your naming convention might, at a later date, bear no relevance to the styles a file contains. For example, you can edit `marine.css` such that all the colors in your web site are changed to ochres, browns, and sandy yellows. This ability to change the web site's design in one action is the whole point of CSS! With the new design, your web site might have an earthy/desert feel to it, yet you could still have 200 or more pages referring to a style sheet by the filename of `marine.css`. Something's not right there, is it? This is why I've chosen an abstract name for the CSS file, and I recommend that you do the same for the web sites you develop.

Recapping our Progress

Time for another breather. What have we learnt? Well, we've learned some more styles that you can apply in CSS, we've seen how you can style certain elements depending on their context, and more recently, we've discussed how you can group elements that need to be styled in the same way. There's one thing that we've touched on only briefly, yet it demands more attention because it's so fundamental to the way the Web functions. That topic is links.

Styling Links

Links are everywhere on the Web: they truly are the basis of everything you see online. Nowadays, we're used to seeing highly decorative web pages adorned by a wealth of different images and features. Take a step back in time, though, and you'll find that the World Wide Web was little more than a collection of linked documents. Go back to the earliest browsers and you'll find that those links were underlined, which remains the case today. By default, a browser uses the following color scheme for links:

blue   an unvisited link

purple   a link to a web page that you've previously visited

red   an active link (one you're clicking on, but, for whatever reason, the next page hasn't quite appeared; we don't see this much in these days of widespread broadband usage, because pages load much faster than they used to!)

This color scheme isn't to everyone's taste, but it's what we're stuck with now. At least, it's what we *would* be stuck with if we couldn't use CSS to redefine those colors.

At its most basic, a CSS style for links might look like this:

```
a {
  font-weight: bold;
  color: black;
}
```

Now, instead of being blue and having a normal font weight, your links appear in bold, black type. Try adding that to your `style1.css` file; save it and see how it affects your web pages—Figure 3.13 illustrates.

Figure 3.13. Styling all the links in our navigation to bold and black

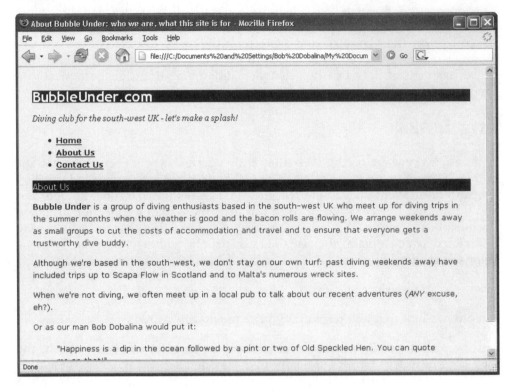

Link States

As I mentioned previously, there are different types of links (unvisited, visited, active) that you'll come across on a web page. There's one other state that I haven't mentioned, but it's one with which you're probably familiar: the **hover** state (which occurs when you pass your cursor over the link). In CSS, you can change the styling of all of these link states using something that sounds complicated but is really fairly straightforward: **pseudo-classes**. Here is some CSS that shows the color/style scheme for the different link states:

```
a {
  font-weight: bold;
}

a:link {
```

```
    color: black;
}

a:visited {
  color: gray;
}

a:hover {
  text-decoration: none;
  color: white;
  background-color: navy;
}

a:active {
  color: aqua;
  background-color: navy;
}
```

The different states are addressed within the CSS through the use of the a element selector, and by applying (with the aid of a colon) the pseudo-classes of link, visited, hover, and active.

Getting your Link States in Order

Browsers usually aren't fussy about the order in which you specify rules in your CSS file, but links should always be specified in the order shown above: link, visited, hover, and active. Try to remember the letters LVHA. The more bitter of us might find it easier to remember this mnemonic with the phrase, "Love? Ha!" We can thank Jeffrey Zeldman for that little gem.[5]

Let's change the styles for different link states in our project site:

❑ If it's not already open, open the project site's CSS file (style1.css), and add the above CSS at the bottom of the file.

❑ Save the CSS file.

❑ Open any of the three web pages in your browser (or hit Reload) to see how the styled links display.

Figure 3.14 shows the three different link states: the home link is unvisited, the link to the About Us page shows that it has been visited previously (shown in

---

[5] *Designing With Web Standards*, Jeffrey Zeldman, New Riders.

gray), and the link to the Contact Us page is being hovered over by the user's cursor.

Figure 3.14. Styling three different link states using CSS

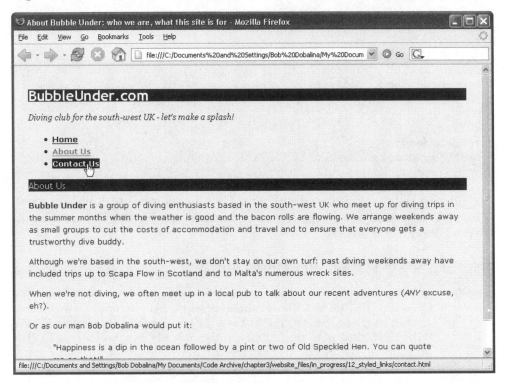

Feel free to experiment in the CSS file with the different foreground and background colors, and other text formatting styles that were detailed in the table earlier in this chapter.

Tip

Clearing your History

Your browser automatically stores a certain amount of your browsing history, and uses this information to decide whether a link has been visited or not (and, hence, how the link should be displayed). If you're building a site and testing links, you might want to check how an unvisited link looks but, because of your browsing history, they may all show as having been visited. This is almost certainly the case with our three-page project site—the links in your navigation list are probably all gray. To reset this, you can clear your browser's history. In IE, select Tools > Internet Options. You'll see a button that reads Clear History, as shown in Figure 3.15; click it, then reload the web page. Any links you may have visited will now appear as unvisited.

Figure 3.15. Clearing the history in IE displays unvisited link styles again

Other browsers have similar options, which may be found in locations such as Tools > Options or Preferences > Privacy. I won't list all the different methods for deleting your history from various browsers here, but if you rummage around, you should be able to find them without too much difficulty.

Class Selectors

To date, we've discussed the ways in which we can style various elements, such as paragraphs and headings; we've also seen how we can style elements in specific areas of the page using the id attribute. However, implementing broad-brush styles, such as coloring the text in all p elements navy, is very much a blanket approach to design. What if you want some of those paragraphs (or any elements, for that matter) to look a little different than the rest? **Class selectors** are the answer.

A class selector lets you define a style that can be used over and over again to style many different elements. So, for example, let's say you wanted to make some parts of your text stand out—to make them look slightly more appealing or fun than other parts of the document. You could do so in your CSS like this:

```
.fun {
  color: #339999;
  font-family: Georgia, Times, serif;
  letter-spacing: 0.05em;
}
```

Here, we've created a style rule for a class called "fun." The fact that it's a class selector is denoted by the period at the beginning of the class name. We've slipped another property into this rule: `letter-spacing` defines the space between each of the letters. We've set a spacing of `0.05em` here. `1em` is the height of the M character in any font, so `0.05em` is 5% of that height. It doesn't sound like much of a difference, but when it comes to typography, subtle changes are usually more effective than extreme ones.

In order to make use of the style, all you need to do is add the `class="fun"` attribute to an element:

```
<p class="fun">A man walks into a bar; you would've thought he'd
   see it coming!</p>
```

Let's apply some classes to our project site. First, we'll need to add the style rule shown above to the style sheet we're working on:

❑ Open `style1.css` and add the CSS from the above block to the bottom of that file.

❑ Save `style1.css`, then open `about.html`.

❑ Find the paragraph that's contained inside the `blockquote` element.

❑ Add the `class="fun"` attribute to the paragraph's opening tag.

This is how your markup should look right now:

File: **about.html** (excerpt)

```
<blockquote>
  <p class="fun">"Happiness is a dip in the ocean followed by a
      pint or two of Old Speckled Hen. You can quote me on
```

```
    - that!"</p>
</blockquote>
```

Note that the `class` attribute was applied at the paragraph level. If there were a few paragraphs in our man Bob's quotation, you'd end up with something like this:

```
<blockquote>
  <p class="fun">"Happiness is a dip in the ocean followed by a
      pint or two of Old Speckled Hen. You can quote me
      on that!</p>
  <p class="fun">"Join us for a weekend away at some of our
      favorite dive spots and you'll soon be making new
      friends.</p>
  <p class="fun">"Anyway, about time I got on with some
      <em>proper</em> work!"</p>
</blockquote>
```

There's a lot of repetition in there. Surely there's a tidier way to apply this style? There sure is!

```
<blockquote class="fun">
  <p>"Happiness is a dip in the ocean followed by a pint or two of
      Old Speckled Hen. You can quote me on that!</p>
  <p>"Join us for a weekend away at some of our favorite dive
      spots and you'll soon be making new friends.</p>
  <p>"Anyway, about time I got on with some <em>proper</em>
      work!"</p>
</blockquote>
```

In this example, we apply that `class` of `fun` to the `blockquote` element, so everything contained in that element inherits the style of the parent container. This saves us from having to apply these different classes all over our pages (an affliction that has become known as class-itis—a not-too-distant relation of div-itis, which we discussed in Chapter 2).

Tip

class vs id

So far, we've looked at both `class` selectors (which involve periods) and `id` selectors (which involve pound signs). Are you confused by them? It's true that these selectors are similar, but there is one important difference: *a specific id can only be applied to one XHTML element*. So, for example, on any web page, there can only be one element with an `id` of `mainnavigation`, and only one with an `id` of `header`. A class, on the other hand, can appear as many times as required.

Limiting Classes to Specific Elements

Imagine you want to italicise any `blockquote` element that has a `class` attribute with the value `fun`, but not other elements with that class value. Think it sounds tricky? Not with CSS!

```css
.fun {
  font-family: Georgia, Times, serif;
  color: #339999;
  letter-spacing: 0.05em;
}

blockquote.fun {
  font-style: italic;
}
```

Now, any text inside a pair of `<blockquote class="fun">` and `</blockquote>` tags will appear in italics.

By prefixing our normal class selector with an element name, we're telling the browser to apply the following declarations to that element-and-class combination only. It's as simple as *element.class*, but make sure you don't leave any spaces!

Specifically Speaking

Those with an eagle eye will have noticed that not all of the `fun` styles in the previous example are actually applied to the quotation. The `font-family` and `letter-spacing` declarations take effect, but the color change does not! The reason for this can be explained with the concept of **specificity**.

Specificity simply means the rule that is the most specific is the one that is applied. "Most specific" really means "most deeply-nested in the document's structure." In our markup, the p element appears inside the `blockquote` element, so any style applied to the p is deemed to be the more specific of the two and, therefore, will always win out. We have such a rule in our project site—the one that states that all paragraphs should be navy-colored—so this is the one that takes effect:

File: **style1.css (excerpt)**

```css
p {
  color: navy;
}
```

Note that, unlike the conflicting rules we encountered in the section called "Which Rule Wins?", this battle between style rules has no relation to the order in which they appear in the style sheet.

Specificity can get confusing, so don't lose too much sleep over it—for now, it's enough just to be aware of the concept, as this may be the reason why one of your styles doesn't take effect when you're convinced it should. Specificity is covered in greater depth in the SitePoint book *HTML Utopia: Designing Without Tables Using CSS*,[6] if you'd like to explore it further.

Styling Partial Text Using span

So, a class can be applied in many different places—perhaps to a specific paragraph, or to a block of several paragraphs contained in a `blockquote`, or to a `div` that holds many different types of content. But what would you do if you wanted to apply the style to a very small section of text—maybe just a couple of words, or even just a couple of letters, within a paragraph? For this, once again, you can use the `span` element.

Earlier in this chapter I showed how you could use the `span` element in conjunction with inline styles to pick out and style specific words within a paragraph. The exact same technique can be used with classes: we simply place an opening `<span>` tag at the point at which we want the styling to begin, and the closing `</span>` tag at the point at which the styling should end. The advantage of this technique over the inline style demonstrated earlier is, of course, that with this technique, the style is defined in a single location, so you could potentially add the "fun" class to many different elements on many different pages with a minimum of hassle. When you decide that you want to have a different kind of fun (so to speak), you need only change your style sheet (`style1.css`) for that new style to be reflected across your site.

```
<p><span class="fun">Bubble Under</span> is a group of diving
    enthusiasts based in the south-west UK who meet up for diving
    trips in the summer months when the weather is good and the
    bacon rolls are flowing. We arrange weekends away as small
    groups to cut the costs of accommodation and travel and to
    ensure that everyone gets a trustworthy dive buddy.</p>
```

Try applying the span element to your "about" page as suggested in the above code. If you save the changes and check them in your browser (remember to hit Reload), your page should look like the one shown in Figure 3.16.

---

[6] http://sitepoint.com/books/css1/

Figure 3.16. Applying the "fun" class to two specific words

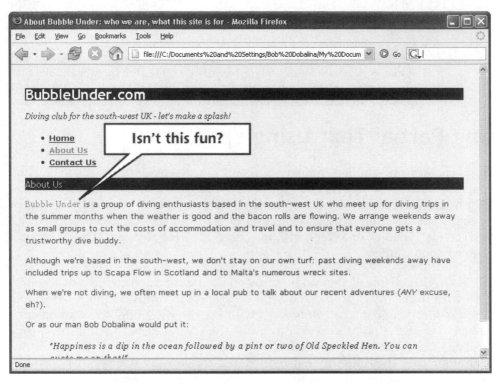

Don't Throw (Needless) spans into the Works

The **span** element is nearly always used with a class attribute. There is not normally a good reason to apply a **span** element to your XHTML on its own, although you may see some web sites that do so.

Before you apply a **span** to any given element on your web page, take a moment to think about whether there's another element that's better suited to the task. For example, you should not use something like this:

```
<p>Do it <span class="shouty">now</span>!</p>
```

A more appropriate choice would be to use the **strong** element:

```
<p>Do it <strong>now</strong>!</p>
```

Think of the meaning of what you're writing, and aim for an XHTML element that suits the purpose. Other examples might be **em**, **cite**, and **blockquote**.

Summary

It's been another busy chapter, but my, how our site's blossoming! A chapter or two ago, we hadn't even built a web page, but now we're at the stage where we know how to apply a (virtual) lick of paint to any type of XHTML element on a page, to a specific section of a web page depending on its `id`, or to arbitrary portions of a page—sometimes in several different places—using class selectors.

The web site is starting to look a little more colorful, but the layout is still fairly basic. In the next chapter, we'll look at how it's possible to change the layout of elements on a page—their position, shape, size, and more—using CSS. Styling text? Been there, done that. Let's move to the next level!

Shaping Up with CSS

For many years, web developers regarded CSS as a tool that could be used to style text on web pages, and add a splash of color here and there, but little more. And for a long time, that was all you could *realistically* use it for, because browser support for CSS was so poor. Thankfully, things have moved on!

You've now reached a point at which many budding web designers stop experimenting with CSS. Not you! In this chapter, we're going to delve a little further into the capabilities of CSS as we use it to:

☐ change the shape and size of specific areas of content

☐ change backgrounds and border styles

☐ position items anywhere on the web page

Let's begin, then, by seeing how we can use CSS to change the shape and size of items on a web page. However, before we can understand this technique, we need to grasp the difference between **block-level elements** and **inline elements**.

Block-level Elements vs Inline Elements

Any given web page comprises two basic types of elements: block-level elements and inline elements. It's important to appreciate the differences between these element types, particularly where CSS is concerned.

The Basic Rules of Block-level and Inline Elements

I'm going to revert to analogies for a moment here—bear with me.

I've been moving house recently! When was the last time you moved? It's amazing how much "stuff" we seem to amass, especially those little trinkets that collect dust on the mantelpiece. You have to find some small boxes to put these bits and pieces in so they don't get damaged, and of course you then need some larger packing boxes into which you can put those smaller boxes.

So on the day before the move—possibly earlier if you're more organized than I am—you start to place your trinkets into small boxes (here's a tip: shoeboxes work well). You then place those shoeboxes into bigger boxes, along with some books and those video tapes of the X-Files that you know you'll never watch but can't bring yourself to throw away. This process continues through the night, and eventually (usually about three minutes before the moving truck is due to arrive) all of your stuff is finally packed and ready to go (whew!).

If you think of the different types of boxes as block-level elements, and your other stuff—the books, videos and trinkets—as inline elements, you'll start to understand the difference between the element types. Armed with that knowledge, we can state the rules for these elements as follows.

A block-level element can contain other block-level elements, as well as inline elements.

An inline element can only contain other inline elements.

Block-level Elements

As I explained above, a block-level element is any element that can contain other elements (block-level and inline). To identify a block-level element, look for any element that:

❑ is normally displayed *on its own line* (or across multiple lines)

Other elements probably appear above or below it, but not on either side (not by default, anyway).

❑ is being used as a *container* for one or more other elements

Here are a few examples of common block-level elements:

❑ h1, h2, h3, and so on, through to h6

❑ p

❑ div

❑ blockquote

❑ ul and ol

❑ form[1]

When you create a paragraph of text, you do not need to tell the browser to add a carriage return, start a new line, then add another carriage return at the end of the paragraph—the opening <p> and closing </p> tags do that for you. Consider the text that appears on our site's "About Us" page:

File: **about.html** (excerpt)

```
<h2>About Us</h2>
<p><span class="fun">Bubble Under</span> is a group of diving
    enthusiasts based in the south-west UK who meet up for diving
    trips in the summer months when the weather is good and the
    bacon rolls are flowing. We arrange weekends away as small
    groups to cut the costs of accommodation and travel and to
    ensure that everyone gets a trustworthy dive buddy.</p>
<p>Although we're based in the south-west, we don't stay on our
    own turf: past diving weekends away have included trips up to
    Scapa Flow in Scotland and to Malta's numerous wreck
    sites.</p>
<p>When we're not diving, we often meet up in a local pub to
    talk about our recent adventures (<em>any</em> excuse,
    eh?).</p>
<p>Or as our man Bob Dobalina would put it:</p>
<blockquote class="fun">
  <p>"Happiness is a dip in the ocean followed by a pint or two
```

---

[1] Forms will be discussed in detail in Chapter 7.

```
       of Old Speckled Hen. You can quote me on that!"</p>
</blockquote>
```

The heading (h2) and the three paragraphs are all block-level elements. They represent blocks of content above and below which clearly defined breaks appear. This is clear in Figure 4.1, where some of the block-level elements are outlined.

Figure 4.1. Blocks of content hinting at XHTML block-level elements

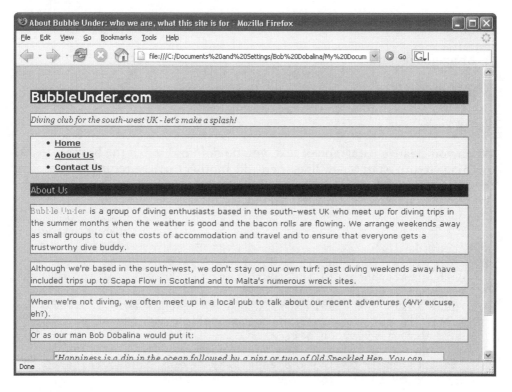

Inline Elements

An easy way to identify an *in*line element is to remember that it sits *in*side another element. As we established in my packing analogy, we can have a box of old photos, or a box containing just one photo, but we can't have a photo full of boxes—it's physically impossible! Similarly, it's against the specifications to use an inline element to contain a block-level element. A good example of an inline element is span, which we used in Chapter 3 to group words together in order to apply a style:

File: **about.html (excerpt)**

```
<p><span class="fun">Bubble Under</span> is a group of diving
    enthusiasts based in the south-west UK who meet up for diving
    trips in the summer months when the weather is good and the
    bacon rolls are flowing. We arrange weekends away as small
    groups to cut the costs of accommodation and travel and to
    ensure that everyone gets a trustworthy dive buddy.</p>
```

Other examples of inline elements include:

❑ em

❑ strong

❑ cite

❑ a

Looking at the example markup above, any one of those inline elements could be applied to the words "Bubble Under":

```
<p><em>Bubble Under</em> is a group of diving enthusiasts…</p>
<p><strong>Bubble Under</strong> is a group of diving
    enthusiasts…</p>
<p><cite>Bubble Under</cite> is a group of diving enthusiasts…</p>
<p><a href="http://www.bubbleunder.com/">Bubble Under</a> is a
    group of diving enthusiasts…</p>
```

In fact, even the image element, img, is inline, although we don't use it in the same way as the elements mentioned above (img doesn't provide any information to the browser about how text should be treated; an image is simply an image).

Inline Begets Inline

It's perfectly okay to nest one inline element inside another. Here's an example of an inline element that contains another inline element:

```
<p><span class="fun"><a href="http://www.bubbleunder.com/">Bubble
    Under</a></span> is a group of diving enthusiasts based in
    the south-west UK who meet up for diving trips in the summer
    months when the weather is good and the bacon rolls are
```

```
flowing. We arrange weekends away as small groups to cut the
costs of accommodation and travel and to ensure that everyone
gets a trustworthy dive buddy.</p>
```

Actually, to refer to the separate examples we saw previously, even the markup shown below would constitute perfectly acceptable and valid XHTML (although it may seem like overkill):

```
<p><strong><em><cite><a href="http://www.bubbleunder.com/">Bubble
    Under</a></cite></em></strong> is a group of diving
    enthusiasts…</p>
```

Watch your Symmetry!

One of the rules of XHTML is that opening and closing tags should be symmetrical: if you open one tag, then another, those tags should be closed in reverse order. In the example above, the tags are correctly opened and closed as follows (indenting is for effect only):

❏ `<strong>`

  ❏ `<em>`

    ❏ `<cite>`

      ❏ `<a>`

        ❏ the text "Bubble Under"

      ❏ `</a>`

    ❏ `</cite>`

  ❏ `</em>`

❏ `</strong>`

This rule of symmetry applies to *any* kind of element—block-level or in-line—and can be checked using online validators (we'll cover this in Chapter 8).

Inline Elements can Never Contain Block-level Elements

The previous example showed the perfectly acceptable usage of an inline element that contained other inline elements. Now, I'm going to turn that on its head and show you what you should *never* do:

```
<span class="fun"><p>Bubble Under is a group of diving enthusiasts
    based in the south-west UK who meet up for diving trips in the
    summer months when the weather is good and the bacon rolls are
    flowing. We arrange weekends away as small groups to cut the
    costs of accommodation and travel and to ensure that everyone
    gets a trustworthy dive buddy.</p></span>
```

Why is this wrong? Well, what we have here is an inline element, span, wrapped around a block-level element, p. Bad, naughty markup! Remember: block-level elements can only be contained within other block-level elements.

Recap: Block-level and Inline Elements

If you think I've belabored the point of differences between these two types of elements, please accept my humble apologies. Often, people don't appreciate the differences between block-level and inline elements. It's a very important point, though, because these two element types have very different capabilities where CSS is concerned. Let's look at this in detail now.

Styling Inline and Block-level Elements

Inline elements allow for a limited range of styling options, as outlined below (this is something of a simplified recap of the discussion from Chapter 3):

❑ changing colors (text and background)

❑ changing font properties (size, font family, and other decorative transformations such as underlining, etc.)

This is all fairly superficial, cosmetic stuff, to be honest. However, with block-level elements, you have a much wider range of CSS tools at your disposal. Here are just some of the things you can do to a block-level element using CSS:

❑ Give a block of text a fixed width or height.

❑ Create padding effects to prevent text from pushing right up against the edge of the block in which it's contained.

❑ Move a block to any location on the web page, regardless of the position in which it appears in the markup.

In this chapter, we'll see examples of all of these techniques, the markup for which is available for download from the code archive. Then, we'll apply the techniques to our project site. Let's begin by looking at how you can shape up and size blocks of content.

Sizing Up the Blocks

By default, a block-level element will take up 100% of the available width (whatever the size of its parent container, be that another `div` element, or even the document's `body`) and whatever height it needs. So far, the paragraphs we've created have fit this description, but, if you wish, you can change these defaults.

Setting a Width

Let's imagine that you have a document that comprises many paragraphs, and you would like to draw attention to one of them in some way other than simply changing the font. For starters, you could try changing the paragraph width. Here's the CSS that does just that (as well as making the font bold):

```
.attentiongrab {
  width: 50%;
  font-weight: bold;
}
```

I've used a class selector here; do you remember it from the last chapter? It will let us apply this particular style as many times as we like. Here's some XHTML to go with the CSS above:

```
<p>We've stayed in quite a few caravan parks and camp sites over
    the last couple of months, and I've started to notice a few
    things that seem to suggest that there are some unwritten
    rules of staying at these places. Unwritten until now, that
    is.</p>
<p>Everyone else on site will be better prepared and better
    equipped than you. It's a fact. No matter what extras you
    might carry, someone a couple of plots down will still have
    more. Utensil envy is rife.</p>
```

```
<p class="attentiongrab">When you first park, the distance
    between the power supply and your van's power socket will be
    precisely 2 inches longer than the inadequate power lead that
    you own.</p>
<p>On the hottest evenings, you will be parked next to someone
    with a very flashy van that's equipped with an air-con unit.
    It will be facing you, blowing out hot air and taunting you
    with its efficient hum.</p>
```

Figure 4.2 shows how the text appears on the screen.

Figure 4.2. Reducing a paragraph's width to 50% of its neighbors'

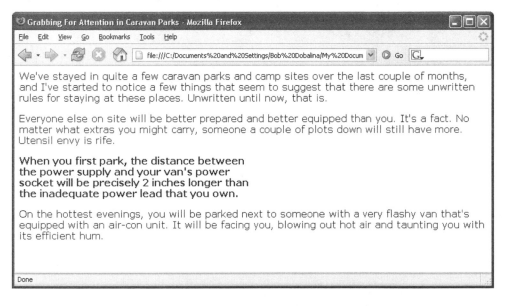

Setting a Height

The process for setting the height of a block of content is just as simple as setting the width, although you probably won't have as much use for `height` as you will for `width` in styling paragraph text. A case in which you may want to set a specific `height` is in a navigation area (assuming that the number of navigation items in the list doesn't vary dramatically between different pages). Consider this XHTML:

```
<div id="mainnavigation">
  <h3>Site Navigation</h3>
  <ul>
```

```
    <li><a href="home.html">Home</a></li>
    <li><a href="recent.html">Recent Work</a></li>
    <li><a href="portfolio.html">Portfolio</a></li>
    <li><a href="testimonials.html">Testimonials</a></li>
    <li><a href="contact.html">Contact</a></li>
  </ul>
</div>
```

As with our project site, the navigation area is contained in a `div` that has an `id` attribute (`mainnavigation`). As we saw at the beginning of this chapter, a `div` is a block-level element and, as such, we can play around with it. Let's specify a height and width for it in CSS:

```
#mainnavigation {
  background-color: #ffcc33;
  color: navy;
  font-weight: bold;
  width: 200px;
  height: 400px;
}
```

Note that I've also added a splash of background color (`#ffcc33`) to make the resized block easier to see.

In the CSS, I've used the `width` *and* `height` properties, applying pixel values to achieve a rectangular shape. Figure 4.3 shows how the page looks in the browser.

Figure 4.3. Displaying the `div` set to 200 pixels wide, 400 pixels high

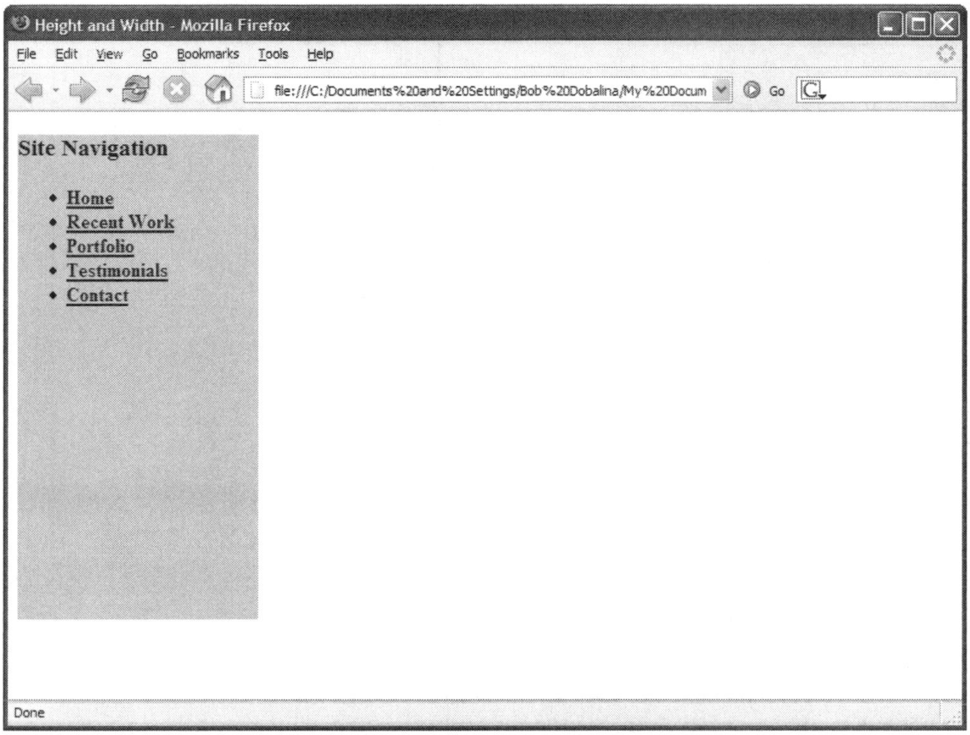

What if the Navigation Area gets too Big?

I mentioned that we could set a height for a navigation block in this way, "assuming that the number of navigation items in the list doesn't vary dramatically between different pages." Well, you know what they say about assumptions! What would happen if the navigation *did* grow too big for the space we'd allowed for it? The answer to this question depends on the browser, actually.

❑ In Firefox, the list items break out of the bottom of that `div`, beyond the yellow background.

❑ In IE, the yellow background area expands vertically as the navigation grows.

Figure 4.4. Firefox and IE behaving differently as content outgrows its allotted area

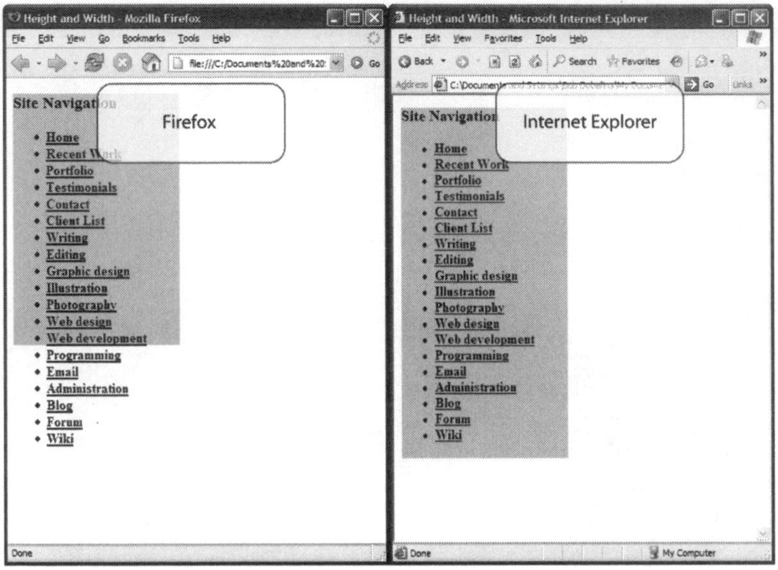

These differences are depicted in Figure 4.4.

Firefox's behavior is probably the least-preferred reaction to this quandary, but remember: you set the height in CSS in just one place. The beauty of this approach is that you can simply make a change in that one place to give your navigation a little more room.[2]

Adding Borders to Block-level Elements

You can use block-level elements to apply a range of border effects, including:

☐ different border thicknesses

☐ various border styles (solid lines, dotted lines, and more)

☐ a range of border colors

---

[2] There is a CSS property that you can use to control the behavior of content that overflows a fixed area. This is best used on sections of a web page in which the amount of content is likely to vary quite a lot. For more information, see "The overflow property" at W3Schools: http://www.w3schools.com/css/pr_pos_overflow.asp.

The CSS properties we can use to achieve these effects are:

❑ `border-width`

❑ `border-style`

❑ `border-color`

Example Borders

Let's see some examples in action.

Simple Black Border

Figure 4.5. A simple black border

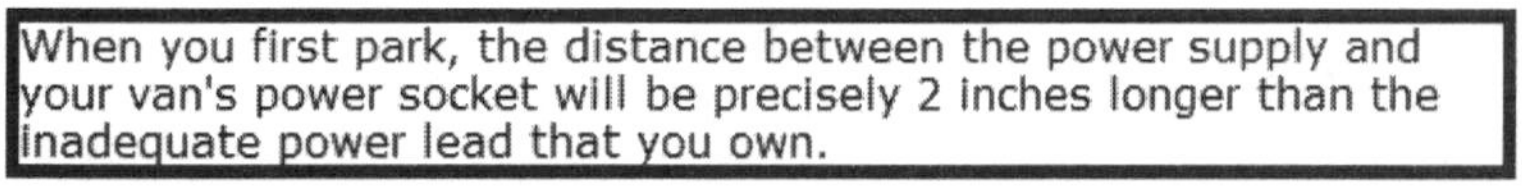

> When you first park, the distance between the power supply and your van's power socket will be precisely 2 inches longer than the inadequate power lead that you own.

Figure 4.5 depicts a basic, entry-level border: a solid black line, five pixels wide. The CSS for this effect is as follows:

```
.simpleblackborder {
  border-width: 5px;
  border-style: solid;
  border-color: black;
}
```

Naming your Classes

You'll notice here that I've given names to our classes to illustrate what the style rules do: "simpleblackborder" is a simple black border. While this is useful for introducing CSS borders, it's not good practice on a site. If I were using this style to highlight a paragraph within a page, a name like "highlight" would be more suitable. That way, at any given point in the future I could change the way that paragraphs were highlighted easily, without being confused by the class names or having to change the class name every time it appeared in the XHTML.

Inset Border

If a solid line doesn't do it for you, you could try an `inset` border, which gives the effect shown in Figure 4.6.

Figure 4.6. An inset border

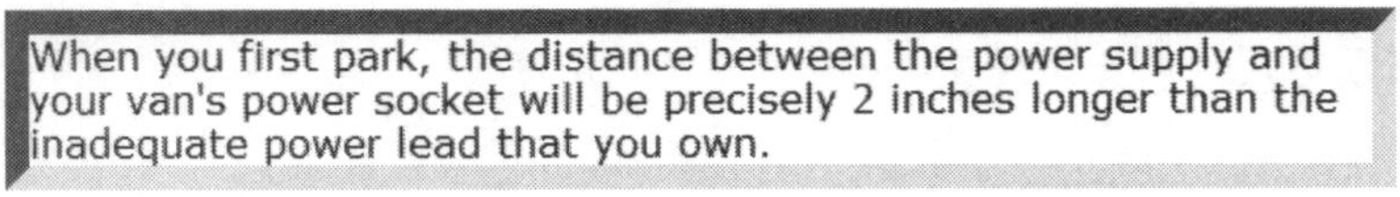

When you first park, the distance between the power supply and your van's power socket will be precisely 2 inches longer than the inadequate power lead that you own.

The color applied in this example is a shade of gray (shown here as a hexadecimal code):

```
.insetborder {
  border-width: 10px;
  border-style: inset;
  border-color: #999999;
}
```

Colored Ridge Border

You can apply some color in combination with a border style to create a two-tone effect. In Figure 4.7, a ridged effect works nicely with the red border color (again, you don't have to take my word for it with regards to the color: check out the file in the code archive for yourself). The code that creates this effect is shown below.

Figure 4.7. A colored ridge border

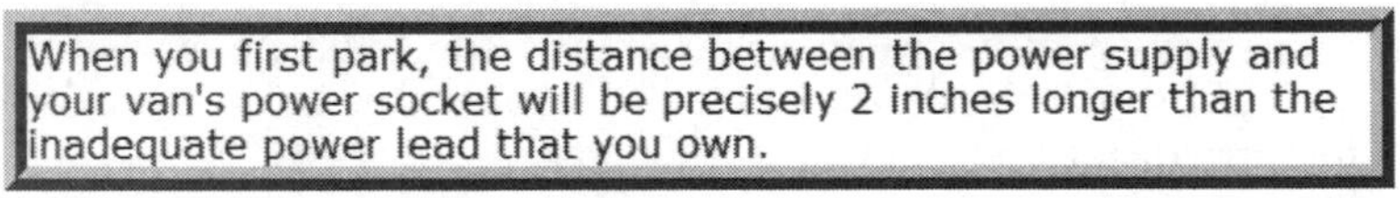

When you first park, the distance between the power supply and your van's power socket will be precisely 2 inches longer than the inadequate power lead that you own.

```
.coloredridgeborder {
  border-width: 10px;
  border-style: ridge;
  border-color: red;
}
```

Bold Border Effects

You're not limited to using solid lines for the border, though. The examples depicted in Figure 4.8 and Figure 4.9 show `dotted` and `dashed` effects respectively; both borders are set to purple with a ten-pixel thickness.

Figure 4.8. A bold, dotted border

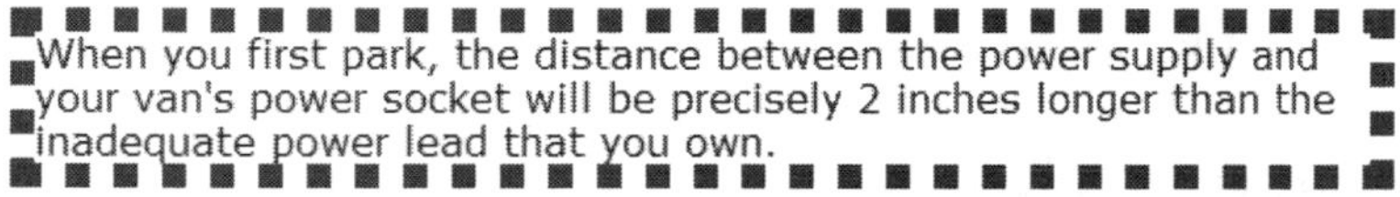

When you first park, the distance between the power supply and your van's power socket will be precisely 2 inches longer than the inadequate power lead that you own.

```
.bolddottedborder {
  border-width: 10px;
  border-style: dotted;
  border-color: purple;
}
```

Figure 4.9. A bold, dashed border

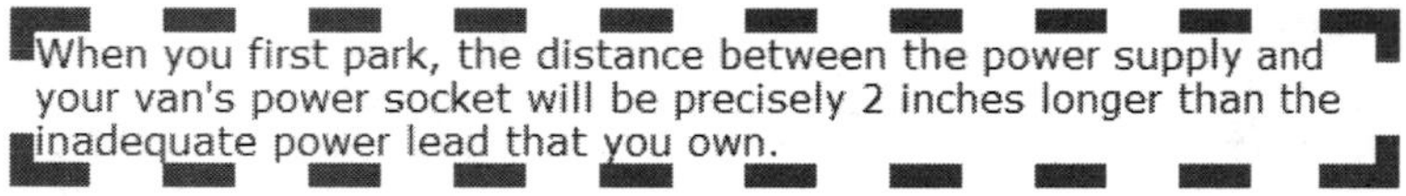

When you first park, the distance between the power supply and your van's power socket will be precisely 2 inches longer than the inadequate power lead that you own.

```
.bolddashedborder {
  border-width: 10px;
  border-style: dashed;
  border-color: purple;
}
```

All the border styles above are a bit intense. Let's have a look at some more refined examples.

Simple Gray Border

Figure 4.10. A simple gray border

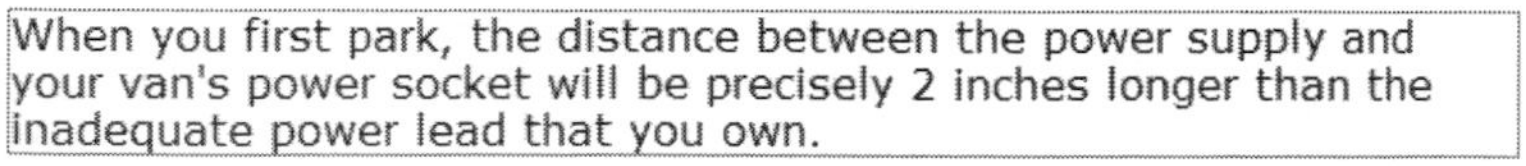

When you first park, the distance between the power supply and your van's power socket will be precisely 2 inches longer than the inadequate power lead that you own.

The example depicted in Figure 4.10 uses a simple, single-pixel, gray border. Here's the CSS that achieves this effect:

```
.simplegrayborder {
  border-width: 1px;
  border-style: solid;
  border-color: gray;
}
```

Simple Gray Border (Version 2!)

Figure 4.11. Another simple gray border

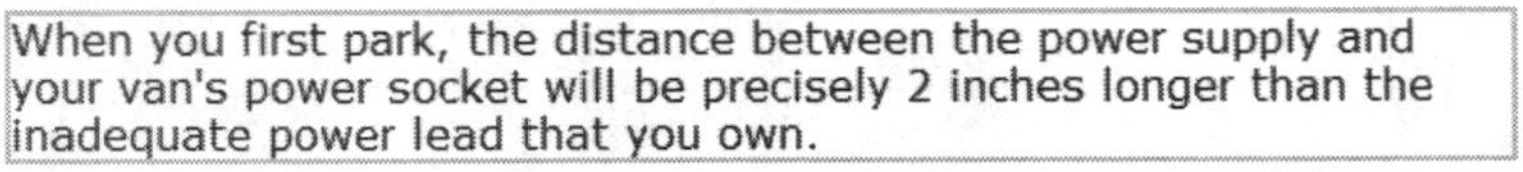

When you first park, the distance between the power supply and your van's power socket will be precisely 2 inches longer than the inadequate power lead that you own.

In Figure 4.11, the border has been thickened a little more (to two pixels), but doesn't appear too bold because we've altered the color to a lighter shade (silver).

```
.simplegrayborder2 {
  border-width: 2px;
  border-style: solid;
  border-color: silver;
}
```

Dotted Red Border

Figure 4.12. A dotted red border

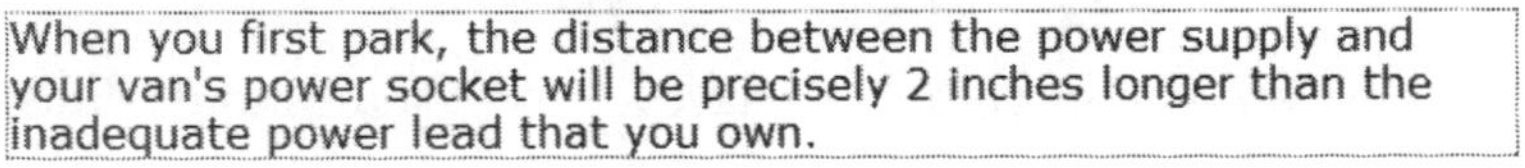

When you first park, the distance between the power supply and your van's power socket will be precisely 2 inches longer than the inadequate power lead that you own.

The red border in Figure 4.12 doesn't seem too severe because it's only one pixel wide; its dotted appearance lightens the effect even more. Here's the CSS for this border:

```
.dottedredborder {
  border-width: 1px;
  border-style: dotted;
  border-color: red;
}
```

Dashed Gray Border

Figure 4.13. A dashed gray border

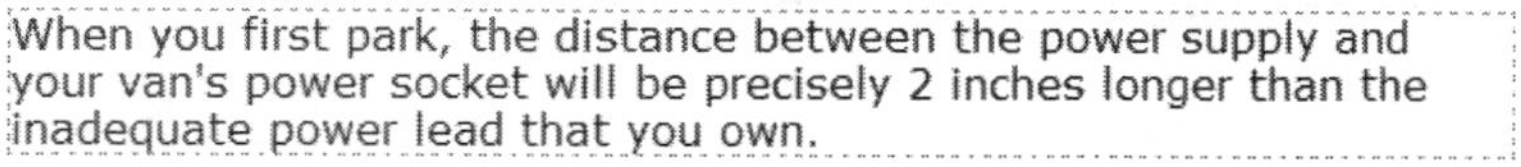

When you first park, the distance between the power supply and your van's power socket will be precisely 2 inches longer than the inadequate power lead that you own.

The difference between `dotted` and `dashed` is more defined in Firefox than in IE. The dotted border shown in Figure 4.12 is made up of a series of single-pixel dots, while the dashed version shown in Figure 4.13 uses slightly longer lines. In IE, the dotted border still has a slightly "dashed" look about it.

```
.dashedgrayborder {
  border-width: 1px;
  border-style: dashed;
  border-color: gray;
}
```

Double Borders

You can set a double border on block-level elements, as Figure 4.14 shows. The markup that creates this effect appears below.

Figure 4.14. Double border

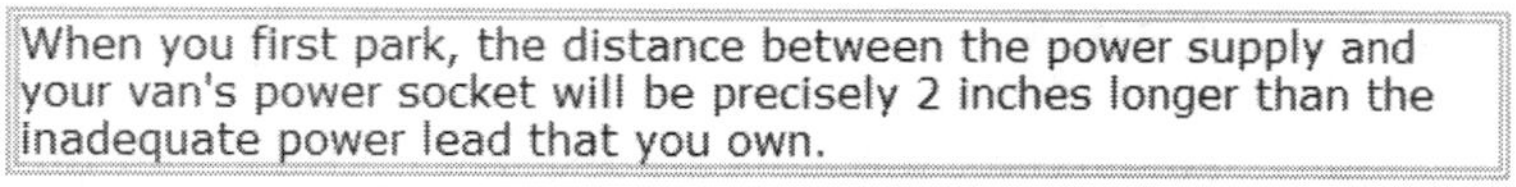

When you first park, the distance between the power supply and your van's power socket will be precisely 2 inches longer than the inadequate power lead that you own.

```
.doubleborder {
  border-width: 5px;
  border-style: double;
  border-color: silver;
}
```

Styling Individual Sides of an Element

As well as applying borders to all the sides of a block-level element, you can style individual edges of the element using `border-top`, `border-bottom`, `border-left`, and `border-right`. Here's an example of a block that has different styles applied to each of its sides:

```
.multiborder {
  border-top-width: 1px;
  border-top-style: solid;
  border-top-color: red;
  border-bottom-width: 3px;
  border-bottom-style: dotted;
  border-bottom-color: blue;
  border-left-width: 5px;
  border-left-style: dashed;
  border-left-color: yellow;
  border-right-width: 7px;
  border-right-style: double;
  border-right-color: fuchsia;
}
```

Figure 4.15. Displaying a different border for each side of the element

When you first park, the distance between the power supply and your van's power socket will be precisely 2 inches longer than the inadequate power lead that you own.

Let's be honest: as Figure 4.15 shows all too clearly, this looks pretty ugly! However, you can use any of those CSS properties on its own. For example, border-bottom is often used quite effectively by itself to create dividing lines between sections of page content.

Shorthand Border Styles

As we saw in the previous example, there are large numbers of CSS declarations. Wouldn't it be nice if you could set up a border using just one declaration, instead of three? Good news: you can!

```
.container {
  border: 5px solid black;
}
```

This is known as a "shorthand" method for styling borders, and browser support for this style of CSS notation is excellent. Given that it saves you a little typing, and also saves on file download sizes (albeit by a pinch), this is the method I recommend for styling borders. You can even use border-top, border-bottom, border-left, and border-right to style individual sides using this shorthand notation.

We can rewrite all of our border styles as shown below.

```
.simpleblackborder {
  border: 5px solid black;
}
.insetborder {
  border: 10px inset #999999;
}
.coloredridgeborder {
  border: 10px ridge red;
}
.bolddottedborder {
  border: 10px dotted purple;
}
.bolddashedborder {
  border: 10px dashed purple;
}
.simplegrayborder {
  border: 1px solid gray;
}
.simplegrayborder2 {
  border: 2px solid silver;
}
.dottedredborder {
  border: 1px dotted red;
}
.dashedgrayborder {
  border: 1px dashed gray;
}
.doubleborder {
  border: 5px double silver;
}
.multiborder {
  border-top: 1px solid red;
  border-bottom: 3px dotted blue;
  border-left: 5px dashed yellow;
  border-right: 7px double fuchsia;
}
```

Border Styles you can Use

The examples above demonstrated most of the styles that you can use. Below is a list of all the different options that are available to you; feel free to experiment with whatever combinations you like.

border thickness

This can be specified using pixels (`px`), points (`pt`), or `ems`.

Alternatively, you could just use one of the border thickness keywords: `thin`, `medium`, or `thick`.

border style

A border can take any of the following styles:

☐ `solid` (the default value)

☐ `double`

☐ `dotted`

☐ `dashed`

☐ `groove`

☐ `ridge`

☐ `inset`

☐ `outset`

border color

Border color is specified in the same way as the colors of other elements—either as a hexadecimal code, or as one of the color keywords.

Recap: what Have we Learned?

In this chapter, we've seen how block-level elements can be shaped and sized, and how the border styles can be changed. Until now, I've been using generic examples to explain the possibilities that are available. Now, we're going to apply some of these styles to our project site, using only a smattering here and there; one thing to be aware of is that the overuse of borders can make a web site look very blocky and, possibly, quite ugly.

Shaping and Sizing our Diving Site

Let's make some minor changes to the project site, beginning with the body element. Open up style1.css and find the rule for the body element (it should be the first item that occurs after the comment). Add a declaration to style the whole of the page with a border, like so:

File: **style1.css (excerpt)**

```
body {
  font-family: Verdana, Helvetica, Arial, sans-serif;
  background-color: #e2edff;
  padding: 15px;
  line-height: 125%;
  border: 4px solid navy;
}
```

Take a look at any of the pages in your browser, and you should see something like the display depicted in Figure 4.16.

Figure 4.16. Surrounding the entire web page with a border

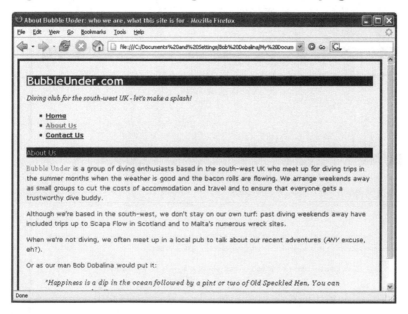

Next, let's make some changes to the navigation area. Earlier, in Chapter 2, I suggested adding `id` attributes to key sections of the web pages. We'll make use of those attributes in this procedure.

In `style1.css`, add a new rule for the `navigation id`. Set the area's width to 180 pixels, and add a dotted navy border that's one pixel wide. Your CSS should look like this:

File: **style1.css (excerpt)**

```
#navigation {
  width: 180px;
  border: 1px dotted navy;
}
```

Save `style1.css`, then take a look at your web site in a browser. Figure 4.17 shows what you should see.

Figure 4.17. The navigation displaying definite dimensions

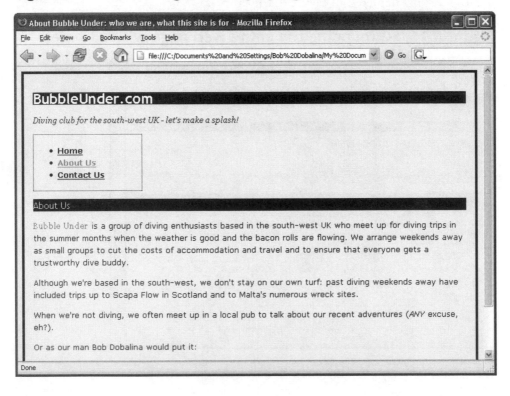

There's another tweak we're going to make to the navigation: let's change the background color.

File: **style1.css (excerpt)**

```
#navigation {
  width: 180px;
  border: 1px dotted navy;
  background-color: #7da5a8;
}
```

I've chosen another shade of blue (remember from Chapter 3 that a range of color picker tools are available to help you find the hexadecimal codes for different colors). The result of this work is shown in Figure 4.18.

Figure 4.18. The navigation displaying as a distinct, functional area of the web page

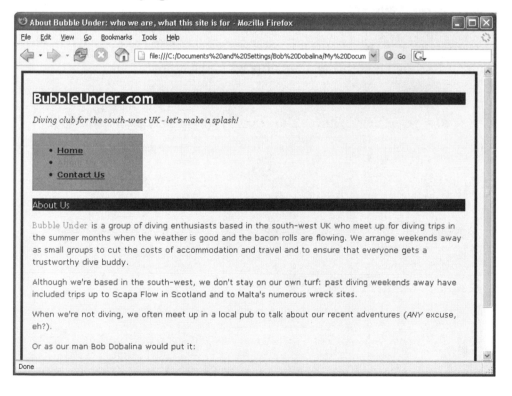

That looks better, but the background color we've chosen makes the `visited` link text a bit difficult to read. Let's fix that by choosing a darker color for the visited link. Find the rule for visited links and change it to the following:

```
a:visited {
  color: navy;
}
```

Much better! Next, let's style the tag line a little more by applying a background color and border effect to set it off nicely. In your style sheet, find the markup that styles the tag line, and add the declaration shown in bold below:

File: **style1.css (excerpt)**

```
#tagline p {
  font-style: italic;
  font-family: Georgia, Times, serif;
  background-color: #bed8f3;
  border-top: 3px solid #7da5d8;
  border-bottom: 3px solid #7da5d8;
}
```

Figure 4.19 shows how this markup displays in the browser.

Figure 4.19. Highlighting the tag line with a border and background color

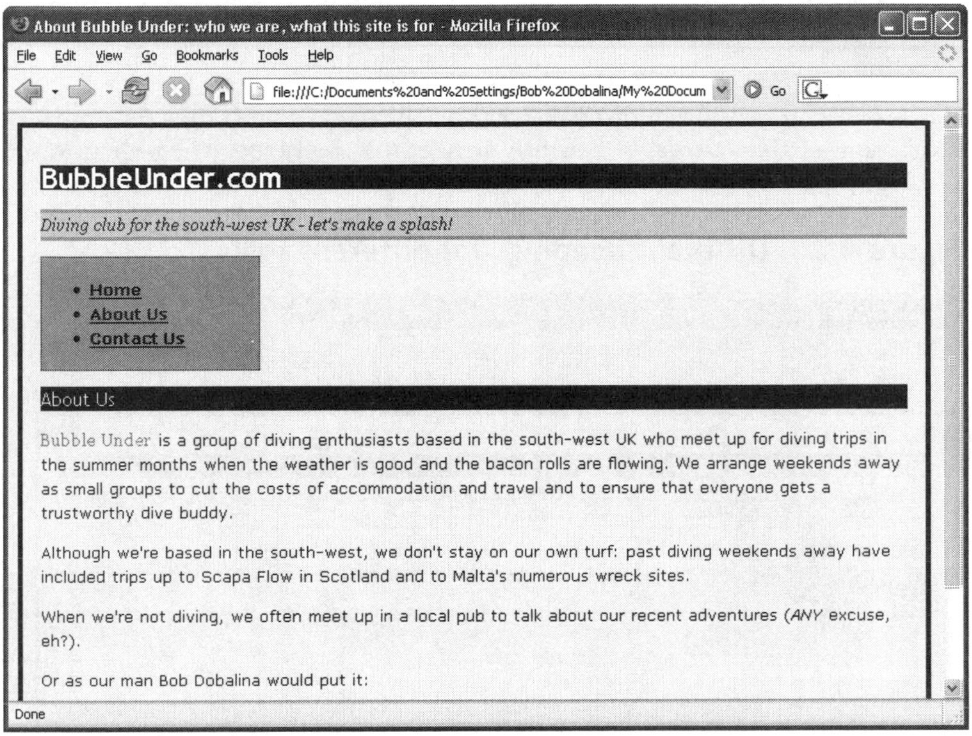

Finally, let's change the styling of the h2 headings so that they look a bit different from the h1s (it *is* possible to go overboard with that dark background effect!). Now is also a good time to rearrange some of our rules which, if you've just been adding to the bottom of the file, may well be jumbled all over the place, rather than appearing in a logical order. Move all of the heading rules so they appear together, to make them easier to locate later on:

```
h1, h2, h3 {
  font-family: "Trebuchet MS", Helvetica, Arial, sans-serif;
}

h1 {
  font-size: x-large;
  background-color: navy;
  color: white;
}
```

```
h2 {
  color: navy;
  font-size: 130%;
  font-weight: normal;
}
```

We've chosen a new height of 130% for our h2 headings, which (in most browsers) is a bit bigger than large, but slightly smaller than x-large. The page now displays like the one shown in Figure 4.20.

Figure 4.20. Different headings for different folks

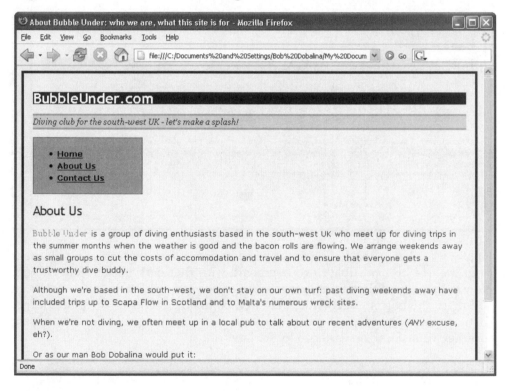

Adding Padding

If you take a look at the headings on the project site, and at the borders that I demonstrated earlier in this chapter, you'll notice that the text sits right next to the border; it looks a little uncomfortable, don't you think? To remedy this, let's add some padding—extra "buffer" space between the border and the text. Not surprisingly, the CSS property for this extra space is padding.

Here are three different ways we can apply padding to a block-level element: using pixels, ems, and percentage values:

```
.pixelpadding {
  padding: 30px;
  border: 1px dashed gray;
}
.empadding {
  padding: 2em;
  border: 1px dashed gray;
}
.percentagepadding {
  padding: 5%;
  border: 1px dashed gray;
}
```

Figure 4.21. Three methods of padding, resulting in equivalent views on the screen

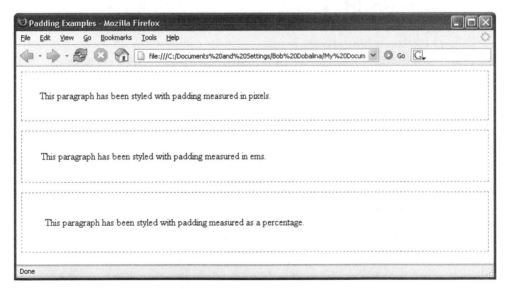

Figure 4.21 shows how these CSS styles render on the screen.

Which Unit of Measurement is Best?

Which method of measurement should you use for your padding: pixels, ems, or percentages? If each of the examples above creates the same effect on the web page, what difference does your choice make? The answer is: it depends on how you want your design to behave.

If you intend for your design to change with the browser window, then percentages is the way to go. Any value that's set using percentages will change as the size of the browser window changes: the bigger the browser window, the bigger your padding will become.

If you want your design to scale well with different font sizes, then you should use ems, because the measurements will be based on how your users set the font size in their browsers. If users increase their browsers' font sizes, then sizes set in ems will also increase accordingly.

If you're after a precise design with graphical elements that line up exactly, regardless of browser window size or font setting, then setting sizes in pixels is the most predictable method of all. A pixel will always, *always* represent a single dot on the user's screen.

Introducing Padding to the Project Site

Adding a bit of breathing space to your layout sure can help. Let's take a moment to address an issue on the project site—namely, the first-level headings.

Find the section in `style1.css` in which you set the color and size of your h1, and add padding as shown below:

File: **style1.css (excerpt)**

```
h1 {
  font-size: x-large;
  background-color: navy;
  color: white;
  padding-top: 2em;
  padding-bottom: .2em;
  padding-left: .4em;
}
```

Next, let's give our h2 headings a bit of head room:

File: **style1.css (excerpt)**

```
h2 {
  color: navy;
```

```
  font-size: 130%;
  font-weight: normal;
  padding-top: 15px;
}
```

Finally, find the tag line, and give that some padding, too. Use the values below:

File: **style1.css (excerpt)**

```
#tagline p {
  font-style: italic;
  font-family: Georgia, Times, serif;
  background-color: #bed8f3;
  border-top: 3px solid #7da5d8;
  border-bottom: 3px solid #7da5d8;
  padding-top: .2em;
  padding-bottom: .2em;
  padding-left: .8em;
}
```

Refresh the view in your browser and you'll see the clear improvement shown in Figure 4.22.

Figure 4.22. Before and after: things looking a lot better with padding applied

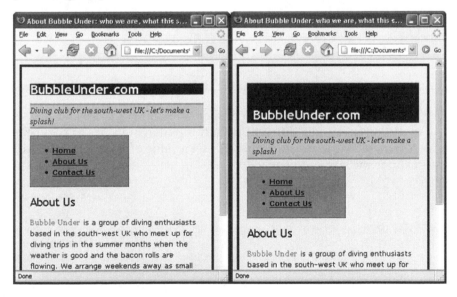

Margins

So, you've learned that you can size a block-level element, give it a border of your choosing, and apply padding to it so that the content it contains doesn't bump right up against its edges. Let's take a look at another very useful CSS property: the `margin` property.

`margin` allows us to specify how much space should exist *outside* an element's border. The only difference between the CSS for the two paragraphs shown in Figure 4.23 is that the declaration `margin: 30px` has been added to the second one.

Figure 4.23. The difference between `padding` and `margin` is clear when a border is present

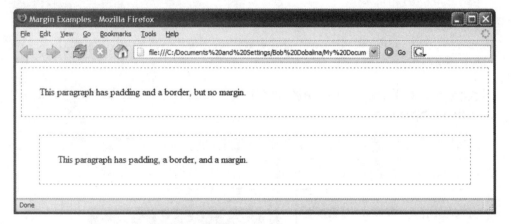

We're going to change the margin of two elements for now: the `ul` and `h2` elements. Different browsers apply different default top margin values to these elements. Rather than relying on the defaults, let's set a value of 15 pixels, so there's no confusion about the size of this margin.

File: **style1.css (excerpt)**

```
h2, ul {
  margin-top: 15px;
}
```

The Box Model

What we've been looking at in this chapter is something that's known as the **box model**. A block-level element can be manipulated using a combination of `margin`, `border`, `padding`, `height`, and `width` values. These properties can be seen together in Figure 4.24.

Figure 4.24. The Box Model explained

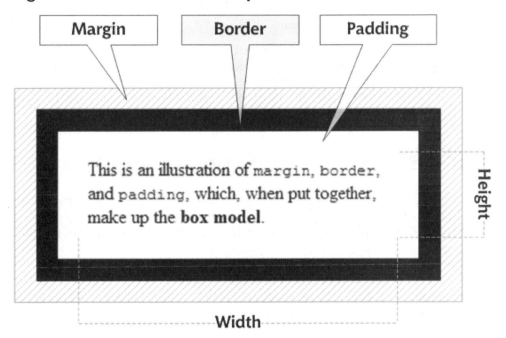

The Broken Box Model

If you're using IE version 6 or later (to check, go to Help > About Internet Explorer and look for Version), you shouldn't have too many problems sizing and manipulating block-level elements as I've described here, as long as you've included a doctype at the beginning of your web page.

If you do not specify a doctype, IE reverts to **quirks mode**.

In quirks mode, IE calculates widths and heights using a different—incorrect—method. This problem arises because IE versions 4 and 5, which were among the first browsers to support CSS, got some of the details, such as the box model, wrong. Microsoft fixed those problems in IE 6, but many sites on the Web had been written to use Microsoft's incorrect interpretation of the CSS rules. Microsoft was in a prickly situation: professional web developers demanded that Microsoft fix the bugs, but if it did that, users would have to battle with a majority of web pages that did not display as intended, sometimes with horrible results.

Microsoft's answer was to use a technique called **doctype switching**. If developers included a doctype, their pages would be displayed according to the correct rules. Pages without a doctype (most of the pages on the Internet at that time didn't bother with doctypes) would be displayed in quirks mode: the same way they appeared in IE version 5.

If you stick to advice given in this book and use the markup provided, you should not experience any problems relating to quirks mode. However, if you do see noticeable differences between web pages viewed in IE and in other browsers, you may be experiencing the "broken box model" problem. If you think this is the case, your best course of action would be to head over to SitePoint's CSS Forum[3] and ask your questions there.

Positioning Elements Anywhere you Like!

Without any intervention, a web browser will simply display the items on the page in the same order as they appear in the source. So, if your markup contains a heading followed by navigation, a second heading, three paragraphs of text, then a quotation, that's precisely what you'll see the on screen, in that exact order. And until now, this has been the way we've approached our project site, adding content in the order in which we wanted it to appear on the page. But in this next section, I'm going to show you some of the really powerful stuff that CSS can achieve: you're going to learn how to position certain sections of the site in very specific areas on the screen.

CSS Layouts: "a Million and One Ways to Skin a Cat"

The one thing you should know about using CSS for the purposes of layout is that there are many, many different ways that you can approach this task. One person may naturally opt for one method, while another will take a completely different approach. I cannot possibly teach you every different available method. If, having read this book, you want to investigate the topic further, I'd recommend that you pick up a copy of another SitePoint book: *HTML Utopia: Designing Without Tables Using CSS.*[4]

---

[3] http://www.sitepoint.com/launch/cssforum/
[4] http://www.sitepoint.com/books/css1/

Showing the Structure

When you're about to lay out your web page using CSS, remember this useful tip: add a border to each section you're planning to move. Borders make it much easier to see the effects of your markup; afterwards, you'll simply need to remove that temporary style. Let's remind ourselves of the specific sections in our web site:

File: **contact.html**

```
<!DOCTYPE html PUBLIC "-//W3C//DTD XHTML 1.0 Strict//EN"
    "http://www.w3.org/TR/xhtml1/DTD/xhtml1-strict.dtd">
<html xmlns="http://www.w3.org/1999/xhtml">
  <head>
    <title>Contact Us at Bubble Under</title>
    <meta http-equiv="Content-Type"
        content="text/html; charset=utf-8" />
    <link href="style1.css" rel="stylesheet" type="text/css" />
  </head>
  <body>
    <div id="header">
      <div id="sitebranding">
        <h1>BubbleUnder.com</h1>
      </div>
      <div id="tagline">
        <p>Diving club for the south-west UK - let's make a
            splash!</p>
      </div>
    </div> <!-- end of header div -->
    <div id="navigation">
      <ul>
        <li><a href="index.html">Home</a></li>
        <li><a href="about.html">About Us</a></li>
        <li><a href="contact.html">Contact Us </a></li>
      </ul>
    </div>
    <div id="bodycontent">
      <h2>Contact Us</h2>
      <p>To find out more, contact Club Secretary Bob Dobalina on
          01793 641207 or email
          <a href="bob@bubbleunder.com">bob@bubbleunder.com</a>.
          </p>
    </div> <!-- end of bodycontent div -->
  </body>
</html>
```

Let's add a new (but temporary) rule to our style sheet (`style1.css`) to apply a border to each of the elements. Insert this rule at the end of the style sheet, so that it overrides any border styles you might have set earlier:

File: **style1.css (excerpt)**

```
#header, #sitebranding, #tagline, #navigation, #bodycontent {
  border: 1px solid red;
  padding: 2px;
  margin-bottom: 2px;
}
```

Here, I've applied some padding, as well as a bottom margin, to make it easier for us to see the items that are nested (the `sitebranding` and `tagline` sections are inside the `header` section). Let's see what that CSS has done to our web pages; Figure 4.25 shows the document displayed in the browser.

Figure 4.25. Revealing the page structure with red borders

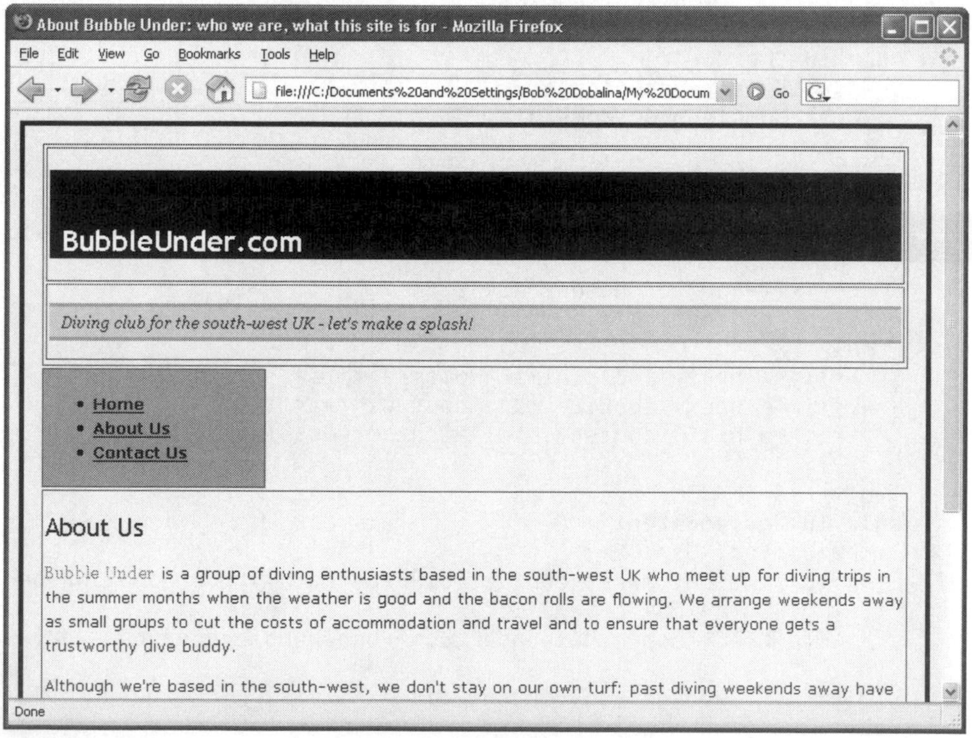

It looks a bit ugly, doesn't it? It's going to get even uglier—for a short while—as we move things about. You know how it is when you move furniture around in your house: while you're halfway through the job, things can seem a little chaotic, but you know that it will all work out in the end. That's exactly what's going to happen with our project site.

Now, let's start moving these boxes around!

Absolute Positioning

Perhaps the easiest method for positioning items using CSS is **absolute positioning**. Using absolute positioning, we specify top and left positions (or coordinates) for the item in question. Imagine directing a store owner to retrieve a piece of jewelry for you from the shop window with the words, "Can I have the watch that's five along and three down?"

Using absolute positioning is as simple as adding a `position: absolute` declaration to your CSS rule, then specifying where you'd like that element positioned. In the following example, we use `top` and `left` to position a `div` 200 pixels from the top of the browser viewport, and 200 pixels from its left edge. Figure 4.26 shows the resulting display.

```
<!DOCTYPE html PUBLIC "-//W3C//DTD XHTML 1.0 Strict//EN"
    "http://www.w3.org/TR/xhtml1/DTD/xhtml1-strict.dtd">
<html xmlns="http://www.w3.org/1999/xhtml">
  <head>
    <title>Absolute Positioning</title>
    <meta http-equiv="Content-Type"
        content="text/html; charset=utf-8" />
    <style type="text/css">
      #redblock {
        position: absolute;
        top: 200px;
        left: 200px;
        color: white;
        background-color: red;
        width: 90px;
        height: 90px;
        padding: 5px;
      }
    </style>
  </head>
  <body>
    <h1>Absolute Positioning</h1>
```

```
    <div id="redblock">This is the red block.</div>
    <p>The red block is positioned 200 pixels from the top and 200
       pixels from the left.</p>
  </body>
</html>
```

Figure 4.26. Absolute positioning in action

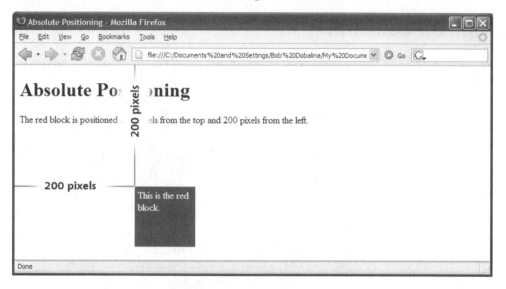

Getting Ready to Move into Position

Because we're going to position every element on our page using fixed coordinates relative to the browser window's top and left sides, it's worth taking the time to undo some stylistic changes that can complicate matters, such as the padding and border properties that we set on the body element earlier.

❏ Open style1.css and remove the padding and border declarations on the body element.

❏ In their place, add two new declarations to set both padding and margin to zero.

The body element rule in your style sheet should now look like this:

File: **style1.css (excerpt)**

```
body
{
  background-color: #e2edff;
  font-family: Verdana, Helvetica, Arial, sans-serif;
  line-height: 125%;
  padding: 0;
  margin: 0;
}
```

note

Nothing is Always Nothing

What's the difference between zero feet, zero meters, and zero furlongs? Well, there's no difference—they're all measuring a zero distance, so the unit is unimportant.

This principle applies in the above CSS—we haven't added a qualifying unit of measurement for the `padding` and `margin` properties. If we want a value of nothing, we don't need to specify a unit of measurement, because whatever the unit might be, it amounts to nothing!

Refresh the view in your browser and you should see a page like the one shown in Figure 4.27.

Figure 4.27. Padding and border removed from the body

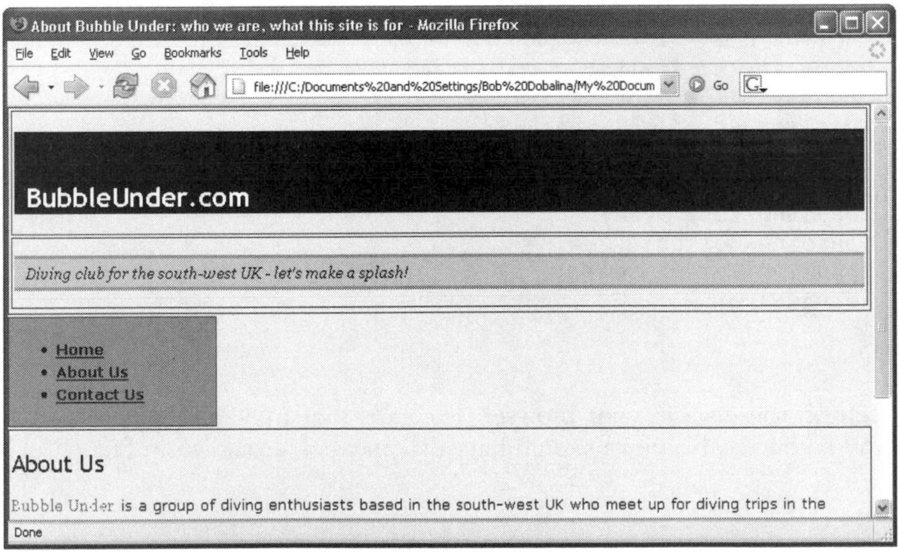

The headings in the page (the h1 that reads "BubbleUnder.com" and the h2 that reads "About Us") are surrounded by margins, which the browser inserts by default if we don't specify margins of our own. It's a good idea to remove them—what we're aiming to do is "trim off the fat" and try to get each heading as close as possible to the top-left of its containing div. This will make the headings easier to position, and ensure that the page looks the same in different browsers.

❏ In style1.css, scroll down the page to find the h1 rule.

❏ Add a declaration to set the margin to zero:

File: **style1.css (excerpt)**

```
h1 {
  font-size: x-large;
  background-color: navy;
  color: white;
  padding-top: 2em;
  padding-bottom: .2em;
  padding-left: .4em;
  margin: 0;
}
```

❏ Locate the #tagline p rule and remove its margins, too:

File: **style1.css (excerpt)**

```
#tagline p {
  font-style: italic;
  font-family: Georgia, Times, serif;
  background-color: #bed8f3;
  border-top: 3px solid #7da5d8;
  border-bottom: 3px solid #7da5d8;
  padding-top: .2em;
  padding-bottom: .2em;
  padding-left: .8em;
  margin: 0;
}
```

❏ Refresh the page in your browser. The gaps that previously appeared above and below the headings should have disappeared, as shown in Figure 4.28.

Figure 4.28. Eliminating spacing around the headings

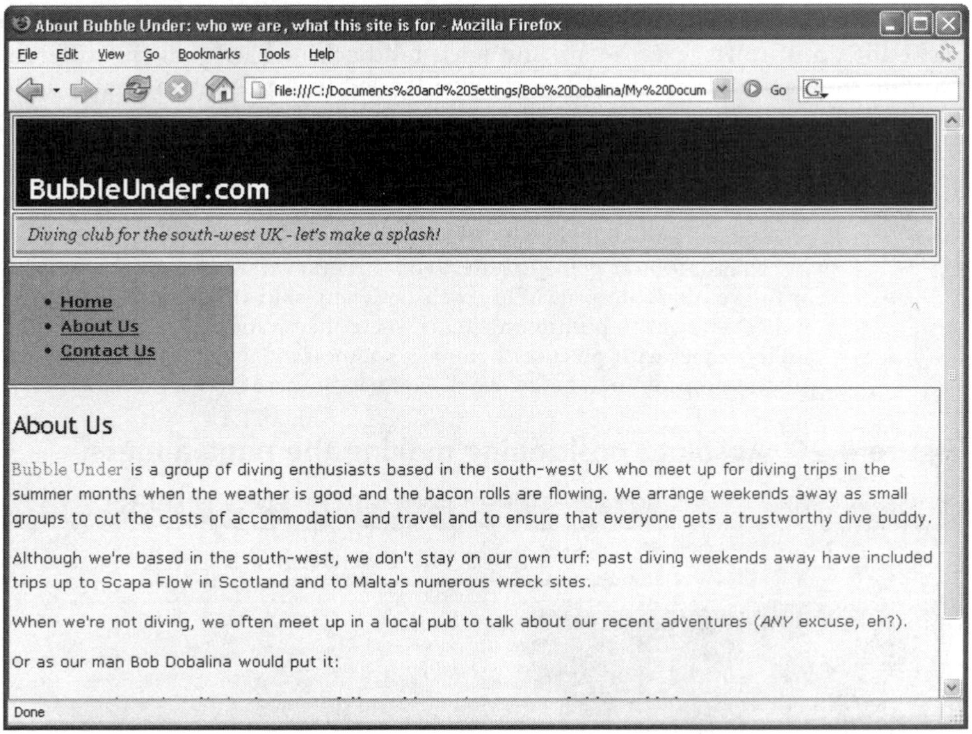

Now, hold your breath: this is where things start to get *really* ugly! Trust me, I'll get you through this quickly and painlessly (and you'll appreciate why I've suggested adding the red borders to the page elements while their positions are shifting).

❑ Add the following to the end of your CSS file:

File: **style1.css** (excerpt)

```
#navigation, #bodycontent, #header {
  position: absolute;
}
```

❑ Save the style sheet.

❑ Refresh the view in your browser.

❑ Enter a state of shock when you see how bad the page looks!

If things have gone according to plan, your page should look like someone has picked it up, thrown it in the air, and let it fall back to Earth: all the different parts of your page should look like they've landed in a pile, as in Figure 4.29. Don't worry: it's all part of the plan!

Avoiding the Messy Part

In case you're wondering why the layout is deliberately being messed up, and whether you're going to have to do this every time you create a web site in future, don't despair. Many web designers skip this intermediate step, and get straight to positioning items where they want them to appear. This ability comes with practice. I think it's important that we understand the process properly first, before we dispense with these basics.

Figure 4.29. Absolute positioning making the page a mess

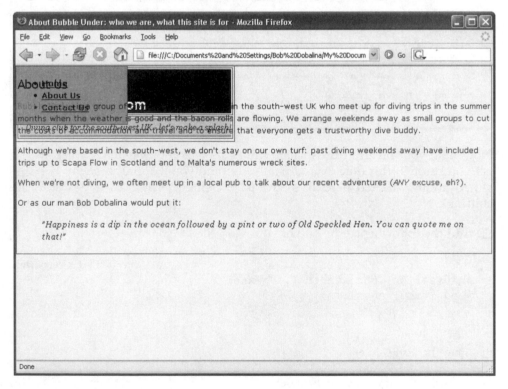

What's happened here? Well, the three sections of the page now sit on top of each other, all absolutely positioned at the top left corner of the page. Why? Because that's what we've told the browser to do with them. All it knows is to position them absolutely; it doesn't know *where* to position them, so they just sit there in a pile: the `header` area first, the `navigation` on top of that, and finally, the `bodycontent` atop that.

Let's begin to put things right by moving the navigation and main content area down so that these appear below the header area.

❑ In `style1.css`, add the following rule:

File: **style1.css (excerpt)**

```
#navigation, #bodycontent {
  top: 120px;
}
```

This should move the blocks down so that the header is no longer obscured. Figure 4.30 shows how the markup displays.

What we've done here is tell the browser to move both the `navigation` and `bodycontent` areas to an absolute position that's 120 pixels from the top of the web page—no questions asked! The browser has honored that request. Now we're going to throw it another request: to move the `bodycontent` area to the right so that it no longer obscures the `navigation`. As the navigation was previously set to a `width` of 180 pixels, let's try moving the `bodycontent` section to the right by 200 pixels: that should easily move it clear (and leave some space between it and the navigation).

Figure 4.30. Pushing the navigation and content down 120 pixels to reveal the header area

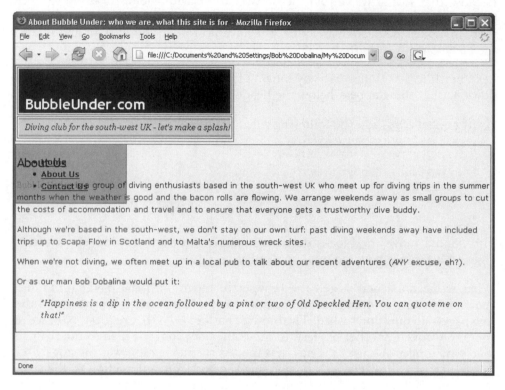

Here's what you need to add to style1.css. I've included all of the CSS relating to position that we added in the previous few steps, so you can check that everything's okay with your style sheet:

File: **style1.css (excerpt)**

```
#navigation, #bodycontent, #header {
  position: absolute;
}

#navigation, #bodycontent {
  top: 120px;
}

#bodycontent {
  left: 200px;
}
```

Let's see how that markup looks in the browser; your page should display as shown in Figure 4.31.

Figure 4.31. Distinguishing navigation from content with the help of positioning

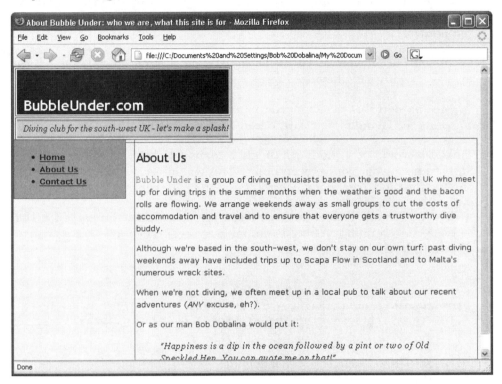

We need to address a few maintenance items before this looks like a finished page:

- ❑ The header area and tag line don't stretch to fill the width of the web page.

- ❑ There is some unnecessary space around the h1 element and the tag line.

- ❑ The red borders and padding between block elements need to be removed (they've served their purpose admirably).

- ❑ It might be an idea to add a comment or two to the CSS, to explain what we've done here.

We're going to complete all these tasks in one go. By now, you should be feeling confident enough to have a go at it yourself (as always, don't worry if you do get a bit stuck: the solution awaits you on the other side of this discussion). Let's get this web site looking completely shipshape!

❑ Position the navigation and body content 107 pixels from the top, instead of 120 pixels. This will allow for things to fit more snugly when we remove the red borders.

❑ Next, tell the browser that the `header div` and the tag line should fill the available width (i.e., they need to take up 100% of the width).

❑ The red borders that were applied to the various `divs` earlier (for the purposes of seeing the layout more clearly) need to be removed. Delete the entire rule.

❑ Finally, it would be a good idea to add a comment above all this positioning stuff to note what you've been doing. This will allow you easily to identify this section's job; note that it controls positioning, rather than cosmetic effects.

How did you get on? Here's the style sheet again (at least, the part of it that we've been concentrating on for positioning purposes). The most recent changes are shown in bold.

```
/*
This section deals with the position of items on the screen.
It uses absolute positioning - fixed x and y coordinates measured
from the top-left corner of the browser's content display.
*/

#navigation, #bodycontent, #header {
  position: absolute;
}

#navigation, #bodycontent {
  top: 107px;
}

#bodycontent {
  left: 200px;
}

#header {
  width: 100%;
}
```

So, the big question is, what's this markup done to our web site? Let's take a look. Does your display resemble Figure 4.32?

Figure 4.32. A very traditional web page layout

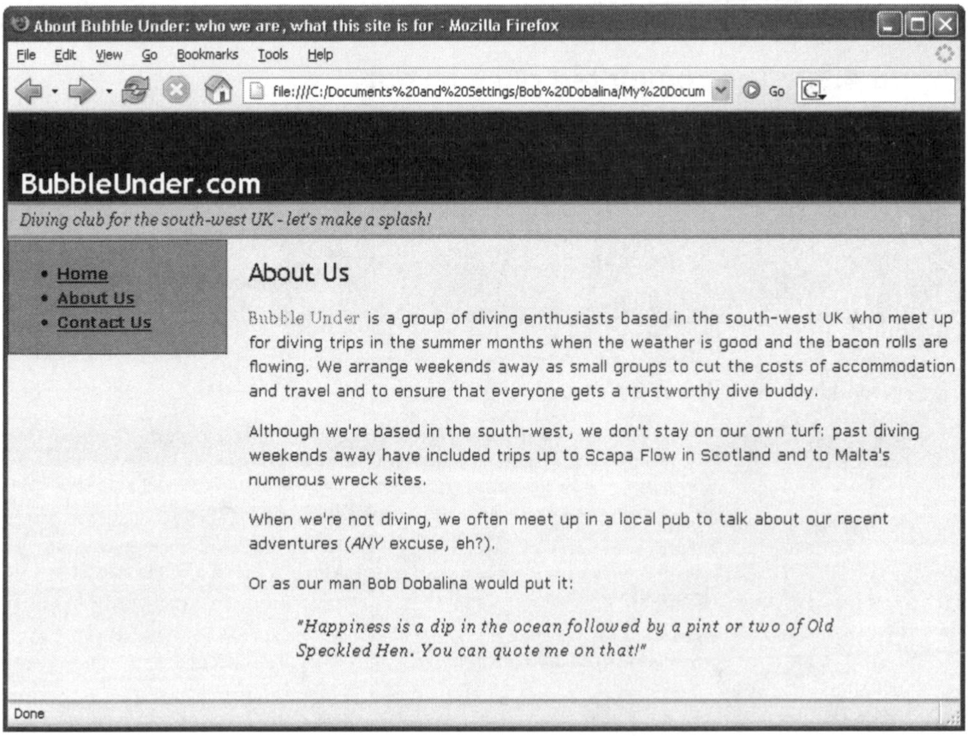

I'm almost happy with it. How about you? The header and tag line might complement each other better if they had matching borders. Give the header a top border of three pixels, using the same shade of blue that we used for the tag line. And let's remove the dotted border around the navigation box—it doesn't quite fit our new design.

Here's the CSS for that:

File: **style1.css (excerpt)**

```
#navigation {
  width: 180px;
  background-color: #7da5d8;
}
```

```
#header {
  border-top: 3px solid #7da5d8;
}
```

Save the changes in `style1.css`, refresh the view in your browser, and see how things look—something like Figure 4.33, I hope!

Figure 4.33. The completed page layout

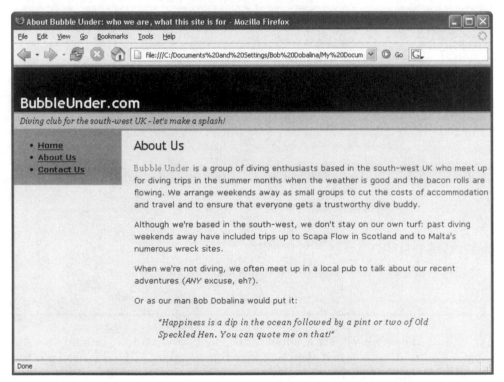

What we've Achieved: Full CSS Layout

Finally, the page is set out as intended, with the navigation on the left (where you'd expect it to be), the content on the right, and a header (and tag line) that stretches all the way along the top. We've achieved a full CSS layout—something that truly will help us out in the future should we want to redesign the look of the site—and it applies to all pages in the site. You may not have noticed, but throughout this whole chapter we haven't touched the page content, or the actual XHTML, once: everything has been changed through the CSS. We've seen how the content can be manipulated using a combination of borders, padding, widths, sizes, and positioning in CSS. Now, use your imagination to visualize this project web site a couple of years from now, with many, many pages of content. Just think how easy it will be to redesign!

Want the navigation to sit on the right-hand side? No problem! Just change the coordinates for the navigation in the CSS, move the content to the left as if you're moving around a piece in a slide puzzle, and before you know it, the whole site will have changed. This is the true power of using CSS to build sites (but then you've never known any other way, you lucky soul!).

Other Layout Options

As I mentioned earlier, there are many different ways that you could approach a CSS layout. In this book, I've opted to choose the simplest, most trouble-free method to get you up to speed with the idea; however, it would be remiss of me not to mention the other positioning techniques you can use. Don't worry—I'm not going to ask you to re-do the web site all over again! Instead, I'll provide some general examples (as I did with the border styles earlier in this chapter). First, let's take a look at one more thing you should know about absolute positioning.

More Absolute Positioning

So far, all our positioning has been relative to the viewport. Whenever you've positioned anything, you've positioned it from the left edge of the page, or from the top of the page. When you start to play around with absolutely positioned elements, and you start putting them inside each other, a different approach is required.

To illustrate, let's take our red box example from before, and add a yellow box:

```
<!DOCTYPE html PUBLIC "-//W3C//DTD XHTML 1.0 Strict//EN"
    "http://www.w3.org/TR/xhtml1/DTD/xhtml1-strict.dtd">
<html xmlns="http://www.w3.org/1999/xhtml">
  <head>
    <title>Absolute Positioning</title>
    <meta http-equiv="Content-Type"
        content="text/html; charset=utf-8" />
    <style type="text/css">
      #redblock {
        position: absolute;
```

```
      top: 200px;
      left: 200px;
      background-color: red;
      width: 100px;
      height: 100px;
    }

    #yellowblock {
      position: absolute;
      top: 20px;
      left: 20px;
      background-color: yellow;
      color: red;
      width: 50px;
      height: 50px;
      padding: 5px;
    }
  </style>
 </head>
 <body>
  <h1>Absolute Positioning</h1>
  <div id="redblock">
    <div id="yellowblock">Yellow!</div>
  </div>
  <p>The red block is positioned absolutely using coordinates of
      200 pixels from the top, and 200 pixels from the left.</p>
  <p>The yellow block inside is positioned 20 pixels from the
      top of its parent element, and 20 pixels to the left.</p>
 </body>
</html>
```

Here, we've put a div with the id yellowblock inside our redblock div, and positioned it absolutely, 20 pixels from the top, and 20 pixels from the left. Where do you think the yellow block is going to appear? The display is illustrated in Figure 4.34.

Figure 4.34. The yellow block appearing inside the red block

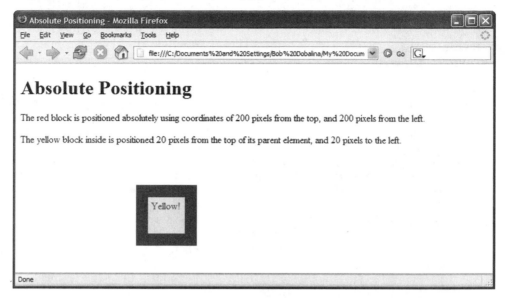

How did it end up there? Well, whenever you absolutely position an element, everything inside that element is positioned in relation to that element. Don't worry if this is a bit confusing—it's a pretty advanced concept, and we won't be using it in our project site. But I wanted to mention it so that you're not confused when you come to play around with positioning on your own sites.

Relative Positioning

With absolute positioning, items are positioned from a very specific start point: the top left corner of the viewport, or the top left corner of a containing element. With **relative positioning**, any value that you apply will be implemented *relative to the item's original location before this positioning rule was applied*. This is best demonstrated with an example:

```
p {
  background-color: yellow;
}

.nudged {
  position: relative;
  top: 10px;
```

```
  left: 10px;
}
```

The nudged class could be applied to any paragraph (or any other block-level element, for that matter). Here's some XHTML in which the class is applied to the middle paragraph:

```
<p>Next came a massage that I was not expecting. It started with a
    bit of manipulation of the temples, followed by the barber's
    attempt to drag the top half of my face down towards my chin
    (and vice-versa) with his big burly hands. I'm sure it's good
    for you. I wasn't sure it was good for me, though. He then
    made his way down to my shoulders and managed to pull me
    around in such a way that I squealed like a girl. This was not
    relaxing -- this was painful! Evidently I was knotted up. I
    must have needed it, I reasoned.</p>
<p class="nudged">There was an audible crack as he grabbed my head
    and twisted it to the right, all of it quite unexpected. To
    the left, no cracking sound. And we weren't quite done
    yet...</p>
<p>To finish off, the barber got a pair of tongs. He took a ball
    of cotton wool and wrapped it tightly around the tip of the
    tongs, so that it looked like a large cotton bud. He then
    doused the cotton wool in what must have been pure alcohol,
    set it on fire, and began to fling it at my face. Using one
    hand to cover the top of my ear and my hair, he flashed it
    against my ear, singeing the small hairs in and around the
    ear.</p>
```

Figure 4.35 shows the effect this markup has on the paragraph (with the paragraph's original position still visible).

Figure 4.35. The middle paragraph positioned relative to the previous element—before and after

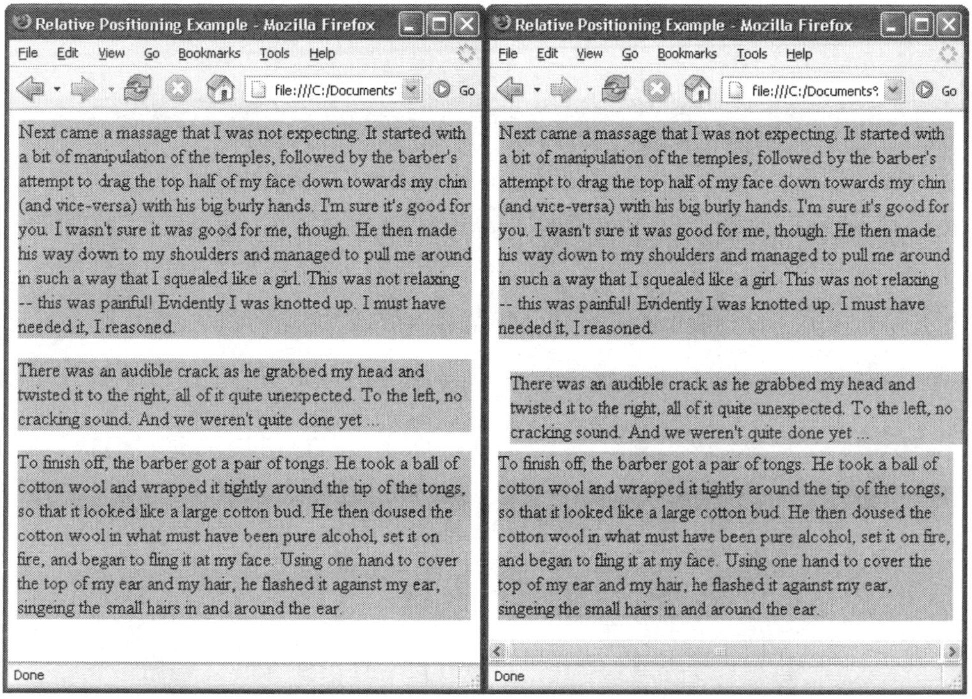

Notice how the markup has moved our paragraph across and down by ten pixels, so that neither the left- nor right-hand sides of that paragraph line up with the others. It really has been "nudged," rather than simply having had an indent applied to the left-hand side.

In case you're wondering, the text in the example above is describing the "joys" of a traditional Turkish shave. It's fun … if you like that kind of thing!

Benefits of Relative Positioning

Relative positioning can offer an improvement over the absolute positioning technique that I proposed in the discussion of our project site. If text sizes are increased in the browser (in IE, you would use View > Text Size > Larger or Largest), the document can re-flow a little more freely if relative positioning is used. With the fixed header area (a space of 107 pixels), a large increase in text sizes could potentially cause text to break out of the allotted space, and intrude onto the content or navigation area, as shown in Figure 4.36.

Figure 4.36. Sometimes, very large font sizes and fixed position layouts don't mix

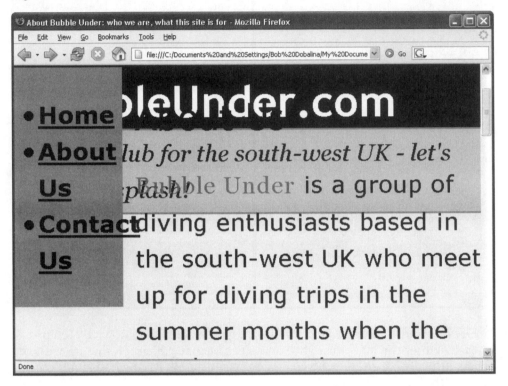

So, why didn't we use the relative positioning method instead of absolute positioning on our project site? Well, using relative positioning for a CSS layout is not an easy thing to accomplish; you might even be put off at an early stage in your CSS career if you get something wrong. In practice, a well-seasoned web developer will use a mixture of absolute, relative, and **floated positioning** schemes.

Stretching your Wings with Elastic Design

There is an approach to building web pages called **elastic** web design, where all measurements are specified using ems—borders, margins, padding, everything. It certainly falls into the realm of "advanced" web design, so we're not going to tackle it in this book. However, as an indication of what is possible, try making this small change to our project's style sheet.

Locate the line that positions our navigation and body content areas 107 pixels from the top of the viewport, and replace it with the following:

File: **style1.css (excerpt)**

```
#navigation, #bodycontent {
    top: 6.54em;
}
```

Save the file and refresh your browser. You shouldn't notice any difference—until you change the font size. Because the `div`s are positioned using `em`s, the design holds together much better, even at large font sizes. The number 6.54 might seem unusual; it was determined by trial and error to be the distance from the top of the viewport to the bottom of the tag line, regardless of the font size in use.

Earlier in this chapter, we discussed the choices available for units of measurement, and here is one case when a definite advantage is gained by using `em`s. Read more in Patrick Griffith's article on elastic design.[5]

Floated Positioning

A technique favored by many web developers is to use CSS floats to lay out a page. Put simply, when you float an area of content, you move it to one side, allowing other content to flow around it. With careful planning, you can float several items on a page, creating effects similar to the multi-column layouts we see in newspapers. Let's take a look at a very simple example of a float:

```
#nav {
  float: right;
  width: 300px;
  background-color: yellow;
}
```

This will move a block with an `id` of `nav` to the right of the web page, setting it to just 300 pixels wide. The text that follows it moves up the page to fill the space that's been vacated by the floated element. Here's the XHTML that achieves this effect:

```
<div id="nav">
  <ul>
```

---

[5] http://www.alistapart.com/articles/elastic/

```
    <li><a href="index.html">This is an area of navigation
        items</a></li>
    <li><a href="index.html">which is floated on the
        right.</a></li>
    <li><a href="turkish.html">Turkish Shaving Stories.</a></li>
    <li><a href="http://www.bubbleunder.com/">Diving
        Stories.</a></li>
  </ul>
</div> <!-- end of nav div -->
<h1>Turkish Shaving Stories</h1>
<p>Next came a massage that I was not expecting. It started with a
    bit of manipulation of the temples, followed by the barber's
    attempt to drag the top half of my face down towards my chin
    (and vice-versa) with his big burly hands. I'm sure it's good
    for you. I wasn't sure it was good for me, though. He then
    made his way down to my shoulders and managed to pull me
    around in such a way that I squealed like a girl. This was not
    relaxing -- this was painful! Evidently I was knotted up. I
    must have needed it, I reasoned.</p>
<p>There was an audible crack as he grabbed my head and twisted it
    to the right, all of it quite unexpected. To the left, no
    cracking sound. And we weren't quite done yet ...</p>
<p>To finish off, the barber got a pair of tongs. He took a ball
    of cotton wool and wrapped it tightly around the tip of the
    tongs, so that it looked like a large cotton bud. He then
    doused the cotton wool in what must have been pure alcohol,
    set it on fire, and began to fling it at my face. Using one
    hand to cover the top of my ear and my hair, he flashed it
    against my ear, singeing the small hairs in and around the
    ear.</p>
```

Figure 4.37 shows the effect as it displays in the browser.

Figure 4.37. A simple float at work

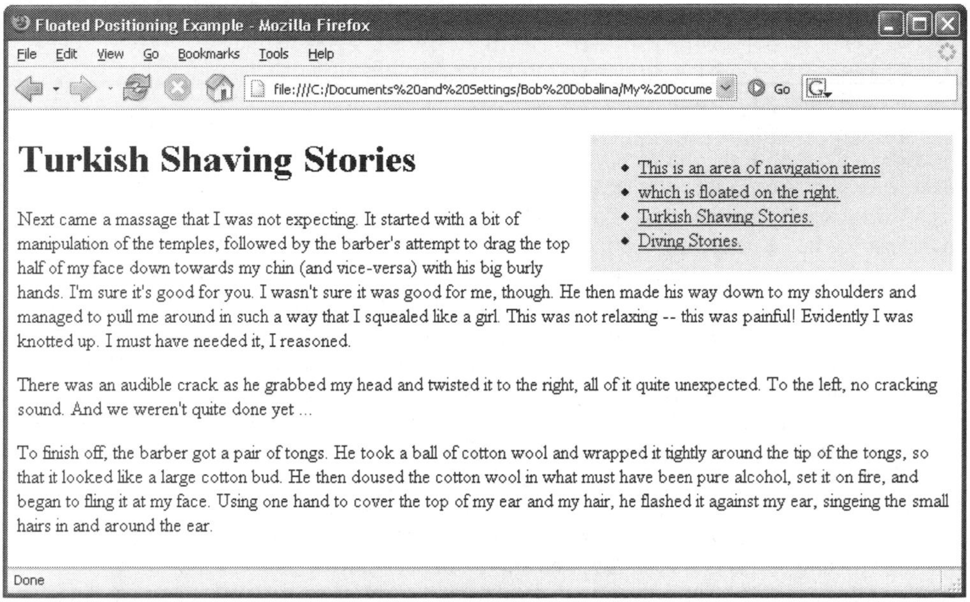

If you want to avoid having the text wrap around the item and create an L shape, apply the CSS `padding` property to the content area. In the example above, the navigation is set to display 300 pixels wide, so the addition of a padding value of 310 pixels on the right of the content area should do the trick. Here's an updated version of the file:

```
#nav {
  float: right;
  width: 300px;
  background-color: yellow;
}

.contentconstrained {
  padding-right: 310px;
}
```

The `contentconstrained` class should be applied to a `div` that can surround all the paragraphs that it needs to affect, like so:

```
<div id="nav">
  <ul>
    <li><a href="index.html">This is an area of navigation
```

```
          items</a></li>
    <li><a href="index.html">which is floated on the
        right.</a></li>
    <li><a href="turkish.html">Turkish Shaving Stories.</a></li>
    <li><a href="http://www.bubbleunder.com/">Diving
        Stories.</a></li>
  </ul>
</div> <!-- end of nav div -->
<div class="contentconstrained">
<h1>Turkish Shaving Stories</h1>
<p>Next came a massage that I was not expecting. It started with a
    bit of manipulation of the temples, followed by the barber's
    attempt to drag the top half of my face down towards my chin
    (and vice-versa) with his big burly hands. I'm sure it's good
    for you. I wasn't sure it was good for me, though. He then
    made his way down to my shoulders and managed to pull me
    around in such a way that I squealed like a girl. This was not
    relaxing -- this was painful! Evidently I was knotted up. I
    must have needed it, I reasoned.</p>
<p>There was an audible crack as he grabbed my head and twisted it
    to the right, all of it quite unexpected. To the left, no
    cracking sound. And we weren't quite done yet ...</p>
<p>To finish off, the barber got a pair of tongs. He took a ball
    of cotton wool and wrapped it tightly around the tip of the
    tongs, so that it looked like a large cotton bud. He then
    doused the cotton wool in what must have been pure alcohol,
    set it on fire, and began to fling it at my face. Using one
    hand to cover the top of my ear and my hair, he flashed it
    against my ear, singeing the small hairs in and around the
    ear.</p>
</div> <!-- end of contentconstrained div -->
```

Figure 4.38 shows the outcome.

Figure 4.38. A tidier use of floats

We won't use floats much on our project site, but we will float the image of the circle of divers on the front page. However, because we don't want to float every image on the site, we can't just apply our CSS to every `img` element. Instead, we'll refer to this image as our "feature image," and name the `img` element accordingly, using a class selector. We'll also give it some margins, so that it sits nicely next to our welcome message.

Edit your homepage (`index.html`) and make the following change to your markup:

File: **index.html (excerpt)**

```
<div id="bodycontent">
  <h2>Welcome to our super-dooper Scuba site</h2>
  <p><img src="divers-circle.jpg" class="feature" width="200"
      height="162" alt="A circle of divers practice their
      skills" /></p>
  <p>Glad you could drop in and share some air with us! You've
      passed your underwater navigation skills and successfully
```

```
           found your way to the start point - or in this case, our
           home page.</p>
  </div> <!-- end of bodycontent div -->
```

Now add the following to our style sheet to float our image to the right of the body content:

File: **style1.css** (excerpt)

```
.feature {
  float: right;
  margin: 10px;
}
```

Save your changes and refresh your browser to see the result:

Figure 4.39. A circle of divers learning how to float

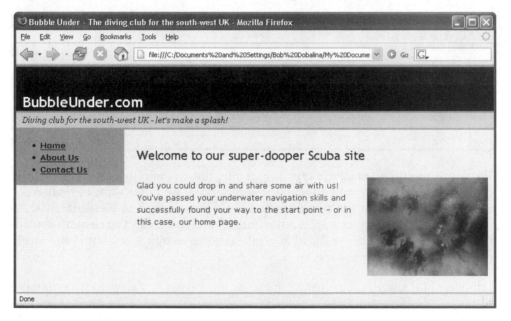

This is as far as I'm going to take you with floats. They have a habit of becoming complex and difficult to get right once you have a few floats on the page. If you want to learn more about using floats to create flexible and exciting layouts, I can recommend two other SitePoint books that go into more detail, namely *The*

CSS Anthology: 101 Essential Tips, Tricks & Hacks[6] and, in particular, *HTML Utopia: Designing Without Tables Using CSS.*[7]

Styling Lists

Our standard navigation list can benefit from a little more styling. By default, the bullet points are small black blobs, but you can change these easily to some different, pre-defined shapes. Let's head back to our project's style sheet, to see how this works.

❑ In `style1.css`, find the `li` element selector.

❑ Add the following declaration (new addition shown in bold):

File: **style1.css (excerpt)**

```
li {
  font-size: small;
  list-style-type: circle;
}
```

❑ Save the CSS file and refresh the view in your browser.

❑ Try changing the value of `list-style-type` to `disc`, `square`, or even `none`. Save the CSS file and check the page display in the browser after each change (we'll go with the `none` option on our project site). You should see something like Figure 4.40.

---

[6] http://www.sitepoint.com/books/cssant1/
[7] http://www.sitepoint.com/books/css1/

Figure 4.40. Applying different list bullet styles in CSS

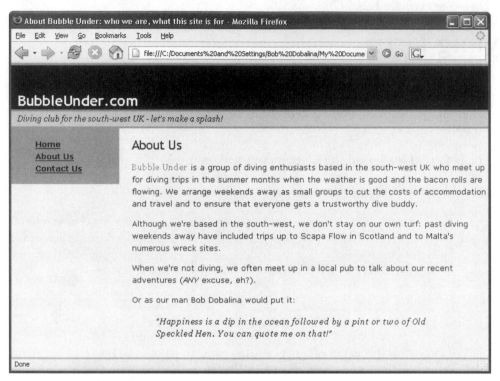

It is possible to use CSS to style lists to a much greater extent, including:

- making the links appear as buttons (using the CSS `border` and `padding` attributes)

- creating a larger clickable area for the link (not just the text itself)

- setting list items out in a horizontal line

These more advanced techniques are discussed and explained thoroughly in *The CSS Anthology: 101 Essential Tips, Tricks & Hacks*[8] by Rachel Andrew. The book devotes almost a whole chapter to styling navigation, in fact, and presents many different styles that you can try out. I strongly advise you to grab a copy if you want to learn some really cool CSS tricks (once you've got the basics under your belt, of course!).

---

[8] http://www.sitepoint.com/books/cssant1/

In the meantime, if you want to play around with some styled lists to see what's possible, please do take a look at the List-O-Matic[9] tool, which I built to make this task a little easier.

Summary

This has been another very productive chapter! We began by learning about the difference between inline and block-level elements. Next, we looked at the various ways in which we can style block-level elements, such as adding a `border`, `padding`, and sizing. This theory was then put into practice as we applied some of these styles to the project web site. Finally, we learned how the entire structure of the web pages could be re-jigged—site-wide—using CSS positioning, and we touched on the styling of list elements.

I hope you now have first-hand experience with the ways in which centralizing all your presentation rules—colors, fonts, or layout schemes—can be such a bonus. In a later chapter, I'll show how you can make use of this technique quickly and easily.

In the next chapter, I'm going to guide you through the use of images on your web site, including background images that are set using CSS, and inline images that you can drop into your web pages as content (like the image of the divers in a circle that we first saw in Chapter 2).

---

[9] http://www.accessify.com/tools-and-wizards/developer-tools/list-o-matic/

Picture This! Using Images on your Web Site

Back in Chapter 2, we made a simple concession to avoid having the web site look bland: we added the image of divers (using the `img` element). This really needed to be done: first and foremost, the Web is a visual medium, and while great writing can keep the audience captivated, the saying "a picture tells a thousand words" is as true as it ever was. The problem is that we glossed over a discussion of all the different things you can do with images in our haste to get that first visual element on the page.

In this chapter, we're going to pick up where we left our discussion of images. We'll see how you can use them to brighten up a site's content, and apply them as decorative backgrounds. I'll also explain some simple techniques for managing and adjusting images using some of the software that I suggested you download in Chapter 2.

Let's begin by taking a look at **inline images**.

Inline Images

Let's take just a brief moment to remind ourselves what the XHTML for an inline image looks like:

```
<p><img src="divers-circle.jpg" width="200" height="162"
    alt="A circle of divers practice their skills" /></p>
```

You've probably seen this line more times than you care to mention since Chapter 2—without paying it any attention. A refresher of its constituent parts is in order.

Anatomy of the Image Element

❑ The element name is `img`.

❑ The `src` attribute defines the "source" of that image: the location at which the browser can find the image file. In this example, it's `divers-circle.jpg`.

❑ The `alt` attribute is an important attribute, which I'll explain in detail below.

Both the attributes above are required: at the very least, they *must* be present in the `img` tag. The following attributes are not required, but as they're extremely useful, few people choose to leave them out.

❑ The `height` and `width` attributes let the browser know the dimensions at which the image should be displayed in the browser (these are particularly useful if the user's web connection speed is a little slow, as the browser can reserve the appropriate space for the image before it has downloaded).

Remember that the `img` element is an empty element. In other words, it has no separate closing tag[1]—the final forward slash tells the browser that everything it needs in order to display that element's content is contained within the "attributes."

The `alt` Attribute: Making Images Useful to All (Even the Blind)

In our diving site example, the `img` element has an `alt` attribute with the value `A circle of divers practice their skills`. What's this for? Well, the `alt` attribute provides an alternative text version of the image that most people see on the screen. I say "most people" because not everyone can see this image. Why not? Here are a few scenarios to consider:

---

[1] If you look at the source of other web sites, you may spot `img` tags that do not have a trailing forward slash. In earlier versions of HTML (such as version 4.01), it was not necessary to close the tag in this way.

☐ The person browsing your site is blind (yes, it is possible to use a computer even if you are completely blind. See the note below, "Screen Readers: Hearing the Web").

☐ The user is accessing your web site on a slow connection and has temporarily disabled images to speed things up.

☐ The user is on a *very* slow connection—so slow, in fact, that images simply take too long to load.

In all of the scenarios above, the `alt` attribute provides another method by which these users can get the information they need. Figure 5.1 shows what the users in the second and third scenarios above will see.

Figure 5.1. A slow connection delaying the image download

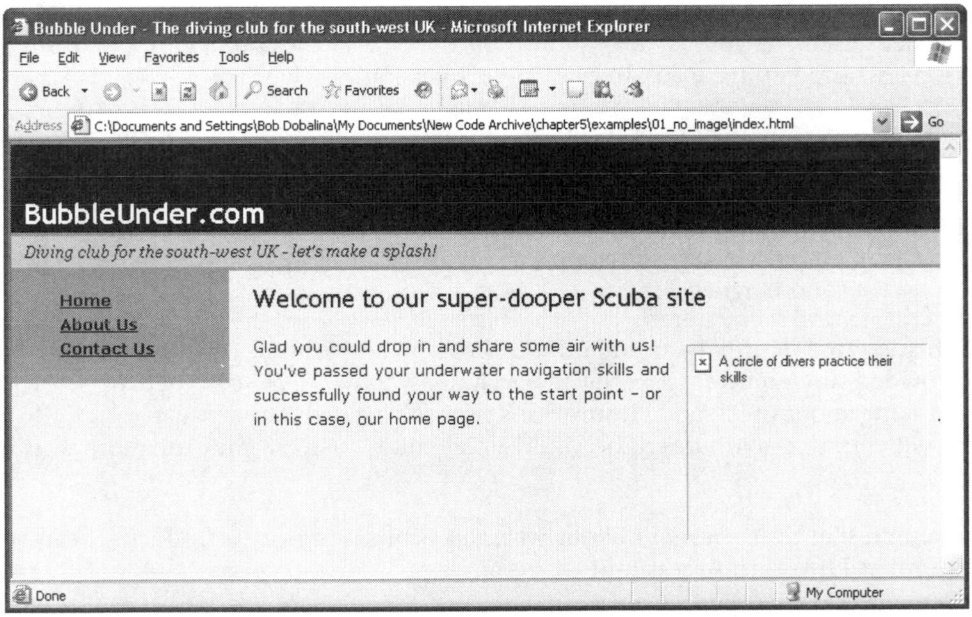

If a user was browsing the site over a very slow connection, and was presented with the screen shown in Figure 5.1, he or she could read the text alternative and, based on that description, decide whether to wait until the image downloaded completely, or click on a link to go elsewhere. The `alt` attribute delivers a similar benefit to users who browse the site with images disabled: if the description seems interesting, the user might choose to switch on images. For a blind user, though, the alternative is not so much an "alternative." In fact, it's an *essential* feature of the image upon which they rely.

Web Accessibility

The practice of making sure that images have appropriate `alt` attributes comes under the general banner of **web accessibility**. This is a specialized area of web design and programming that concerns itself with creating web sites that can be accessed and used by everyone, including users with a wide range of disabilities. Here are some examples:

❑ people with poor vision (Are your font sizes too small? Can they be scaled up?)

❑ blind users (Do your `alt` attributes explain the visual elements on your page?)

❑ deaf users (If you use any sounds on the site—for example, an audio interview—do you have an alternative, text version?)

❑ mobility-impaired users (Can the user move a mouse around easily, if at all? If not, can your site be navigated using the keyboard alone?)

❑ people with reading difficulties (Could you have worded things to be more easily understood by someone with dyslexia, or by people for whom English is a second language?)

This is most definitely an area that's beyond the scope of this book. I haven't provided any solutions for the few examples above; I've just tried to get you thinking about the issues. However, it's generally agreed that if you make an effort to get your `alt` attributes right, you're doing much to make your site more accessible.

If you'd like to learn more about web accessibility, a great introduction can be found at Dive Into Accessibility.[2]

note

Screen Readers: Hearing the Web

Once upon a time, blind users had to rely on Braille alternatives to web site content, or they had to ask a friend to read web content aloud to them. Now, blind users have an excellent and far more immediate alternative: the **screen reader**. A screen reader is a piece of software that provides a sound-based

---

[2] http://diveintoaccessibility.org/

replication of a web page. It reads aloud the text that appears on-screen, so users hear the page, rather than see it. Some screen readers are used only to access web sites, while others provide audible feedback for the entire operating system plus many other applications, including office and email programs.

For the sake of these users, it's especially important that you take care with your `alt` attributes: the screen reader will read these aloud when it comes across images on your web pages. As Figure 5.2 shows, including a description of the image that doesn't provide any insight (for example, just writing the word "IMAGE") isn't terribly helpful to anyone.

Figure 5.2. An `alt` attribute that leaves everyone in the dark

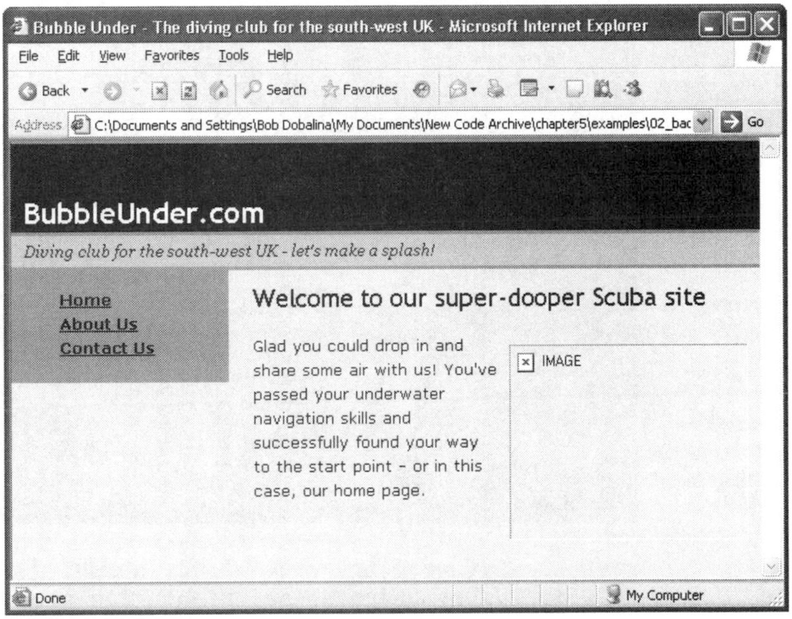

If you'd like to learn more about the way screen readers work, and in particular, how they deal with images on your web pages, you could try the WebAIM screen reader simulation.[3] If you want to try a screen reader on your own web site, download a trial version of JAWS (for Windows).[4]

---

[3] http://www.webaim.org/simulations/screenreader
[4] http://www.freedomscientific.com/fs_downloads/jaws.asp

What Makes a Good alt?

I could write a lot about the topic of `alt` attributes, as it can be quite a subjective field. What one person believes is an appropriate description of an image may not be seen as such by others. However, there are a few simple rules that you can use as guidelines:

❏ If the image conveys useful information, describe the image as briefly but accurately as possible. This rule is exemplified in Figure 5.3 and the code that follows.

Figure 5.3. Describing the image you see

```
<img src="sydney.jpg" width="500" height="354"
    alt="Sydney Opera House, night-time shot with the
    Harbour Bridge in the background" />
```

❏ If the image is purely decorative, and provides no useful information, use an empty `alt` attribute (`alt=""`). This informs screen readers that the image isn't relevant, and that they needn't read anything out.

❏ If the image is being used as a link, do not describe the image as it appears; instead, describe the *function* of that image. So, if you're using an image of Sydney Harbour Bridge as a call to action, the `alt` attribute should reflect just that. See below the `alt` text that's used to describe the function of Figure 5.4.

Figure 5.4. Using an image as a link

```
<a href="win-holiday.html"><img src="win-a-trip.jpg"
    width="500" height="354" alt="Win a trip to
    Sydney!" /></a>
```

There are many other aspects of web accessibility—the discipline of making your web pages accessible to people with a wide range of disabilities—and you might like to learn more about these in due course. For our purposes, though, taking care of the `alt` attributes used with images will be of great benefit.

GIF vs JPG vs PNG

You may have wondered why some images have a `.gif` file extension while others use `.jpg`. Even if you haven't thought about this, I'm going to explain the difference, because it's extremely important.

The image formats that are most commonly used on the Web are **GIF** and **JPEG**. Both have their uses, but if we were to summarize to the absolute essentials of applying these formats, they would be as follows:

❑ JPEG images, or JPEGs, are great for photographic images. JPEG images achieve small file sizes by using "lossy compression," which, as the name suggests, means that some of the detail is lost from the original image during the compression process. In photographs, the effect of this lossy compression is minimal, but in images with clear, crisp lines (such as illustrations or logos, for example), this compression can make the image appear blurred.

❑ GIF images, on the other hand, are great for illustrations and logos, and images that have large areas of a single color. They're not great for photographs, though, because GIFs can only show 256 colors. This might sound like a lot, but a colorful photograph can contain millions of different colors. GIFs also offer transparency, which is the ability to make part of the image see-through.

One alternative to these formats is to use the PNG format. This is an excellent choice that has taken the good points of each of the image formats mentioned above, and added even more. However, there is one niggling problem: IE does not (at the time of writing) fully support the PNG format. Most people still use only GIFs and JPEGs.

Transparency

When you save an image, it will most likely be rectangular and fill the entire space. However, imagine that you have an image that's not a regular shape—for instance, an oval-shaped company logo. The straight edges of image files don't really lend themselves to tasks such as placing that image on a background. The GIF format allows you to specify the transparent portions of an image. Of the 256 colors that make up a GIF, just one can be set to transparent, as is illustrated in Figure 5.5.

Figure 5.5. The differences between JPEG and GIF support for transparency

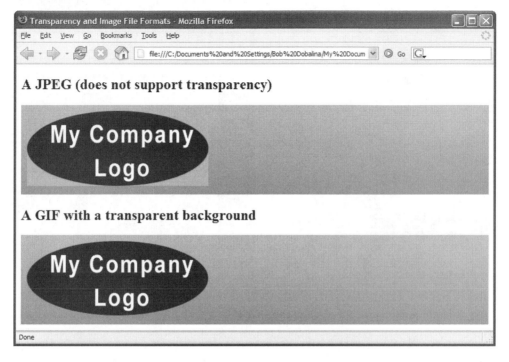

PNG: King of Transparency

Undoubtedly the best image format for dealing with transparent images is PNG, which is capable of handling something called **alpha channel** transparency. To the layperson, what this means is that PNG can handle different levels of transparency—it doesn't just turn transparency "on" or "off" the way GIF does.

A good example is demonstrated on Audion's web site.[5] Audion is a media player (for Macintosh) that's "skinnable"—you can choose different "looks" for the program's interface. The Audion site displays PNG images for users to try out. For as long as I can remember, this web page has looked horrible when viewed in IE; this display is shown in Figure 5.6 (they probably weren't too worried about IE, given that Audion's audience is restricted to Mac users whose browsers support PNG).

---

[5] http://www.panic.com/audion/faces.php

Figure 5.6. Firefox getting it right; IE 6 handling PNG transparency poorly

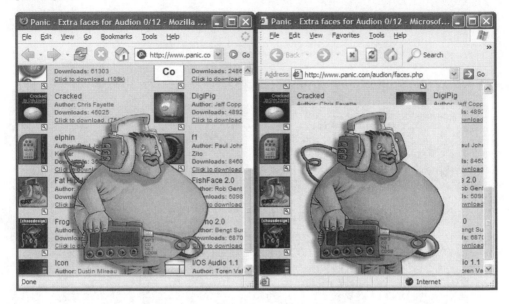

Figure 5.7 emphasizes how nicely the drop-shadow sits over the background in Firefox.

Figure 5.7. A drop-shadow demonstrating that different levels of transparency are at play

Microsoft has fixed its handling of PNG images in IE version 7, but until it's been released and most people have it installed on their computers, we're stuck with using GIFs if we want transparency.

Adding an Image Gallery to the Site

One of the great joys of diving is getting up close and personal with all the beautiful creatures that live in the sea. You can try to explain the wonder of all this to a non-diver but, usually, they just don't get it. Our web site provides a great opportunity to show people just how beautiful these underwater sights can be.

It's time to grow the project site a little by adding a new page: a simple image gallery. Before we start looking at the images themselves, we need to re-jig the existing web site files slightly to accommodate the new page.

Updating the Navigation

❏ Open `index.html` in your text editor.

❏ Find the navigation section and add another link to your list of links, like so:

File: **index.html (excerpt)**

```
<div id="navigation">
  <ul>
    <li><a href="index.html">Home</a></li>
    <li><a href="about.html">About Us</a></li>
    <li><a href="contact.html">Contact Us</a></li>
    <li><a href="gallery.html">Image Gallery</a></li>
  </ul>
</div> <!-- end of navigation div -->
```

❏ Save the file, then glance over it in the browser to make sure the link appears appropriately.

❏ Repeat the steps above for `about.html` and `contact.html`.

The navigation in all your pages should look like that shown in Figure 5.8.

Figure 5.8. Adding the Image Gallery to the navigation list

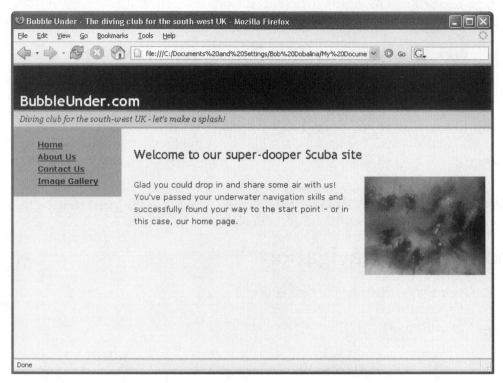

There's just one small problem: the gallery page doesn't exist! Let's rectify that now.

Adding the New Gallery Page

❏ Create a copy of contact.html and rename it gallery.html, just as we did back in Chapter 2.

❏ Open the newly-created gallery page in your text editor, and change the level 2 heading (h2) content to read "Image Gallery."

❏ Remove the single paragraph that appears below that heading, and replace it with the following:

File: **gallery.html (excerpt)**

```
<p>Below are some of the great views that club members have
    captured on film (or digital memory!) on various dive
    trips.</p>
<p>Please do drop me (that's Bob) a line if you would like to
    <a href="mailto:bob@bubbleunder.com">submit an image</a> to
    this gallery.</p>
```

❑ Finally, change the `title` content to read "Image Gallery - Underwater Photography from Bubble Under's members."

❑ Save the amendments and check the page in your browser.

Adding the First Image

Finally, we're ready to add the first picture to our gallery: a picture of a turtle. Unfortunately, though, it appears that a local shark has taken quite a chomp out of his side—Figure 5.9 reveals all.

Figure 5.9. Ouch! That must have hurt!

I've made a point of commenting on that image—after all, it's quite a sight, isn't it? This image deserves a descriptive `alt` attribute—something a little better than `A picture of a turtle`, which doesn't really tell the full story. Here's the markup we'll use for this image:

```
<p><img src="gallery/turtle-bite.jpg" width="400" height="258"
    alt="A turtle swims comfortably among the coral, despite its
    old injury - a large shark bite on one side" /></p>
```

 Get the Picture

Tip

You'll find this image—and all the others that we'll use in this chapter—in the code archive (see the preface for details about how to access it).

Note that the value of this `src` attribute is a little different than the others we've seen so far. Those slashes just tell the browser that the image is inside a folder. In this case, `gallery/turtle-bite.jpg` tells the browser that the image file (`turtle-bite.jpg`) is inside a folder named `gallery`. So, before you go to add this image to the gallery, create the `gallery` folder inside your web site's folder (we learned how to create a folder back in Chapter 1: in Windows, select File > New > Folder; on a Mac, select File > New Folder), and put the image inside it.

When you have saved the image inside the folder, add the markup above to `gallery.html`, like so:

File: **gallery.html (excerpt)**

```
<div id="bodycontent">
  <h2>Image Gallery</h2>
  <p>Below are some of the great views that club members have
      captured on film (or digital memory!) on various dive
      trips.</p>
  <p>Please do drop me (that's Bob) a line if you would like to
      <a href="mailto:bob@bubbleunder.com">submit an image</a> to
      this gallery.</p>
  <p><img src="gallery/turtle-bite.jpg" width="400" height="258"
      alt="A turtle swims comfortably among the coral, despite its
      old injury - a large shark bite on one side" /></p>
</div> <!-- end of bodycontent div -->
```

Save the page and make sure it appears as expected in your browser—something like Figure 5.10.

The size of the photo is sensible: at a width of 400 pixels, it fits quite well on the page without any further adjustment. Soon, I'll show you how to re-size larger photos (as most of the photos you take on a digital camera will be far too large to simply drop into the gallery page).

Figure 5.10. The gallery page taking shape

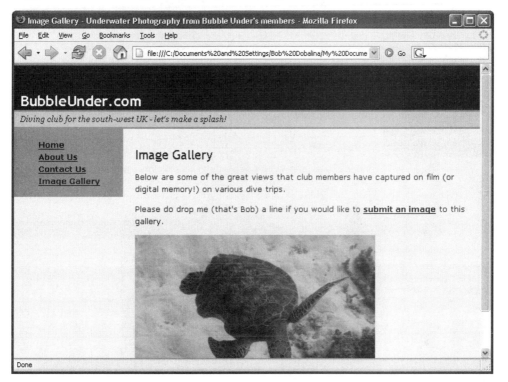

Formatting the Picture with CSS

A common mistake that many people make as they create image galleries is to use a graphics program to create borders around their images. As we saw in the previous chapter, we can use CSS to create border effects; let's use this technique now. How about a reasonably thick white border, reminiscent of Polaroid snaps?

❑ Open `style1.css` and add a new rule for the `img` element, like so:

File: **style1.css (excerpt)**

```
img {
  border: 15px solid white;
}
```

☐ Save the CSS file, then go back to your web page (`gallery.html`) and refresh it. You should be looking at something like the view shown in Figure 5.11.

Figure 5.11. The white border gives a Polaroid-like effect to the photo

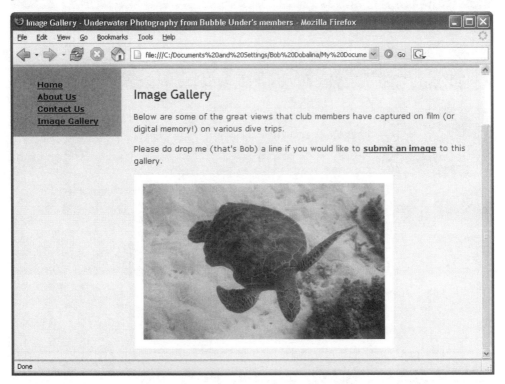

Of course, you're free to try out any effect you like—perhaps you'll experiment with some of the effects we discussed in Chapter 4. For the purposes of this project site, I'm going to stick with the white borders. I know it's not very adventurous, but you *can* overdo things if you're not careful!

Beware of the Flow-on Effects

Note that if you go to the homepage now, the image there will also have a thick white border around it. Well, we did ask for *all* images to have a white border—the browser's just following orders! If you'd rather have only the images on the gallery page appear with the white borders, you can move the style rule from `style1.css` into an embedded style sheet inside `gallery.html`. That way, the rule will take effect only on this page.

File: **gallery.html (excerpt)**

```
<head>
  <title>Image gallery - Underwater Photography from
      Bubble Under's members</title>
  <meta http-equiv="Content-Type"
      content="text/html; charset=utf-8" />
  <link href="style1.css" rel="stylesheet"
      type="text/css" />
  <style type="text/css">
    img {
      border:15px solid white;
    }
  </style>
</head>
```

Let's do just that, and delete the white border image style from our style sheet.

Captioning the Picture

Pick up any newspaper, flick through the pages, and you'll notice that the photos are accompanied by captions. It's a standard practice, and I'm going to show you how we can implement image captions here. First, let's think about what information might appear beneath this photo. You'll probably want a description of the photo, perhaps a location, and almost certainly a credit for the photographer. All these items could be styled in the same way, but I'm going to use two new styles.

 Tip

When's a caption not a Caption?

Strangely, there is no such thing as a picture caption element in XHTML—which seems like an oversight, really—but there is a `caption` element. If someone tells you that you can use this `caption` element for image captions, give them a smug look and say, "Actually, the caption is used with tables, not images." We'll be looking at tables in Chapter 6.

☐ In `gallery.html`, remove the opening and closing paragraph tags that surround the picture of the turtle, and replace them with `<div class="galleryphoto">` and `</div>` tags instead:

File: **gallery.html (excerpt)**

```
<div class="galleryphoto">
  <img src="gallery/turtle-bite.jpg" width="400"
      height="258" alt="A turtle swims comfortably among the
      coral, despite its old injury - a large shark bite on
```

```
      one side" />
</div>
```

❏ Next, add a paragraph after the image (but inside the containing div), like so:

File: **gallery.html (excerpt)**

```
<div class="galleryphoto">
  <img src="gallery/turtle-bite.jpg" width="400"
      height="258" alt="A turtle swims comfortably among the
      coral, despite its old injury - a large shark bite on
      one side" />
  <p>This turtle was spotted swimming around the Great Barrier
      Reef (Queensland, Australia) quite gracefully, despite
      having had a large chunk taken out of its right side,
      presumably in a shark attack. [Photographer: Ian
      Lloyd]</p>
</div>
```

❏ Finally, let's add a span element around the photo credit part of the caption, so that we can style it differently.

File: **gallery.html (excerpt)**

```
<p>This turtle was spotted swimming around the Great Barrier
    Reef (Queensland, Australia) quite gracefully, despite
    having had a large chunk taken out of its right side,
    presumably in a shark attack. <span
    class="photocredit">[Photographer: Ian Lloyd]</span></p>
```

❏ Save gallery.html and take a look at the page in your browser. It should resemble Figure 5.12. You won't see any real stylistic changes, but it's important to look at the page first, so you can understand why I suggest the changes I'm about to recommend.

Figure 5.12. The picture is captioned but as yet unstyled

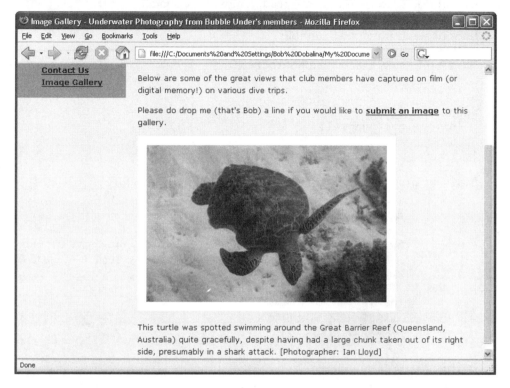

It's common for a picture caption to display in a font that's different from the document's main body text, and possibly in a different font weight and size, too. That's the first thing we'll change. Secondly, the gap between the text and the photo is a little too big; I'll show you how we can fix that using the `margin` property. Finally; I'm going to show you how we can add a stylistic touch beneath the photo and caption that will help us once we add more photos to the gallery.

❑ Open `style1.css` and add the following markup:

File: style1.css (excerpt)

```css
.galleryphoto p {
  font-size: 65%;
  font-weight: bold;
  margin-top: 0;
  width: 430px;
  line-height: 1.4em;
}
```

This markup makes the necessary changes to the font, reduces the width of the caption to make it easier to read, removes the spacing immediately above the paragraph that describes the photo, and reduces the spaces between the lines to something more suitable.

❏ Next, add a new class called `photocredit`:

File: **style1.css (excerpt)**

```
.photocredit {
  font-weight: normal;
  color: gray;
}
```

This will affect the text contained in the `span` element only.

An Alternative Approach

Incidentally, you could use some selector trickery to achieve the same effect without having to use the `photocredit` class at all. It would look like this:

```
.galleryphoto p span {
  font-weight: normal;
  color: gray;
}
```

If you did that, you could remove the **class** attribute from the **span** element. I've suggested using a class in this instance for future-proofing purposes: you might want to use a photo credit elsewhere in the site, outside the photo gallery.

❏ Save the CSS file, refresh the web page once more, and review your work. It should look like the page shown in Figure 5.13.

Figure 5.13. The caption displaying with style rules applied

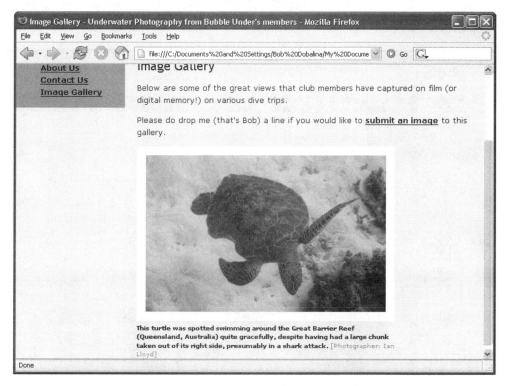

Lastly, we're going to add some style declarations to the `galleryphoto` class (that's the class we applied to the `div` that contains the image and all associated text). This class will be used to help separate the many different photos that this page will eventually hold.

❑ Add the following to `style1.css`:

File: **style1.css (excerpt)**

```css
.galleryphoto {
  padding-bottom: 20px;
  border-bottom: 1px solid navy;
  margin-bottom: 10px;
}
```

❑ The CSS should speak for itself. If not, save the CSS file, then refresh the view in your browser once more. You should see something similar to Figure 5.14.

Figure 5.14. A custom divider providing a nice separation between our photos

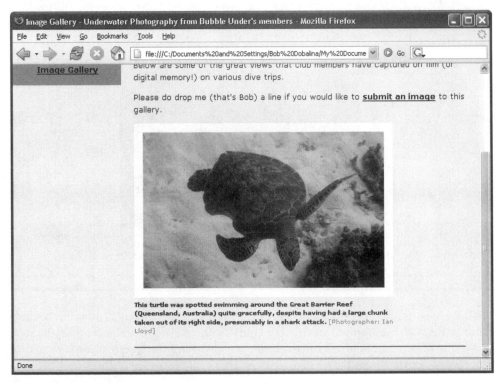

Basic Image Editing

Image Cropping

An easy mistake to make when preparing images for display on web pages is to resize the image to fit the available space without cropping the image in some way first (note that we'll discuss resizing shortly). It's all too easy to end up with small images that try to pack in far too much detail—detail that, ultimately, gets lost. It's much better to crop first, *then* resize. In the image shown in Figure 5.16, the blue water around the fish isn't really required. We can make the image smaller—but keep the fish the same size—by cropping it.

Picasa

In Chapter 1, I suggested that Windows users may want to download Picasa for the purposes of managing photos (be they your own happy snaps, or photos used on the project site). Among other features, Picasa offers a range of special effects that you can apply at the touch of a button. Imagine that another two images have been added to our `gallery` folder (thus trebling the gallery size!). Any image that is added to this folder will automatically appear in Picasa's library, as have the two (a jellyfish and another unidentified fish) shown in Figure 5.15.

Figure 5.15. The gallery is positively booming, as shown by Picasa

If you double-click on one of the images, a range of new options will appear on the left-hand side, as illustrated in Figure 5.16.

Figure 5.16. The range of basic photo fixes offered by Picasa

Perhaps the most important tool you'll use here is Crop. With it, you can remove any extraneous clutter, and focus on the most important part of the image.

Just press the Crop button, then drag a rectangle around the area to which you want to crop the image, as shown in Figure 5.17. You can also choose to crop the image to a pre-determined aspect ratio by selecting 10×15, 13×18, or 20×25. When you're done, click the Apply button to crop the picture.

Figure 5.17. A fishy pic gets a good, solid cropping!

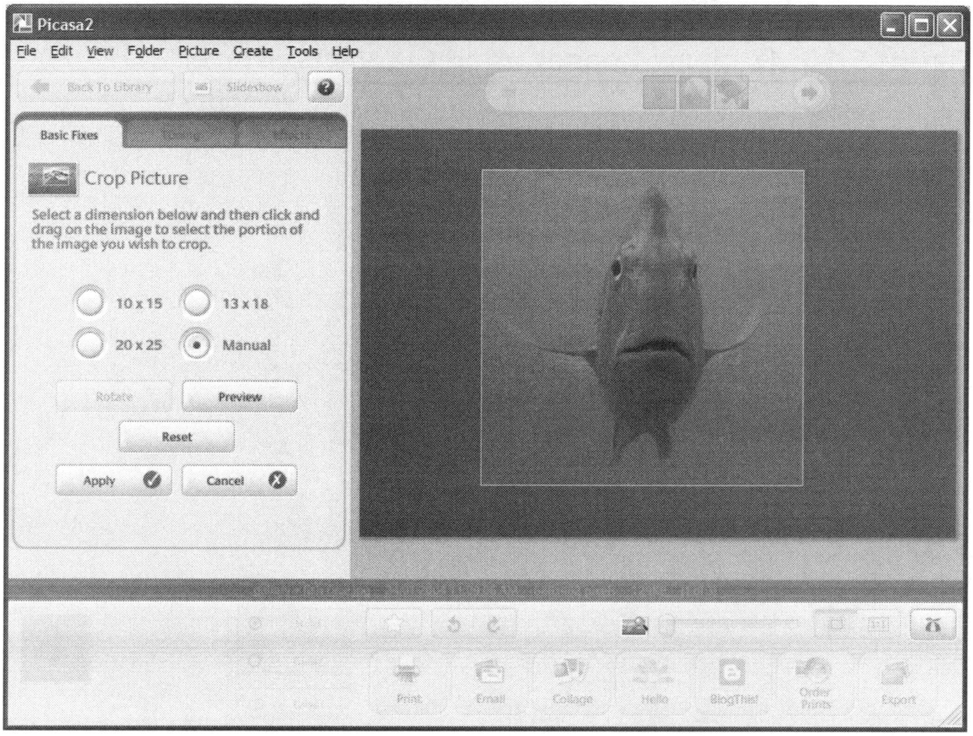

GraphicConverter

We mentioned this handy little program for Mac users who don't have iPhoto back in Chapter 1. Despite its name, GraphicConverter is useful for far more than simply converting pictures from one format to another. One thing I didn't mention, though, is that GraphicConverter is not the most intuitive program in the world. Powerful, yes. But the finding of some of these powerful features requires a bit of poking around, and quite often the problem is simply one of terminology. Let me explain.

Cropping an image in GraphicConverter is fairly straightforward. But if you go looking for the "crop" menu option, you'll be searching all day.

To crop an image, open your image and select the Selection tool from the toolbox to the right of your image. Click and drag your mouse so that the area of your image to which you wish to crop is selected, then choose the Edit > Trim Selection option from the menu bar, as shown in Figure 5.18. Voila!

Figure 5.18. Cropping images using GraphicConverter

Special Effects

Programs like Photoshop offer a wide variety of special effects, and whole books are devoted to explaining the various techniques you can use. Needless to say, we don't have the space for such discussions, but our photo editing programs do have some nifty tools that you should explore for yourself.

Picasa

Figure 5.19 shows our recently cropped picture of the fish; under the Effects tab to its left are a number of available effects, such as black and white, sepia tone, and soft focus.

Figure 5.19. Selecting effects in Picasa

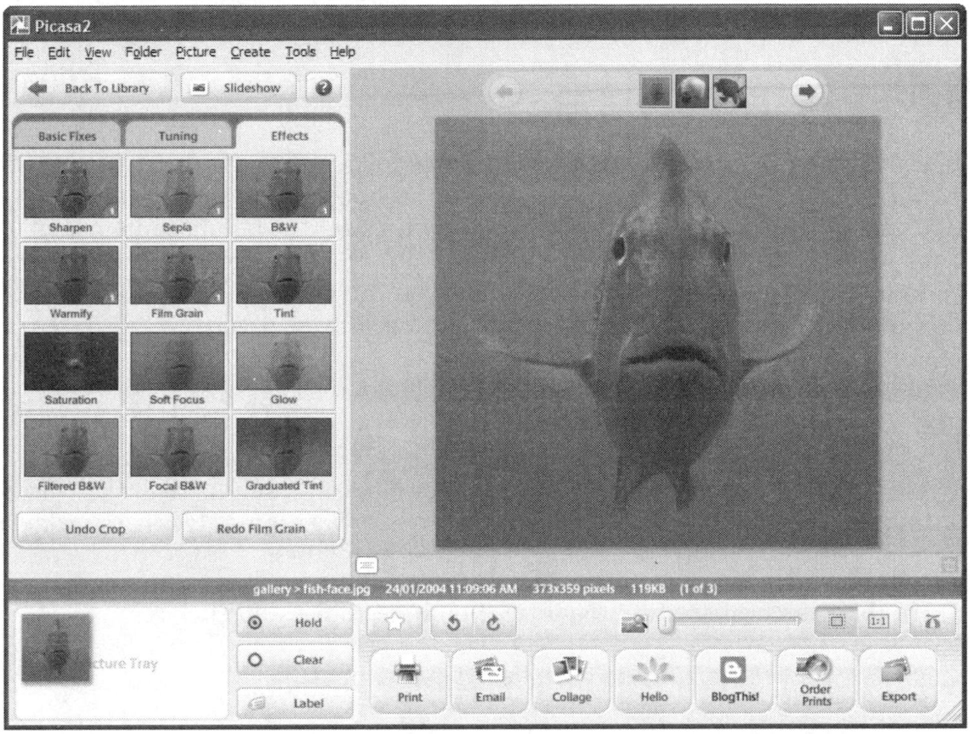

I'm going to leave this image just as it is. But, now that you know where to find the effects, why not go and experiment for yourself?

GraphicConverter

Some of the effects we revealed to Picasa users are also available to GraphicConverter users. The tools included in GraphicConverter range from "really useful" to "not sure what I'd use *that* for." It's probably best just to experiment so that you can get a feel for which tools you might use most. Try and guess what each of the following menu options does, then try the different effects on one of your images to see if they behave as you expected!

❑ Picture > Simple Brightness/Contrast...

❑ Picture > Colors > Grayscale > 256 Grays

❑ Picture > Colors > Change To Sepia

❑ Effect > Red Eye

Resizing Large Images

It's highly unlikely that everyone will submit images that are the right size for use in our gallery. Let's take an image from this book's code archive (I know it's not really code, but let's not split hairs!) and resize it. The image you want is jellyfish.jpg. It's a giant image with a width of 1359 pixels—it needs some serious knocking down in size! Here's how you can do the job using a couple of different programs (in the procedures below, I've assumed you already have the file open).

Picasa

If you already have images available somewhere on your hard drive, they'll automatically appear in the Picasa library. An easy way to use Picasa to create a web-page-friendly image from a larger photo is as follows:

❑ In the Picasa gallery, find the image you want to use and click on it.

❑ Select File > Export Picture to Folder from the menu.

❑ You will be presented with the dialog pictured in Figure 5.20; here, you can choose from a series of pre-set widths (don't be fooled by the text box and slider control; you can choose widths of 320, 480, 640, 800, and 1024 pixels only—but these are all sensible sizes for web pages). You can also use another slider control to select the amount of JPEG compression you want to use (the lower the number, the smaller the file size ... and the worse the photograph will look).

Figure 5.20. Exporting a large image for the Web using Picasa

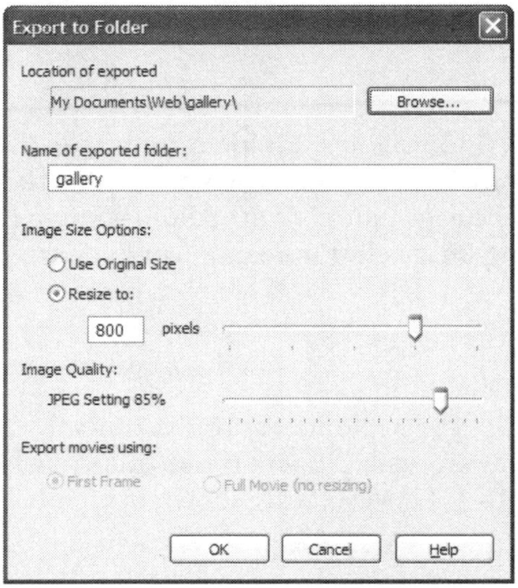

- ❑ Click the Browse... button and select your Web folder inside My Documents. Don't select the gallery folder; if you do, Picasa will create another folder named gallery inside your gallery folder!

- ❑ In Name of exported folder:, enter the name of the folder to which you'd like the resized image saved. In this case, enter **gallery**.

- ❑ Click OK and the resized picture will be saved.

GraphicConverter

- ❑ From the menu, select Picture > Size > Scale....

- ❑ In the drop-down list next to the Width textbox, select Pixel if it's not selected already, and enter **400**. Click OK.

- ❑ Save the file by selecting File > Save as....

- ❑ Select the format in which you want to save the file from the Format drop-down list—you'll probably want JPEG for a photo or GIF for a logo image—and click Save. If you save as JPEG, GraphicConverter will pop up a dialog that offers an overwhelming array of options. The only one you're likely to need to worry about is the quality slider at the top of the window. As with Picasa, the lower this number, the lower the quality of the image.

Other Software

The instructions above cover Picasa (Windows) and GraphicConvertor (Mac) only, but most other graphics applications will do something very similar. If you can't find the equivalent process in your image editor, try the built-in help files, or search the Web for tutorials ("resizing images in Photoshop" or similar).[6]

Filling Up the Gallery

With the wave of a magic wand—and the techniques you've already seen (XHTML, CSS, and image editing)—we can easily finish off our gallery (which, of course, is available from the code archive). The results are shown in Figure 5.21.

File: **gallery.html (excerpt)**

```
<div class="galleryphoto">
  <img src="gallery/turtle-bite.jpg" width="400" height="258"
      alt="A turtle swims comfortably among the coral, despite
      its old injury - a large shark bite on one side" />
  <p>This turtle was spotted swimming around the Great Barrier
      Reef (Queensland, Australia) quite gracefully, despite
      having had a large chunk taken out of its right side,
      presumably in a shark attack. <span
      class="photocredit">[Photographer: Ian Lloyd]</span></p>
</div>
<div class="galleryphoto">
  <img src="gallery/jellyfish.jpg" width="400" height="300"
      alt="A jellyfish flanked by smaller fish" />
  <p>Jill was just snorkelling when she took this picture - the
      jellyfish was only a couple of feet under the surface,
      hence the light is excellent. Jill assures us that the
      jellyfish had no "nasty, stingy, dangly bits"!
      <span class="photocredit">[Photographer: Jill
      Smith]</span></p>
</div>
<div class="galleryphoto">
```

---

[6] A quick search on Google found these tutorials for Photoshop, Paint Shop Pro and iPhoto: Resizing Images with Photoshop [http://its.uwrf.edu/support/apps/design/pshop-resize.php], Rotating, Cropping and Resizing Photos for the Web using Jasc Paint Shop Pro at about.com [http://graphicssoft.about.com/od/digitalphotography/l/blpsp_prep.htm], and Apple's excellent iPhoto Tutorial [http://www.apple.com/support/iphoto/tutorial/].

```
  <img src="gallery/turtle-face.jpg" width="400" height="300"
      alt="A close-up, straight-on shot of a turtle feeding on the
      coral" />
  <p>"I was right next to him as he bit chunks of coral off for
      dinner - what a sound!" So describes club member Paul who
      took this shot in Fiji. <span
      class="photocredit">[Photographer: Paul Spencer]</span></p>
</div>
<div class="galleryphoto">
  <img src="gallery/what-a-star.jpg" width="400" height="318"
      alt="Black and white patterned starfish" />
  <p>You're a star - and don't let anyone tell you any different!
      <span class="photocredit">[Photographer: Helen
      Cranfield]</span></p>
</div>
<div class="galleryphoto">
  <img src="gallery/reef2.jpg" width="400" height="285"
      alt="Another beautiful example of the Great Barrier Reef" />
  <p>Another cracking shot of the reef from Mark.
      <span class="photocredit">[Photographer: Mark
      Williams]</span></p>
</div>
```

Moving Beyond a Simple Gallery

This is a simple example of an image gallery. As you add more images, the page will take longer and longer to download. For this reason, most people opt for a two-layer approach: a page containing **thumbnails** (small copies of the image that are linked to full-size versions). If you think that this aspect of your site might grow beyond all manageability, you might want to look into an automated system of some kind; many are available (including plenty of free services!).[7]

---

[7] Completely free tools that you can use include Slideshow Refinery (Windows) [http://slideshow-refinery.com/allthumbs.html], Easy Thumbnails (Windows) [http://www.fookes.com/ezthumbs/], and TimeSaviour (Mac) [http://www.kalleboo.com/details.php?list=program&sw=psts]. There are many more tools that are "Free to Try, $30 to Buy," and so on. Try searching on http://www.download.com for "thumbnail gallery generator" or similar, and you'll generate lots of results. Mac users, if you have iPhoto, you can make use of the Export (or "Share" in later versions) facility to create a thumbnail gallery. More info and tips are available at http://www.peachpit.com/articles/article.asp?p=30217.

Figure 5.21. The complete gallery

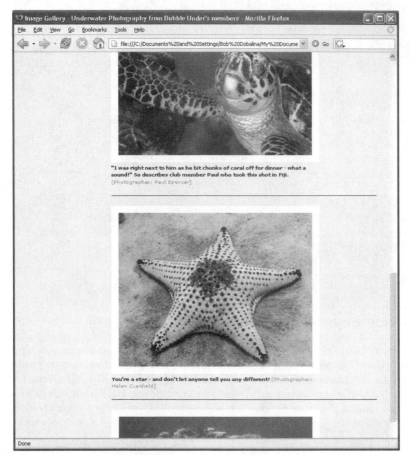

Sourcing Images for your Web Site

The creation of an online gallery is all well and good if you have a large collection of suitable photos at your disposal, but what if you need an image that isn't in your collection? There are numerous web sites that allow you to download and use images royalty-free, such as iStockphoto[8] and Fotosearch.[9] Note that royalty-free does not mean that the image itself is free to use: you may have to pay a

---

[8] http://www.istockphoto.com/
[9] http://www.fotosearch.com/

once-only download fee, but if the image is really good, you probably won't be all that worried about spending a dollar or two.

Another potential source of images is Flickr,[10] where you can search images based on how people have "tagged" them. For example, you could search for all photos tagged with the word "scuba"[11] and look for a suitable image in the search results.

IMPORTANT

Using Images from Flickr

Flickr is a photo-sharing service, not a professional photo stock library, and every poster has a different policy on how his or her photos can be used. The licensing details are clearly marked on each photo's page. But even if the photo is marked "All Rights Reserved," you could try dropping the photographer a line—many people will quite happily let you use one of their photos if it's not for personal financial gain (indeed, many people will actually be quite flattered to have been asked).

Background Images in CSS

So far, we've dealt purely with "inline" images: those that appear inline with the rest of the page content. These kinds of images constitute an integral part of a page's content, but there's another way that you might use images in a web site: as decorative backgrounds.

In the last chapter, we learned how to specify background colors for any block element. We can assign background images in a similar way. In practice, we can do both: provide a background image for those who are browsing normally, and a suitable color as an alternative for those using slow web connections. In fact, this color can also be displayed for the first group of users while the background image is loading. Let's take a look at a simple example.

Repeated Patterns

```
#repeatedclouds {
  border: 1px solid black;
  padding: 20px;
  background-color: #aebbdb;
  background-image: url(clouds.jpg);
}
```

---

[10] http://www.flickr.com
[11] http://www.flickr.com/photos/tags/scuba/

Here's the XHTML that refers to this CSS:

```
<div id="repeatedclouds">
  <p>Content of some kind goes here.</p>
  <p>Some more content goes here.</p>
</div>
```

With this code, the browser will simply repeat the selected background image, filling the available space (I've added a `border` and `padding` to make it easier to see the shape of the box and the background peeking through around the edges). Figure 5.22 shows how the effect displays on the screen (remember that you can get this example from the code archive).

Figure 5.22. A simple repeated cloud pattern

Notice that this rule also includes a background color. Whenever you choose a background image, you should also choose a suitable color "alternative" in case images are not downloaded with your page for some reason. If the browser finds the image you've referred to, it will use it, but if not, it will display the specified background color—something like the page shown in Figure 5.23. This is an important point. Imagine that, in one section of your page, you had a dark background image with white text displayed on it. If the user disables images, or the background image does not download for some reason, you'll need to have a dark background color in place. Otherwise, the user may be presented with white text on a white background, which would render that section of the page unreadable.

Figure 5.23. Displaying a simple gray background in place of an image

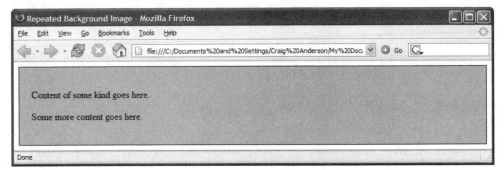

Horizontal Repeats

It is possible to set a background so that it repeats only in one direction—horizontally, for example, from left-to-right. You may remember the process of plotting graphs along the x-axis (left-to-right) or the y-axis (going up) from your school days spent learning mathematics. We use the same x and y notations to specify direction in CSS. For example, you could use the following code to repeat an image along the horizontal axis. The effect is depicted in Figure 5.24.

```
#verticalfade {
  border: 1px solid black;
  padding: 20px;
  padding-top: 300px;
  background-color: #e3e3e3;
  background-image: url(vert-fade.gif);
  background-repeat: repeat-x;
}
```

Figure 5.24. Repeating a background horizontally

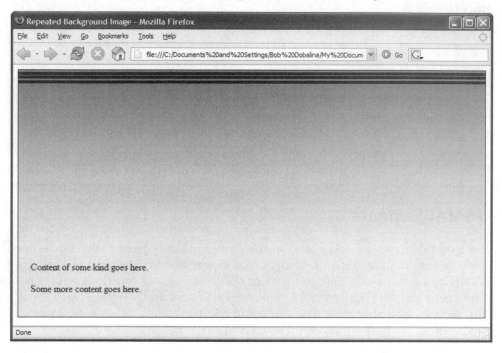

Figure 5.25. The vertical image used for the horizontal repeat

Ironically, an image that you want to repeat horizontally will usually be taller than it is wide. Such images provide a very efficient way to create interesting effects using what are, generally, small (in terms of download overhead) image sizes. The image used to create the effect we saw in Figure 5.24 is shown in Figure 5.25.

When background images are repeated in one direction only, setting the background color becomes even more important. For instance, consider what would happen if we removed the background color from the previous example—Figure 5.26 shows the resulting display. As you can see, once the background image ends, the background color is displayed, so it's important to make sure the colors match.

Figure 5.26. The vertical fade effect without a background color

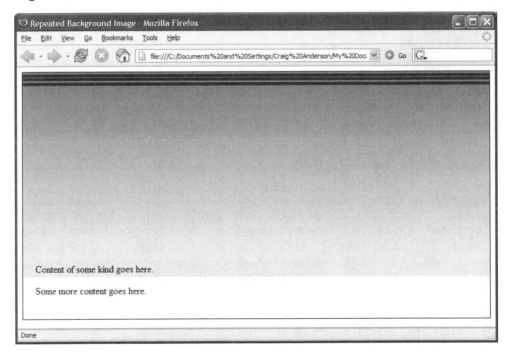

Vertical Repeats

You shouldn't be too surprised to learn that it's just as easy to create the same repeat effect vertically.

```
#horizontalfade {
  border: 1px solid black;
```

```
    background-color: white;
    background-image: url(hori-fade.gif);
    background-repeat: repeat-y;
    padding: 20px;
    padding-left: 180px;
}
```

Figure 5.27 shows the resulting display.

Figure 5.27. Repeating a background vertically

Non-repeating Images

You may simply want to display a background image once, and once only. Some use the "non-repeating" image technique to drop a company logo behind text (like a watermark effect). Whatever your plans, the CSS that displays a background image once is simple and very similar to the examples above. In such cases, you need to use no-repeat to tell the browser not to repeat the image at all, and specify the location at which the image should appear. Figure 5.28 shows the effect.

```
#palmtree {
  border: 1px solid black;
  background-color: white;
  background-image: url(palm-trees.jpg);
  background-repeat: no-repeat;
  background-position: top right;
  padding: 60px;
  padding-right: 210px;
}
```

Figure 5.28. Palm trees as a non-repeating background image

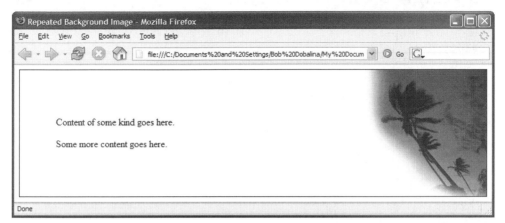

The `background-position` property requires two values: the vertical position (`top`, `center`, or `bottom`) and the horizontal position (`left`, `center`, or `right`). If you use `no-repeat` without a `background-position`, the browser puts the image in the top-left corner.

Shorthand Backgrounds

In the same way that we can set the color, style, and thickness of a border using the `border` shorthand property, we can set a background image and color with the `background` property.

```
#repeatedclouds {
  border: 1px solid black;
  padding: 20px;
  background: #aebbdb url(clouds.jpg);
}

#palmtree {
  border: 1px solid black;
  background: white url(palm-trees.jpg) no-repeat top right;
  padding: 60px;
  padding-right: 210px;
}
```

Fixed Heights and Widths

One final example remains before we start to apply some of this knowledge to our project site: artistic effects with fixed dimensions. In Chapter 4, we saw how we can fix a block-level element to a certain size. Here, I'll show how you can achieve the same end using a background image rather than a solid background color. When this solution is combined with a contrasting text color, you can create an interesting and artistic text overlay effect (note that, in this example, I've used padding to move the line of text away from the top of the containing div element). Here's the CSS:

```css
.sunset {
  border: 1px solid black;
  color: white;
  font-weight: bold;
  font-size: 300%;
  background: black url(sunset.jpg);
  width: 650px;
  height: 125px;
  padding-left: 50px;
  padding-top: 400px;
}
```

The XHTML for this effect couldn't be simpler!

```html
<div class="sunset">Sunsets are a gift of nature.</div>
```

The effect of the XHTML and CSS working in harmony produces the display shown in Figure 5.29.

Figure 5.29. A sized `div` with a background image

Looks good (the effect, that is, though I have to agree that the sunset is pretty spectacular, too).

I think we're done with the theory here. Let's roll up our sleeves and integrate these techniques into the project site!

Setting a Background for our Navigation

The evolution of our site continues apace! The first thing that I'd like to make look a little prettier is the navigation area. The image I want to use is shown in Figure 5.30 (it's available from the code archive, of course).

Figure 5.30. Decorative background for the left-hand navigation

I know what you're thinking: this image is the correct width, but it's far too tall for our current navigation area. Don't worry: the size of the navigation area can easily be set within the CSS to match the height of our new background image. Here's the modified markup:

```
#navigation {
  width: 180px;
  height: 484px;
  background: #7da5d8 url(backgrounds/nav-bg.jpg) no-repeat;

}
```

Figure 5.31. The new-look navigation bar

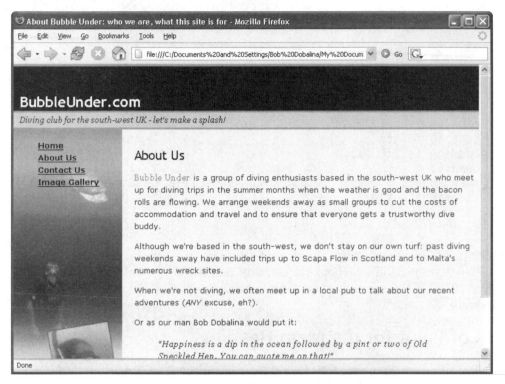

Figure 5.31 shows the effect in context.

Applying a Fade to the Tag Line

The tag line under the main heading does its job just fine, but it's a little simple and, perhaps, too blocky. One way that we can reduce this blockiness is to apply a background image that has some kind of smoothing effect. Let's use the graduated fade shown in Figure 5.32 and apply it to the right-hand edge of the tag line.

Figure 5.32. The tag line background image

For the effect we're after, the image should be locked to the right-hand edge of the tag line paragraph. This can be achieved easily using CSS:

File: **style1.css (excerpt)**

```
#tagline p {
  font-style: italic;
  font-family: Georgia, Times, serif;
  border-top: 3px solid #7da5d8;
  border-bottom: 3px solid #7da5d8;
  padding-top: .2em;
  padding-bottom: .2em;
  padding-left: .8em;
  margin: 0;
  background: #bed8f3 url(backgrounds/tagline-fade.jpg) repeat-y
      right bottom;
}
```

The position keyword `right` is all you need to use to keep the image hugging the tag line's right-hand side; `repeat-y` ensures that the image will repeat downwards (vertically) if the font size is increased, thereby boosting the size of the tag line overall.

A Lick of Paint for the Main Heading

Using the technique we just saw, I'm going to show you how the main header (h1) can be livened up a little. Once again, I've opted for an image that's going to hug the right-hand side. This time, though, it's not a fade, and it can't be repeated. Instead, it's the medium-sized image shown in Figure 5.33, only some of which will be visible in the header.

Figure 5.33. The background image for our main heading

The image is quite dark (ensuring that the white text that reads "BubbleUnder.com" will be readable over the top) and the left edge fades out nicely to match the navy background color that the h1 headings use. We discussed this technique when we applied the graduated fade to the tag line. And the best way to appreciate the technique is try it out: either type the example out or extract it from the code archive. Be sure to try resizing your browser window, so that you can see the effect such changes have on the background image.

We've used an image that's taller than the main page heading to ensure that the page displays well if users re-scale their fonts, causing the height of the container to grow. Yes, you *do* need to think about these things!

Let's look at the CSS for this effect. Make sure that the code below appears after the grouped h1, h2, h3 rule; we want to redefine the simple blue background that was applied in Chapter 4 with this more funky version.

File: **style1.css (excerpt)**

```
h1 {
  font-size: x-large;
  color: white;
  padding-top: 2em;
  padding-bottom: .2em;
  padding-left: .4em;
  margin: 0;
  background: navy url(backgrounds/header-bg.jpg) repeat-y right;
}
```

The effect is shown in Figure 5.34.

Figure 5.34. Background images applied liberally to finish off the effect

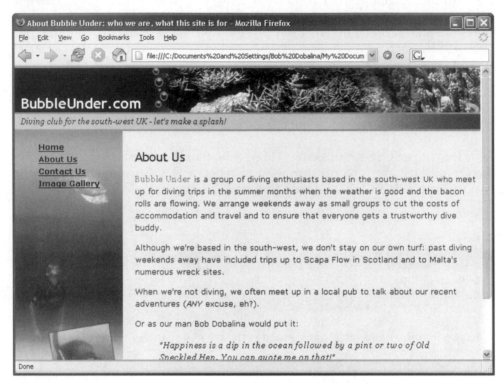

Summary

In this chapter, we've seen how you can source free images from the Web, or use your own photos, to compile an image gallery for your site. We've discussed the processes of resizing images to suit your specific needs and applying various effects. I've also explained how you can use CSS to add creative effects to your images (for instance, defining colored borders in a style sheet, rather than producing them in image editing software), and how you can use images as decorative backgrounds that can be repeated or used just once on a page.

It's amazing how much a web site can be improved by a liberal sprinkling of imagery. Just a couple of chapters back, our project site was a fairly dull-looking collection of documents; now it really is starting to look more like a proper web site—one that we could very easily re-style by making a few changes in our CSS file.

In the next chapter, we'll learn all about **tables**, as I show you how you can use these to display data in a clean, easy-to-understand format.

6

Tables: Tools for Organizing Data

The title of this book is Build Your Own Web Site *The Right Way*. It's important to emphasize this point as we begin this chapter because in the "Bad Old Days," the content of this chapter—concerning tables—would have been right up near the front of the book as the author taught you how to use tables to create exciting page layouts! This approach has since been recognized as bad, bad, *bad*! But, you know what? There are still books that teach you to use tables for layout. Thankfully, you didn't pick up one of those books: bonus points to you!

As the name suggests, tables are designed to present *tabular data*, like the information you'd expect to see if you were looking at a calendar of events or a spreadsheet that showed how pitiful your bank balance is this month (or am I just speaking for myself here?). In fact, there are many different circumstances in which tables are a sensible choice; laying out an entire web page is definitely not among them.

What is a Table?

Several times in the preceding chapters, I compared web techniques with tools that you might use in Microsoft Word, and in the case of tables, there's another direct correlation. If you've used this Microsoft Office program, you've almost certainly had to "insert a table" before, probably using one of the toolbar icons shown in Figure 6.1.

Figure 6.1. The Insert Table icon in Microsoft Word

You can use this tool to create a display like the one in Table 6.1 very easily.

Table 6.1. An table example

Name	Contact (Home)	Contact (Work)	Location
Jane Bradley	02380 123123	02380 577566	Southampton
Fred Bradley	01273 177166	01273 946376	Brighton
Lionel Rundel	01793 641207	01793 626696	Swindon

A table really is the most sensible, tidy way to organize this kind of data. You can easily scan down a column, or along a row, and see what's what. Exactly the same effect can be achieved on a web page.

Before we embark on table creation, though, let's make a couple of essential changes to our project site so that we have an appropriate place to use tables. What sort of data would warrant the use of tables on a diving web site? How about a table of forthcoming club events? That'll do nicely!

❑ First, we need to add some links to *all* of the web site's files. We need to make just one addition to the navigation that appears on the left of the page. I think this new navigation item should appear between the "About Us" and "Contact Us" page navigation links. Be sure to add it to all of the files in the web site, as shown below:

```
<div id="navigation">
  <ul>
    <li><a href="index.html">Home</a></li>
    <li><a href="about.html">About Us</a></li>
    <li><a href="events.html">Club Events</a></li>
    <li><a href="contact.html">Contact Us</a></li>
    <li><a href="gallery.html">Image Gallery</a></li>
```

```
    </ul>
  </div> <!-- end of navigation div -->
```

❑ Next, take a copy of index.html, and rename it in Windows Explorer (or Finder, if you're using a Mac) to events.html

Open events.html and make the following changes:

❑ Change the content between the opening <title> and closing </title> tags to read, "Forthcoming club diving events and trips with Bubble Under."

❑ Change the page heading (the h2 element) to read, "Forthcoming Club Events."

❑ Delete everything except the heading inside the div whose id is bodycontent.

❑ Beneath that heading, add a new paragraph that reads:

> Bubble Under members love meeting up for dive trips around the country. Below are all the dive trips that we currently have planned. For more information about any of them, please get in contact with that event's organizer.

If you've completed all those steps, your code should look like this:

```
<!DOCTYPE html PUBLIC "-//W3C//DTD XHTML 1.0 Strict//EN"
    "http://www.w3.org/TR/xhtml1/DTD/xhtml1-strict.dtd">
<html xmlns="http://www.w3.org/1999/xhtml">
  <head>
    <title>Forthcoming club diving events and trips with Bubble
        Under</title>
    <meta http-equiv="Content-Type"
        content="text/html; charset=utf-8" />
    <link href="style1.css" rel="stylesheet" type="text/css" />
  </head>
  <body>
    <div id="header">
      <div id="sitebranding">
        <h1>BubbleUnder.com</h1>
      </div>
      <div id="tagline">
        <p>Diving club for the south-west UK - let's make a
            splash!</p>
      </div>
    </div> <!-- end of header div -->
```

```
    <div id="navigation">
      <ul>
        <li><a href="index.html">Home</a></li>
        <li><a href="about.html">About Us</a></li>
        <li><a href="events.html">Club Events</a></li>
        <li><a href="contact.html">Contact Us</a></li>
        <li><a href="gallery.html">Image Gallery</a></li>
      </ul>
    </div>
    <div id="bodycontent">
      <h2>Forthcoming Club Events</h2>
      <p>Bubble Under members love meeting up for dive trips
        around the country. Below are all the dive trips that we
        currently have planned. For more information about any
        of them, please get in contact with that event's
        organizer.</p>
    </div> <!-- end of bodycontent div -->
  </body>
</html>
```

Why Tables are Bad and CSS Rules ... but *Only* for Layout!

It's time for a very short history lesson.

The reason why web designers used to use tables for layout was quite simple: in the early days of web development, tables were the only way to achieve a layout that resembled a magazine- or newspaper-like grid. Designers wanted to have a heading at the top of the page, a column on the left for navigation, a column in the middle for content, and a third column on the right for more links. The problem was that using tables to achieve such effects was an abuse of the markup—a hack—but it worked at the time, and people didn't see anything wrong with it.

Today, CSS is so well-supported that there really is no excuse for using tables for layout, and CSS is most definitely the better tool for the job. Nevertheless, many web sites still use table-based layouts. This doesn't mean that this approach is right: it's simply an old habit that refuses to die quietly in the corner as it should (although that's something you can help redress!). But just what are the advantages of using CSS instead of tables? Here are a few for you to consider:

Design and Redesign Flexibility

A CSS-based layout ensures that you place all your styles (from cosmetic touches such as font styling, to the major structural/layout rules) in one location. Change the layout rules you set in that style sheet, and you affect every page that refers to it. Using a table-based layout locks your page design in at page-level, so changing a layout becomes a major problem—one that cannot be resolved simply by changing the style sheet.

Better Accessibility

A table is supposed to be used for tabular data only. For this reason, some assistive devices (such as screen readers, which we discussed in Chapter 5) get a bit confused when the content is not presented as expected. In other words, these kinds of devices expect to access tabular data inside a table; if the table is being used for a purpose for which it was never intended, all bets are off, and accessibility may be the first casualty. If you use a table for the purposes of layout, content that may appear to be located logically on the screen may not be logical at all when read out by a screen reader. This is a phenomenon known as "table linearization," which we'll explore in detail shortly.

Quicker Downloads (or Perception of Download)

A table-based page layout often loads more slowly than an equivalent CSS-based layout (this is especially true with pages that have quite a lot of content). There are a couple of reasons for this. The first is that a table-based layout will generally require much more markup—"scaffolding," if you like—to hold the page together. With a table-based layout, it's not just a matter of marking up sections of the page with `div` elements. This extra markup adds to the page file size, and therefore, the amount of time it takes to download the file.

The second reason is related to the user's *perception* of download speed. Browser's don't download entire web pages in one go: when they ask for a web page, they receive it as a trickle of information. And the browser tries to render that information as it arrives. In the case of our site, the browser would render the header, then the navigation, and finally the body content. If the trickle of information is so slow that there's a pause halfway through the body content, the browser is still able to display the first half of the body content without any trouble. This isn't the case with table-based layouts. In a table-based layout, the browser needs to have downloaded *all* the content in the table before it knows how to render that information on the screen. As such, a CSS-based page layout will usually appear on the screen faster than a table-based layout.

If there's one thing I hope you remember from this chapter, it's this: despite what anyone tells you, using tables is not a sin. Tables are not evil in and of themselves. They should not be used for page layout (that's where they get their bad reputation from), but it is *perfectly okay to use tables for their originally intended purpose*: the presentation of data in a grid.

Anatomy of a Table

Before we start adding the table to our Events page, let's take a step back and look at the general example we saw in Table 6.1: the simple telephone contact details table. At a glance, we can identify some specific areas of the table, namely the headers, rows, columns, and table data cells. Figure 6.2 explains things a lot better than my ham-fisted attempts at clear English!

Figure 6.2. The anatomy of a table

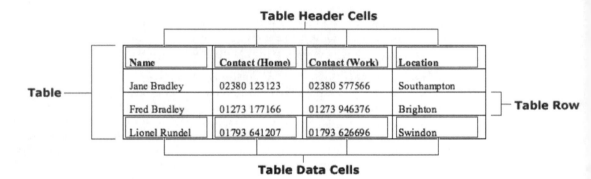

Although I mentioned columns, you do not need to indicate these in the XHTML. At its most basic level, a table is put together using commands that tell the browser where to start a new row, or a new cell within any given row (the columns are a natural by-product of this approach, so you don't need to declare each new column). The areas marked in the image above have the following direct equivalents in XHTML:

table   contains the entire table

tr   contains an entire row of a table (hence table row)

th   signifies a table header cell

td   a general table data cell

Let's see how the example table looks in XHTML:

```
<table>
  <tr>
    <th>Name</th>
```

```
      <th>Contact (Home)</th>
      <th>Contact (Work)</th>
      <th>Location</th>
    </tr>
    <tr>
      <td>Jane Bradley</td>
      <td>02380 123123</td>
      <td>02380 577566</td>
      <td>Southampton</td>
    </tr>
    <tr>
      <td>Fred Bradley</td>
      <td>01273 177166</td>
      <td>01273 946376</td>
      <td>Brighton</td>
    </tr>
    <tr>
      <td>Lionel Rundel</td>
      <td>01793 641207</td>
      <td>01793 626696</td>
      <td>Swindon</td>
    </tr>
</table>
```

Can you see how the two marry up? The various elements that make up a table can seem a little daunting when you first encounter them, but like so many XHTML elements, their names are quite easy to remember.

Styling the Table

The table element is pretty simple: it's the element that contains all of the data that makes up the table ... though, as Figure 6.3 shows, it *is* fairly ugly.

Figure 6.3. The uninspiring default appearance of a table

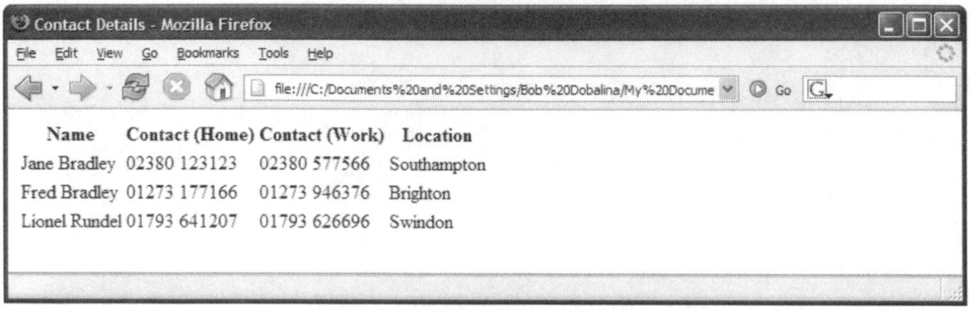

How can we jazz this up? If you're thinking "CSS," give yourself a pat on the back: CSS is definitely the way to go!

Borders, Spacing, and Alignment

Let's start by putting some borders around these cells. Figure 6.4 shows the impact of the following markup.

```
td {
  border: 1px solid black;
}
```

Figure 6.4. One-pixel borders around each cell

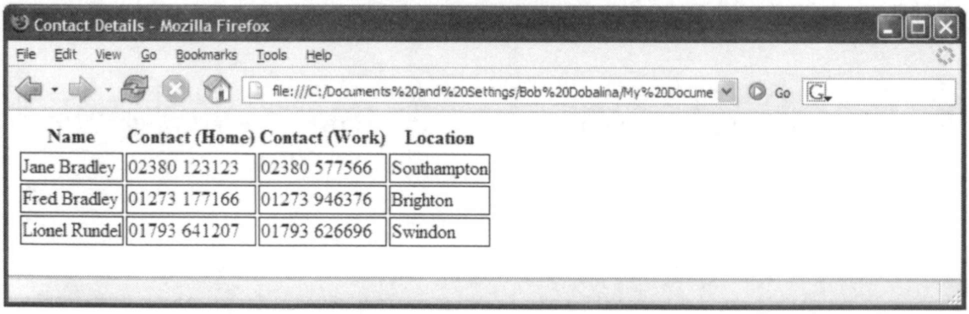

Perhaps this is not quite what you expected. That space between each of the cell's borders is called **cell spacing**, and you can turn it off using the `border-collapse: collapse;` declaration.[1]

Let's turn off the cell spacing, and add a little more decoration to our table. We'll also set the table headings to align to the left of the cell. By default, they're aligned to the center, which can get very confusing. Figure 6.5 shows the results of this code:

```
table {
  border-collapse: collapse;
  border: 1px solid black;
}

th {
  text-align: left;
  background: gray;
  color: white;
  padding: 0.2em;
}

td {
  border: 1px solid black;
  padding: 0.2em;
}
```

Figure 6.5. Applying style rules to the table

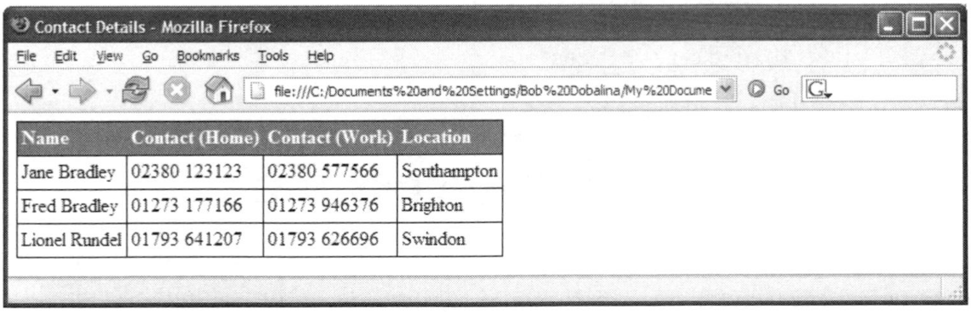

It's looking a little nicer, isn't it?

---

[1] Netscape didn't support `border-collapse` until version 7. However, on a positive note, Netscape users are inclined to update their browsers more frequently than IE users, so don't expect this to be a problem for a large proportion of your site's visitors.

class-ifying your Tables

Tables can be used for a variety of purposes, each of which may warrant a different look. For this reason, it may be a good idea to use classes in your CSS selectors for tables.

For example, imagine your site includes the following types of tables:

❑ rates

❑ schedule

❑ events

You could set different style rules for each table type in your CSS:

```
table.rates {
  /* declarations for rates tables */
}

table.schedule {
  /* declarations for schedule tables */
}

table.events {
  /* declarations for events tables */
}
```

Then, when you added a `table` to your XHTML, all you'd need to do would be to give it the appropriate `class` attribute.

```
<table class="rates">
```

A little forethought goes a long way!

Making your Tables Accessible

I introduced the idea of web accessibility in Chapter 5 to emphasize the importance of the `img` element's `alt` attribute. It's important to think about accessibility when it comes to tables, too. The question that all web designers ask themselves as some point in their careers is, "How the heck does a screen reader read out a table?"

Linearization

In reading out the content of a table, a screen reader **linearizes** that content. "Linearization" simply means that the screen reader reads the content in the order in which it appears in the table's markup. As an example, consider Table 6.2, which displays TV listings. Visually, it's very easy to associate a time-slot with the associated program.

Table 6.2. An example of TV listings set out in a table

9:30 p.m. – 10:00 p.m.	10:00 p.m. – 11:00 p.m.	11:00 p.m. – 11:45 p.m.
Regional News	Lost	Big Brother

With a visual scan, we can quickly and easily see when each program starts and ends. Let's take a look at the markup:

```
<table>
  <tr>
    <td>9:30 p.m. - 10:00 p.m.</td>
    <td>10:00 p.m. - 11:00 p.m.</td>
    <td>11:00 p.m. - 11:45 p.m.</td>
  </tr>
  <tr>
    <td>Regional News</td>
    <td>Lost</td>
    <td>Big Brother</td>
  </tr>
</table>
```

The linearized interpretation of this would be: "9:30 p.m. – 10:00 p.m., 10:00 p.m. – 11:00 p.m., 11:00 p.m. – 11:45 p.m., Regional News, Lost, Big Brother". That's not the most comprehensible piece of content! We can fix this problem either by changing the orientation of the table (i.e., making the program names run down the left and the time slots run down the right), or by marking up the cells that contain the names of the programs with th instead of td and adding a scope attribute to each of the th elements. We'll take a look into this second solution later in this chapter, when we discuss some advanced table concepts.

summary

No, I'm not about to summarize what we've just discussed! Instead, it's time to introduce the table's summary attribute. This is an invisible attribute (it doesn't render on the screen or, for that matter, when you print the web page) that can be used to provide extra information about the table to people who use assistive devices such as screen readers. Here's an example of a summary:

```
<table summary="Area representatives, and their home and work
    telephone numbers">
```

When you add a summary, be brief but descriptive. This attribute is a bit like the alt attribute we use for images: it needs to be brief, but not so brief that it begs more questions.

Captioning your Table

If you think the summary attribute seems like a bit of a wasted opportunity because it doesn't appear in the table's on-screen display, don't worry. You can use the caption element for this purpose. Many people would insert a heading (e.g., h2, h3) in the XHTML above a table, but the caption element is really the right element for the job. Also, you can use CSS to style it, just as you style headings:

```
<table summary="Area representatives, and their home and work
    telephone numbers">
  <caption>Contact details</caption>
  <tr>
    <th>Name</th>
    <th>Contact (Home)</th>
    <th>Contact (Work)</th>
    <th>Location</th>
  </tr>
```

Recap

So far, we've looked at some of the basics of tables, and discussed some examples that demonstrate the key concepts. I've shown you how to use CSS to style the table content, and how to make the table content accessible, but it's best to see this in practice, not in theory. So, let's move along to our project site and see how we can apply some of this knowledge.

Adding an Events Table

You've learned about the various elements that make up a table. Now, you're going to build one of your own.

- [ ] Open up `events.html` in your text editor.

- [ ] Type the following code beneath the paragraph you added earlier:

File: **`events.html` (excerpt)**

```html
<table class="events" summary="Details of upcoming club events and
    dive trips">
  <caption>Club events/dive trips for the next six
      months</caption>
  <tr>
    <th>Date</th>
    <th>Event Description</th>
    <th>Approximate Cost</th>
    <th>Contact</th>
  </tr>
  <tr>
    <td>12 July</td>
    <td>Committee meeting, deciding on next year's trips</td>
    <td>N/A</td>
    <td>Bob Dobalina</td>
  </tr>
  <tr>
    <td>19 July</td>
    <td>7-day trip to Hurghada (package deal) - limited
        spaces</td>
    <td>&pound;260 pp (all inclusive), departing Luton</td>
    <td>Bob Dobalina</td>
  </tr>
  <tr>
    <td>5 August</td>
    <td>Ocean &amp; Sports Diver Theory Course</td>
    <td>Call for details</td>
    <td>Jeff Edgely</td>
  </tr>
  <tr>
    <td>12 August</td>
    <td>Murder Mystery Weekend, Cotswolds (no diving!)</td>
    <td>&pound;65 pp (accommodation included)</td>
    <td>Jill Smith</td>
  </tr>
</table>
```

Remember that you don't *have* to type this all out yourself—you can cheat a little by grabbing the markup from the code archive.

Note that all the features we've covered in the chapter are present here: the table `summary` attribute, the `caption` element, table headers (`th`), and the basic items of construction that you need for every table: the `table`, `tr`, and `td` elements. But, never mind the markup; how does it look in the browser? Figure 6.6 illustrates!

Figure 6.6. The basic, unstyled table

This display can be summed up in one word: yuck! Like the unstyled table we saw earlier, this one doesn't look too good, nor is it very easy to interpret. Fortunately, it's CSS to the rescue once again! The first thing we should do to make our table more legible is add some borders to it:

❑ Open `style1.css` and add a new rule for the `th` and `td` elements. Here's the CSS you need:

File: **style1.css (excerpt)**

```css
table.events {
  border-collapse: collapse;
}

table.events th, table.events td {
  padding: 4px;
  border: 1px solid #000066;
}

table.events th {
  font-size: x-small;
}

table.events td {
  font-size: small;
}
```

Here, we've created four rules. The first affects all `table` elements that have a `class` attribute set to `events`. The rule uses the `border-collapse` property to turn off the cell spacing effect we saw earlier. The second rule uses a selector that's slightly more complicated: `table.events th, table.events td` affects all `th` and `td` elements between the `<table class="events">` and `</table>` tags. Unfortunately, a simpler-looking declaration such as `table.events th, td` affects the `th` elements inside our table and *all* `td` elements. We're killing a couple of birds with one stone here, those proverbial birds being the `border` and `padding` for each cell.

The last two rules take care of the `font-size` for our cells and headers.

Figure 6.7 shows the effect of the above CSS on our web page.

Figure 6.7. Borders improving the table

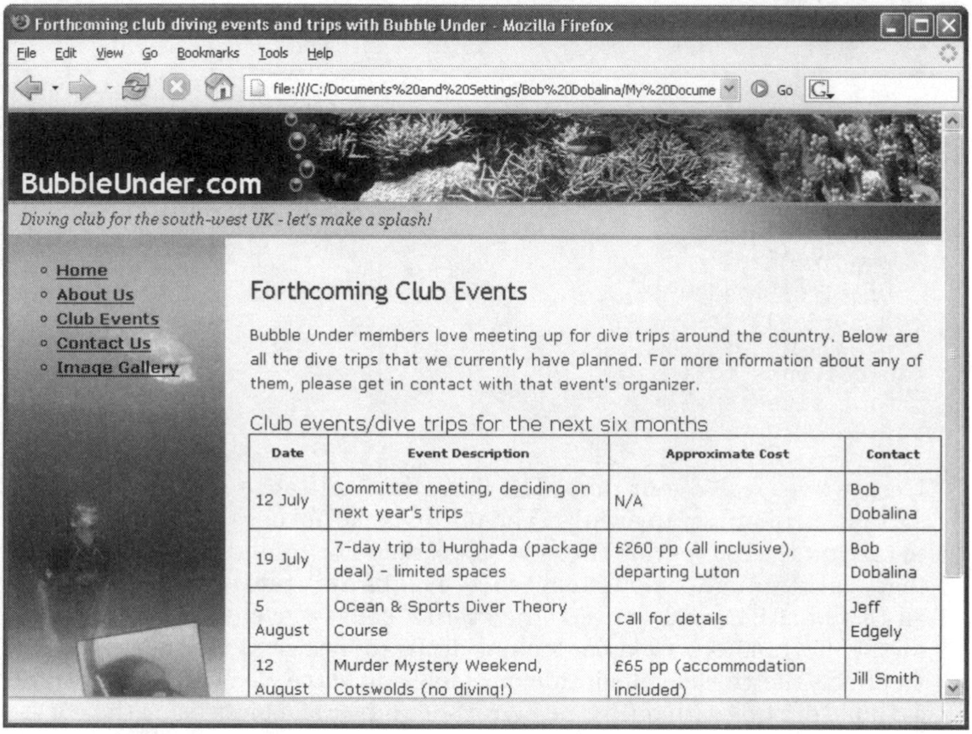

The next thing we'll improve in our table is the alignment of the table header text. As I mentioned before, the default setting for th centers the header text, which prevents the majority of your content from lining up with that header. It's crazy, I know. Let's fix it quickly and easily.

❑ In `style1.css`, modify the declaration for the table header (th) element, like so:

File: **style1.css (excerpt)**

```
table.events th {
  font-size: x-small;
  text-align: left;
}
```

That should solve the problem, but let's go a little further to make the table header look more attractive.

❑ Add some more declarations to the `table.events th` rule: one to change the foreground (or text) color to white, one to direct the background to take an image, and a few padding rules:

File: **style1.css (excerpt)**

```
table.events th {
  font-size: x-small;
  text-align: left;
  background: #241374 url(backgrounds/header-bg.jpg);
  color: #ffffff;
  padding-top: 0;
  padding-bottom: 0;
  padding-left: 2px;
  padding-right: 2px;
}
```

❑ While we're here, we might as well spruce up the table's caption:

File: **style1.css (excerpt)**

```
table.events caption {
  color: #000066;
  font-size: small;
  text-align: left;
  padding-bottom: 5px;
  font-weight: bold;
}
```

❑ Save the style sheet and do the whole browser refresh thing one more time to see how it looks. Compare your work with Figure 6.8.

Figure 6.8. A much improved table header

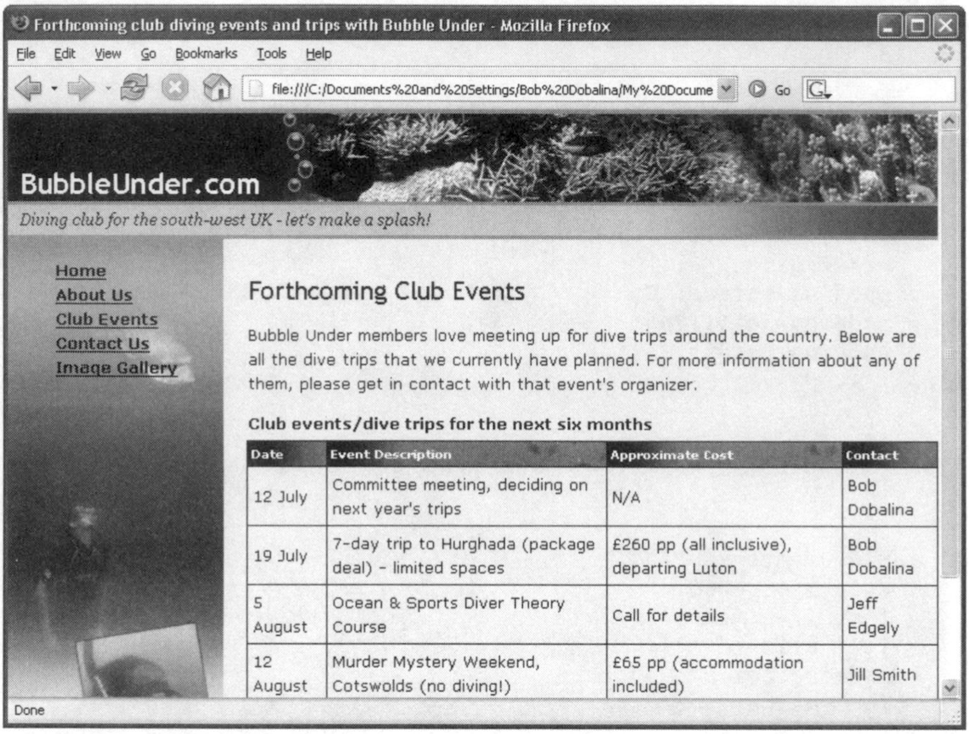

I want to draw your attention to two points in that last addition. First, the background image is actually the same as the one we used in the page header (beneath the BubbleUnder.com text right at the top), but it looks very different here. Why? In the header, we positioned the image so that it hugs the bottom right-hand edges; in the `th` declaration, we haven't specified any positioning, so the image starts at the top left, and that portion of the image is quite different. By using an image that's already used elsewhere in the web site, we can save ourselves a little download time (because the image will already have downloaded, the computer does not have to request a different image file for this background).

The second point I want to make is about the text color. Here, I've specified a color of `#ffffff`. This is the hexadecimal color specification for white, and although it may be easier to remember the word "white" than an obscure hex value, it's important to be familiar with a handful of hex values so you don't get confused the next time you see one. Another hex value that you'll come across often is

#000000, which means black (the red, green, and blue values are 0, 0, and 0—in other words, there's no light at all—so #000000 represents black).

Stylish Table Cells

I've got just one more suggestion for our Events table. While it looks fine now, I'd like to give it that extra bit of polish. Once again, I'm going to suggest using a background image for this effect: a very subtle faded background that will be positioned at the top of each table cell. Here's the markup:

File: **style1.css (excerpt)**

```
table.events td {
  font-size: small;
  background: #e2edff url(backgrounds/td.jpg) repeat-x top;
}
```

That background color—yet another obscure-looking hex value—is a very light blue that matches the blue that appears in the top of the image. The background image repeats horizontally (as demonstrated in Chapter 5) and is positioned along the bottom of the cell, giving our data table the very polished look depicted in Figure 6.9.

It's up to you to decide how far you want to take your table styling—you are limited only by your imagination (or, in my case, skill with graphics applications!). If you're interested in this area, have a look at Veerle Pieters' example of a CSS-styled table,[2] for starters.

---

[2] http://veerle.duoh.com/?id=P315

Figure 6.9. The final presentation of the data table

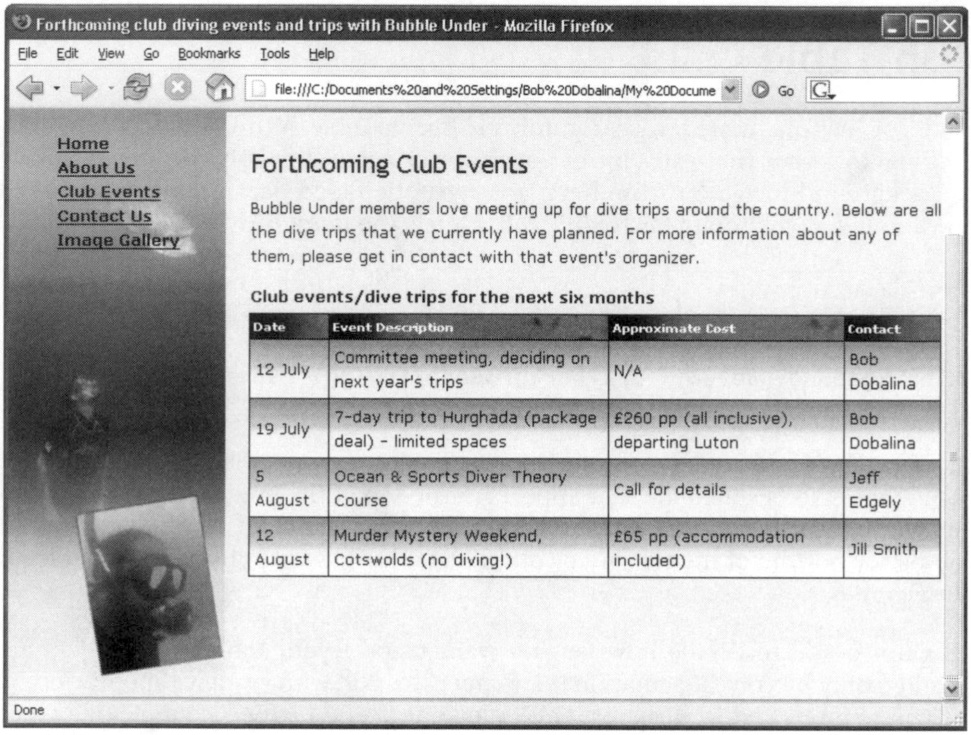

Advanced Tables

In the examples we saw earlier in the chapter, and in the table we've created in the project web site, the tables' structures have been quite simple: we have straight columns and rows, and no complications. What kinds of complications *could* we encounter?

Merging Table Cells

The complication that you're most likely to encounter as you work with tables arises within merged table cells. Let's consider the table from the project site again, and imagine it has the slightly different layout shown in Table 6.3 (I've removed the formatting to make things a little clearer).

Table 6.3. A more complicated table construction

Date	Event Details		Contact
	Event Description	Approximate Cost	
12 July	Committee meeting, deciding on next year's trips	N/A	Bob Dobalina
19 July	7-day trip to Hurghada (package deal) – limited spaces	£260 pp (all inclusive), departing Luton	Bob Dobalina
5 August	Ocean & Sports Diver Theory Course	Call for details	Jeff Edgely
12 August	Murder Mystery Weekend, Cotswolds (no diving!)	£65 pp (accommodation included)	Jill Smith

rowspan and colspan

In the example above, the headings of the first and last columns ("Date" and "Contact") span across two rows of the table. Along the top, the table header that has the text "Event Details" takes up the space of two columns. To achieve this effect, we use the following XHTML attributes:

❏ rowspan

❏ colspan

The example above would be marked up as follows (the code is abbreviated somewhat):

```
<table>
  <tr>
    <th rowspan="2">Date</th>
    <th colspan="2">Event Details</th>
    <th rowspan="2">Contact</th>
  </tr>
  <tr>
    <th>Event Description</th>
    <th>Approximate Cost</th>
  </tr>
  <tr>
    <td>12 July</td>
    <td>Committee meeting, deciding on next year's trips</td>
```

```
    <td>N/A</td>
    <td>Bob Dobalina</td>
  </tr>
```

Note that the first row appears to have three cells (1 column + 2 columns + 1 column = 4); the second row has only two table headers, but because the left- and right-most cells in the previous row have been set with a `rowspan` of 2, everything adds up quite nicely.

Are you feeling confused? If so, you're not the first person to find `rowspan` and `colspan` tricky; many a web designer has tripped over this in the past. If you get your `rowspan` and `colspan` mathematics wrong, your table constructions can do some very weird (and not so wonderful) things! That's why I placed this exercise in the "advanced" section of this chapter. If you want to merge table cells, there are two ways that you can approach it:

❑ Use a dedicated web development tool that's capable of handling and creating tables visually (such as Dreamweaver[3]).

❑ Rough it out on paper! Start with a simple table that has no merges, and simply cross out the lines you don't need. As you do so, make a note of the increased numbers of rows or columns that these cells span. Only when you're finished with your paper layout should you start translating this back to XHTML.

Advanced Accessibility

Badly constructed tables cause some of the biggest accessibility headaches. While it's beyond the scope of this book to tell you everything about web accessibility, there is one extra feature that you can easily add to your tables to improve your site visitors' chances of accessing tabular content with assistive technology (such as screen readers).

The scope Attribute

When you look at a table of data on the screen, it's very easy to glance at a header, then scan down the column and see the data that relates to that header. For a blind user who relies on a screen reader to interpret that table data and read it back, it can be tricky to associate data stored deep within a table with its appropriate header. The `scope` attribute can make this easier.

---

[3] http://www.macromedia.com/software/dreamweaver/

The scope attribute is applied to a header and has two possible values: row and col. Essentially, the scope attribute says to the browser (and any other piece of technology that needs to make use of it), "Hey, see this header cell? Well, everything below it is related to this cell, and don't you forget it!" The code below puts this a little more formally:

```
<tr>
  <th scope="col">Date</th>
  <th scope="col">Event Description</th>
  <th scope="col">Approximate Cost</th>
  <th scope="col">Contact</th>
</tr>
```

The table we're using on our project web site has headers at the tops of the columns only, but you might use tables that have headers down the left-hand side as well, like the one shown in Figure 6.10.

Figure 6.10. Applying scope="row" and scope="col" to table headers

Here's the XHTML for the above example (which is available from the code archive):

```
<table>
  <caption>Train times and departures</caption>
  <tr>
    <td></td> <!-- empty cell in the top-right corner -->
    <th scope="col">Departure Time</th>
    <th scope="col">Platform</th>
    <th scope="col">Buffet Coach</th>
  </tr>
  <tr>
    <th scope="row">Southampton</th>
    <td>13:03</td>
    <td>12</td>
    <td>Yes</td>
```

```
    </tr>
    <tr>
      <th scope="row">Edinburgh</th>
      <td>14:47</td>
      <td>4</td>
      <td>Yes</td>
    </tr>
    <tr>
      <th scope="row">Newcastle</th>
      <td>15:55</td>
      <td>7</td>
      <td>No</td>
    </tr>
</table>
```

If you start to merge cells (using the aforementioned `colspan` and `rowspan`), it gets incredibly tricky to mark the table up in a way that ensures its accessibility. Tools are available to help, though—namely the `headers` and `id` attributes, which are explained in the article *Bring on the Tables*, by Roger Johansson.[4] At this point, I'll simply say that it's far better to keep your tables simple because, at the time of writing, even using the correct techniques (according to the W3C documentation) for such complicated tables does not work with most assistive devices. This really is a topic that you can leave for now!

Summary

When you need to present information in a tidy, organized fashion, tables really are the right technique for the job, and with XHTML, you have all the necessary tools at your disposal. In this chapter, we've seen how you can use combinations of simple XHTML elements to provide the necessary order, and employ CSS to style tables in such a way that they can be visually appealing. We've also covered some of the basic considerations that you need to take in order to make tabular information accessible to a much wider audience.

Now that we've given tables their due attention, we can move on to another topic that's essential to grasp if you're going to have people interact on your web site with one another and with you. That topic is forms. If you're done here, the next chapter will "fill you in" on the details!

---

[4] http://www.456bereastreet.com/archive/200410/bring_on_the_tables/

7

Forms: Interacting with your Audience

One of the great things about the Internet is the apparently never-ending wealth of information it puts at your disposal. The term "web surfing" came about because, like real-world surfers, users never know which path they're going to take: if something piques their interest, that's the direction they'll take. But the process of simply reading, clicking on a link, and reading some more is very passive—users aren't really getting involved. They're simply on the receiving end of all that information. At some point, users need to interact in some way with the web site, ending that one-way flow of information.

Imagine this scenario: you're looking to book a holiday—perhaps a surfing trip or a diving holiday—and the first steps you take are to search for information about resorts, read other people's reviews, and look at some stunning pictures. You make a decision fairly quickly about which resort you'd like to visit, then you decide to find a site through which you can book a trip, arrange your flights, and so on. As you book the holiday, you'll need to enter details such as your name and address; you may have to select travel dates from a drop-down list; you might also need to specify certain features that you want to include in your holiday using checkboxes. To make these kinds of selections, you use HTML forms.

In this chapter, you'll learn about the various elements that make up a form, the tasks for which those elements should and should not be used, and how you can make sense of information submitted through forms. As part of the practical work of this chapter, we're going to add a simple form to the diving project site to allow users to notify the webmaster of forthcoming diving events. But, to start, let's investigate the different parts that comprise a form.

Anatomy of a Form

It might not surprise you to learn that a form begins with an opening `<form>` tag and ends with a closing `</form>` tag. Inside that `form` element, the browser can expect to find some special XHTML elements that can capture data in some way. Though the `form` element doesn't have any visual characteristics to speak of, it's a block-level element, and as such, will cause the browser to create breaks before and after its opening and closing tags.

Before we move any further into a description of what a `form` does, it's probably a good idea to review an example of a `form` as we'd see it in the browser. Take a look at the example in Figure 7.1.

Figure 7.1. A basic form

The `form` element is a special kind of container. It contains a variety of XHTML elements that can exist only inside the `form` element, including:

- `fieldset`

- `legend`

- `input`

- `textarea`

❑ select

I'll explain all of these elements through the course of this chapter, but let's start at the beginning with a very basic form that you can build for yourself. Then, we'll start to talk about all the different elements we might want to use in our forms.

A Simple Form

Let's get a feel for what a form does. Open your text editor and enter the following markup:

File: **simpleform.html**

```
<!DOCTYPE html PUBLIC "-//W3C//DTD XHTML 1.0 Strict//EN"
    "http://www.w3.org/TR/xhtml1/DTD/xhtml1-strict.dtd">
<html xmlns="http://www.w3.org/1999/xhtml">
  <head>
    <title>A Simple Form</title>
    <meta http-equiv="Content-Type"
        content="text/html; charset=utf-8" />
  </head>
  <body>
    <h1>A Simple Form</h1>
    <form method="get" action="simpleform.html">
      <p>
        <label for="yourname">Enter your name:</label>
        <input type="text" name="yourname" id="yourname" />
      </p>
      <p><input type="submit" /></p>
    </form>
  </body>
</html>
```

Save the page as simpleform.html, then open it in your browser. You should see a very basic example of a form, like the one shown in Figure 7.2, which has:

❑ one text input in which you can enter your name

❑ a submit button that sends the details that were entered into the form

Figure 7.2. A very simple form

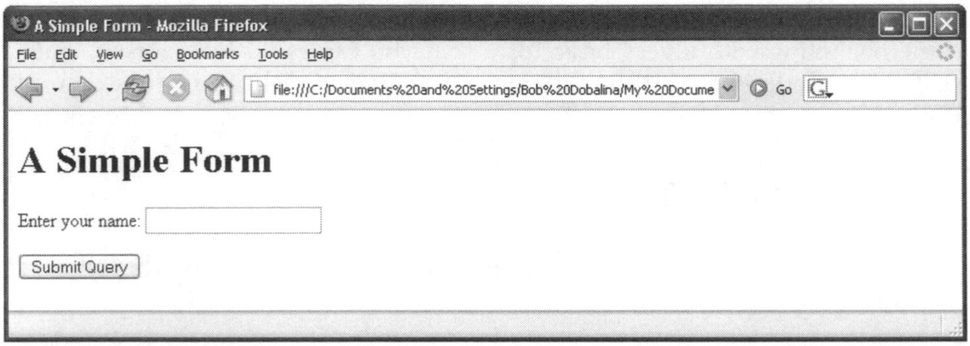

Now, enter your name in the text input and click on the submit button (it's usually labeled Submit Query or just Submit). The page should reload, your name should disappear from the text box, and if you look in the address bar, you'll see that the data you entered has been appended to the address for that page. It should look something like this:

```
file:///C:/Documents%20and%20Settings/Bob%20Dobalina/My%20Document
s/Web/simpleform.html?yourname=Bob
```

We haven't done anything with that data yet, but you can appreciate even with this basic example that the entered data is there for the taking (and manipulating).

Let's start looking at the different elements you can place in a form, and their uses.

The Building Blocks of a Form

The `form` Element

As we've already seen, a form begins with the `form` element. You'll see a few important attributes in an opening `<form>` tag, and these are:

method   This tells the browser *how* to send the data in the form when the user clicks the submit button. The options are `get` and `post`. The option you use will depend on what you're doing with the data (see the tip below, titled "Get it or Post it?" for more on this). For now, don't worry too much about `method`; we'll use `get` for our simple examples.

action This attribute tells the browser *where* to send the data that was collected in the form. Normally, this will specify another web page that can read and interpret the data entered.

Get it or Post it?

The decision about whether to use `get` or `post` in the `method` attribute of your `form` normally won't be yours if you want to avoid writing computer code. As you'll see later on, we'll use an external form processor to do something useful with our form, and that will dictate which method we use. However, there are a couple of points about these different methods that are useful to know:

❑ If you specify a `get` method, your form data will appear in the address bar of the page to which you submit that form. This can be useful: if you want to, you can bookmark that page[1] with those pieces of information included. For example, because Google's search form includes `method="get"`, you can bookmark a search for "cake shops Southampton." Then, every time you call up that bookmark, Google will give you an up-to-date list of cake shops in Southampton.

❑ Sometimes, you won't want users to be able to bookmark the results of their form usage, nor will you want the information in the form to be visible to anyone who happens to walk past the users' computers. A good example of a form that meets both these criteria is the login form for an Internet banking site. You'd want to make sure that only the actual bank account holder (not another family member, for example) can access the details for the account in question, and you certainly wouldn't want people to see the user's password. In cases like these, we use the `post` method.

It's also worth noting that if you're sending a large amount of data, `post` is the preferred method.

As usual, there's more to this topic if you're interested,[2] but we won't need to concern ourselves with it any more in this chapter.

The `fieldset` and `legend` Elements

These two elements really do go hand in hand: the `fieldset` element provides the ability to group related elements within a form together (by drawing a line

---

[1] Or, if you use IE, add it to your favorites.
[2] A good place to start is *Methods GET and POST in HTML forms—what's the difference?* by Jukka Korpela [http://www.cs.tut.fi/~jkorpela/forms/methods.html].

around them), while the legend element lets you caption that group of elements appropriately. Here's the XHTML for using this dynamic duo:

```
<form method="get" action="simpleform.html">
  <fieldset>
    <legend>All About You</legend>
    <p>
      <label for="yourname">Enter your name:</label>
      <input type="text" name="yourname" id="yourname" />
    </p>
    <p><input type="submit" /></p>
  </fieldset>
</form>
```

Figure 7.3 shows how the form looks with the addition of these elements.

Figure 7.3. A form to which a **fieldset** and **legend** have been applied

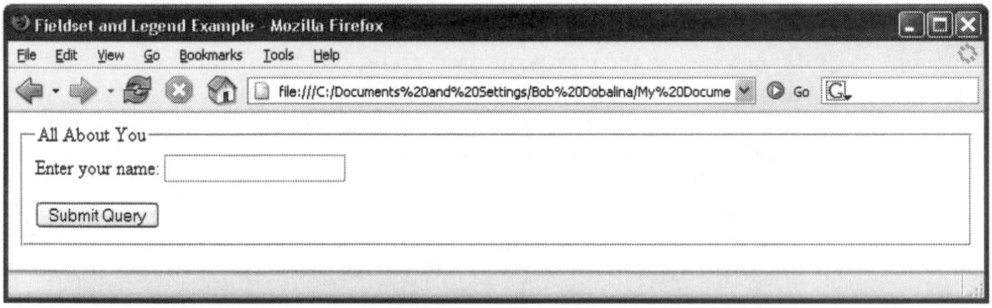

Nesting fieldsets

Tip

You're not limited to using just one **fieldset** and **legend**. On more complex forms, you can "nest" these elements to provide more clarity about certain sections within the form, as Figure 7.4 shows.

Figure 7.4. Nested `fieldsets` helping to organize form inputs

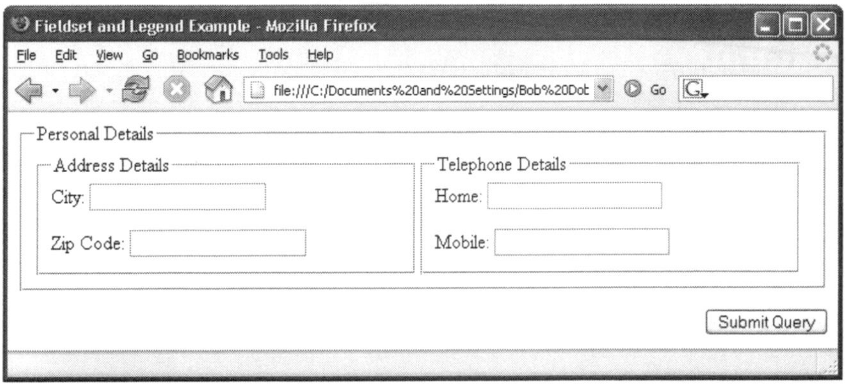

The input Element

With the preamble out of the way, we can get into the nuts and bolts of the form: the section in which we actually capture data from users. The first element that you'll learn to use is the `input` element, which is used to insert into the form **controls** with which the user can interact.

The `input` element is very versatile; its appearance and behavior can be changed dramatically using the `type` attribute. Some of the most common values of the `type` attribute are:

☐ `text`

☐ `password`

☐ `checkbox`

☐ `radio`

☐ `hidden`

☐ `submit`

Each of these values causes a dramatically different control to be placed on your page. Let's start by looking at the most commonly-used type of control: the **text input** control.

Text Input

You've seen this control countless times on web pages. The text input, depicted in Figure 7.5, is the most basic type of form data that users can enter.

Figure 7.5. A simple text input

Enter your name:

The XHTML for this control is really very simple:

```
<p>
  <label for="yourname">Enter your name:</label>
  <input type="text" name="yourname" id="yourname" />
</p>
```

Let's look at each of these components in turn:

the `label` element
> The `label` is used to provide a label for a control so that users know what kind of data they should enter. The `label` element is linked directly to the `input` to which it relates using the `for` attribute. The value of the `for` attribute should be the same as the `id` attribute of the `input` element.

the `type` attribute
> We set the `input` element as a simple text input control by setting the `type` attribute to `text`.

the `name` attribute
> Remember, when we submitted our very first form, that the name we entered appeared at the end of the text in the address bar?
>
> ```
> file:///C:/Documents%20and%20Settings/Bob%20Dobalina/My%20Docum
> ents/Web/simpleform.html?yourname=Bob
> ```
>
> The `yourname` part came from the `name` attribute of the `input` element, which can be used to identify which piece of data came from a given control.

the **id** attribute

At first glance, the `id` attribute seems identical to the `name` attribute, and for some types of controls, it is. However, as we'll see later, some controls can share the same `name`, and it is in these cases that the `id` is used to distinguish between individual controls on the page.

The `id` attribute is referred to by the `label` element's `for` attribute. An `id` attribute can be used for many different purposes (you've already seen it used in this book to aid the styling of layouts created with CSS). However, in this example, its purpose is to give the `label` something to refer to.

You might also want to add a couple of optional attributes to a text input:

size   tells the browser how many characters the text box should display

maxlength   places an upper limit on how many characters the user can enter into the text box

Setting the Value of a Text Box

If you'd like to set the initial value of a text box, you can use the `value` attribute to do so. Load the following markup into a form, and a text box with the value "Bob" (without the quotation marks, of course) will be displayed.

```
<p>
  <label for="yourname">Enter your name:</label>
  <input type="text" name="yourname" id="yourname" value="Bob" />
</p>
```

Password Input

The **password input** control is almost identical to the text input, with one notable exception: the characters that are typed into the control are not displayed on the screen. Instead, they're replaced by asterisks, as shown in Figure 7.6.

```
<p>
  <label for="password">Your password:</label>
  <input type="password" id="password" name="password" />
</p>
```

Figure 7.6. A password input control displaying entered characters as asterisks

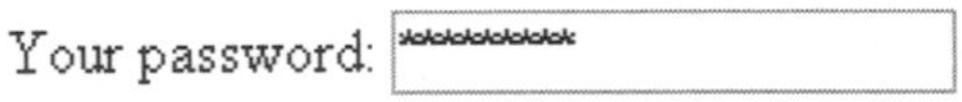

Your password: [∗∗∗∗∗∗∗∗∗∗]

A Password INPUT Does Not A Secure Form Make

Although the password input control helps to stop people from looking over your users' shoulders and seeing the passwords they're typing in, it does not make the form any more secure during the actual data submission. For that, you'd need to consider security a little more seriously. To ensure that data in your forms is sent securely, you'll need to send it using a protocol called HTTPS. Although you may not know it, HTTPS is used when you fill in a form on an ecommerce web site such as Amazon or eBay—it's this that causes the little padlock icon to display in the status bar on your browser (usually at the bottom).

Hidden Inputs

As the name suggests, a **hidden** input is one that doesn't appear in the page at all. "Input" is a confusing name in this case, because the user doesn't actually input anything into it; its value can be set only by the page's author (or by some JavaScript, but that technique is beyond the scope of this book). Why would you want to set the value of a hidden input? We'll answer that question when we process our form. For now, all you need to understand is that the following markup won't cause anything to appear on the screen:

```
<input type="hidden" name="peekaboo" value="hereiam" />
```

However, it will have an effect when the user submits the form:

```
file:///C:/Documents%20and%20Settings/Bob%20Dobalina/My%20Document
s/Web/hidden.html?peekaboo=hereiam
```

Checkbox Input

Checkboxes are an excellent tool for gathering answers to "yes or no" questions. A text input is completely free and open, but with a checkbox. the user's choice is a straightforward yes or no, as the example in Figure 7.7 demonstrates.

Figure 7.7. Adding checkboxes to the form

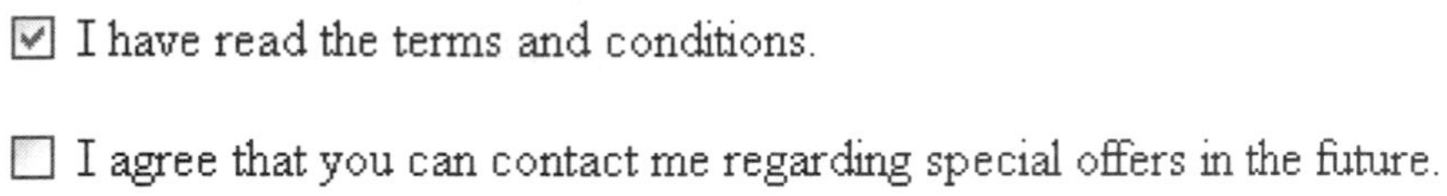

☑ I have read the terms and conditions.

☐ I agree that you can contact me regarding special offers in the future.

Here's how you can achieve that effect in XHTML:

```
<p>
  <input type="checkbox" name="terms" id="terms" />
  <label for="terms">I have read the terms and conditions.</label>
</p>
<p>
  <input type="checkbox" name="offers" id="offers" />
  <label for="offers">I agree that you can contact me regarding
      special offers in the future.</label>
</p>
```

Preselecting Checkboxes

Often, when you're working with checkboxes, you might want them to be checked (or selected) when the page loads, and let users uncheck them as they see fit. To achieve this, we use the checked attribute. Strangely, the value you need to use for checked is checked (not checked="yes" or checked="true"):

```
<p>
  <input type="checkbox" name="terms" id="terms" />
  <label for="terms">I have read the terms and conditions</label>
</p>
<p>
  <input type="checkbox" name="offers" id="offers"
      checked="checked" />
  <label for="offers">I agree that you can contact me regarding
      special offers in the future</label>
</p>
```

Radio Buttons

The checkbox option is great when you have many different options to which you want the user to answer "yes" or "no"—they could say "yes" to none, some, or all of the options. However, what would you do if you wanted the user to select only one option? For this scenario, we use **radio buttons** like those shown in Figure 7.8.

Figure 7.8. Inserting radio buttons into the form

⦿ In the morning
◯ In the afternoon
◯ In the evening

This code creates the radio buttons:

```
<p>
  <input type="radio" name="timeslot" id="morning"
      value="morning" />
  <label for="morning">In the morning</label>
  <br />
  <input type="radio" name="timeslot" id="afternoon"
      value="afternoon" />
  <label for="afternoon">In the afternoon</label>
  <br />
  <input type="radio" name="timeslot" id="evening"
      value="evening" />
  <label for="evening ">In the evening</label>
</p>
```

The key difference between this and the checkbox example is that, in this case, we have three different options, *yet the* `name` *attribute is the same for all three inputs*. This is essential: it's this value that binds the three inputs together. They share the same `name`, but each has a different `value` attribute. As a user selects an option and submits the form, the appropriate value is sent to the server.

Note also that each `input` has a different `id`. In fact, *any* `id` that is assigned to an element in the document must be unique, whether it is a form element, an image or some other XHTML element. In this case, it also benefits the `label` elements, which must refer to unique identifiers.

"Hey, these things don't look like buttons! And what have they got to do with radios?"

Old car radios had buttons with which listeners could select the station. You could only press one button in at a time, and when you did, the previously selected button would pop out. This is the origin of the name for these form controls: selecting one makes the currently selected one "pop out" (deselects it). Younger readers will just have to take my word on the subject!

Preselecting Radio Inputs

The technique we use to preselect a given radio button is exactly the same as that used for checkboxes:

```
<p>
  <input type="radio" name="timeslot" id="morning" value="morning"
      checked="checked" />
  <label for="morning">In the morning</label>
  <br />
  <input type="radio" name="timeslot" id="afternoon"
      value="afternoon" />
  <label for="afternoon">In the afternoon</label>
  <br />
  <input type="radio" name="timeslot" id="evening"
      value="evening" />
  <label for="evening ">In the evening</label>
</p>
```

The `select` Element

Radio buttons allow you to choose only one item from a range of options, which is great ... up to a point. But what would happen if you had 20 or more options? Do you really want to display them all on the screen if only one is required? Probably not. A better option might be to use the `select` element. This control lets users choose from a range of options, but takes up just a single line on your web page; users view the options by clicking on the drop-down arrow (using a mouse or keyboard). You've probably used this form control, which is illustrated in Figure 7.9, countless times.

Figure 7.9. Choosing an option from a drop-down list, or `select` element

Which best describes you? | Web Designer ▾ |

The `select` element contains an array of `option` elements. Each `option` correlates to an option in the drop-down list. Here's the XHTML for this type of form control:

```
<p>
  <label for="role">Which best describes you?</label>
  <select name="role" id="role">
    <option>Secretary</option>
```

```
    <option>Web Designer</option>
    <option>Manager</option>
    <option>Cleaner</option>
    <option>Other</option>
  </select>
</p>
```

Preselecting Options

Like checkboxes and radio buttons, it's possible to have one of the options in a drop-down list preselected. However, rather confusingly, to preselect an option in the case of drop-down lists, we need to use a **selected** attribute with a value of **selected**. Who knows what they were thinking when they came up with *that* idea?

Here's the **select** again, this time with the "Web Designer" option pre-selected:

```
<p>
  <label for="role">Which best describes you?</label>
  <select name="role" id="role">
    <option>Secretary</option>
    <option selected="selected">Web Designer</option>
    <option>Manager</option>
    <option>Cleaner</option>
    <option>Other</option>
  </select>
</p>
```

Making Multiple Selections

It's actually possible to create a list that allows several items to be selected, but this technique isn't used very often. The main reason why many developers don't take this route is that it requires the user to hold down the **Ctrl** key and click on the items required—something that's not exactly obvious (it's also very difficult to make multiple selections using the keyboard alone).

textarea

A text input control is good for capturing short pieces of information, but the viewable area is not really suited to anything more than a few words (you've probably experienced the limits of text inputs first-hand when typing more than a handful of words into a search engine: the words start to disappear from view). The better choice for longer text inputs is the **textarea** shown in Figure 7.10.

Figure 7.10. Making longer text inputs usable with the text area

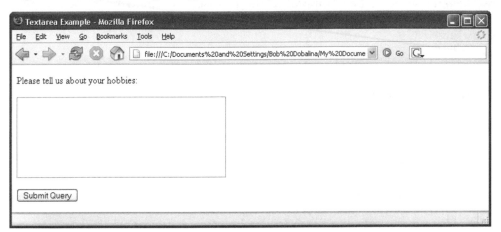

Here's some code that displays a `textarea`:

```
<p><label for="hobbies">Please tell us about your
    hobbies:</label></p>
<p><textarea name="hobbies" rows="7" cols="40"
    id="hobbies"></textarea></p>
```

Submit Buttons

Users must click on the submit button to send the data they've entered into the form. Strangely, it's also a type of `input`. That's strange because you can't really put anything *into* it at all! All you can do is activate it by clicking on it.

Although this is another type of `input`, I left this one until last—rather than grouping it with the text box, password, radio button, and checkbox controls—for the simple reason that the submit button will almost always be the last element in your form.

Inserting a submit button is a cinch. The code below produces the display shown in Figure 7.11.

```
<p><input type="submit" /></p>
```

Figure 7.11. The humble submit button

Submit Query

The wording on this button is a little cryptic, isn't it? The reason for this is that we haven't set a `value` attribute, so the browser uses its default. Adding in a `value` helps to make the button a little more friendly and intuitive, as Figure 7.12 illustrates.

```
<p><input type="submit" value="Send Your Feedback"/></p>
```

Figure 7.12. A more friendly-looking button

Send Your Feedback

No Mouse Required!

Tip

Not many people realize this, but you don't have to use a mouse to submit a form: it's not always necessary to click that button. Usually, you can fill in the form data and simply hit **Enter**.

The Default Control Appearance

It's worth noting that forms can look quite different when displayed on different browsers and operating systems. Throughout this book, we've used Firefox for Windows for most of our screen shots, but it's important to be aware of how users of other systems will see your forms. Imagine that we combined all of the different form elements we've just looked at into one big form; let's see how it looks in different browsers.

Figure 7.13 shows a form displayed in Firefox on Windows.

Figure 7.13. Firefox for Windows displaying our combination mega-form

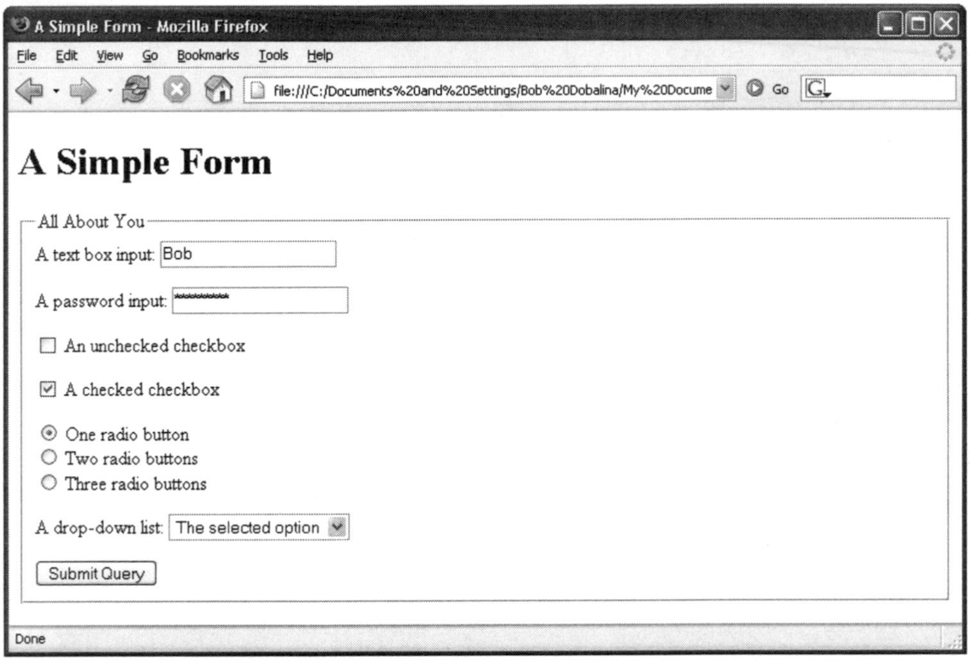

This is very similar to the world's most popular browser, Internet Explorer. However, IE's default `fieldset` appearance is a little more polished than Firefox's, thanks to its blue text and rounded corners. The submit button is a bit larger in IE, too, as Figure 7.14 shows.

Figure 7.14. IE looking *almost* the same as Firefox: the `fieldset` and submit button look different

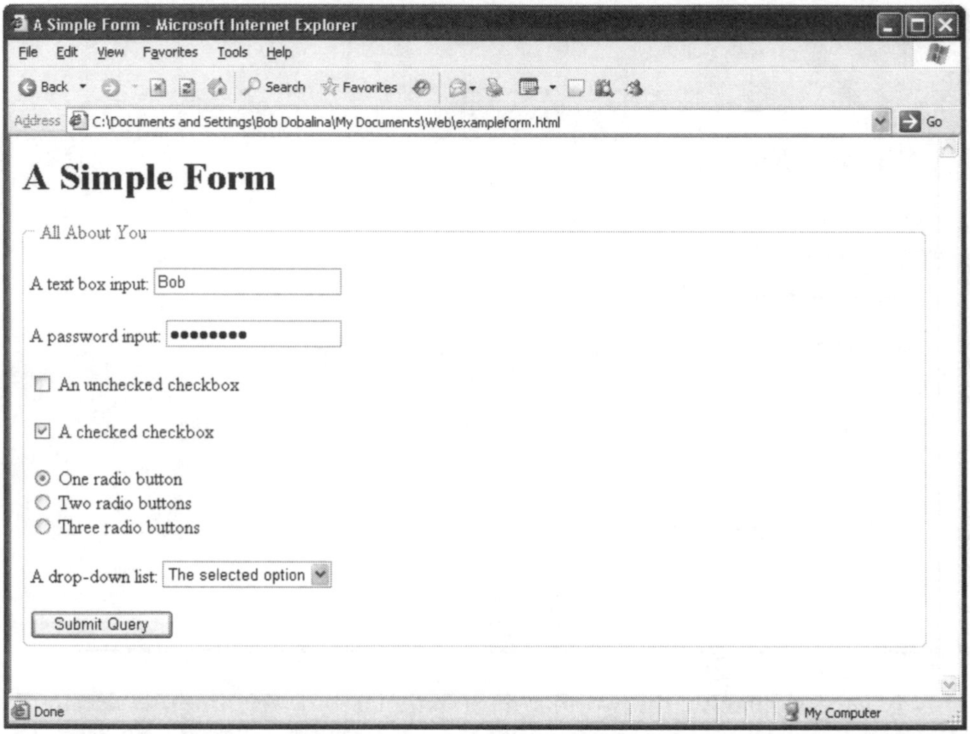

Firefox on Mac OS X isn't too different from its Windows cousin. Some of the controls look a little basic, but they're pretty close to their Windows counterparts, as Figure 7.15 illustrates.

Figure 7.15. Firefox on Mac OS X: a reasonable approximation of its Windows cousin

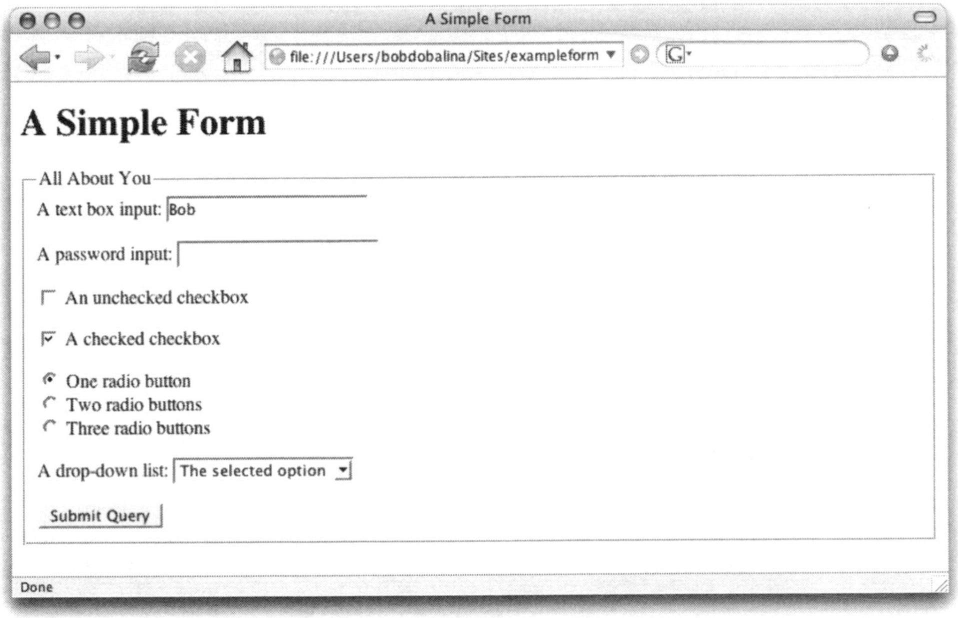

When we switch over to Safari, we see that our form is given a bit more of a Mac OS X flavor (if you've never used a Mac, you'll just have to trust me). The selected checkboxes and radio buttons are blue, the drop-down has changed to a Mac OS X-style list, and our submit button has nice rounded ends, as Figure 7.16 shows.

Figure 7.16. Safari looking very Mac OS X-ish

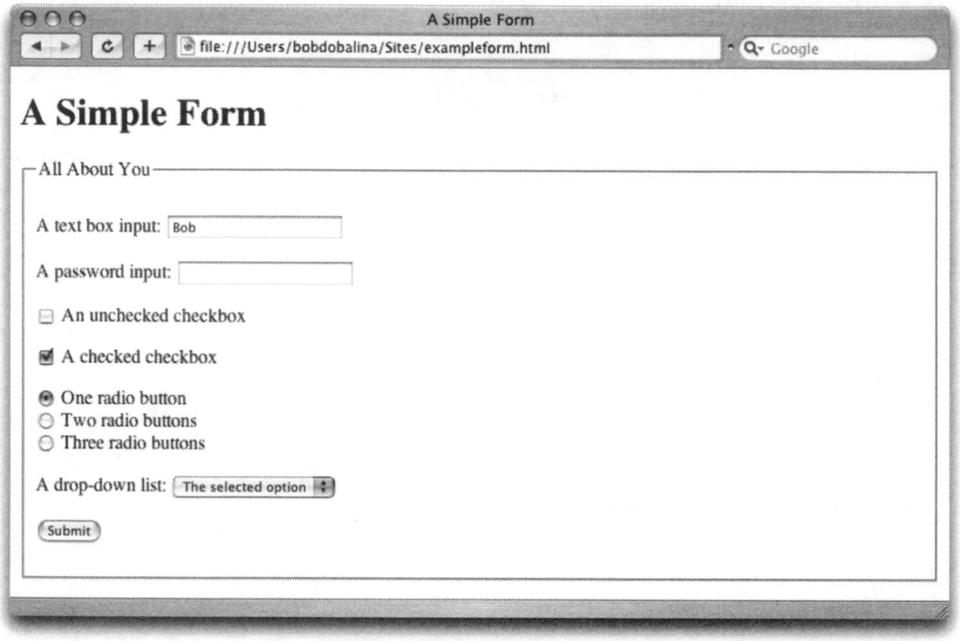

As you can see, there's a fair degree of variation between the controls that different browsers can display. We can customize the appearance of many of these controls for most browsers, with the major exception of Safari. Safari doesn't allow developers to change the appearance of its controls at the time of writing, though Apple is working to add this feature. So if you do style your controls, they should eventually display in Safari as you intended.

Building a Contact Page

Let's apply some of our new-found knowledge by adding a contact form to the project site. In the process, I'll show you, once again, how you can use CSS to spruce up the otherwise plain-looking default styling of these XHTML elements. This time around, we won't need to add any new pages to the project site; instead, we'll expand on the existing Contact Us page.

Processing the Data: it's Coming!

A problem I've had with many web design and development books in the past was that, when forms were mentioned, there was never any real explanation of how you might *use* the data the user entered. I would merrily build a form, click the submit button, then say, "Great, now what?"

Processing form data is not a trivial task: it requires programming know-how or, at the very least, web hosting with *truly* helpful support resources that can explain to the beginner how to set up form handling. As you're reading this book, the chances are that your programming skills have yet to develop, but don't despair! By the end of the chapter, I will have demonstrated an easy method for getting hold of your form data. This form-building exercise will *not* be a purely cosmetic affair that leaves you wanting to know more about the black art of handling form data!

Editing the Contact Us Page

☐ In your text editor, open `contact.html`.

☐ We need to edit the wording that exists in the body of the page. It's useful to have an email address or telephone number on the page, just in case the visitor prefers to contact you via those means. With this in mind, let's replace the paragraph in the page with the following:

File: **contact.html** (excerpt)

```
<p>To let us know about a forthcoming dive event, please use
    the form below.</p>
<p>If you need to get in touch urgently, please call Bob
    Dobalina on 01793 641207. For anything else, please <a
    href="mailto:bob@bubbleunder.com">drop us a line by
    email</a>.</p>
```

Adding a `form` and a `fieldset` Element

Next, let's set up the basics for the form, using the `form`, `fieldset`, and `legend` elements.

☐ In `contact.html`, add an opening `<form>` tag and a closing `</form>` tag in between the two paragraphs that you just added to the page.

☐ In the opening `<form>` tag, add the following attributes:

□ `action=""` (We'll be filling in the blanks later.)

□ `method="post"` (We're using post because we intend to submit a fair bit of data through this form.)

□ `class="contact"` (We'll use this when it comes to applying styles to our form.)

□ Next, add a `fieldset` and a `legend`. Remember that the `fieldset` is contained inside the `form` element, and the `legend` immediately follows the opening `fieldset` tag.

□ For the `legend`, use the phrase, "Tell us About a Dive Event."

Does your XHTML look like this?

File: **contact.html (excerpt)**

```
<p>To let us know about a forthcoming dive event, please use the
    form below.</p>
<form action="" method="post" class="contact">
  <fieldset>
    <legend>Tell us About a Dive Event</legend>
  </fieldset>
</form>
<p>If you need to get in touch urgently, please call Bob Dobalina
    on 01793 641207. For anything else, please <a
    href="mailto:bob@bubbleunder.com">drop us a line by
    email</a>.</p>
```

If so, save `contact.html`, then take a look at it in the browser. It should appear similarly to Figure 7.17.

Figure 7.17. An empty form

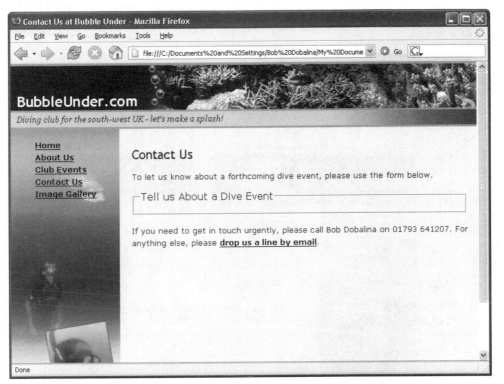

IE and Empty `fieldsets`

If you're using IE, don't worry if you don't see the `fieldset` border. In IE, the `fieldset`'s border won't show up if there's nothing (apart from the `legend`) inside the `fieldset`; other browsers will show the border even when `fieldset` doesn't contain any content.

IE users can add some temporary content, just so you can see the border. Then, we can start to play around with it:

File: **contact.html (excerpt)**

```
<form action="" method="post" class="contact">
  <fieldset>
    <legend>Tell Us About a Dive Event</legend>
    <!-- some temporary content -->
    <p>Form elements go here</p>
```

```
   </fieldset>
</form>
```

Figure 7.18 shows the basic unstyled `fieldset` as it appears in IE on Windows XP.

Figure 7.18. An unstyled `fieldset` displaying in IE

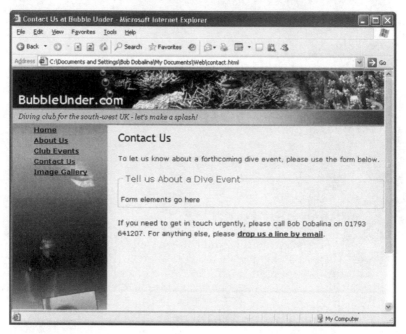

Styling `fieldset` and `legend` with CSS

If you wish, you can leave the styling of form controls until later (i.e., after you've built the actual form and have all the controls in place). However, I prefer to get right in there and apply CSS to forms as I go, mainly because I use CSS to set the widths of text boxes and so on, and I like to make sure each part looks right before I move to the next.

While the default appearance of the `fieldset` doesn't look all that bad in Figure 7.18, other browsers don't display the curved border that IE provides, and as a result, things can look a little bland. With CSS, though, it is possible to apply some styles that improve the look of our form and help to standardize the page's appearance across different browsers. Let's sort out the `fieldset` and `legend` in one hit.

❑ Open `style1.css` in your text editor.

❑ Add the following style rules:

File: **style1.css (excerpt)**

```
form.contact fieldset {
  border: 2px solid navy;
  padding: 10px;
}

form.contact legend {
  font-weight: bold;
  font-size: small;
  color: navy;
  padding: 5px;
}
```

class-ified Forms

Note that we're using the `contact` class to style the elements in this form in the same way that we used the `events` class to style our table in Chapter 6. We're doing this in case we decide to add other kinds of forms to the site later on. For example, we may add a search form in future, and we may wish that form to have a very different appearance from this one.

Save `style1.css`, then take a look at the Contact Us page in your browser. The result should look like Figure 7.19.

Figure 7.19. The `fieldset` styled in CSS

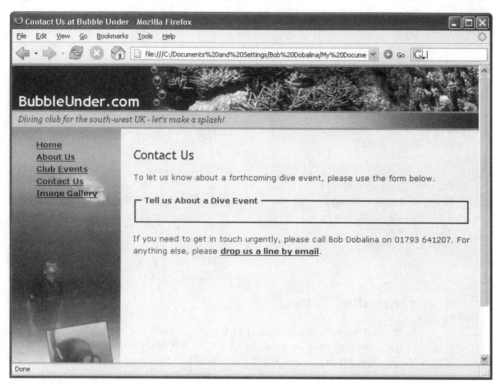

The only problem I can see with this page is that there seems to be a little too much space between the first paragraph and the form. This can be fixed with a negative margin, which we apply to the `form` element like so:

File: **style1.css** (excerpt)

```
form.contact {
  padding: 0;
  margin: 0;
  margin-top: -15px;
}
```

In the above rule, I've also taken the opportunity to remove any default `padding` or `margin` values that the browser might want to set on the `form` element.

Adding Text Input Controls

Now we're going to add to the form a couple of items that will allow us to get some information—such as a contact name, telephone number, and so on—from the user.

- [ ] In `contact.html`, add a `div` element just after the `legend`. If you added some temporary content for IE, you should remove it now.

- [ ] Inside that `div`, add an `input` with `type="text"`.

- [ ] Give that `input` element `name` and `id` attributes, both with a value of `contact-name`.

- [ ] Place a `label` that reads "Contact Name" before that `input`. Remember to add the `for` attribute, and to give it a value that matches up with the `id` attribute of the `input` element.

- [ ] Save the web page, then take a look at it in your browser.

How does it look? Do you see something that resembles a text input? If not, check your XHTML to see if you got it right:

File: **contact.html (excerpt)**

```
<form action="" method="post" class="contact">
  <fieldset>
    <legend>Tell Us About a Dive Event</legend>
    <div>
      <label for="contactname">Contact Name</label>
      <input type="text" name="contactname" id="contactname" />
    </div>
  </fieldset>
</form>
```

The `div` element will keep those items together and cause line breaks to appear before and after them; we'll be using this approach on all the form elements on this page.

Next, I'm going to address the styling of the text that sits inside the label element. Just a couple of minor tweaks are required:

File: **style1.css** (excerpt)

```css
form.contact label {
  font-weight: bold;
  font-size: small;
  color: blue;
  line-height: 150%;
}
```

Figure 7.20 shows our progress so far.

Figure 7.20. Adding a contact name text input control to the form

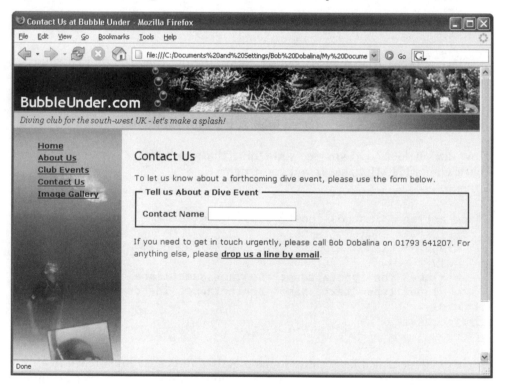

Okay, let's add a bunch of other text input controls in one fell swoop. Here's the XHTML you need (new parts are shown in bold):

File: **contact.html** (excerpt)

```html
<form action="" method="post" class="contact">
  <fieldset>
    <legend>Tell us About a Dive Event</legend>
```

```
  <div>
    <label for="contactname">Contact Name</label>
    <input type="text" name="contactname" id="contactname" />
  </div>
  <div>
    <label for="telephone">Telephone Number</label>
    <input type="text" name="telephone" id="telephone" />
  </div>
  <div>
    <label for="email">Email Address</label>
    <input type="text" name="email" id="email" />
  </div>
  <div>
    <label for="eventname">What's the event called?</label>
    <input type="text" name="eventname" id="eventname" />
  </div>
  <div>
    <label for="eventdate">When's the event happening?</label>
    <input type="text" name="eventdate" id="eventdate" />
  </div>
 </fieldset>
</form>
```

Figure 7.21 shows how it looks.

Figure 7.21. Building up the form with several text inputs

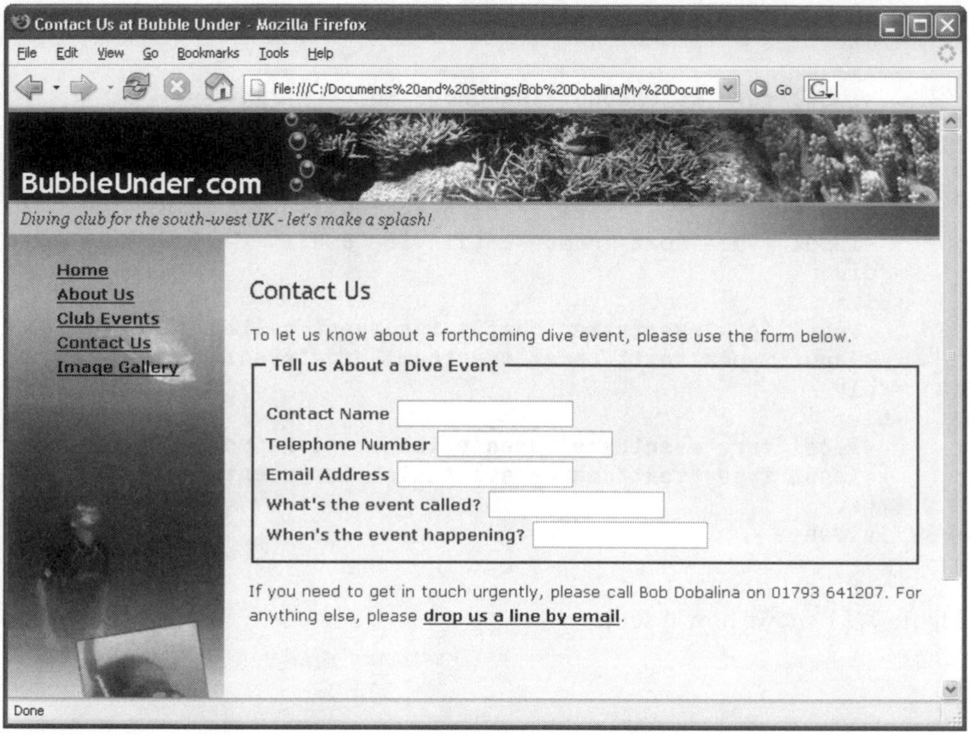

Tidying up `label` Elements with CSS

That form might work well, but the misalignment of the text input controls is kind of ugly. Thankfully, you can correct this issue using CSS. Rather than apply the style to *all* `label` elements inside the form, we'll add a `class` attribute to all of the `label` elements so that we can style only these `label`s (we'll need to add some different style rules to other `label`s later on). Add the following code to `style1.css`, just after the previous `label` selector:

File: **style1.css (excerpt)**

```
form.contact label.fixedwidth {
  display: block;
  width: 240px;
  float: left;
}
```

Next, add the `class` attribute to the `label`s that you have in `contact.html`. Your XHTML should now look like this:

```
<form action="" method="post" class="contact">
  <fieldset>
    <legend>Tell us About a Dive Event</legend>
    <div>
      <label for="contactname" class="fixedwidth">Contact
        Name</label>
      <input type="text" name="contactname" id="contactname" />
    </div>
    <div>
      <label for="telephone" class="fixedwidth">Telephone
        Number</label>
      <input type="text" name="telephone" id="telephone" />
    </div>
    <div>
      <label for="email" class="fixedwidth">Email Address</label>
      <input type="text" name="email" id="email" />
    </div>
    <div>
      <label for="eventname" class="fixedwidth">What's the event
        called?</label>
      <input type="text" name="eventname" id="eventname" />
    </div>
    <div>
      <label for="eventdate" class="fixedwidth">When's the event
        happening?</label>
      <input type="text" name="eventdate" id="eventdate" />
    </div>
  </fieldset>
</form>
```

Refresh the page your browser, and it should look like Figure 7.22.

Figure 7.22. More regimented labels

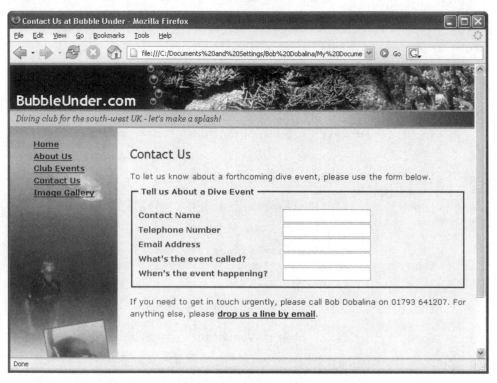

What Just Happened There?

Sorry—I glossed over that CSS a bit! What we did above was a little clever (even if I do say so myself, ahem)—it veers into "advanced CSS" territory. Essentially, the declarations we used told the browser to display the following:

display: block   This declaration converts an inline element (such as a `label` element) into a block-level element. Once it's treated as a block-level element, we can start doing a little more to it, for instance, setting a `width`.

width: 240px   Ah, there we go! By setting the `width`, we've reserved a certain amount of space for the `label` text. Nothing's going to encroach upon that. However, normally a break appears before and after a block-level element.

float: left   Remember this? We used it on the home page to move the feature image over to the right. In this case, we'll use it to place the `label` on the left; the content that immediately follows it is bumped over to the right, in much the same way text in a newspaper wraps around photos in the page layout. Without this declaration, the text input control would appear beneath the `label` text.

Adding a `select` Element

Now, let's add a `select` element. Where could we use this on our page? We could make a control to specify the region of the country in which the diving event or trip will take place.

❑ Add another `div` at the end of your `form` in `contact.html`.

❑ Insert a `select` element into the `div` element you just added.

❑ Give the `select` element `id` and `name` attributes with the value `region`.

❑ Add a `label` that has some appropriate text.

❑ Add an `option` element inside the `select` element for each of the following regions:

    ❑ South-west

    ❑ South-east

    ❑ Central

    ❑ East

    ❑ North

    ❑ Scotland

    ❑ Northern Ireland

    ❑ Overseas (see details below)

Your XHTML should now look like this:

```
<div>
  <label for="region" class="fixedwidth">What region is the event
    in?</label>
  <select name="region" id="region">
    <option>South-west</option>
    <option>South-east</option>
    <option>Midlands</option>
    <option>Central</option>
    <option>London</option>
    <option>East</option>
    <option>North</option>
    <option>Scotland</option>
    <option>Northern Ireland</option>
    <option>Overseas (see details below)</option>
  </select>
</div>
```

And, of course, Figure 7.23 shows the obligatory screenshot.

Figure 7.23. Activating the drop-down list (or `select` element)

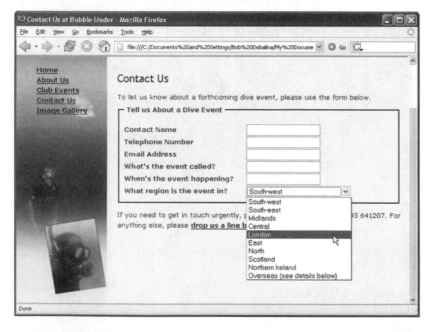

Adding a **textarea** Element

We've got the basics. Now it's time to let the user go a bit wild! Let's move beyond the somewhat restrictive inputs we've created so far. The textarea will let the user enter as much text as they like, so we'll need to create a little extra space for this element.

Because a textarea is an "anything goes" kind of input, you might like to insert some guideline text before it, just to let people know what they should enter:

> Please provide any other details you think will be useful to us in the text area below (it may save us calling or emailing you, and help avoid delays).

Now, let's add a textarea to the form:

- ❑ In contact.html, add an opening <textarea> tag and a closing </textarea> tag, leaving *no space between them* (any spaces or carriage returns in the source code will appear inside the textarea, which can be an annoyance).

- ❑ Add the following attributes with the values indicated:

  - ❑ id="details"

  - ❑ name="details"

  - ❑ cols="30"

  - ❑ rows="7"

- ❑ As before, add a label element just before the textarea and tie that in with the id and name attributes in the textarea element (use the value details).

- ❑ Give the label a class attribute with the value fixedwidth.

- ❑ Save your work, then take a look at the web page in your browser.

The XHTML for this text area is as follows:

File: **contact.html** (excerpt)

```
<div>
  <p>Please provide any other details you think will be useful to
      us in the text area below (it may save us calling or
```

```
      emailing you, and help avoid delays).</p>
  <label for="details" class="fixedwidth">More details (as much as
      you think we'll need!)</label>
  <textarea id="details" name="details" cols="30"
      rows="7"></textarea>
</div>
```

Figure 7.24 shows the intended result.

Figure 7.24. The `textarea` providing freedom to type

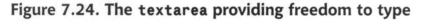

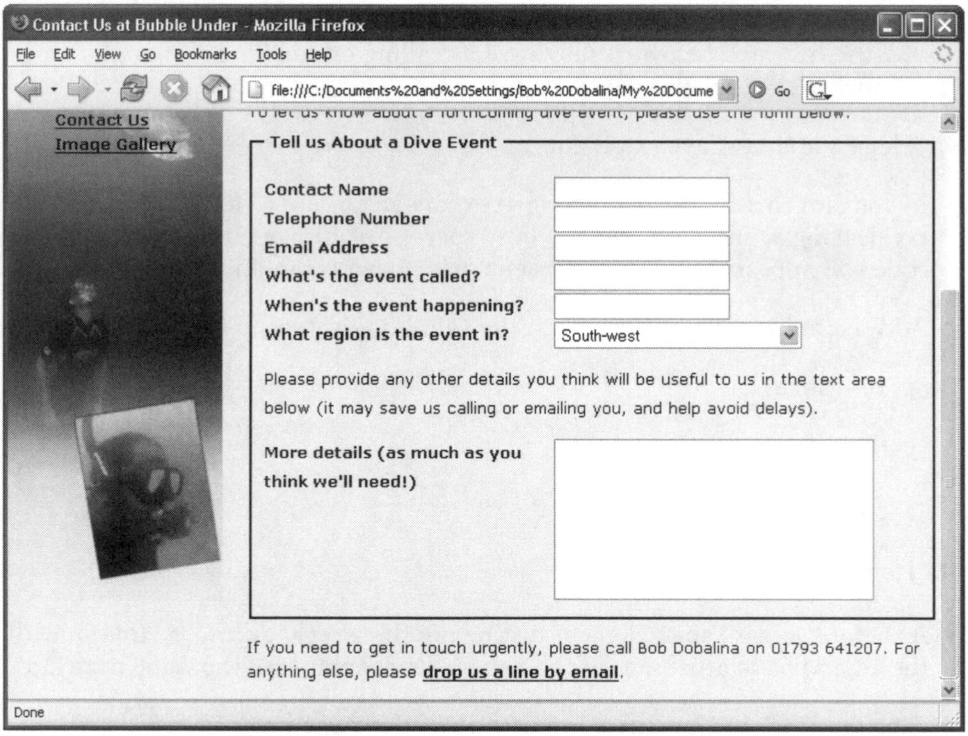

Our form's nearly complete. Truth be known, it's probably detailed enough in its current state, but it's better to see a working example of all the input controls that you're likely to want to use, than to stop now. So, let's fast-track through the last task: adding checkboxes and radio buttons.

Adding Radio Buttons and Checkboxes

As you know, we use radio buttons to allow users to choose one option only from a group of options. With checkboxes, each option is independent of the others, so, if you have ten checkboxes, your users may check:

❑ all of them

❑ none of them

❑ any number of them

We're going to use radio buttons to allow users to choose a convenient time for a call-back (just in case the information they supplied in the form is not clear). A checkbox will be used to let the user confirm that he or she is happy for the information entered in the form to be shared (a very common use for this particular form control).

As I mentioned a moment ago, I'm going to fast-track through this section. Here's the XHTML you need to add for the radio buttons:

File: **contact.html** (excerpt)

```
<div>
  <p>If we need to call you back for any more info, what would be
     the best time to call you on the number supplied?</p>
  <input type="radio" name="timetocall" id="morning"
     value="Morning" />
  <label for="morning">In the morning</label>
  <br />
  <input type="radio" name="timetocall" id="afternoon"
     value="Afternoon" />
  <label for="afternoon">In the afternoon</label>
  <br />
  <input type="radio" name="timetocall" id="evening"
     value="Evening" />
  <label for="evening">In the evening</label>
  <br />
  <input type="radio" name="timetocall" id="never" value="Never"
     checked="checked" />
  <label for="never">No calls please</label>
</div>
```

Here's the final part of code, which deals with the checkbox:

File: **contact.html** (excerpt)

```
<div>
  <p>Bubble Under may share information you give us here with
      other like-minded people or web sites to promote the event.
      Please confirm if you are happy for us to do this.</p>
  <input type="checkbox" name="publicize" id="publicize"
      checked="checked" />
  <label for="publicize">I am happy for this event to be
      publicized outside of and beyond BubbleUnder.com, where
      possible</label>
</div>
```

Figure 7.25. Radio buttons and checkboxes displaying in the form

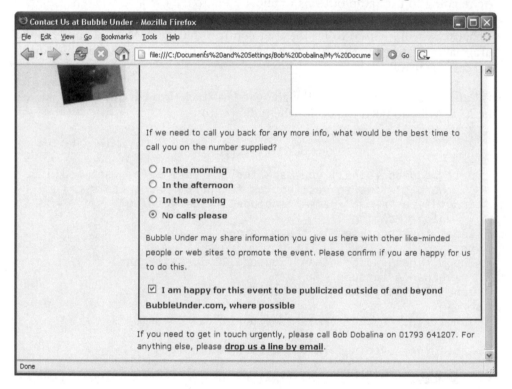

Now, go type that lot in! Seriously, though, there's only one thing here that you haven't already seen: when you use a checkbox or a radio button, the control comes *before* the text that's associated with it. This is common practice with forms;

please don't break the convention by putting your text first, before the form control—no matter how much you might be tempted.[3]

Let's take a look at how the form displays in Firefox: Figure 7.25 shows its appearance.

Completing the Form: a Submit Button

This really is the last step, and it will take but a moment. Simply add the following markup before the closing `</fieldset>` tag:

```
<div class="buttonarea">
  <input type="submit" value="Send Us the Info" />
</div>
```

I've added a `class` attribute to the `div` that contains the submit button, and I've given it the appropriate value: `buttonarea`. I've done this because I want to be able to style the button area (the button and its containing `div`) in CSS. In most browsers, buttons look a little bland by default (as we saw when we looked at a few examples earlier in this chapter).

❑ In `style1.css`, add a new contextual selector for the button. We want it to affect an `input` that's contained in a `div` that has a `class` of `buttonarea`.

❑ Set the background color to navy.

❑ Set the text color to white.

❑ Make the font bold.

❑ Add a little padding around the button: five pixels should do it.

❑ Finally, add a one-pixel border on the button to make the border solid and white.

The CSS that achieves these steps is shown here:

File: **style1.css (excerpt)**

```
form.contact .buttonarea input {
  background: navy;
  color: white;
```

---

[3] Read more on how the order of a control's text affects form accessibility at http://webstandards.org/learn/tutorials/accessible-forms/01-accessible-forms.html.

```
    font-weight: bold;
    padding: 5px;
    border: 1px solid white;
}
```

Check the effect of this markup by saving `style1.css`, then refreshing the view in your browser. Are you looking at a blue button instead of a gray one? If you're looking at a gray button, are you using Safari? Sorry folks: Safari won't pay attention to any CSS styles you might throw at buttons (but, hey, they still look nice, right?).

Our button looks a little lost, though. I like to create a "special area" for buttons like this. After all, they're special: they're the final part of the form, and a "special area" helps to draw attention to the fact that they're there to be clicked. Let's add a class selector for the button area:

```
form.contact .buttonarea {
    text-align: center;
    padding: 4px;
    background-color: #0066ff;
}
```

The button now sits in the middle of an eye-catching blue strip, rather than displaying at the bottom of the form and looking a little lost. Figure 7.26 shows the final product: our form from start to finish.

Figure 7.26. Highlighting the submit button with CSS styling

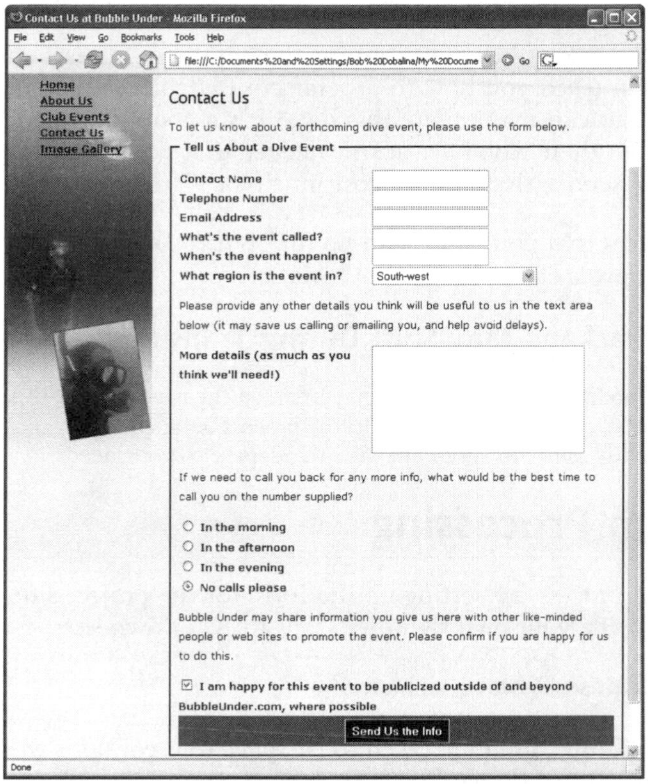

What Have we Achieved?

In this chapter, you've learnt what different form elements are used for, and which types of controls are suitable for particular purposes. Together, we've stepped through the process of building a real form, and we've styled it with CSS along the way. But, what now? Where's this data going?

For the last part of this chapter, I'll walk you through the process involved in signing up for a free form processing service that will handle your data for you.

Processing the Form

Handling form data is a skill that requires programming. I mentioned this earlier, and there's no way that I can teach you how to program in PHP, Perl, or some other server-side language that can manipulate this data. It's a good job, then, that there are other people out there who have acknowledged that there's a need for a simple form-processing service that doesn't cost much, or is free.

There are a number of services that you could sign up for,[4] but the one that I'm going to walk you through now is called Response-O-Matic.

Contents of Package May Shift During Transit

That's my rather pompous way of saying that between the time I wrote this book and the time at which you're reading it, the process detailed below may have changed slightly. But you should be able to adapt it to your needs.

Signing Up for Form Processing

The steps below explain the process for setting up the form for the project site. Naturally, you'll need to provide your own sign-on details for your own site.

❑ Head on over to the Response-O-Matic web site.[5]

❑ Click on the Create a Form link. You'll be taken to the page that contains the Response-O-Matic Form Wizard shown in Figure 7.27.

---

[4] Other free services are available from sites such as
http://www.prospector.cz/Free-Internet-services/Webmaster-services/Forms-processing/ and
http://cgi.resourceindex.com/Remotely_Hosted/Form_Processing/.
[5] http://www.response-o-matic.com/

Figure 7.27. The Response-O-Matic Form Wizard

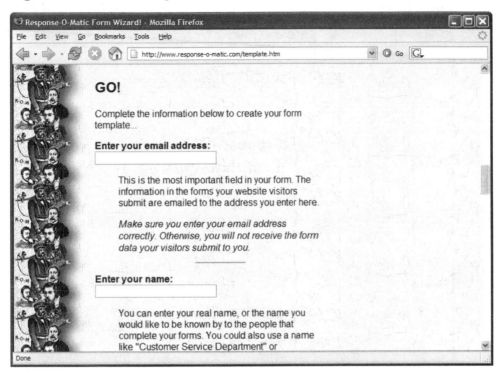

❑ Go through the form, entering the details for your web site as you go. Don't worry if you're not sure about any particular detail—it's very easy to test and change these settings at any time.

❑ Once you've filled out the form, click the Submit button. You'll be taken to the page shown in Figure 7.28, and your template will be generated.

Figure 7.28. Confirmation that your template has been generated

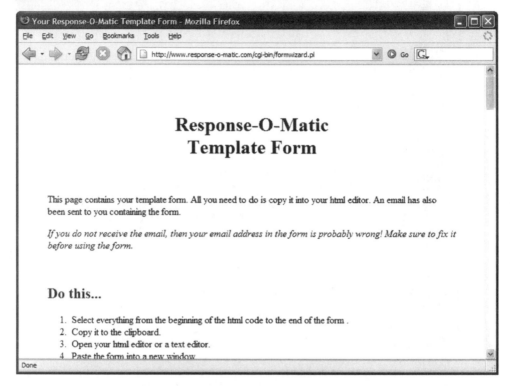

The page shown in Figure 7.28 advises you to copy the HTML that Response-O-Matic has generated for you and paste it into your text editor. If you take a look at it, though, you'll see that the HTML looks quite different from the XHTML we've been writing: all of the tags and attributes are in uppercase, it uses h3 elements instead of label elements, it's using tables for layout, and there are a few mysterious, empty h4 elements floating about. Instead of using this markup, let's take what we need from the code and place it into our own form.

Inserting the Form Code

Having worked through the form wizard, I'm provided with the code below:

```
<!--    INSTRUCTIONS    -->
<!--1. Select this entire file.-->
<!--2. Copy and paste it into Notepad or a similar text editor-->
<!--3. Save this to your web site as an HTML file.-->
<!--4. Have fun!-->

<HTML>
<HEAD>
<TITLE>Response-O-Matic Form</TITLE>
</HEAD>
<BODY BGCOLOR="#FFFFFF">
<FORM action="http://www.response-o-matic.com/cgi-bin/rom.pl"
    method="POST">
<H1><CENTER> </CENTER></H1>
<H1><CENTER><FONT COLOR="#000000">Thanks for visiting my
    site!</FONT>
</CENTER></H1>
<H3><CENTER>

<INPUT TYPE="hidden" NAME="your_email_address"
VALUE="bob@bubbleunder.com">
<INPUT TYPE="hidden" NAME="your_name"
VALUE="Bob Dobalina">
<INPUT TYPE="hidden" NAME="email_subject_line"
VALUE="Upcoming Event">
<INPUT TYPE="hidden" NAME="required_fields"
    VALUE="your_email_address">
<INPUT TYPE="hidden" NAME="thank_you_title"
VALUE="Thanks for submitting your event to Bubble Under">
<INPUT TYPE="hidden" NAME="return_link_url"
VALUE="http://www.bubbleunder.com/">
<INPUT TYPE="hidden" NAME="return_link_name"
VALUE="Back to the Home Page">
<INPUT TYPE="hidden" NAME="background_color"
VALUE="#FFFFFF">
<INPUT TYPE="hidden" NAME="text_color"
VALUE="#000000">
<INPUT TYPE="hidden" NAME="link_color"
VALUE="#0000FF">
<INPUT TYPE="hidden" NAME="visited_link_color"
VALUE="#8000FF">
<INPUT TYPE="hidden" NAME="active_link_color"
VALUE="#0000FF">
</CENTER></H3>
<H3><CENTER>Your comments are appreciated!</CENTER></H3>
```

```
<P><CENTER>Just complete this form. Click on Submit when ready to
send.</CENTER></P>
<H4> </H4>
<BLOCKQUOTE><P><TABLE BORDER=0 CELLSPACING=0>
<TR>
<TD WIDTH=116>
<H3>Your name:</H3>
</TD><TD>
<H4><INPUT TYPE="text" NAME="visitor_name" VALUE="" SIZE=50>
</H4>
</TD></TR>
<TR>
...
```

Eugh! I hope that, by looking at this HTML, you can see the advantage in
building your web site *the right way*—we could do all this in about half as much
markup, and our markup would make much more sense!

Response-O-Matic's idea is that you insert your input, select, and textarea
elements into that form markup. I'm going to suggest the opposite: instead, pick
out what you need from the markup above and apply it to our already-built form.
Below, the parts you need have been marked in bold:

```
<!--    INSTRUCTIONS    -->
<!--1. Select this entire file.-->
<!--2. Copy and paste it into Notepad or a similar text editor-->
<!--3. Save this to your web site as an HTML file.-->
<!--4. Have fun!-->

<HTML>
<HEAD>
<TITLE>Response-O-Matic Form</TITLE>
</HEAD>
<BODY BGCOLOR="#FFFFFF">
<FORM action="http://www.response-o-matic.com/cgi-bin/rom.pl"
    method="POST">
<H1><CENTER> </CENTER></H1>
<H1><CENTER><FONT COLOR="#000000">Thanks for visiting my
    site!</FONT>
</CENTER></H1>
<H3><CENTER>

<INPUT TYPE="hidden" NAME="your_email_address"
VALUE="bob@bubbleunder.com">
<INPUT TYPE="hidden" NAME="your_name"
VALUE="Bob Dobalina">
```

```
<INPUT TYPE="hidden" NAME="email_subject_line"
VALUE="Upcoming Event">
<INPUT TYPE="hidden" NAME="required_fields"
    VALUE="your_email_address">
<INPUT TYPE="hidden" NAME="thank_you_title"
VALUE="Thanks for submitting your event to Bubble Under">
<INPUT TYPE="hidden" NAME="return_link_url"
VALUE="http://www.bubbleunder.com/">
<INPUT TYPE="hidden" NAME="return_link_name"
VALUE="Back to the Home Page">
<INPUT TYPE="hidden" NAME="background_color"
VALUE="#FFFFFF">
<INPUT TYPE="hidden" NAME="text_color"
VALUE="#000000">
<INPUT TYPE="hidden" NAME="link_color"
VALUE="#0000FF">
<INPUT TYPE="hidden" NAME="visited_link_color"
VALUE="#8000FF">
<INPUT TYPE="hidden" NAME="active_link_color"
VALUE="#0000FF">
</CENTER></H3>
<H3><CENTER>Your comments are appreciated!</CENTER></H3>
<P><CENTER>Just complete this form. Click on Submit when ready to
send.</CENTER></P>
<H4> </H4>
<BLOCKQUOTE><P><TABLE BORDER=0 CELLSPACING=0>
<TR>
<TD WIDTH=116>
<H3>Your name:</H3>
</TD><TD>
<H4><INPUT TYPE="text" NAME="visitor_name" VALUE="" SIZE=50>
</H4>
</TD></TR>
<TR>
<TD WIDTH=116>
<H3>Email address:</H3>
</TD><TD>
<H4><INPUT TYPE="text" NAME="visitor_email_address" VALUE=""
SIZE=50></H4>
</TD></TR>
</TABLE></P>
<H3>Where do you want to go today?</H3>
<P><INPUT TYPE="radio" NAME="Where to?" VALUE="I don't know">I
    don't know<BR>
<INPUT TYPE="radio" NAME="Where to?"
VALUE="Disneyland">Disneyland<BR>
```

```
<INPUT TYPE="radio" NAME="Where to?" VALUE="Bill Gate's house"
CHECKED>Bill Gate's house<BR>
<INPUT TYPE="radio" NAME="Where to?" VALUE="Back to bed">Back to
    bed
</P>
...
```

Well, let's get cracking!

❏ Open contact.html in your text editor.

❏ Take the value of Response-O-Matic's action attribute and paste it into the currently empty action attribute in the opening <form> tag in contact.html.

❏ Take all of the hidden inputs just after Response-O-Matic's opening <form> tag and paste them inside the form element in contact.html.

File: **contact.html (excerpt)**

```
<form action="http://www.response-o-matic.com/cgi-bin/rom.pl"
    method="post" class="contact">
  <INPUT TYPE="hidden" NAME="your_email_address"
      VALUE="bob@bubbleunder.com">
  <INPUT TYPE="hidden" NAME="your_name" VALUE="Bob Dobalina">
  <INPUT TYPE="hidden" NAME="email_subject_line"
      VALUE="Upcoming Event">
  <INPUT TYPE="hidden" NAME="required_fields"
      VALUE="your_email_address">
  <INPUT TYPE="hidden" NAME="thank_you_title"
      VALUE="Thanks for submitting your event to Bubble Under">
  <INPUT TYPE="hidden" NAME="return_link_url"
      VALUE="http://www.bubbleunder.com/">
  <INPUT TYPE="hidden" NAME="return_link_name"
      VALUE="Back to the Home Page">
  <INPUT TYPE="hidden" NAME="background_color" VALUE="#FFFFFF">
  <INPUT TYPE="hidden" NAME="text_color" VALUE="#000000">
  <INPUT TYPE="hidden" NAME="link_color" VALUE="#0000FF">
  <INPUT TYPE="hidden" NAME="visited_link_color"
      VALUE="#8000FF">
  <INPUT TYPE="hidden" NAME="active_link_color"
      VALUE="#0000FF">
  <fieldset>
```

❏ You'll need to make a couple of tweaks to make the supplied code XHTML-compliant: you'll need to change the <INPUT> tags and TYPE, NAME, and VALUE attributes to be lowercase, and you'll need to close the empty `input` elements. These changes are highlighted below:

File: **contact.html (excerpt)**

```
<form action="http://www.response-o-matic.com/cgi-bin/rom.pl"
    method="post" class="contact">
  <input type="hidden" name="your_email_address"
      value="bob@bubbleunder.com" />
  <input type="hidden" name="your_name" value="Bob Dobalina" />
  <input type="hidden" name="email_subject_line"
      value="Upcoming Event" />
  <input type="hidden" name="required_fields"
      value="your_email_address" />
  <input type="hidden" name="thank_you_title"
      value="Thanks for submitting your event to Bubble
          Under" />
  <input type="hidden" name="return_link_url"
      value="http://www.bubbleunder.com/" />
  <input type="hidden" name="return_link_name"
      value="Back to the Home Page" />
  <input type="hidden" name="background_color"
      value="#FFFFFF" />
  <input type="hidden" name="text_color" value="#000000" />
  <input type="hidden" name="link_color" value="#0000FF" />
  <input type="hidden" name="visited_link_color"
      value="#8000FF" />
  <input type="hidden" name="active_link_color"
      value="#0000FF" />
  <fieldset>
```

On the Case

Some text editors will include a "change selection to lowercase" function. If you're the lucky user of such a program, now might be a good time to use it. All you need to do is select the text you want changed, then click the appropriate menu item. If you're stuck using Notepad or TextEdit, my apologies—you're all alone on this one.

When an `input` is Not an Input

Remember when we looked at hidden inputs, and I told you that I'd explain their applications a little later? Well, now that we're knee-deep in them, I guess I've got some explaining to do!

Whenever a user submits our form to Response-O-Matic, the form needs to tell Response-O-Matic who we are, and how we want the page to look.

For example, the following hidden inputs describe the colors we want to appear on the page.

File: **contact.html** (excerpt)

```
<input type="hidden" name="background_color"
    value="#FFFFFF">
<input type="hidden" name="text_color"
    value="#000000">
<input type="hidden" name="link_color"
    value="#0000FF">
<input type="hidden" name="visited_link_color"
    value="#8000FF">
<input type="hidden" name="active_link_color"
    value="#0000FF">
```

We set these colors when we went through the form wizard, but we're free to change them as we wish. The same is true for all of the other hidden inputs—the email address, email subject line, the Thank You page message, and other details are all customizable—just change the **value** attribute.

❑ The last thing we need to do is to change the value of the **name** attribute on the email address and name text inputs so that they match up with the names that Response-O-Matic expects.

File: **contact.html** (excerpt)

```
<div>
  <label for="contactname" class="fixedwidth">Contact
      Name</label>
  <input type="text" name="visitor_name" id="contactname" />
</div>
<div>
  <label for="telephone" class="fixedwidth">Telephone
      Number</label>
  <input type="text" name="telephone" id="telephone" />
</div>
<div>
  <label for="email" class="fixedwidth">Email Address</label>
  <input type="text" name="visitor_email_address" id="email" />
</div>
```

❑ Save the page, then try it out in your browser—and this time, I mean *really* try it out! Try entering data and then submitting the form (assuming that you're online, of course!). If you've done it correctly, you should be redirected to a Thank You page.

Figure 7.29. Response-O-Matic doing its thing

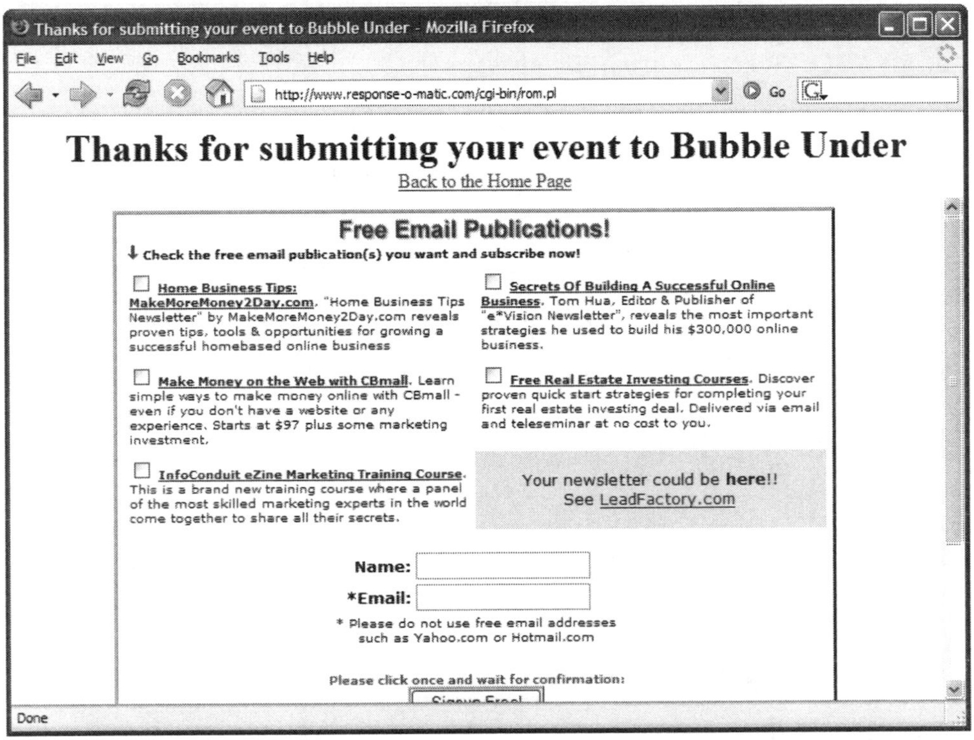

Unfortunately, a big fat ad takes up most of the screen, and there's not a whole lot you can do about that. Like everyone else, Response-O-Matic needs to pay the bills, and the company's revenue comes from displaying these ads to the users that submit their forms.

Feedback by Email

You've built your form and submitted some data. Now all you have to do is open up your mail client and wait for the mail to arrive. Based on the form that we've been building in this chapter, and using the form processing service, this is what you can expect to receive:

```
To: Bob Dobalina <bob@bubbleunder.com>
From: Jill Smith <jsmith@someisp.net>
Reply-To: Jill Smith <jsmith@someisp.net>
Subject: Upcoming Event

### Here's an email that YOU requested, with information
### from YOUR web site visitor, sent to you using the
### FREE Response-O-Matic service!


A visitor to your web site submitted this information from your
form at:

================================================================


Date: Tuesday, December 6, 2005
Time: 11:40 PM EST

Submitted by:  Jill Smith
Email address: jsmith@someisp.net
Subject: Upcoming Event


telephone: 01793 654834

eventname: Murder Mystery Weekend

eventdate: 12th August

region: South-West

details: Murder Mystery Weekend, Cotswolds (no diving!) £65 per
person, accom. included.

timetocall: Afternoon

publicize: on

================================================================

End of submission
Thank you for using RESPONSE-O-MATIC!
http://www.response-o-matic.com
```

Notice that the data is prefixed with the `name` attributes you applied on the form. If you want this email to read more nicely, you could amend the `input` elements' `name` attributes accordingly, but bear in mind that you cannot use spaces in them. For example `publicize` could be `Publicize_On_Site`.

Summary

In this chapter, we've explored the different types of form input controls, discussed what we'd use them for, and understood their limitations. You've stepped through the process of building a practical form, before styling it with CSS to make it a little more pretty. Finally, you've discovered that you don't need to be a programming whiz to be able to deal with form data—but if you *do* want to have more control over how form data is handled (for example, you might want it stored in a database somewhere), you could consider learning a language like PHP. SitePoint published a book on that very topic, written by Kevin Yank, entitled *Build Your Own Database Driven Website Using PHP & MySQL*[6]—you might want to check it out.

For now, though, the bulk of the work on our project site is done. We've got some content, some pretty pictures, some tabular information, a working form, and it's all styled in CSS, offering great flexibility for future redesigns. All that's left is to get these files live, so that the world at large can see our web site. Let's set those wheels in motion right now!

---

[6] http://www.sitepoint.com/books/phpmysql1/

Getting your Web Site Online

Creating web pages can be great fun. It's a relatively easy thing to learn (compared to brain surgery and rocket science, neither of which I'd advise practicing in your spare time) and you can experiment until your heart's content with little more than a standard home computer and some fiendishly good typing fingers. You can spend as little or as much time as you like building web pages and viewing them on your computer, but in the end you'll have to make these babies "live" on the Internet. How you do that—and the tools you'll need to make it happen—are the subject of this chapter. Let's begin by reminding ourselves about some of the basics of the Internet and how it's possible for us to see all these lovely web pages.

The Client-server Model

The relationship between the browser that you use at home and the web sites you visit is known in technical circles as the "Client-server Model," and is depicted in Figure 8.1.

Figure 8.1. The Client-server Model

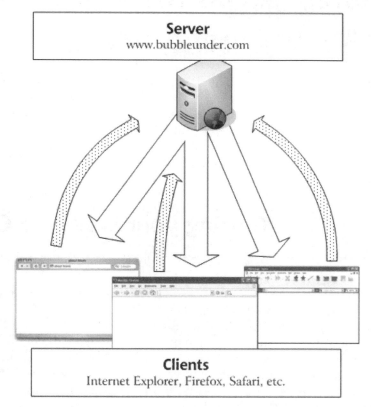

Server
www.bubbleunder.com

Clients
Internet Explorer, Firefox, Safari, etc.

The Client That's you. You're the demanding client (or rather, your browser is) and you demand web pages. You send those demands via your ISP (Internet Service Provider), which provides the connection between you and the server.

The Server That's the other guy. Okay, it's another computer (and probably a hugely complicated, big fat beastie of a computer, at that) and its job is to meet all your demands for web pages.

That's the basics of the relationship. You and many other people can ask that server for many different web pages and other files at the same time—it's a very busy machine! The busier the web site, the greater the demands placed on that server, and the more expensive things can get, but your web site would need to get *a lot* of visitors for this to become a problem. But that's not for you to worry about now—after all, we're trying to do this on the cheap!

Web Hosting Jargon 101

To start with, here are a few words of jargon that it'll help you to understand up-front (I'll be expanding on each of them a little further on):

Bandwidth

This is the size of the "pipe" that runs between the client and the server, and along which all the data travels. The wider the pipe, the more data can fit through it. The size of the pipe is usually measured in megabytes or gigabytes per month. You can now see where the term *broadband* comes from—it means you have a big fat data pipe!

FTP

This is the method used for transferring files from the client to the server and vice versa—it's very useful for getting your web site onto the server in the first place! FTP stands for **File Transfer Protocol**.

Domain Name

This is the "bubbleunder.com" part in the web address `http://www.bubbleunder.com`. You can buy the rights to use a domain name for a fixed period of time—usually 1 or 2 years at a time (it's not yours to own forever). This is referred to as **registering** the domain.

Hosting

Hosting refers to the storage of your web site files on an Internet-connected server somewhere. This hosting service is entirely separate from the registering of your domain name, although many hosting companies offer both services. Site owners use web hosts to store the files for their site so that the site owners themselves don't have to expose their own personal computers' hard drives to potentially malicious web surfers who request the web site's pages over the Internet. Oh, and it beats having to make sure that their own computers are constantly up and running for everyone to access!

Hosting your Web Site—Finding Server Space

The expression that there's no such thing as a free lunch is mostly true. Mostly. However, you can get many things for free on the Web, including hosting. Okay, you can get hosting almost for free. We have to be realistic about this!

The cost for web hosting can vary from around US$10, to hundreds of dollars, each month. You get what you pay for, it has to be said.

❑ A cheap hosting plan is likely to have a limited monthly bandwidth allowance and may not offer advanced features (such as web site statistics that allow you to see how many visitors your web site has attracted, and so on).

❑ A more expensive hosting plan will offer all the basics, should give you more advanced features (like those statistics!), and usually will allow you to do more with your web site as it grows, or your web programming skills improve and you want to try out something more complex.

However, it's folly to spend lots of money on features or bandwidth that you won't use—especially in the case of a small web site that you don't expect will attract masses of visitors. It's a bit like buying a double-decker coach with a multimedia entertainment unit in the back of every seat, when all you need to do is run your auntie a short distance to work and back each day. I'll be pointing out the web hosting features you'll need to consider very shortly.

Free Hosting—with a Catch!

A sensible approach to take with your first foray into web hosting is to sign up for a free hosting service. Conditions will still apply to your usage of the service—perhaps you'll have popup ads forced upon your users, or maybe you'll be asked to include a link to the hosting company, probably in the form of a little graphic, on your web site. However, these shouldn't be big obstacles (although if the free hosting service causes a popup ad to appear on every page of your site, that might well deter visitors from returning, so be sure to check out the conditions thoroughly before you sign up). Regardless, free hosting can at least get your "foot in the door" and let you share your web site with others.

Of course, it pays to shop around! The best advice would be to perform a search in your search engine of choice for the phrase **free hosting "no ads"** (be sure to wrap the "no ads" part in quotes), then to check out the options available—they change quite frequently. To go back to the "free lunch" scenario, many companies that offer free hosting close their virtual doors after they've had enough sign-ups. The best deals don't last long!

Beware of Ugly Addresses

If you do decide to go for free hosting, you may find that the web site address for your files is a little on the ugly side: something like http://www.freespaceforall.net/users/~bubbleunder/, for example. However, there are ways to mask this ugliness—as I'll explain later in the section "Web Forwarding"—so don't let this rule you out of using free hosting.

Free Hosting with Your ISP

If you already have a web connection, the chances are that your Internet Service Provider already offers you some free web space. Again, one could argue that this is not truly "free," but if you're already happily paying for the connection, having the hosting thrown in will at least mean you can host your web site at no extra cost. Well, almost—you will still have the issue of an ugly domain name to deal with, but that issue can be resolved using a web forwarding service.

Try the Forums

Make use of the expertise already out there and be sure to pay a visit to SitePoint's online forums. One area is dedicated specifically to web hosting deals,[1] while in another, users discuss general hosting issues.[2] Here, you can ask for advice about reliable free hosts, and any other questions that you might have about hosting.

Free Hosting—with a Domain Name at Cost

Another free hosting option is to use a service that provides free hosting on the condition that you first register a domain name with them. This may be an economical way of doing things, as you'll have to pay for a proper domain name at some point (that's unavoidable, unless you're happy using one of the longer, less friendly, and less professional domain names that you'll get through the "free-with a catch!" services mentioned above).

---

[1] http://www.sitepoint.com/launch/webhostingforum/
[2] http://www.sitepoint.com/launch/hostdealsforum/

Be a little wary, though: a service may claim to offer free hosting if you register the domain name with them, through you may find that the cost of registering the domain name is a little higher than usual, to offset the lack of hosting charges. In short, "free" may not be anything of the sort!

As an example, Oh-ic.com was, at the time of writing, offering free hosting on the basis that the site owner registered a domain name with the organization, and re-registered each year at a cost of $29.95 US. This is still likely to be cheaper in the long run than a paid hosting plan, but be sure to do some research before you commit.

What is Web Forwarding?

If you decide to take an ultra-low-cost approach to hosting by using web space offered by your ISP (or another free hosting service), your web site's address will probably be something ugly (like the fictional `http://www.freespacefor-all.net/users/~bubbleunder/` address I mentioned earlier). That's hardly something that rolls off the tongue, is it?

What web forwarding allows you to do is register a sensible domain name and nothing else—there's no hosting to be paid for—and to have that domain name point to the address at which your web pages are *really* hosted. You can then quite happily tell people that your web site is at an easy-to-remember address (e.g. www.bubbleunder.com), and when users enter this address in the browser's address bar, your pages will be delivered successfully.

Many small businesses use web forwarding, and it seems to do the job for them. Cheap (or free) hosting combined with a paid-for domain name keeps the costs down and provides an outwardly professional appearance. However, while this seems like a good solution for a new venture, there are some caveats of which you should be aware.

The Downsides of Web Forwarding

Often, web forwarding will make use of an older feature of HTML called **frames**. These are normally used so that you can split the browser display into more than one area, a bit like cutting up a cake. It's a technique that is used less and less frequently though, (and is not even covered in this book—most sensible people agree that frames are generally a bad idea, for a number of different reasons[3]). If you use web forwarding services, your web site will actually be displayed in a single frame; that frame will contain all your web pages. On the surface, everything will seem okay to the casual observer, as Figure 8.2 illustrates. But really, your site's hiding a dirty little secret.

Figure 8.2. A web site making use of a web forwarding service; notice the subtle problems?

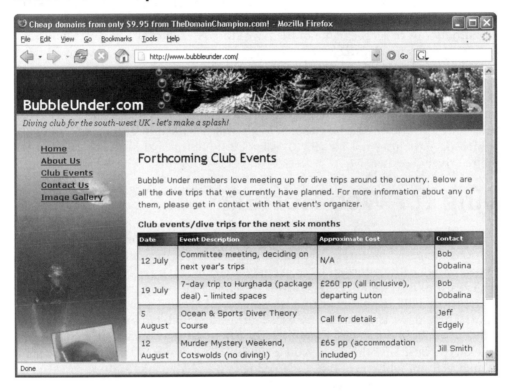

There are a couple of anomalies in Figure 8.2 that, if you've got a keen eye, you might have noticed. The first is the URL: normally, the filename of each page of a web site appears at the end of the domain name. For example, the address of the Club Events page (`events.html`) would be `http://www.bubbleunder.com/events.html`. However, as Figure 8.2 shows, web forwarding with frames

---

[3] A good discussion of why frames are bad can be found in the article "Who framed the web: Frames and usability" by Roger Johansson
[http://www.456bereastreet.com/archive/200411/who_framed_the_web_frames_and_usability/].

means that all of our pages will appear to have the same address: `ht-tp://www.bubbleunder.com/`. As this is the address that the browser uses when a users bookmarks a page, it's difficult to bookmark a specific page within this site. It also makes things a bit trickier for other sites that want to link directly to a specific page in your site. However, as our site has just five pages at the moment, this mightn't be such a big issue.

The second anomaly is the `title` that we so carefully crafted for every page of our site. Using this web forwarding service, no matter which page of our site the users visit, they see the same title—and we aren't able to change it! So when users bookmark our page, the name of the page stored in their favorites lists will be an advertisement for the web forwarding service we signed up for, not the name of our site, or the specific page they bookmarked!

There's a third drawback to domain forwarding that's not very obvious in Figure 8.2: web forwarding breaks the browser's Refresh button. When a user clicks the Refresh button, the page that reloads will be our home page, regardless of which page the user was viewing. It's a good thing that paid-for web hosting can be relatively inexpensive.

Paying for Web Hosting

If you are willing to put your hand in your pocket and pay for your hosting, your options increase immensely. You will not be hobbled by restrictions such as forced links to the hosting provider's site, weird address behavior, or compulsory domain registration. And don't be fooled into thinking that paying for hosting is going to be financially crippling, or that it's something that only big businesses can afford. These days, there are many excellent hosting plans to be had, and for a relatively small amount (less than $10 US per month) you can get quite a good package. Naturally, the more you pay, the more features you'll get—most of which will probably seem like a whole lot of gobbledygook if you're new to this arena. However, as we mentioned before, there's no need to pay for masses of features that you'll never use (think "people carrier" not "double-decker coach"!).

Based on what you've learned so far in this book, and what our project site will require, I'll outline briefly the features you'll need to look for as you research hosting providers.

Hosting Essentials

If you want to get your web site online quickly and easily, you're going to need the following:

FTP Access to your Server

FTP stands for File Transfer Protocol, but nobody ever says it in full. It's a bit like saying you're going to find an Automated Teller Machine instead of an ATM. Stick to FTP and you won't mark yourself as a freak! But what is FTP?

FTP is a method of transferring data over a network, and it's the preferred method of transferring files between the server on which you'll host your web site, and your home computer. Using an **FTP Client**—a program that helps manage these transfers—you can drag and drop files to your server as easily as if you were moving files from one place on your hard drive to another (albeit a little more slowly). In this chapter, I'll show how you can use a selection of FTP clients to upload your files to the Web.

Adequate Storage Space

Once you've finished building your site, it's a good idea to work out the total size of all your site files together. You can find this out quite easily:

Windows   Right-click on the folder on your hard drive that contains all of your web site's files (that's the Web folder inside My Documents), then choose Properties. You will be presented with a dialog like the one depicted in Figure 8.3.

Figure 8.3. Windows' file properties dialog

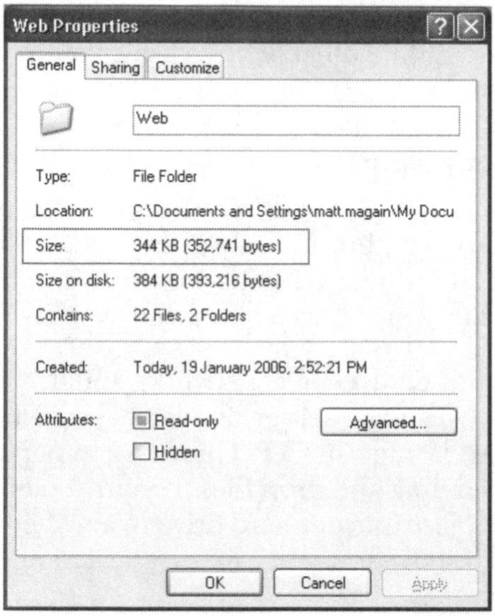

Look for the number next to Size (not the one that says Size on disk—that will give you a skewed figure that's actually more focussed on how efficiently the file has been saved on your hard drive!)

Mac OS X ## Figure 8.4. File properties in Mac OS X

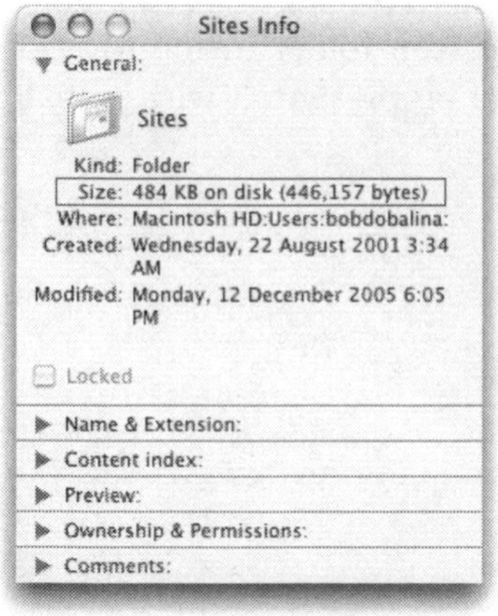

In Finder, select the folder containing your web site files and select File > Get Info. Figure 8.4 shows the Get Info dialog on the Mac, showing files that add up to almost 500KB.

Armed with this knowledge, you can consider how many files you have in your completed web site, and try to work out how much your site is likely to grow. I know that this is not an exact science. Let's try a simple exercise to see how this might work in practice.

Multiply the total size of your existing web site files by ten, then add a little extra for luck. Now, make sure that your host will allow you that amount of storage space. These days, most hosts will give you more than you need for your first web site. A free host may provide 30MB, while a low-cost paid-for service may offer hundreds of megabytes.

Calculating File Sizes

In the examples above, the combined size of the files used in the web site was a measly 480KB (or kilobytes). No hosting company will tell you how many kilobytes they will offer—it will be referred to in megabytes (MB) or gigabytes (GB). As you perform your calculations, bear these figures in mind:

❑ 1 kilobyte = 1,024 bytes

❑ 1 megabyte = 1,024 kilobytes

❑ 1 gigabyte = 1,024 megabytes

A Reasonable Bandwidth Allowance

This is a little bit trickier to assess: it's the proverbial "how big's a piece of string" scenario. If you have 20MB of files on your web site and you access each of them once a month, then you'd need a 20MB monthly bandwidth allowance. Well, that's about as unlikely a figure as you'll ever find—after all, you'll want others to be able to view the web site as well! But how many? Ten? 100? 1,000? What happens if someone links to your site and you suddenly have thousands of people visiting in a single day? Your bandwidth usage shoots up, that's what!

You should expect to have a monthly bandwidth allowance of at least 5GB—this should be quite a comfortable allowance for your first web site, unless people are downloading large photos or video files from your pages.

You need to be careful about exceeding your monthly bandwidth allowance (although, arguably, it's beyond your control—it's the other people visiting your web site that pushes your bandwidth usage up). Some hosting companies won't warn you if you've exceeded your bandwidth allowance: they'll simply block any further traffic to your site until the next calendar month or billing period starts. Others will allow the excess traffic, but they'll charge you a premium for their "flexibility." It pays to check the fine print in your hosting agreement. Most hosts will notify you if you exceed your bandwidth allowance, give you some leeway, and provide you with the opportunity to buy a chunk of extra bandwidth to see you through the dizzy heights of your new-found popularity!

Hosting Nice-to-haves

Email Accounts

A free hosting service is likely to offer some email facilities but, like the domain name that such hosts provide, the email addresses you'll get for free are not often very professional. For example, which of these looks better?

- ❏ bob.bubbleunder@freespaceforall.net

- ❏ bob@bubbleunder.com

It's amazing, but even the email address you provide to others says a lot about the kind of operation you run. This may be reason enough to shell out for hosting.

When you're looking at the email services provided by a host, make sure they offer the following features:

POP3/IMAP   If the hosts offer either of these services (and they should), you will be able to download email to your computer using an **email client** such as Outlook Express, Mail, or Thunderbird.

Webmail   Ifyou think you may need to keep in touch with others about the site while you're away from your home PC, check to see whether the host offers a **webmail** facility. This facility allows you to log in to a web site and check your email from any computer, just as you might with a Yahoo! or Hotmail account.

Email Forwarding If you already have an email address, you may want to have any mail for your new web site sent directly to your existing email address. This is called **email forwarding**. It's a bit like an electronic version of the mail redirection service you can use when you move house, but it has no expiry date!

The advantage of this service is obvious—you don't have to check multiple email addresses. The downside is that someone who emails you at your web site email address (bob@bubbleunder.com, for example) will get a reply from your usual email address. Again, this might make you look a little unprofessional, or confuse the person who receives the reply.

Server Side Includes (SSIs)

You'll already be aware that in building the project site you've had to do a lot of copying and pasting—a change to the navigation in one file necessitates a change in all of them. That may be manageable for sites with a handful of pages, but if you have more than that—or if you can foresee your web site growing—it will become increasingly difficult to keep on top of these kinds of site-wide changes.

One solution is to use **Server Side Includes** (SSI), which let you create a file that's included automatically in all of your web pages, so that a change to that one file will be reflected on every page of your site. Trust me: this is a very useful feature that will save you time in the long term, but it also requires you to learn about setting up your own computer to act as a personal web server. This is not the most straightforward of tasks, so this is one topic that you'll have to investigate in your own time. A good place for Windows users to start would be to download the Apache web server software.[4] Apache is an open-source product, and is used for running web servers that serve web sites of all sizes. Mac OS X users are likely already to have Apache installed; if that's you, you'll need to start Personal Web Sharing, which is accessible from the Sharing screen of System Preferences.

Support for Scripting Languages and Databases

This is another facility that you won't need for anything that we've learned in this book. But, if you ultimately want to make your web site more dynamic, you

---

[4] http://httpd.apache.org/

may want to make use of a **server-side scripting** language such as PHP. With a scripting language, you can start to apply a little bit of logic within your pages, so that content can be displayed differently depending on particular circumstances. For example:

```
If it's after 8pm or before 6am then
  Show the night-time image
Else
  Show the day-time image
End
```

If you can, sign up with a host that supports a scripting language. Even if it's not something that you're using right now, it will make life easier later on should you decide to dabble in server-side scripting and start to add dynamic content.

Often, database support goes hand in hand with support for a scripting language. If you start experimenting with a scripting language, you'll probably find that you need somewhere to store and read data—most likely, a database. A database is a collection of data that you can access and present in many different ways. For example, if you had a database of customers, you could have one web page that lists them all alphabetically, another that lists them by location, and another that lets you know who owes you money (that's useful information to have!). By updating your database, you then make it available to any of these web pages, and any new pages that you create can also tap into the stored information in many different ways.

If you want to learn more about creating dynamic web sites, SitePoint has it all covered for you—you can learn online from the community in the various dedicated forums (PHP[5] and MySQL[6]—a database technology), or pick it all up in one book—Kevin Yank's *Build Your Own Database Driven Website Using PHP & MySQL*[7] is a great place to start.

It's fair to say that the very cheapest hosting services (and most free ones) will not provide database access or allow you to use a scripting language.

What if my Hosting Requirements Change?

 Tip

The features that I've suggested you research here will almost certainly suit the requirements of your first web site. However, if later you find that you outgrow your hosting plan, don't worry—you won't be locked in with that

---

[5] http://www.sitepoint.com/launch/phpforum
[6] http://www.sitepoint.com/launch/mysqlforum/
[7] http://www.sitepoint.com/books/phpmysql1/

company forever. You can transfer your domain name between different hosts as your needs change (although you may incur a small transfer fee, depending on the terms of service of the host whose services you no longer require).

Likewise, don't be fooled into thinking that you need to pay for services early on just *in case* you need them later. For example, don't go paying for PHP and MySQL on the off-chance that you might need these technologies in eight months' time. When you actually need those facilities, you should simply be able to upgrade your current hosting plan or, alternatively, move to another hosting company.

Pre-flight Check—How Do your Pages Look in Different Browsers?

If you build your web pages according to **web standards** (and if you've been following the advice in this book so far, you most definitely have!), you should find that your web site works quite nicely on all or most of the browsers in which you view it—no tweaks required! Still, you should check your page design as early as possible, just in case you spot anything. It's better to fix your prototype or template in as many browsers as possible before you create lots of web pages based on that first page. You should then check your entire site in a range of browsers before you put those files on a live web server for everyone else to see. Here are the browsers that I'd recommend you test against; the most important ones appear at the top of the list for each operating system. In cases where no version number is stated, grab a copy of the latest version available for download:

Windows
- Internet Explorer version 6[8] (IE 7 is due to be released soon after this book goes to print, so it would be best if you could check your site in both IE 6 *and* IE 7.)
- Firefox[9]
- Opera[10]

Mac OS X
- Safari[11]

---

[8] http://www.microsoft.com/windows/ie/
[9] http://www.mozilla.com/firefox/
[10] http://www.opera.com/
[11] http://www.apple.com/safari/

❑ Firefox[12] (You could try the Mac-only Camino,[13] which is based on the same open-source code as Firefox.)

Uploading Files to your Server

So, you've done a bit of homework, and you've settled upon a hosting plan that you can afford and that does everything you need. You've filled out countless forms and received lots of confirmation emails—containing all kinds of gobbledygook—from your hosting service. Let's filter through that to focus on one specific piece of gobbledygook: your FTP details.

FTP Settings

Your host will give you FTP details that look something like those below. This example shows some *fictional* settings for the Bubble Under site (try as you might, entering these details won't get you access to the live files—they're for demonstration purposes only!).

```
Hello Bob Dobalina,

Your FTP account 'bubbleunder' has just been activated, and you
can begin uploading your web site's files to it.

When you have your software and are ready to connect, you will
need to provide it with a few settings: your username, password,
and where you want it to connect to.

        Hostname: ftp.bubbleunder.com
        Username: bobdobalina
        Password: fl1bbertyg1bbet
            Path: /home/bobdobalina
```

The host name, username, and password will always be required, but the path may not be necessary; in fact, it may not even be supplied. Carefully check the instructions provided by your host.

Now that we have these details handy, let's upload some files.

---

[12] http://www.mozilla.com/firefox/
[13] http://www.caminobrowser.org/

Uploading with FileZilla for Windows

You can download numerous free FTP clients for Windows, but one of the most popular is the open source program FileZilla. To download FileZilla, visit the FileZilla home page[14] and click on the Download link to go to the page shown in Figure 8.5. From this page, you can download any past version of FileZilla, or the FileZilla source code, but we're interested only in the setup program. Click the Download link for FileZilla and grab the file named `FileZilla_x_y_z_setup.exe` (where x, y, and z make up the version number).

Figure 8.5. The FileZilla download page

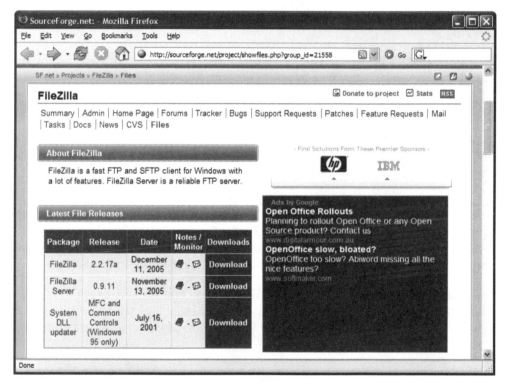

Once you've downloaded this file, run it to install FileZilla. In most cases, the default settings should serve you fine. Once FileZilla has finished installing, start it by selecting Start > All Programs > FileZilla > FileZilla. The FileZilla window shown in Figure 8.6 should appear.

---

[14] http://filezilla.sourceforge.net/

Figure 8.6. FileZilla

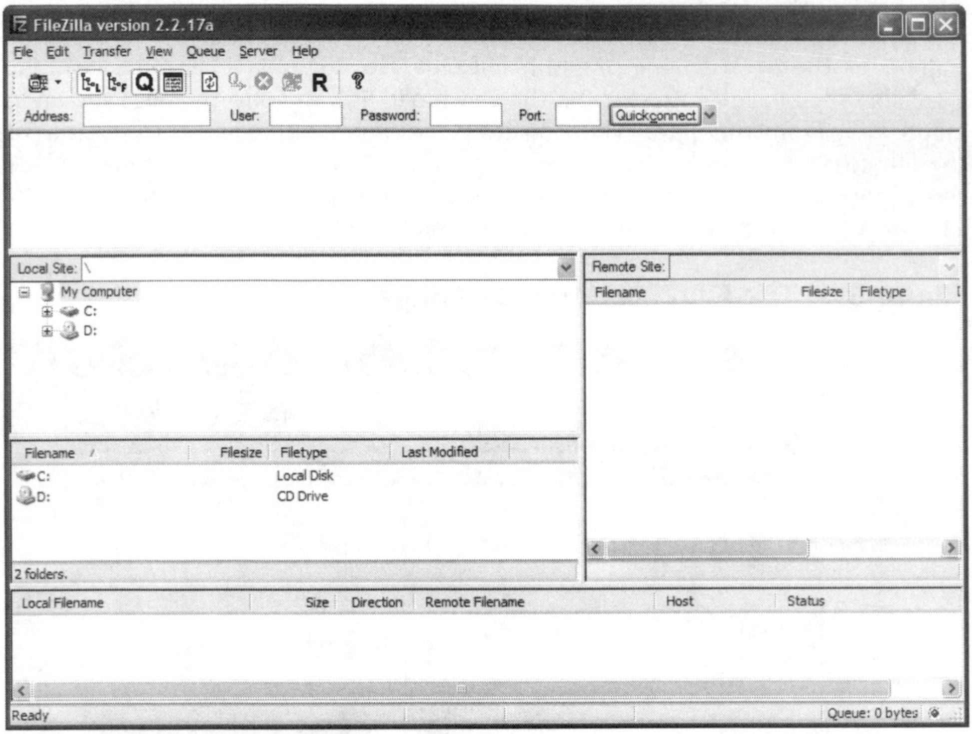

To connect to your FTP server, enter the host name, username, and password into the Address, User, and Password text boxes at the top of the FileZilla window, and click Quickconnect. The Port text box will be filled in automatically.

You should now be connected to your FTP server. The files that reside on your computer will appear on the left-hand side under Local Site; the files on the FTP server will be shown on the right, under Remote Site, as you can see in Figure 8.7.

Figure 8.7. FileZilla, showing local files on the left, and files on the server on the right

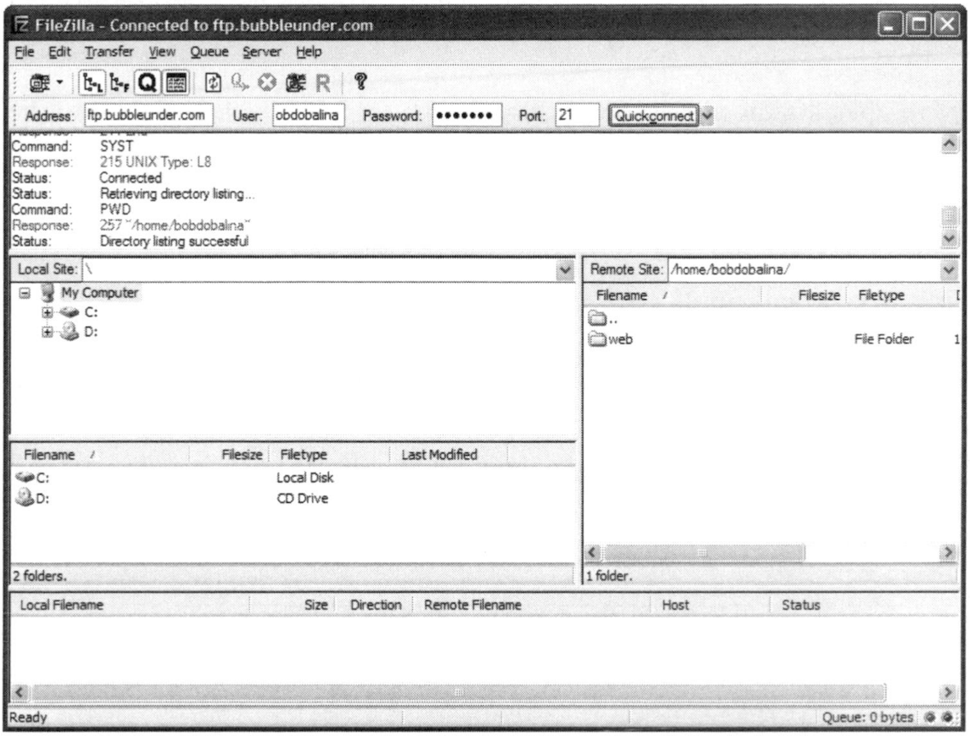

To upload files, you need to follow three steps:

❑ Locate the files that you want to upload using the left-hand pane.

Where's My Documents?

Unfortunately, FileZilla doesn't display the My Documents folder in a location that's easy to find. To get to My Documents in Windows XP, expand the C: icon (click the little plus sign to the left of the icon) to show the folders that are saved on your hard drive. Expand the Documents and Settings folder in the same way, then locate the folder that has your name (our example user would find a folder named Bob Dobalina). Expand that folder, and you'll see My Documents, which will contain the Web folder you created back in Chapter 1.

☐ In the right-hand panel, navigate to the folder on the server to which you want to upload the files. You'll need to refer to the hosting company's instructions to find out where your files need to go, but if you see a folder named `web` or `public_html`, it's a pretty safe bet that your web site files should go there.

☐ To upload a file to the server, click and drag it from the left panel into the right panel, similarly to the way that you would copy files in Windows Explorer. The progress of your upload will be displayed in the bottom of the FileZilla window, as shown in Figure 8.8. Also, you can drag an entire folder across; everything inside the folder will be copied over to the server.

Figure 8.8. FileZilla uploading the backgrounds folder

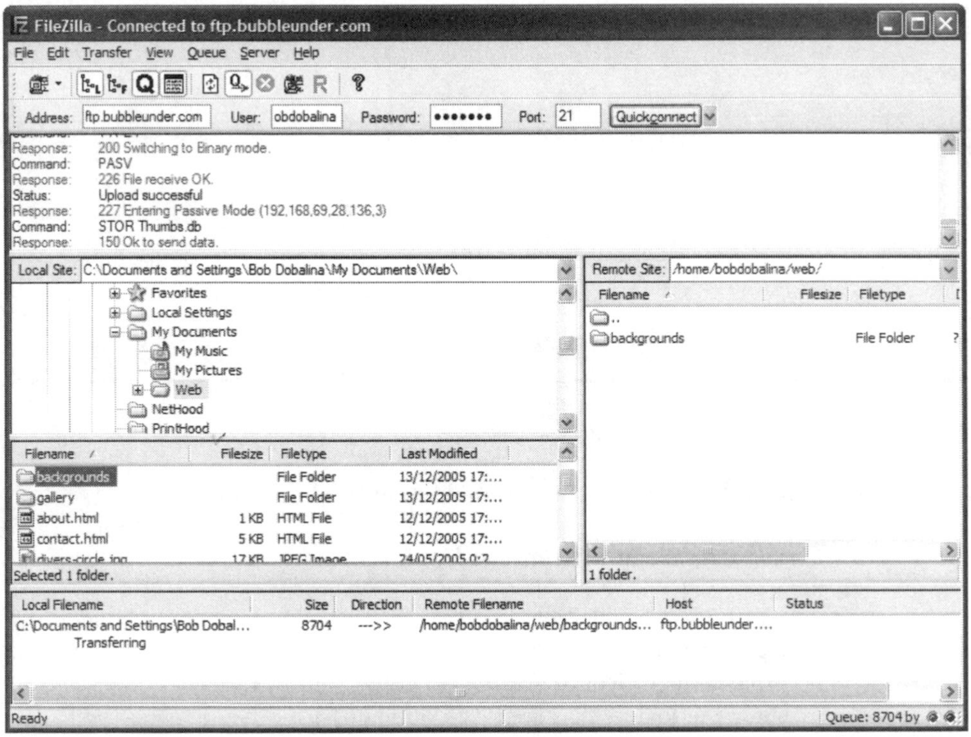

A handy feature of FileZilla is the **Quickconnect recent servers list**. This remembers the usernames and passwords used for the last ten FTP servers you've connected to, so you don't need to re-enter all of those details every time you want to update your web site. To activate this list, simply click the little down-arrow next to the Quickconnect button, and select the appropriate option—in our case, it would be bobdobalina@ftp.bubbleunder.com.

Uploading with Cyberduck—Mac OS X

The Mac platform has fewer freely available FTP clients, but there is one nice tool (with an oh-so-cute icon!) called Cyberduck.[15] Just like FileZilla (assuming you read the previous section, dear Mac user), Cyberduck will remember your login details, but in Cyberduck, you need to create an **FTP bookmark**. Here's how you do it:

❑ When you open Cyberduck, you need to display the bookmarks drawer. Click on the Bookmarks button in the tool bar and it will slide out to the side of the window, as Figure 8.9 illustrates.

Figure 8.9. The Cyberduck Bookmarks drawer

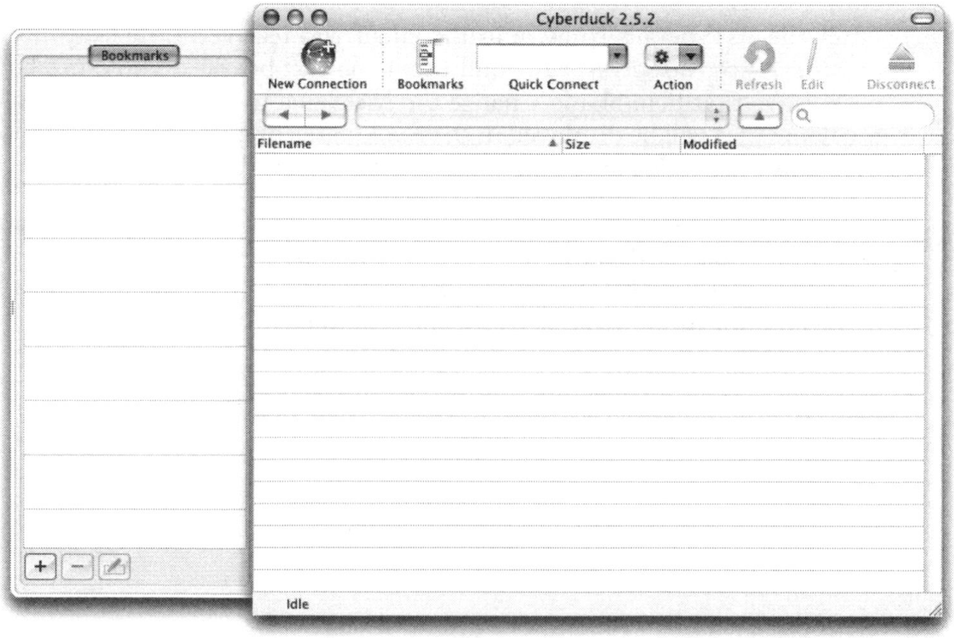

---

[15] http://cyberduck.ch/

❏ Next, add a bookmark. Click on the little + button at the bottom of that drawer, and you'll be presented with the dialog shown in Figure 8.10.

Figure 8.10. FTP Server settings as seen in Cyberduck

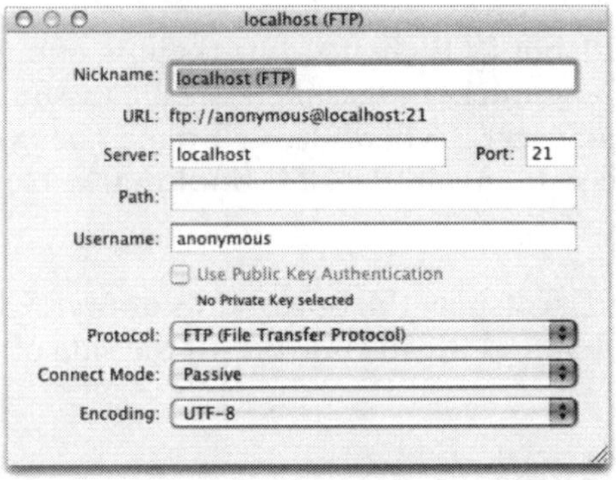

❏ Enter the FTP details (they're in the email you received from your hosting provider) into the Server, Path, and Username text boxes. If you don't have a path, leave that field blank. Change the Nickname to anything you like—it's the name that will be displayed in the Bookmarks drawer. When you've done that, close the dialog and the bookmark will be saved for future use.

❏ To connect to the server, you simply need to double-click on the bookmark. You'll get a message saying Login failed—this is because you have not yet provided a password. Here's your chance to do it (if you want it to be remembered for future reference, tick the Add to Keychain checkbox).

Figure 8.11. Cyberduck's password prompt

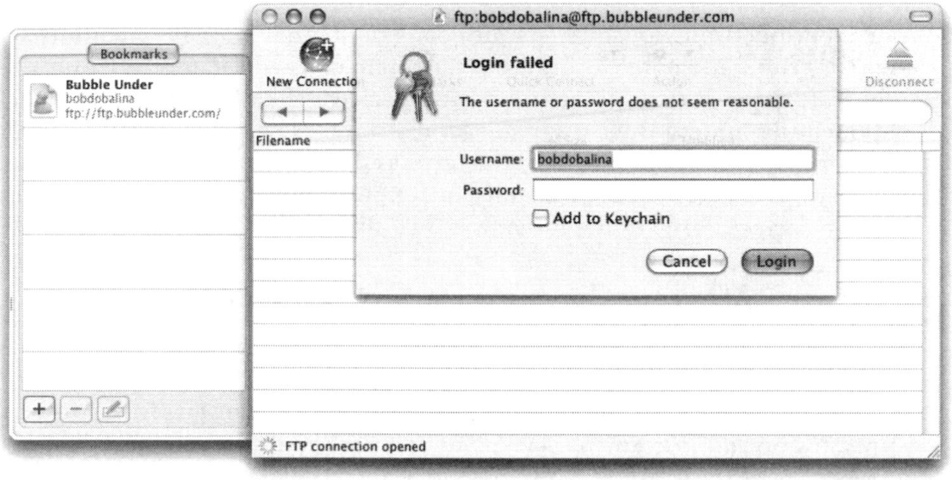

☐ If all the details are correct, you should connect straight through to your server, and the main window of Cyberduck should have changed to display the files and folders stored on the server, as Figure 8.12 shows.

Figure 8.12. Files on the live server, as displayed in Cyberduck

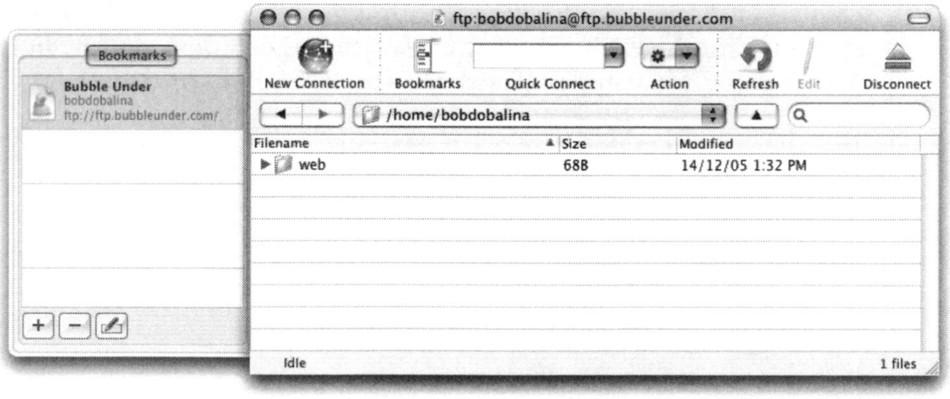

Uploading files to the server is now a simple case of dragging files or folders straight onto the Cyberduck window—if you treat the window above as a special Finder window, you won't go wrong.

Other Uploading Tools

As I mentioned previously, there are loads of standalone FTP clients that you could use (by standalone, I mean that's all their job is—FTP and FTP only). More fully-featured web development software packages like Dreamweaver[16] include FTP facilities among their site management tools. The procedure for uploading files using these services is exactly the same as the process I've outlined here—just make sure you enter the right details, as supplied by your web hosting company, into the correct boxes in the program's FTP dialogs.

Recap—Where's your Site At?

Where's it at? It's on the Internet, that's where! If you've installed and run an FTP client, and uploaded your files, they should now be online for all to see. But your job's not done quite yet—you can't sit back and put your feet up so soon! You need to do just a few more jobs: you must make sure you don't have any broken links, and that your XHTML and CSS are up to scratch.

Checking Links

In our project site, there aren't too many web pages, nor images, to deal with. However, it only takes one careless typing error to break a link between your web pages, or a reference to an image. Many web design and authoring programs include built-in link checkers, but you don't need to go out and buy an expensive piece of software to get this facility. Once again, there are oodles of free link checkers that you can download, or you can use an online service free of charge.

The first choice for checking your web pages is the W3C's Link Checker.[17] Simply enter the address for the web site in the box and press the Check button (I've used one of my personal sites in the example in Figure 8.13).

---

[16] http://www.macromedia.com/software/dreamweaver/
[17] http://validator.w3.org/checklink/

Figure 8.13. The W3C Link Checker service

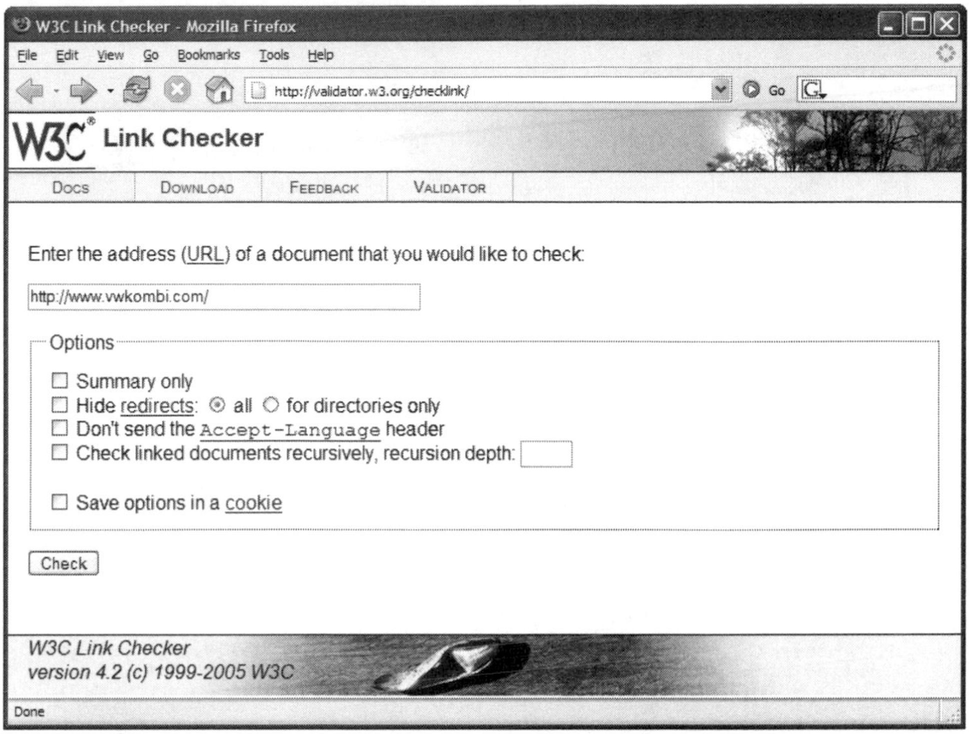

The service will go off and investigate all of your links, and provide you with a report of all the links it found. More importantly, it will tell you about any links that were broken, in a report like the one shown in Figure 8.14.

Figure 8.14. Link checker results for one of my personal sites

Tip — Get a Summary Version

The report may be quite long if you have a lot of web pages, images, style sheets, or other dependencies linked to the page that you submit. In such cases, you might like to check the "Summary" option—then you'll only be told what's broken.

Validating Your Web Pages

Another important step to take before telling the masses to visit your new web site is to **validate** your web pages. This is the process of checking your markup to see if it conforms to the rules of the language that you specified in the Document Type Declaration (otherwise known as the doctype). The Document Type Declaration is the first line of your file's XHTML:

File: **index.html (excerpt)**

```
<!DOCTYPE html PUBLIC "-//W3C//DTD XHTML 1.0 Strict//EN"
    "http://www.w3.org/TR/xhtml1/DTD/xhtml1-strict.dtd">
```

For the project site, we're using XHTML Strict. By validating your site, you're checking that your pages follow the rules of XHTML Strict, and confirming that you haven't made any errors that might cause your page to fail in any given browser. This is important to check, because although a web page may *appear* to be fine to you, if there is an error in the XHTML document, it may not appear correctly for someone using a different browser. Validation gives you a "heads-up"—a warning about anything that might not work in a browser on which you haven't checked your web site.

Another reason why it's very important to validate your XHTML is because the associated CSS is intrinsically linked to it. An error in the XHTML can cause problems with the CSS that can range from the minor—like the wrong link color displaying—to the much more drastic, such as a broken page layout!

How to Validate your Live Web Pages

Again, advanced tools like Dreamweaver have this kind of functionality built-in, but there's always the W3C Markup Validation Service[18] if you don't have access to other tools. As with the link checker, to use this service, simply type into the Address text box the address of the live web page that you want to check, then click the Check button. If you've followed the instructions in this book, you should see a nice message like the one depicted in Figure 8.15.

---

[18] http://validator.w3.org/

Figure 8.15. A pass mark for your markup!

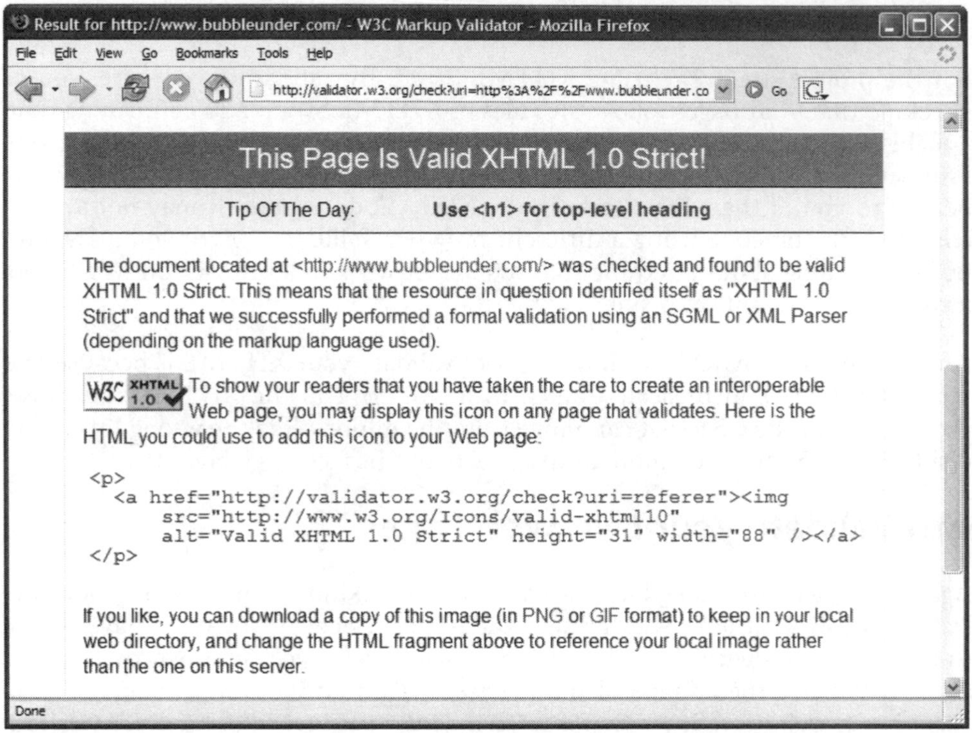

If you aren't seeing this (try scrolling down a little, just in case it's off-screen), your web page probably has errors that need to be fixed. The good news is that the validator will point you in the direction of the problem, telling you what's wrong, and providing some explanation about why it's wrong. A typical validation failure looks like the page shown in Figure 8.16.

Figure 8.16. Highlighting and explaining validation failures

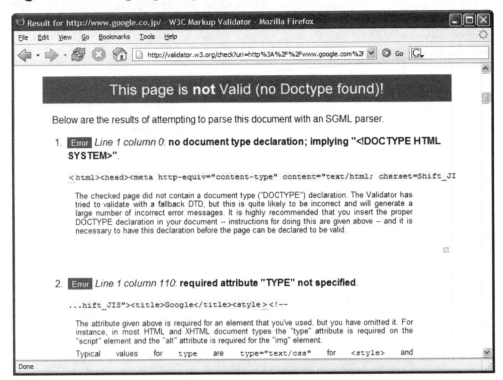

You will need to check more than just one page on your web site, and this is a one-page-at-a-time affair; unfortunately, it's not possible to check an entire site at once using this validator. To ensure that your site is valid, you'll need to validate every page individually.[19]

Validate Everything

Validation is not just about your XHTML—you can (and should) also validate you site's CSS using the W3C's CSS Validator.[20] You can even run an automated test to see if your page is accessible to people with disabilities,[21] although it must be pointed out that no automated test can ever really tell you if your web page is *truly* accessible—it can only point out possible problems. Once again, if you

---

[19] The W3C validator is not the only online tool; the Web Design Group's HTML Validator [http://www.htmlhelp.com/tools/validator/] offers the ability to validate an entire site in one pass.
[20] http://jigsaw.w3.org/css-validator/
[21] The most popular accessibility validator is Cynthia Says [http://www.contentquality.com/].

find that the results you get are too detailed to make sense of (it's a common complaint), try seeking clarification in an online forum. SitePoint's CSS forum[22] members will be able to explain any CSS validation failures; for answers to web accessibility problems, you should register an account at the Accessify Forum[23] and post your question there.

What are all these Errors?

Tip

An automated validation service has no feelings. If you were to ask it, "How's my hair looking?" it wouldn't be tactful. It might bluntly tell you, "Well, it's not right—it's wonky at the back, there are tangles here, here, here, here, here, and *here*, and the color at the back doesn't match the front." Of course, you can't ask that question, but the point is that an automated service of this type won't go easy on you—all errors will be reported in a matter-of-fact way.

Don't let this get you down: it happens to all web designers and programmers. And don't be annoyed with yourself if you don't understand everything you're being told—it really can be a case of information overload.

The trick is to fix the obvious faults—those that you can easily identify—first. Then, when you've uploaded the amended pages, try validating again. You may find that fixing some simple problems also resolves some others that you didn't quite understand. One simple problem is often the cause of many other problems.

If you still can't quite get your web page to pass validation, make your way over to the SitePoint forums, specifically the HTML and XHTML forum,[24] and post your question there. Tell the people you're a "newbie" after some advice, and you should get that more caring, tactful approach that the validator so sorely lacks!

Promoting your Web Site

If you've confirmed that your web pages are using valid XHTML and CSS, you're confident that they're accessible to a wide audience, and you're happy that the pages look good on all the browsers on which you've viewed it, you should start to think about how you're going to promote your web site.

---

[22] http://www.sitepoint.com/launch/cssforum/
[23] http://www.accessifyforum.com/
[24] http://www.sitepoint.com/launch/htmlforum/

Promoting your site can become something of a project in its own right. SitePoint offers kits for those with a bit of marketing budget, including *The Search Engine Marketing Kit*[25] and *The Web Design Business Kit*.[26] As a newcomer to the world of web design, though, these are probably too ambitious for the time being—I mention them merely to make a point that this can be a big topic in its own right (not to give you the big sales pitch!). So, what promotions can you undertake that won't cost you an arm and a leg?

Submit your Web Site to Search Engines

An extremely high percentage of all visitors to my personal web sites find those sites through searches on Google, MSN, and Yahoo! (in that order), and the same will probably be true for your web site. However, a search engine will not know that your web site is there unless either:

❑ there is a link to your web site from another web site that the search engine knows about (this is how search engines "crawl the web"—by finding links in pages that it knows about, and adding these pages to its database of pages)

❑ you fill in a form on the search engine to instruct it to visit and index the content of your web site; Google,[27] MSN,[28] and Yahoo![29] offer such pages

Another good place to get started is the Open Directory Project,[30] which aims to become a comprehensive directory of the Internet. This site is structured hierarchically, so you'll need to work out where your site fits in the hierarchy before you submit it.

These are just a few tips to get you started. For further advice about search engine submissions, pay a visit to SitePoint's Promotion Techniques forum.[31]

Cleaner Markup, Better Search Results

It's worth noting that by writing web pages that conform to standards, and are lightweight and accessible, you almost always improve your chances of getting good search engine results. Without going into too much detail, the search engines find it easier to retrieve search terms from a well-structured

---

[25] http://www.sitepoint.com/books/sem1/
[26] http://www.sitepoint.com/books/freelance1/
[27] http://www.google.com/addurl/
[28] http://search.msn.com/docs/submit.aspx
[29] http://search.yahoo.com/info/submit.html
[30] http://dmoz.org/add.html
[31] http://www.sitepoint.com/launch/promoforum/

and simple web page than from a non-standards-compliant web page. You can learn more about how and why this is the case from the forum mentioned above.

Tell your Friends and Colleagues

Well, it seems like an obvious idea, but it's worth mentioning. Your friends and colleagues could be your biggest fans (even if they've never seen your web site!), and if you give them your web site address on a handy-to-keep piece of card or something similar, you never know how many times they might visit, or who they might mention it to further down the line.

Craft an Email Signature with your Web Site Details

Consider creating a default signature that is applied to every email message that you compose. It's a simple marketing technique that's basically a no-brainer. Something simple at the end of each email you send, as shown below, can generate a surprising number of visits to your web site.

```
Hi Dad,

What time should we should expect you for dinner on Tuesday? Also,
have you had a chance to check out the new web site? Pretty
spiffy, eh?

--
Bob Dobalina
President of Bubble Under -- the diving club for the south-west UK
Visit our web site at http://www.bubbleunder.com/
```

Once you've added it to your signature, you don't need to update it, and there's no maintenance overhead—every message you send could attract a new visitor to your web site!

Post on a Related Forum

Similarly to the way you can add a signature to an email, you can usually add a signature to posts you make in discussion forums that are related to the topic of your web site. The advantage of this is that the other people lurking on, posting to, and reading the messages on that forum will be interested in the same thing.

So, rather than the signature being a hit-and-miss affair, suddenly your signature (which could even include a clickable link to your web site) is being presented to people who will be most inclined to take a look.

Of course, this means that you'll need to start getting a little more prolific with your posting on such sites, but that shouldn't be a great hardship if it's a topic that's of interest to you.

Link Exchange

Finally, I'd recommend that you look into swapping links with similar web sites. It is not considered good etiquette to email someone and say, "Hey, can you link to my web site—it's really good!" However, if you have already included a link to someone else's web site, and you approach them on the basis that you've already linked to them and ask them nicely if they would they be willing to link back, you're likely to have more luck.

Link exchange programs that automate the process are available, but I don't recommend you use them. You cannot be sure of the quality of links that will appear automatically on your web site, nor the quality of sites that link to you, through these services. Also, link exchange programs often require you to display ugly banner ads or badges that can make your web site look unprofessional. It's better to remain a little choosy and stay in control of your site.

Summary

In this chapter, we've focused on the process of getting your web site files online, from the initial choices you'll need to make about where to host your web site, to the nuts and bolts of getting your files up on to the live server. I've explained how you can use free online services to check whether your web pages are in good shape, and suggested some ways that you can begin to promote your new online venture.

It may have been fun building your site. Perhaps at times you've found things difficult, yet you've battled on and seen your way through to the end result. But is this the end of your web site's development? Probably not—shortly after making your files live, you'll no doubt think of new things you'd like to add. There are only so many hours in the day, though—how can you continually add new content to your web site without it getting in the way of all the other things you have to juggle in your busy schedule?

One way of ensuring fresh content is to add a **weblog** (or just **blog**) to your site. In the next chapter, I'll explain what a blog is, what it can do for your web site, and how you can set one up and continue to manage it. Let's find out about blogging!

9

Adding a Blog to your Web Site

Building web sites is something from which many of us get a lot of enjoyment, just as some people enjoy knitting sweaters or carving sculptures from old tree trunks. So updating our web site may not be viewed as a "chore"—rather, it may actually be good fun. However, if you update the content regularly, you'll almost certainly need to go back to the files on your computer, alter them, and upload them using FTP each and every time you want to make a change. In short, content updates require you to have everything there at the ready, which is perhaps a little complicated if all you want to do is make some simple text changes.

For instance, what happens if you feel like updating the web site when you're on holiday? This could well be the case with our diving project site—you might want to make a report on a dive trip while the events are still fresh in your mind. Even if you have your project files set up on a laptop, will you actually be able to get it connected at a local Internet café? What if you're always updating the web site yourself, yet as part of a committee, you think that the other members should do their share? Can you really let them come to your house and amend the web site on your computer every time there's an update to post? Definitely not!

The solution to these problems is to add a **blog** to your site. Hang on, though! What exactly is a blog?

note

What is a Blog?

Blogs started off life being known as **weblog**s—a concatenation of the words "web" and "log." As the name implies, they started off as online logs or diaries that individuals published on the Web. These days, though, it's increasingly common to find pages on business and other organizations' web sites that could readily be described as blogs.

Blogs often feature a comments facility that permits two-way communication between bloggers (those who post to blogs) and their readers—and among the readers themselves—which is often one of the main reasons why organizations introduce blogs rather than publishing static web pages: suddenly, a faceless organization gets a personality!

A key feature of blogs is that typically they allow bloggers to log into a central location, from anywhere in the world—you don't need to manage the web site from your own computer. This is what makes blogging so accessible to people who, in the past, might not have been able to publish a web site.

A word of caution: although the word "blog" is becoming more prevalent, there are still a lot of people who have never heard the term before, so you might need to explain yourself when discussing the topic with others.

Where to Get a Blog

There are numerous services that you can use to set up and manage a blog. Each has its advantages and disadvantages, the fine details of which I won't go into here. Suffice to say that if you are looking to set up a blog as quickly and painlessly as possible, any one of the following services would be suitable:

Blogger[1]

This was one of the first services to appear, and is the one that truly popularized the whole blogging format. Blogger is easy to set up and can be configured to integrate closely with your web site's look and feel. This is the service I'll be using in this chapter as we add a blog to our project site.

LiveJournal[2]

Another service that's been around a while (since 1999), LiveJournal was set up by Brad

---

[1] http://www.blogger.com/
[2] http://www.livejournal.com/

Fitzpatrick as a way of keeping high school friends up-to-date with activities, but is now a fully-featured blogging service.

MSN Spaces[3]

A relative newcomer to the scene (MSN Spaces launched late in 2004), this is Microsoft's offering to the world of free blogging tools.

Self-hosted Blogging Services

note

In addition to the blogging services above, there are several tools that you can set up on your own web site—that is, you host all the "mechanics" of the blog yourself (which would include a control panel of some kind, as well as a database). The advantage of this option is that you can tweak a self-hosted system more to your own liking, to make it work specifically for you. However, the downside is that with a self-hosted service, you must do all the hard work of setting the system up; also, the correct functioning of your blog relies on your web host being able to support certain technologies (which are different for each system). If you feel confident enough to try such a system out, here are a few worth investigating:

Movable Type[4]

An erstwhile favorite amongst the blogging community, Movable Type is a very powerful tool that also supports a range of **plug-ins** (these are little pieces of code that extend the functionality of the system).

WordPress[5]

WordPress mightn't have been around as long as some other services, but it, too, boasts plug-in support and a simple user interface. It also provides a great deal of flexibility around the management and publication of content.

Textpattern[6]

Like the others mentioned here, Textpattern offers plug-in support, but it goes one step further in that it allows you to create multiple templates for the same site. It's a great service for team environments and

---

[3] http://spaces.msn.com/
[4] http://www.movabletype.org/
[5] http://www.wordpress.org/
[6] http://textpattern.com/

lets users customize blogs extensively to
suit their web sites.

For reasons of simplicity and speed, in this chapter I'm going to show you how
to set up an account and start publishing with Blogger. I've chosen Blogger over
the others for a couple of reasons. Firstly, it's the one with which I'm most familiar (I'll hold my hands up and admit to that—it's probably best that I write based
on experience!). The second reason is that Blogger is a service that's fairly simple
to use, yet offers some great customization options for those who want to dig
below the surface.

By the end of this chapter, you'll have set up a system that will allow you easily
to write and publish new content on your home page, making it look something
like this:

Figure 9.1. The finished result: a blog on the home page

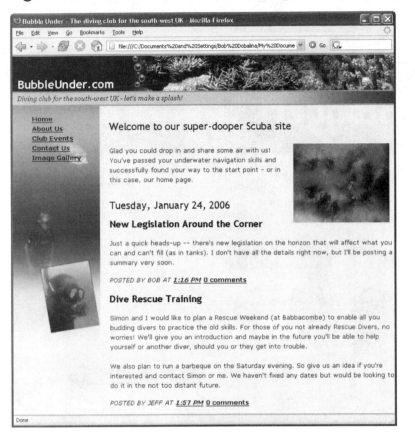

Signing up for Blogger

Settingup a blog on your web site won't take long at all. And the time you have to take at the beginning of the process will easily be offset by the simplicity and speed of publishing content to your web site in the future. To get started with Blogger, head over to Blogger's home page[7] and look for the CREATE YOUR BLOG NOW link as shown in Figure 9.2.

---

[7] http://www.blogger.com/

Figure 9.2. Blogger's home page (at January 2006)

On the next page, you'll be asked for a username, password, email address, and a "display name," which will appear as the blog author's name. You'll also be asked to accept Blogger's terms of service. Complete this form, as illustrated in Figure 9.3, then click CONTINUE.

Figure 9.3. Complete username and password details first

Create an **account**		
Choose a user name	bobdobalina	You will use this to sign in for future visits.
Enter a password	********	Must be at least 6 characters long.
Retype password	********	Enter it again just to be sure.
Display name	Bob Dobalina	The name used to sign your blog posts.
Email address	bob@bubbleunder.com	We will never share your address with third parties without your permission.
Acceptance of Terms	☑ I accept the **Terms of Service**	Indicate that you have read and understand Blogger's Terms of Service

CONTINUE

The next page, Name Your Blog, provides the simplest possible setup procedure for your blog. It assumes that Blogger will provide the hosting for your blog (using an address like `http://bubbleunder.blogspot.com/`). We're going to skip this easy setup procedure and go for the more advanced setup options, so click the Advanced Blog Setup link.

Easy vs Advanced Setup

Most users who sign up for Blogger avoid the Advanced Setup options, but just what is the difference between a simple and an advanced setup?

Using the simple method (the one that Blogger normally guides you toward), you can quickly create a blog that looks the part, and to which you can post quickly and easily. There's very little configuration for you to do, as Blogger does it all for you. The procedure is made simpler by the fact that Blogger publishes your blog pages to its own servers—all you need to do is choose your address in the format *yourname*.blogspot.com. Any files hosted by Blogger will have this blogspot.com address.

In the advanced setup procedure, you're given a choice about where you want to host your blog. Instead of publishing to Blogger's own servers, you can ask it to publish to your own server—a great solution if you want to be in total control of the presentation of your blog.

Note that most people who sign up for Blogger don't choose the advanced route (it's no coincidence that Blogger doesn't promote that route very obviously to new users!). However, I'm guiding you down that path so that you can integrate your blog right into your home page, giving it a much more professional look.

The advanced setup page, shown in Figure 9.4, asks you for more information about the location to which you want to have your blog published. Many of these details you'll already know from the stage when you set up your FTP service to upload your files to your web site.

Figure 9.4. The advanced setup page

This is the information that you'll need:

Blog Title   The title can be anything you like. We'll call ours the "Bubble Under Blog."

Listing	Blogger automatically creates a list of recently updated blogs, which appears on the Blogger home page. If you choose Listed, your blog will appear on that list. Well, why not? It gives you a little extra exposure, and another avenue through which your web site might be discovered.
FTP Server	Use the address that you used in Chapter 8, for example: ftp.bubbleunder.com.
FTP/SFTP	Here, specify whether your host supports Secure FTP (SFTP). Unless your host has specified otherwise, select FTP here.
FTP Path	Once again, refer to the settings that you used in the last chapter to fill in this item. For the Bubble Under web site, I've used the path of web.
Blog Filename	You need to choose a file to which you want Blogger to save your blog. Since we're going to get Blogger to save the blog to the Bubble Under home page, we'll enter index.html here.
Blog URL	Enter the address of the blog page. On the project site, the blog is going to be on our home page, so I've entered our home page's address.
Word Verification	In this final step, enter the characters that appear in the image. This option is here to deter automated spam-bots from abusing the Blogger service.

When you've entered all the details above, click Continue. Unless you've mistyped or left any items on this page blank (I always seem to mess up on the word verification part!), you should be presented with the "Choose a Template" page depicted in Figure 9.5.

The templates here are actually very good, and were designed by people who really know their stuff. However, we're not really very interested in these designs, as good as they are, because we're going to change the template later to fit in with the look and feel of the rest of our site. By all means, investigate to see what's on offer, but don't get hung up on these choices. I chose Minima, but only because it was the first template in the list. Follow the CONTINUE link.

Figure 9.5. Choose any template; we'll be changing it later on to fit the Bubble Under look and feel

All things being well, you should receive notification like that shown in Figure 9.6, to tell you that your blog is being created.

Figure 9.6. An encouraging sign

The service is actually uploading to your server the various files that you'll need for your blog (images, CSS, and so on). You'll get another message, like the one shown in Figure 9.7, once the process has finished.

Figure 9.7. A blog is born—yours!

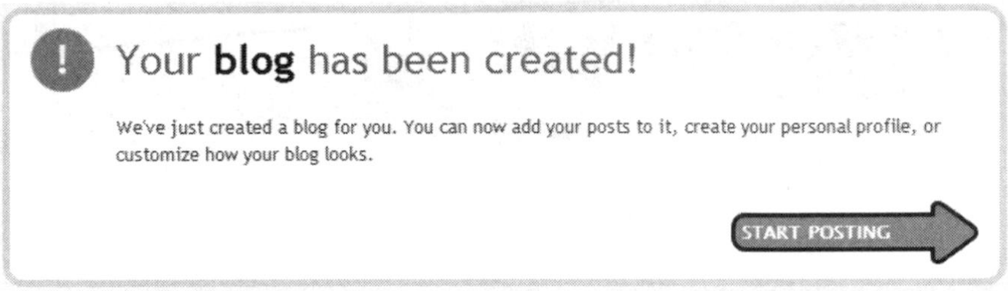

Follow the link that says START POSTING, and we'll create a first test post for your blog. On the next page, enter something simple in both the title and the body of your post, as illustrated in Figure 9.8, then click the Publish Post button.

Figure 9.8. Typing something simple for your first post—it's only a test

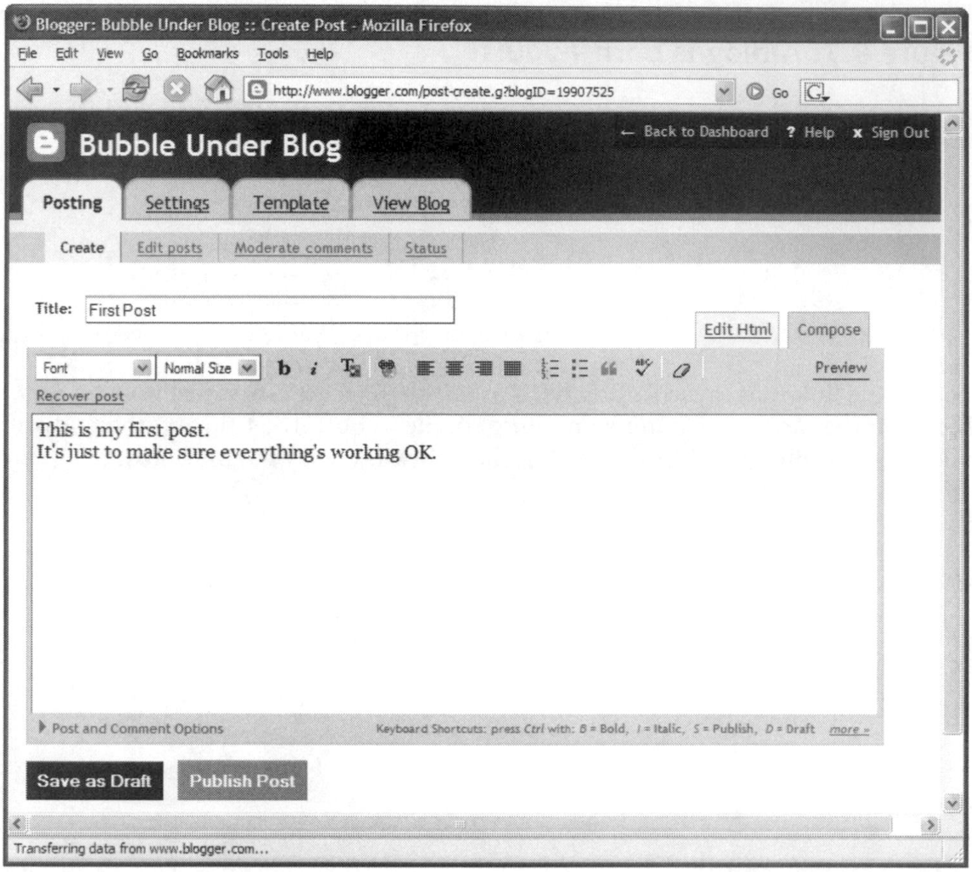

Next, you'll be asked for your FTP login details, as Figure 9.9 shows. Once again, refer to the settings you used when setting up FTP in the last chapter.

Figure 9.9. Blogger asking for FTP login details

Please Sign In To Your FTP Server

Username

bobdobalina

Password

****

Login

Enter the login details for your host's FTP server, then click the Login button. Blogger will remember these details for future reference—you don't need to enter this information every time you publish a post.

This is the point where the magic happens! You should now have notification, like that shown in Figure 9.10, to say that your blog entry was published successfully.

Figure 9.10. Success! The blog entry published with no errors

Your blog published successfully. (Details ...)

Files published... **100%**

View Blog (in a new window)

Republish Index Only   Republish Entire Blog   ⊙

Having Trouble Publishing?

Tip

You may find that your host only allows one FTP connection to your server at a time. If you have trouble publishing your blog, try closing your FTP program (FileZilla or Cyberduck) if it's still open.

You should see a link that reads, View Blog. Try it out. Can you see a page like Figure 9.11? And is it at the right location?

Figure 9.11. The blog created successfully, with a post showing

The blog created successfully, with a post showing — browser window titled "Bubble Under Blog - Mozilla Firefox" at http://www.bubbleunder.com/index.html

> # BUBBLE UNDER BLOG
>
> THURSDAY, DECEMBER 15, 2005
>
> First Post
>
> This is my first post.
> It's just to make sure everything's working OK.
>
> POSTED BY BUBBLE UNDER BLOG AT 4:12 PM   0 COMMENTS
>
> ABOUT ME
>
> BUBBLE UNDER BLOG
> VIEW MY COMPLETE PROFILE
>
> LINKS
>
> Google News
> Edit-Me
> Edit-Me
>
> PREVIOUS POSTS
>
> First Post
>
> ARCHIVES

IMPORTANT

Don't Panic!

At this point, you may be worrying where your homepage has gone. Your choosing to publish the blog to the same location as your homepage has allowed Blogger to overwrite your homepage file. But, like the title of this note says, there's no need to panic—you still have the local copy (the one stored on your hard drive). What we've done here is confirm that the process or publishing from Blogger to your web hosting service is working properly. The fact that it looks so different from the rest of your web site is not a problem—this is just a temporary stage in the process.

How Blogger Creates a Web Page

For many people, this is where the process of creating a blog ends. The off-the-shelf designs are fine—they do the job, and look pretty. But, as I mentioned before, you and I will take things a step further. You now have in place the basic mechanics for publishing blog entries to your site. Next, I'm going to show you how to customize the Blogger template so that it fits perfectly with your web site.

At this point, it's worth taking a step back to learn exactly how Blogger is able to publish your web pages. The basic process, illustrated in Figure 9.12, is this:

❑ Take a base document written in good old XHTML.

❑ Introduce a set of Blogger-specific tags. Some of these look like XHTML elements (for example, there's a `<BlogItemTitle>` opening tag and a `</BlogItemTitle>` closing tag), but other Blogger tags look nothing like XHTML (`<<$BlogItemTitle$>>`, for example). These tags are *not* XHTML, and they're meaningless to the browser, but they are applied in the template that Blogger uses.

❑ Save the document as a template in Blogger.

❑ When you save or publish your post on the Blogger web site, it's saved to Blogger's database. If you save the post (by clicking on the Save as Draft button), it won't be displayed to the public.

❑ When you publish a post, Blogger takes your template, finds the Blogger-specific tags, and replaces them with the related entry for that page in the database. The end result is a complete web page in which all of the Blogger-specific tags have been replaced.

❑ Blogger then sends this new XHTML page to your web server (using the details that you provided during the sign-up procedure).

Figure 9.12. How Blogger creates a web page

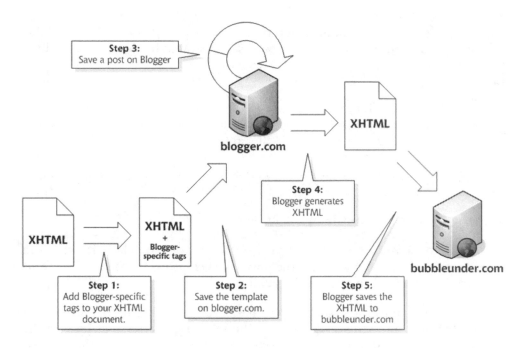

We're going to see how this works in practice with the project web site now. The first thing you need to do is write your Blogger template.

Writing a Blogger Template

The wonderful thing about publishing systems such as Blogger is that they can give you a considerable amount of freedom to customize the display of your content. If you're familiar with blogs, you may have noticed that some blogs have comments, while others don't. Those that do may display the comments directly beneath the post, or they might display comments in a side panel of some kind. However, if you want to customize your blog to such a level, you'll have to get your hands dirty, so to speak, with those Blogger template tags we touched on earlier. This can be quite a confusing task for a newcomer to blogging, so my advice is simple: just take one of the existing Blogger templates, note the parts that contain the Blogger-specific tags, and leave them as they are for the time being. We'll do a little tweaking now, just to build a bit of confidence, but you're encouraged to go ahead and fiddle around with your Blogger template to your heart's content. If you mess things up, you can always reset the original template and start again.

To get to one of these Blogger templates, sign on to Blogger from the home page by filling in the Username and Password text boxes (this assumes that you've signed off between setting up the account and this point; otherwise, select the Back to Dashboard link). Figure 9.13 shows this step.

Figure 9.13. The Blogger sign-in box

When you get to the Dashboard, select the Change Settings icon (a little cogwheel), which you can see in Figure 9.14.

Figure 9.14. Changing the settings of your blog

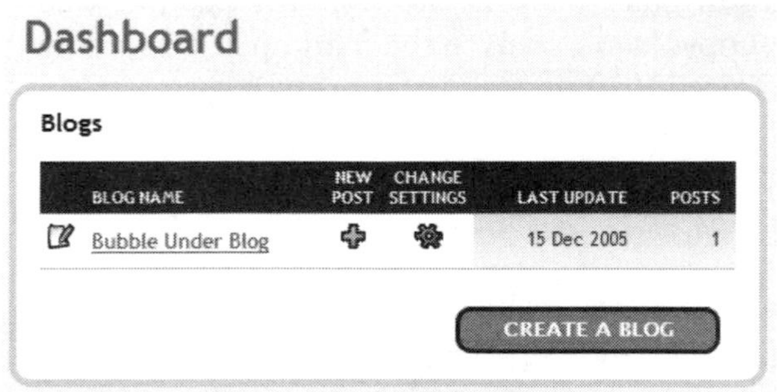

351

Figure 9.15. The markup for your template is in the large text area

On the next page, click on the Template tab. You'll be presented with the template editor shown in Figure 9.15. Here you can see the markup for the Minima template, including the Blogger-specific tags that instruct Blogger how to use the template. Note that the indenting of the markup is a little haphazard, but this doesn't affect the display on the screen—we indent our markup only so that it's easier for humans to read.

On the Blogger template page, select all of the markup that begins with a `<Blogger>` tag and ends with a `</Blogger>` tag, as shown in the example below, and copy it by selecting Edit > Copy. Don't analyze the markup at all—it might make your head hurt! We don't need to understand all of the Blogger tags now; we just need to copy them.

File: **Markup for the Blogger Minima Template (excerpt)**

```
<Blogger>

  <BlogDateHeader>
 <h2 class="date-header"><$BlogDateHeaderDate$></h2>
 </BlogDateHeader>
```

```
<!-- Begin .post -->
<div class="post"><a name="<$BlogItemNumber$>"></a>
      <BlogItemTitle>
  <h3 class="post-title">
<BlogItemUrl><a href="<$BlogItemUrl$>" title="external
    link"></BlogItemUrl>
<$BlogItemTitle$>
<BlogItemUrl></a></BlogItemUrl>
  </h3>
  </BlogItemTitle>

        <div class="post-body">
<div>
    <$BlogItemBody$>
  </div>
  </div>

  <p class="post-footer">
    <em>posted by <$BlogItemAuthorNickname$> at <a
        href="<$BlogItemPermalinkUrl$>" title="permanent
        link"><$BlogItemDateTime$></a></em>
    <MainOrArchivePage><BlogItemCommentsEnabled>

    <a class="comment-link" href="<$BlogItemCommentCreate$>"<$B
logItemCommentFormOnclick$>><$BlogItemCommentCount$> comments</a>

    </BlogItemCommentsEnabled><BlogItemBacklinksEnabled>
<a class="comment-link" href="<$BlogItemPermalinkUrl$>#links"
   >links to this post</a>
</BlogItemBacklinksEnabled>
</MainOrArchivePage>  <$BlogItemControl$>
  </p>

</div>
<!-- End .post -->


<!-- Begin #comments -->
<ItemPage>
<div id="comments">

<BlogItemCommentsEnabled><a name="comments"></a>
      <h4><$BlogItemCommentCount$> Comments:</h4>
```

```
      <dl id="comments-block">
    <BlogItemComments>
    <dt class="comment-poster" id="c<$BlogCommentNumber$>"><a
name="c<$BlogCommentNumber$>"></a>
      <$BlogCommentAuthor$> said...
    </dt>
    <dd class="comment-body">

      <p><$BlogCommentBody$></p>
    </dd>
    <dd class="comment-timestamp"><a href="#<$BlogCommentNumber$
>" title="comment permalink"><$BlogCommentDateTime$></a>
  <$BlogCommentDeleteIcon$>
  </dd>
    </BlogItemComments>
  </dl>
 <p class="comment-timestamp">

  <$BlogItemCreate$>
  </p>
  </BlogItemCommentsEnabled>
  <BlogItemBacklinksEnabled>
  <a name="links"></a><h4>Links to this post:</h4>
  <dl id="comments-block">
  <BlogItemBacklinks>
    <dt class="comment-title">
    <$BlogBacklinkControl$>
    <a href="<$BlogBacklinkURL$>" rel="nofollow"><$BlogBacklin
kTitle$></a> <$BlogBacklinkDeleteIcon$>
    </dt>
    <dd class="comment-body"><$BlogBacklinkSnippet$>
    <br />
    <span class="comment-poster">
    <em>posted by <$BlogBacklinkAuthor$> @ <$BlogBacklinkDateT
ime$></em>
    </span>
    </dd>
  </BlogItemBacklinks>
  </dl>
  <p class="comment-timestamp"><$BlogItemBacklinkCreate$></p>
  </BlogItemBacklinksEnabled>

 <p class="comment-timestamp">
 <a href="<$BlogURL$>">&lt;&lt; Home</a>
  </p>
```

```
      </div>

</ItemPage>

  <!-- End #comments -->

</Blogger>
```

Merging the Blogger Code with your Existing Web Page

What we need to do is take the markup above and insert it into a sensible location in one of our existing pages. Below is the current homepage of the Bubble Under web site—I've marked the place where the Blogger template tags need to go (see the comment in bold type):

File: **index.html** (excerpt)

```
<body>
  <div id="header">
    <div id="sitebranding">
      <h1>BubbleUnder.com</h1>
    </div>
    <div id="tagline">
      <p>Diving club for the south-west UK - let's make a
         splash!</p>
    </div>
  </div> <!-- end of header div -->
  <div id="navigation">
    <ul>
      <li><a href="index.html">Home</a></li>
      <li><a href="about.html">About Us</a></li>
      <li><a href="events.html">Club Events</a></li>
      <li><a href="contact.html">Contact Us</a></li>
      <li><a href="gallery.html">Image Gallery</a></li>
    </ul>
  </div> <!-- end of navigation div -->
  <div id="bodycontent">
    <h2>Welcome to our super-dooper Scuba site</h2>
    <p><img src="divers-circle.jpg" alt="A circle of divers
         practice their skills" width="200" height="162" /></p>
    <p>Glad you could drop in and share some air with us! You've
         passed your underwater navigation skills and successfully
         found your way to the start point - or in this case, our
         home page.</p>
```

```
    <!-- Insert Blogger code template tags here -->
  </div> <!-- end of bodycontent div -->
</body>
```

Open `index.html`, and just prior to end of the bodycontent `div`, paste the Blogger template markup by selecting Edit > Paste. Here's the page once the Blogger markup is inserted (I've formatted the Blogger markup so it's easier to identify):

File: **index.html** (excerpt)

```
<div id="bodycontent">
  <h2>Welcome to our super-dooper Scuba site</h2>
  <p><img src="divers-circle.jpg" alt="A circle of divers practice
      their skills" width="200" height="162" /></p>
  <p>Glad you could drop in and share some air with us! You've
      passed your underwater navigation skills and successfully
      found your way to the start point - or in this case, our
      home page.</p>
  <Blogger>
    <BlogDateHeader>
      <h2 class="date-header"><$BlogDateHeaderDate$></h2>
    </BlogDateHeader>
    <!-- Begin .post -->
    <div class="post">
      <a name="<$BlogItemNumber$>"></a>
      <BlogItemTitle>
        <h3 class="post-title">
          <BlogItemUrl><a href="<$BlogItemUrl$>"
              title="external link"></BlogItemUrl>
            <$BlogItemTitle$>
          <BlogItemUrl></a></BlogItemUrl>
        </h3>
      </BlogItemTitle>
      <div class="post-body">
        <div>
          <$BlogItemBody$>
        </div>
      </div>
      <p class="post-footer">
        <em>posted by <$BlogItemAuthorNickname$> at
            <a href="<$BlogItemPermalinkUrl$>"
            title="permanent link"><$BlogItemDateTime$></a></em>
        <MainOrArchivePage>
          <BlogItemCommentsEnabled>
            <a class="comment-link"
                href="<$BlogItemCommentCreate$>"
```

```
                    <$BlogItemCommentFormOnclick$>>
                    <$BlogItemCommentCount$> comments</a>
          </BlogItemCommentsEnabled>
          <BlogItemBacklinksEnabled>
            <a class="comment-link"
                href="<$BlogItemPermalinkUrl$>#links">links to
                    this post</a>
          </BlogItemBacklinksEnabled>
        </MainOrArchivePage>
        <$BlogItemControl$>
    </p>
</div>
<!-- End .post -->
<!-- Begin #comments -->
<ItemPage>
    <div id="comments">
      <BlogItemCommentsEnabled>
        <a name="comments"></a>
        <h4><$BlogItemCommentCount$> Comments:</h4>
        <dl id="comments-block">
          <BlogItemComments>
            <dt class="comment-poster"
                id="c<$BlogCommentNumber$>">
                <a name="c<$BlogCommentNumber$>"></a>
              <$BlogCommentAuthor$> said...
            </dt>
            <dd class="comment-body">
              <p><$BlogCommentBody$></p>
            </dd>
            <dd class="comment-timestamp">
              <a href="#<$BlogCommentNumber$>"
                  title="comment permalink">
                  <$BlogCommentDateTime$></a>
              <$BlogCommentDeleteIcon$>
            </dd>
          </BlogItemComments>
        </dl>
        <p class="comment-timestamp">
          <$BlogItemCreate$>
        </p>
      </BlogItemCommentsEnabled>
      <BlogItemBacklinksEnabled>
        <a name="links"></a>
        <h4>Links to this post:</h4>
        <dl id="comments-block">
          <BlogItemBacklinks>
```

```
            <dt class="comment-title">
              <$BlogBacklinkControl$>
              <a href="<$BlogBacklinkURL$>" rel="nofollow">
                  <$BlogBacklinkTitle$></a>
              <$BlogBacklinkDeleteIcon$>
            </dt>
            <dd class="comment-body"><$BlogBacklinkSnippet$>
              <br />
              <span class="comment-poster"><em>posted by
                  <$BlogBacklinkAuthor$> @
                  <$BlogBacklinkDateTime$></em></span>
            </dd>
          </BlogItemBacklinks>
        </dl>
        <p class="comment-timestamp"><$BlogItemBacklinkCreate$>
            </p>
      </BlogItemBacklinksEnabled>
      <p class="comment-timestamp">
        <a href="<$BlogURL$>">&lt;&lt; Home</a>
      </p>
    </div>
  </ItemPage>
  <!-- End #comments -->
</Blogger>
</div> <!-- end of bodycontent div -->
```

If you were to save these changes and open index.html in your browser now, it would look a bit of a mess (as you can see in Figure 9.16). It's still full of strange Blogger tags, and the browser's not too sure what to do with them. What we need to do is get this page back into Blogger, so that it can make sense of those tags. Then we can give the browser something that it will understand.

Figure 9.16. Bubble Under is a bit of a mess at the moment

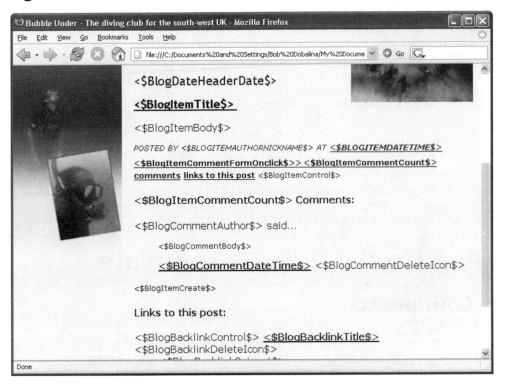

In Blogger's template editor, delete all of the text from the template (most browsers will have an Edit > Select All function; select this menu item and hit the **Delete** key to get rid of the existing template). Now, paste in the contents of `index.html`, and then hit the Save Template Changes button.

The next page will tell you that your changes have been saved, and that you'll need to republish the blog in order for them to take effect. Click the Republish button on this page and Blogger will once again upload the necessary files to your web server. Assuming that there were no errors in the publishing process, you should get a confirmation page like the one in Figure 9.17, which includes a View Blog link.

Figure 9.17. The Blogger confirmation page

Excellent! You've successfully set up a blog on your web site. Now, updating the content on that home page is going to be easy—there's no need to lug a laptop around with you, and no restrictions about using your desktop PC at home to make updates. As long as you're connected to the Internet, you can head over to Blogger, sign in, and update your site. However, we do have a couple more things to look at before we break out the champagne.

Tidying Up the Blogger Template

Blog Comments

Getting people to comment on your blog is easy. All they need to do is follow the link that says "0 comments." This will take them to the Blogger web site, as shown in Figure 9.18, where anyone can leave a comment on your blog. Follow that link, add a comment, and you'll see the number of comments on your post increase by one.

Tip

Anonymous Comments

To make a comment on your blog, your site visitors will need to sign up as users on the Blogger web site. You can allow anonymous comments, but that will leave you open to **comment spam**, a terribly annoying version of email spam in which spammers will leave comments on your blog exalting the benefits of online poker, cheap pharmaceuticals, and bargain stocks. I'd recommend that you choose not to allow anonymous comments, lest your web site should become flooded with junk.

Figure 9.18. The Blogger comment form

In the background, Blogger will republish your home page so the number of comments stays up to date.

Viewing Comments

Blogger also publishes for each post a separate page on which your site's visitors can view the comments that others have left. Whenever a post is published or a comment is made, this page will be updated along with the home page.

You can access this page by following the first link below your post (the link shows the time at which the post was first published). When you visit this page, you might get a shock—all of your CSS style rules have disappeared! Figure 9.19 shows this sorry state of affairs. Don't worry, though: it's a cinch to fix.

Figure 9.19. The comments page has lost its style

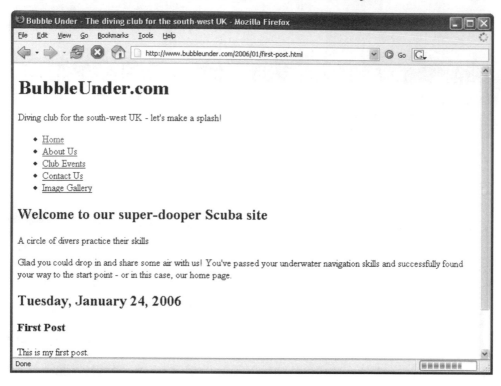

This problem arises as a result of the location to which Blogger writes our page: `http://www.bubbleunder.com/2006/01/first-post.html`. This isn't like the addresses of our other pages; they have addresses like `http://www.bubbleun-der.com/events.html` and `http://www.bubbleunder.com/contact.html`. Blogger has put the `first-post.html` file inside another two folders that it has created—2006 and 01.[8]

Why does this matter? Well, remember the `link` element that we used to include our style sheet?

File: **first-post.html** (excerpt)

```
<link href="style1.css" rel="stylesheet" type="text/css" />
```

---

[8] These folder names relate to the date on which the post was published—it was posted in January, 2006.

That tells the browser to load the CSS file `style1.css` from the *current* directory. This works when all the files are in the same directory, but fails when the CSS file is in a different directory from the pages to which it applies. What we need to do is make these Blogger pages look for the style sheet file in its correct location—http://www.bubbleunder.com/style1.css—regardless of where the page calls it from.

Open up Blogger's Template Editor, locate the `link` element, and change it to the full address of the CSS file, as shown here:

File: **Blogger Template (excerpt)**

```
<link href="http://www.bubbleunder.com/style1.css"
    rel="stylesheet" type="text/css" />
```

Before you save your changes, there's another element whose location also needs to be updated—the image that shows the circle of divers. Modify the `img` tag as follows:

File: **Blogger Template (excerpt)**

```
<h2>Welcome to our super-dooper Scuba site</h2>
<p><img src="http://www.bubbleunder.com/divers-circle.jpg" alt="A
    circle of divers practice their skills" width="200"
    height="162" /></p>
<p>Glad you could drop in and share some air with us! You've
    passed your underwater navigation skills and successfully
    found your way to the start point - or in this case, our
    home page.</p>
```

Finally, the same prefix needs to be added to our menu items. The navigation menu should look like this in your template:

File: **Blogger Template (excerpt)**

```
<div id="navigation">
  <ul>
    <li><a href="http://www.bubbleunder.com/index.html">Home</a>
        </li>
    <li><a href="http://www.bubbleunder.com/about.html"
        >About Us</a></li>
    <li><a href="http://www.bubbleunder.com/events.html"
        >Club Events</a></li>
    <li><a href="http://www.bubbleunder.com/contact.html"
        >Contact Us</a></li>
    <li><a href="http://www.bubbleunder.com/gallery.html"
        >Image Gallery</a></li>
```

```
    </ul>
  </div> <!-- end of navigation div -->
```

Save the changes to the template in Blogger, republish your blog, and reload the page to see it in its fully styled glory. Does your page look like the one in Figure 9.20?

Figure 9.20. Each post's comments page now has style!

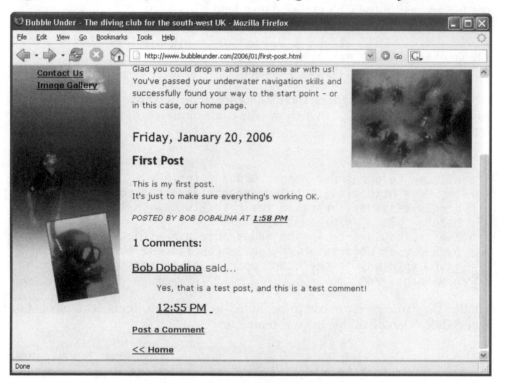

That's it! You've set up a blog on your site, configured it so that visitors can leave comments, and the entire site is composed entirely of valid, well-structured XHTML, so it's accessible to any browser ... or is it?

Validating your Blog

If you now run your homepage through the W3C Markup Validator[9] that we saw in Chapter 8, you'll find that a couple of errors have been introduced, as Figure 9.21 reveals. These errors may cause problems for some browsers.

Figure 9.21. The Blogger template has introduced some problems

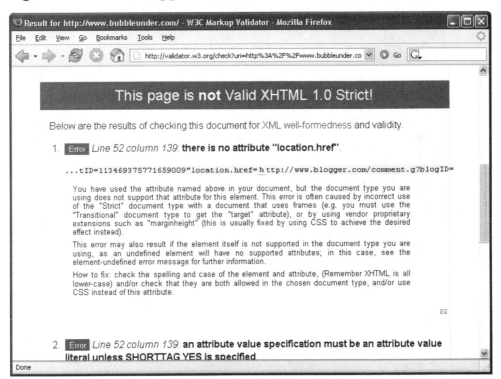

Here, the validator is complaining that there's no attribute called `location.href`, which is very true. Thankfully, we're able to hunt down this invalid attribute and remove it from our Blogger template.

Take a look at the markup of the page that Blogger has created: load the homepage in your browser, and select View > Source (or View > Page Source). You'll see that all of the Blogger-specific tags have been replaced with the *almost* valid XHTML generated by Blogger. It's in this markup that you'll find the offending

---

[9] http://validator.w3.org/

location.href attribute, which I've highlighted below (again, the markup here has been formatted for readability—the formatting won't affect how it's displayed in the browser).

File: **index.html (excerpt)**

```
<div id="bodycontent">
  <h2>Welcome to our super-dooper Scuba site</h2>
  <p><img src="divers-circle.jpg" alt="A circle of divers practice
      their skills" width="200" height="162" /></p>
  <p>Glad you could drop in and share some air with us! You've
      passed your underwater navigation skills and successfully
      found your way to the start point - or in this case, our
      home page.</p>
  <h2 class="date-header">Thursday, January 20, 2006</h2>
  <!-- Begin .post -->
  <div class="post">
    <a name="113469375771659009"></a>
    <h3 class="post-title">First Post</h3>
    <div class="post-body">
      <div>
        <div style="clear:both;"></div>
        This is my first post.<br />
        It's just to make sure everything's working OK.
        <div style="clear:both; padding-bottom: 0.25em;"></div>
      </div>
    </div>
    <p class="post-footer">
      <em>posted by Bob Dobalina at <a
          href="http://www.bubbleunder.com/2006/01/first-post.html"
          title="permanent link">4:12 PM</a></em>
      <a class="comment-link" href="http://www.blogger.com/comment
.g?blogID=19907525&amp;postID=113469375771659009" location.href=ht
tp://www.blogger.com/comment.g?blogID=19907525&amp;postID=11346937
5771659009;>
          0 comments</a>
      <span class="item-control admin-594974497 pid-2135550719">
        <a style="border:none;" href="http://www.blogger.com/post-
edit.g?blogID=19907525&amp;postID=113469375771659009&amp;quickEdi
t=true" title="Edit Post">
          <span class="quick-edit-icon"> </span>
        </a>
      </span>
    </p>
  </div>
  <!-- End .post -->
  <!-- Begin #comments -->
```

```
  <!-- End #comments -->
</div> <!-- end of bodycontent div -->
```

We can locate the corresponding markup in the template by looking for the <a> tag with the class="comment-link" attribute, which is highlighted in the following code:

File: **Blogger Template (excerpt)**

```
<p class="post-footer">
  <em>posted by <$BlogItemAuthorNickname$> at
      <a href="<$BlogItemPermalinkUrl$>"
      title="permanent link"><$BlogItemDateTime$></a></em>
  <MainOrArchivePage>
    <BlogItemCommentsEnabled>
    <a class="comment-link"
        href="<$BlogItemCommentCreate$>"
        <$BlogItemCommentFormOnclick$>>
        <$BlogItemCommentCount$> comments</a>
    </BlogItemCommentsEnabled>
    <BlogItemBacklinksEnabled>
      <a class="comment-link"
        href="<$BlogItemPermalinkUrl$>#links">links to this
        post</a>
    </BlogItemBacklinksEnabled>
  </MainOrArchivePage>
  <$BlogItemControl$>
</p>
```

Comparing the two versions of the markup side-by-side, we can see that the <$BlogItemAuthorNickname$> tag has been replaced with the author's name, <$BlogItemCommentCount$> has been replaced with the number of comments that have been left on this blog post, and so on.

But what's introducing this mysterious location.href attribute? It looks like it's been slotted in just after the normal href attribute, so I'd bet my last dollar on the <<$BlogItemCommentFormOnclick$> tag being the one at fault. Let's delete that tag from our Blogger template (as shown below), click the Save Template Changes button and republish our blog. The page should now validate, as Figure 9.22 indicates.

File: **index.html** (excerpt)

```
<a class="comment-link"href="<$BlogItemCommentCreate$>">
  <$BlogItemCommentCount$> comments
</a>
```

After doing this, try the W3C Markup Validator again.

Figure 9.22. Success! The home page generated by Blogger is valid XHTML Strict

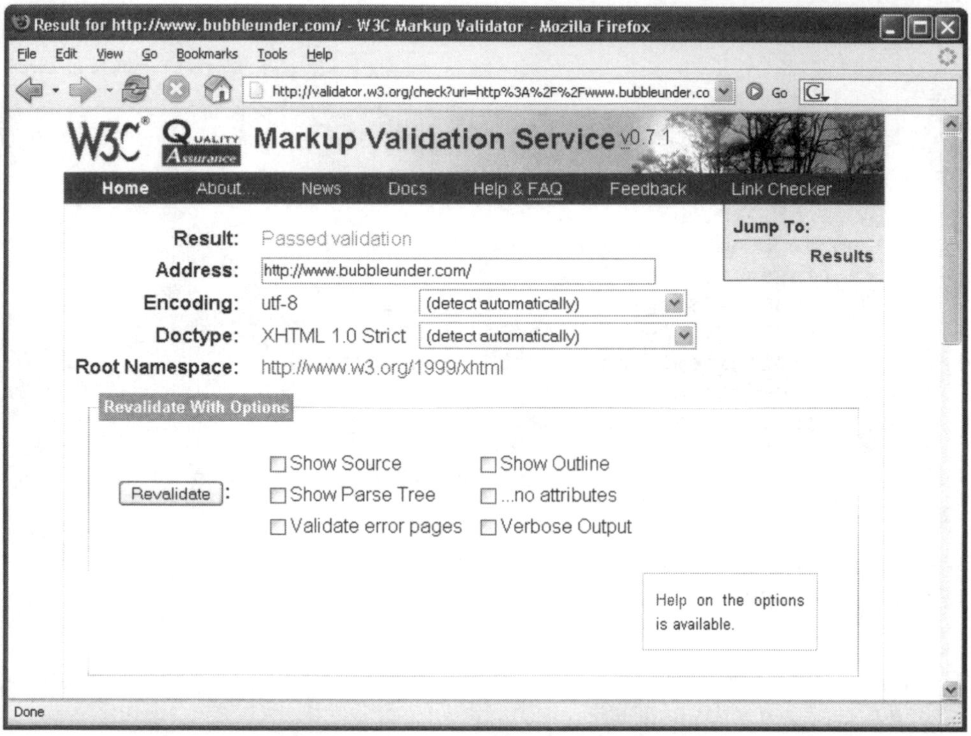

Now, updating the content on our web site using Blogger will produce valid markup, which is a worthwhile goal for all those reasons we discussed in Chapter 8. And, thanks to Blogger, we also have a way for our web site's readers to interact with the site: they can leave comments on each post's page. What's next? It's time to put some real content into our blog!

Managing your Blogger Posts

Let's add a more realistic post to the site (we'll delete our simplistic test post, too). In Blogger, click on the Postings tab—you should find yourself at the Create Post page shown in Figure 9.23. Type whatever you want into the area provided, then click the Publish Post button.

Figure 9.23. The text area where you type posts in Blogger

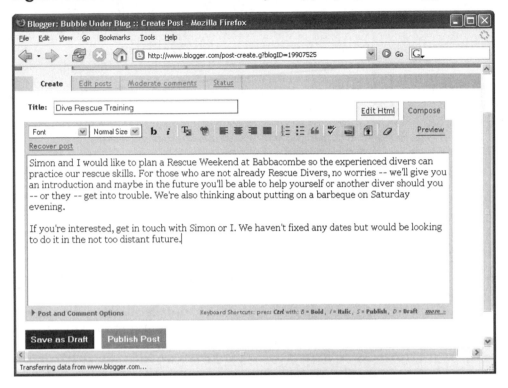

Again, Blogger will automatically update all of the necessary files on your web server. There's just one more thing left to do—let's delete our test post. Go back to the Blogger dashboard and, under the Postings tab, select Edit Posts to access the list of all of your blog posts. Locate the test post and click Delete. The next page will ask if you really want to delete the test post; click the Delete It button to get rid of it for good.

Now, at last, you can go and admire the web page on your live site. Finally, the site looks great, the markup validates,[10] and adding new content from any computer is a piece of cake. Give yourself a pat on the back!

---

[10] Unfortunately, our markup may not pass W3C validation once we start to receive comments on our blog. As of February 2006, Blogger's comments engine introduced invalid characters (uppercase tags and unencoded ampersands) that prevented pages from validating. There isn't much we can do about this, unfortunately. Having greater control over our markup is one advantage of using a self-hosted blogging solution. When Blogger fixes these problems, our site will inherit the changes. Follow their progress at http://validxhtml.blogspot.com/.

Tip

Blogging with `class`

If you want to change the style of certain elements of the Blogger-generated markup, such as the post title or the comments link, you can. You may have noticed that many of these elements have `class` attributes with reasonably intuitive names, such as `post-title` or `comments-link`. Simply add a rule for these classes to your style sheet, and by applying the CSS you've learnt in this book, you'll have complete control over how those elements are displayed! Unfortunately, Blogger doesn't wrap the paragraphs typed in a post with `<p>` tags, the way it really should. To have this text display the same as other paragraphs throughout our site, expand the rule for `p` elements in our style sheet to read as follows:

```
.post-body div, p {
  font-size: small;
  color: navy;
}
```

Getting Others to Contribute to your Blog

Arguably, one of the best features of managing and updating your site content via a blog is that it gives you the ability to let others contribute. If you want to take a week or two off, or go on holiday, a friend or colleague can continue to update the web site easily. Even if you're not holidaying, it's great to have a few other people pitching in with their own writing styles and contributions. In this section, I'll show you how easy it is to add another author to your blog.

Click the Settings tab in Blogger, then click the Members link. You'll arrive at a page that shows a list of the current "members" (or authors) of your blog. Click the Add Team Member(s) button.

You'll be presented with the page shown in Figure 9.24. Enter the email addresses of the people you want to invite, and any other explanatory notes you feel will be useful.

Figure 9.24. Sending an invitation to potential scribes, and halving your workload in the process!

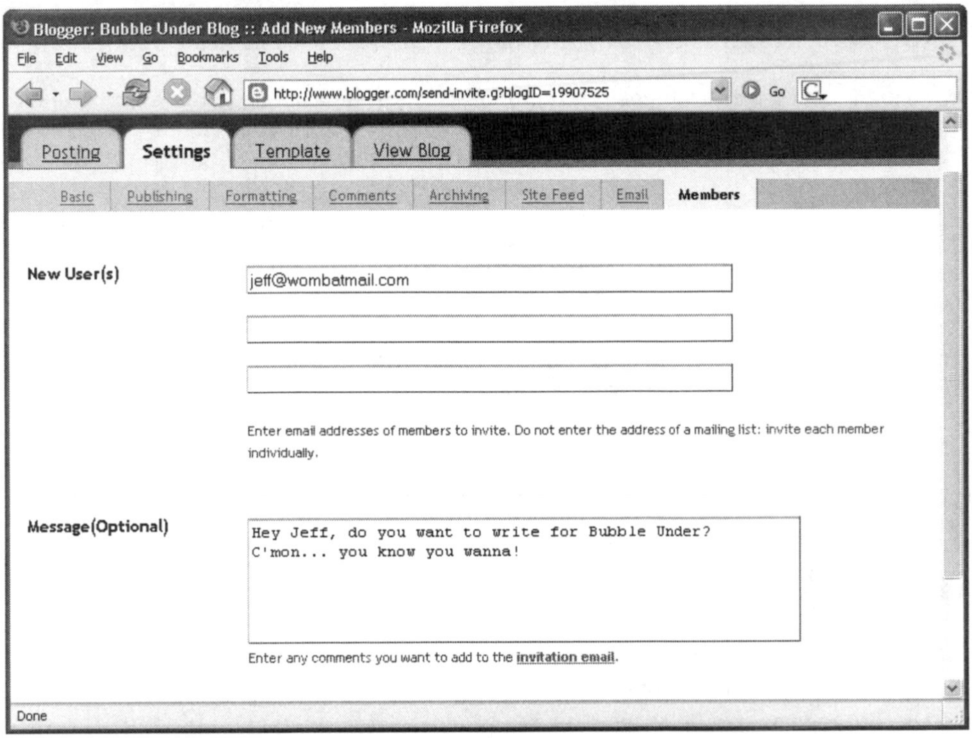

The invitee will receive an email that explains how to contribute, just like the one shown here:

```
Bubble Under Blog wrote:

Hey Jeff, do you want to write for Bubble Under? C'mon... you know
you wanna!
-----------------------------------------

You have been invited by Bob Dobalina to join a blog called Bubble
Under Blog

Blogger is a free service for easily communicating and sharing
ideas on the web.

Next Steps:
```

```
1. Please follow the link below. If you do not follow this link,
you will not be able to logon to the correct blog.

http://www.blogger.com/i.g?invID=4213817513204124315&lh=en

Note: If this link wraps in your email (not all of it is on one
line) copy and paste the entire link into your browser's location
bar. Be sure to include characters that may have wrapped to the
next line.

2. If you already have a Blogger account, you will be asked to
either accept or decline this invitation.

3. If you do not have a Blogger account, you can create one for
free in less than a minute. Just click the link and press the
"Create an Account" button.

Thanks!
```

Now, just sit back and wait for your budding team of writers to do their thing!

Summary

In this chapter, I've told you a little bit about what blogging is, and how it can help you keep your web site content fresh. I freely admit to limiting my discussion to the Blogger hosted service—this really makes it easy to get a blog up and running, and Blogger does not require any major technical knowledge beyond a bit of XHTML. You won't need to install and configure anything on your own server! However, if you find that Blogger is limiting you in any way, be sure to check out the other options available, and remember: if you get stuck with anything, you can always post a question on the SitePoint Forums.

If you've got this far, you should have a nicely rounded web site that's built to meet current standards, is accessible to a wide audience, is easy for search engines to index, is quick to download, and, now, is an absolute cinch to update. To refer to my analogies about building a car in the early chapters of this book, your job is basically complete—you've built yourself a great car! But, no matter how cool your shiny new ride is, few motor heads can resist adding the odd feature here and there—dare I say it, adding a touch of "bling!" In the next chapter, I'll introduce you to some of the add-ons that you might consider clipping onto your web site to finish it off nicely. Bring on the chrome!

10

Pimp my Site: Cool Stuff you can Add for Free

Your web site looks great, everything seems to be going tickety-boo, and maybe you've even got regular news updates happening thanks to a group of budding bloggers who contribute regularly. Your work's done, right? Well, no. There's always something else to do!

When you first set up your web site, you probably had a good idea of the audience you were building it for (at least, I hope you did), and you may well have catered admirably to that audience. But within a couple of weeks of launching your web site and promoting it to the world (using some of the suggestions I made in Chapter 8), you'll start to receive emails from people you don't know asking questions about the site that you really hadn't expected:

> "Can you tell me where I can get my air regulators serviced in North Devon?"

> "I can't find details of your training courses—do you offer any?"

> "My name is Abdul Akinbobola and I am the son of the recently deposed president of Burkino Faso and..."

Okay, so that last message has nothing to do with your web site, but trust me, you'll certainly get emails like this! The point I'm making is that no matter what sort of planning you've undertaken, people beyond your expected audience will find your web site one way or the other, and you'll likely need to be able to cater to them, too. This is where you should consider some add-ons to your site—extras that will:

❑ let you *discover how people are arriving at your web site* (e.g., through a search on Google, or via a referral—or link—from another web site in which you've promoted your own site)

❑ reveal *which search terms people used* to get to your web site, and provide some statistics about the most common ones

❑ let the visitor *search the contents of your web site* (rather than click around the navigation in the hope of finding what they need)

❑ allow the visitor to *search a group of related web sites* from the comfort of your web site

❑ provide a way for you to *manage a list of your favorite web sites* related to the topic in your own web site, and provide them as a links resource for others

❑ let your visitors become part of your web site community by *providing a discussion forum*

All of these goals can be achieved using free services, and in this chapter, I'm going to provide step-by-step instructions to help you add these services and truly pimp your site![1]

Getting the Low-down on your Visitors

How can you be absolutely sure that what you've got on your web site is the right content for your audience? Well, the truth is that you can't know for sure—everyone's different, after all, and each person's needs are unique. However, you can get some indication about whether your web site is serving the audience's needs through some simple statistics.

Some hosting companies will provide statistics software as part of your hosting package, so be sure to check. If your package includes a statistics service, you can safely skip over this next section—instead, make use of the tools your host has

---

[1] For those who don't get the reference, Pimp My Site is my little pun based on the MTV show Pimp My Ride, [http://www.mtv.com/onair/dyn/pimp_my_ride/series.jhtml] in which old, neglected cars are renovated (or "pimped") for their owners.

already provided. However, most free hosting services, and many of the cheaper hosting plans, will not provide statistics for you. It's up to us to fill that gap.

Choosing a Statistics Service

As with a number of services I've mentioned elsewhere in this book, there are two ways that you could introduce a statistics service to your site:

❑ You could install and configure a statistics service on the web server that hosts your site. The web server keeps detailed records of every visit to your web site: it records the time of the visit, which pages were viewed, which browsers were used, how visitors found the site, and much, much more. There are many programs you can install onto your web server that will produce easy-to-read graphs based on this data. Installing this software is no easy feat, though, and is not really something I'd recommend for beginners.

❑ Thankfully, the second option is much easier—you can sign up for a third-party solution that collects and stores the data on your behalf. All you're required to do is add a link to an image or script file (hosted by the service provider) into your web pages.

Many third-party statistics services are available, but to narrow things down a little, I advise you to look for one that offers the following features:

list of referring web sites (recent referrers and totals)
This information will tell you how your visitors found your web site.

number of visitors
You should be able to view a count of the numbers of visitors your site receives each day and each month, as well as the total number of visitors who have stopped by since the site launched.

information about your visitors' computer setups
This data will tell you whether your visitors are using PCs or Macs, which browsers they're using, and so on.

Any information beyond that is probably overkill for a small-scale web site (as you can probably imagine, too many statistics can end up muddying the waters—there's a lot to be said for simplicity!). Some of the hosted services you might want to consider using include StatCounter,[2] Extreme Tracking,[3] and AddFreeStats.[4]

In the past, I've always used the Extreme Tracking service—it's easy to set up and does its job. However, I'm going to break with my own habits and show you the process for setting up an account with StatCounter. Why? Because the reporting looks good, there's lots of additional help on each report page that will lead you to discover more, and—a real selling point for me—the service generates standards-based markup for its visitor tracking code (most services are not all that thoughtful, and it would be a shame to undo the good work you've completed on your web site so far by introducing invalid markup).

Registering an Account with StatCounter

There are just a few forms to fill in—soon, you'll be ready to add a statistics service to your site! Here's what you need to do:

❑ Head over to StatCounter's home page[5] and click on the Register Now link.

❑ Fill in your account and personal details into the registration page shown in Figure 10.1. Be sure to make your username and password easy to remember.

---

[2] http://www.statcounter.com/
[3] http://www.extreme-dm.com/tracking/
[4] http://www.addfreestats.com/
[5] http://www.statcounter.com/

Figure 10.1. StatCounter's registration page

ACCOUNT DETAILS	
Username	bobdobalina
Email	bob@bubbleunder.com
Password (case sEnSitive)	*******
Confirm Password	*******
PERSONAL DETAILS	
First Name	Bob
Last Name	Dobalina
Company Name (optional)	
Country	United Kingdom
Date Format	21st December 2005
Time Format	23:18:39

☐ I accept the terms and conditions.

REGISTER MY ACCOUNT >>

❏ You'll be asked to select your time zone before proceeding to the project setup process—Figure 10.2 shows how it's done. A StatCounter Project is a single web site whose statistics are collected by StatCounter. You can collect statistics for multiple web sites, but each web site must have its own separate project.

Figure 10.2. Selecting a time zone

Congratulations! Your account has been created successfully!

Please select your timezone:

GMT0:00 Europe/London (GMT)

The next step toward tracking your visitors is to create a StatCounter Project for your website. A Project relates to one website - if you have multiple websites you can create a Project for each, and manage them all from your account. Click the button below to set your timezone and start creating a StatCounter Project:

PROCEED & ADD A PROJECT >>

If you don't wish to create a project now, you can simply log in again at a later time to continue the process.

❏ The first step in setting up a project is to select the type of project you want to create. At the time of writing, only one project type is available—the Standard StatCounter Project—but that's all we need anyway. Select the

Standard StatCounter Project, as shown in Figure 10.3, and click the Next > button.

Figure 10.3. Only a standard StatCounter project is available

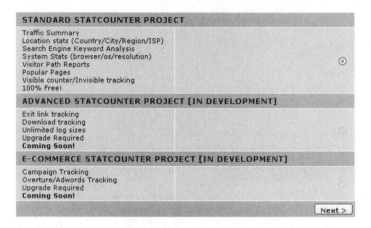

On the project setup page illustrated in Figure 10.4, you'll need to provide details such as the web site's name, the web address (URL), the site's category, and so on. You'll also be asked whether you want these statistics to be available to others. The choice is yours, but personally, I'd choose to hide the statistics, just because the link tends to look a little ugly on the page. Fill in the necessary details, then press the Next > button.

Figure 10.4. Selecting your project settings

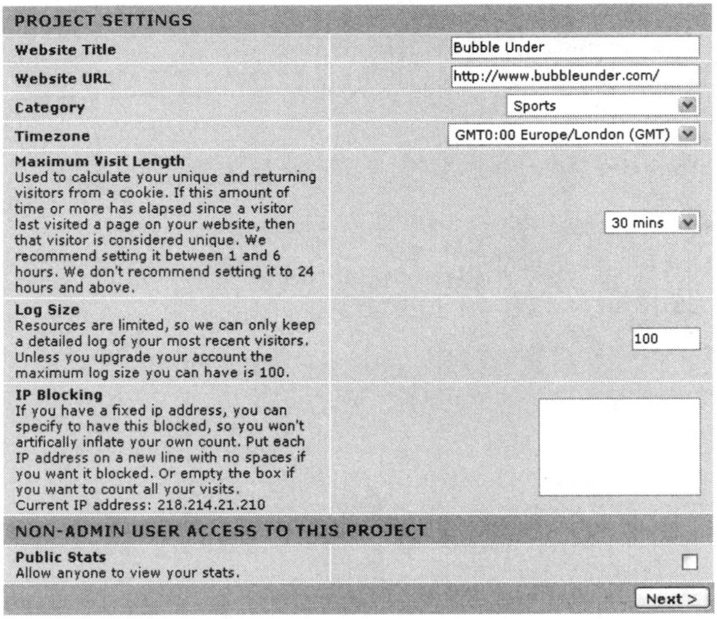

PROJECT SETTINGS	
Website Title	Bubble Under
Website URL	http://www.bubbleunder.com/
Category	Sports
Timezone	GMT0:00 Europe/London (GMT)
Maximum Visit Length Used to calculate your unique and returning visitors from a cookie. If this amount of time or more has elapsed since a visitor last visited a page on your website, then that visitor is considered unique. We recommend setting it between 1 and 6 hours. We don't recommend setting it to 24 hours and above.	30 mins
Log Size Resources are limited, so we can only keep a detailed log of your most recent visitors. Unless you upgrade your account the maximum log size you can have is 100.	100
IP Blocking If you have a fixed ip address, you can specify to have this blocked, so you won't artificaly inflate your own count. Put each IP address on a new line with no spaces if you want it blocked. Or empty the box if you want to count all your visits. Current IP address: 218.214.21.210	
NON-ADMIN USER ACCESS TO THIS PROJECT	
Public Stats Allow anyone to view your stats.	
	Next >

❑ You'll receive a confirmation message to tell you that your project has been created. The next step is to get the XHTML that you need to put onto your web site. Click Configure & Install Code to continue.

❑ As Figure 10.5 indicates, you'll be asked to choose a display style for the counter—do you want people to see how many visitors you've had, or do you want to keep that information hidden? Once again, I'd choose to hide it (showing your visitor numbers is *so* 1998!). Besides, until your web site has been running for a while, the visitor figures may be quite low, and there's no need to advertise the fact. Make your choice, then continue once again.

Figure 10.5. Selecting the counter type

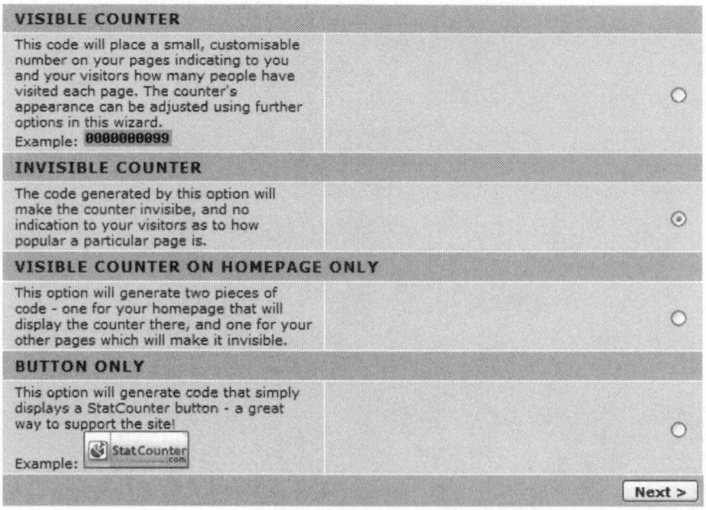

☐ Next, you're asked about the make-up of your web site through the form shown in Figure 10.6. Do you use frames? If you've followed my advice so far, the answer should be No, unless you're using a web forwarding service. This page also gives you the option of making the counter W3C- and XHTML-compliant. Ignore the overly fussy warnings about compatibility and check both options—we don't need to worry about these warnings because everything we've covered in this book follows W3C recommendations.

Figure 10.6. Settings relating to your web site's technical make-up

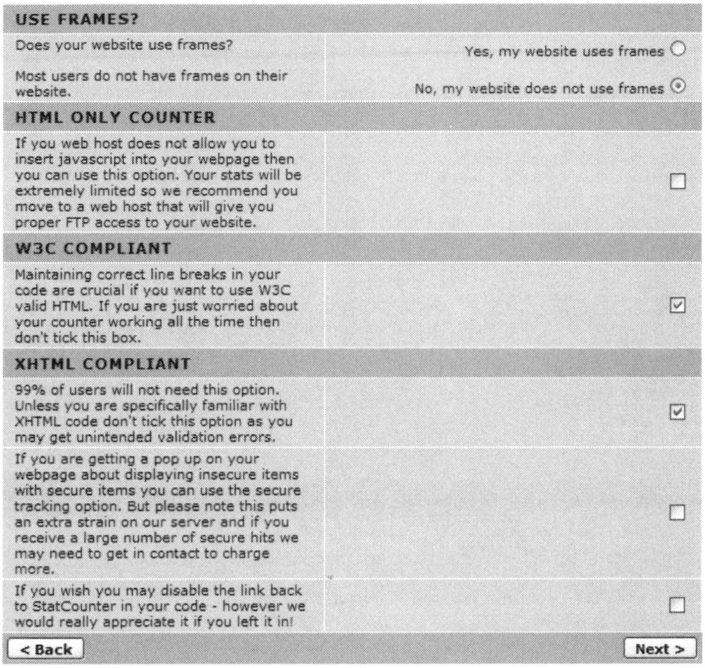

The next page asks you if you use a web page editor (by which is meant a simple web page builder offered by the likes of AOL, or a program like Dreamweaver or FrontPage). Answer No and carry on.

On the next page, depicted in Figure 10.7, you'll be given the code that you need to insert into your web pages so that StatCounter can keep track of your site's traffic.

Figure 10.7. The final markup is easily copied and pasted into your web pages

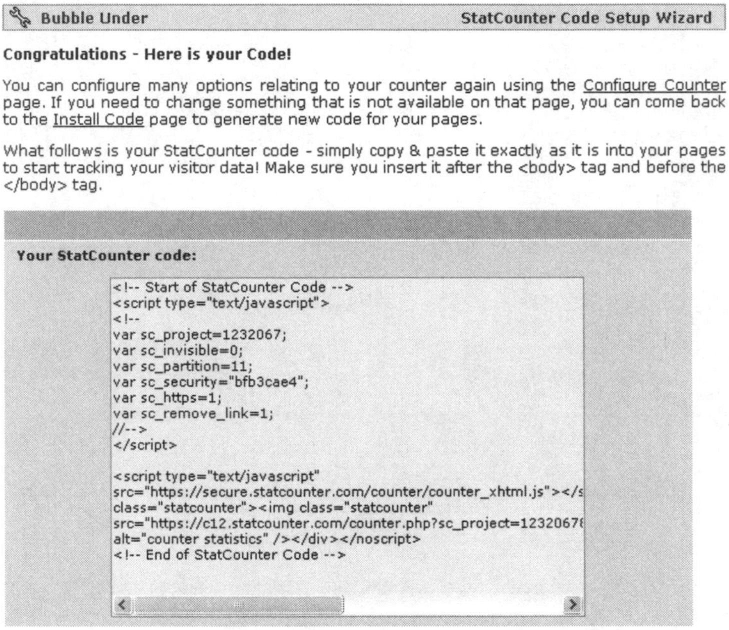

That's it for the sign-up process. Now all you need to do is put the generated code into your web pages.

Adding the Statistics Code to your Web Pages

Your statistics code should look something like this (though specific details relating to your account will differ):

```
<!-- Start of StatCounter Code -->
<script type="text/javascript">
<!--
var sc_project=1143403;
var sc_invisible=1;
var sc_partition=10;
var sc_security="bb4d77e9";
//-->
</script>
```

```
<script type="text/javascript"
    src="http://www.statcounter.com/counter/counter_xhtml.js">
</script>
<noscript>
  <div class="statcounter">
    <a class="statcounter" href="http://www.statcounter.com/">
      <img class="statcounter" src="http://c11.statcounter.com/cou
nter.php?sc_project=1143403&amp;java=0&amp;security=bb4d77e9&amp;i
nvisible=1" alt="web statistics" />
    </a>
  </div>
</noscript>
<!-- End of StatCounter Code -->
```

To get yourself up and running, simply paste this code in your web page just before the closing `</body>` tag (because we've chosen a tracker that's invisible, we needn't concern ourselves with its position on the page). Here's how it looks in the context of the "About" page (which I've truncated somewhat):

File: **about.html (excerpt)**

```
<p>
  Or as our man Bob Dobalina would put it:</p>
  <blockquote>
    <p class="fun">"Happiness is a dip in the ocean followed
        by a pint or two of Old Speckled Hen. You can quote
        me on that!"</p>
  </blockquote>
</div> <!-- end of bodycontent div -->
<!-- Start of StatCounter Code -->
<script type="text/javascript">
  <!--
  var sc_project=1143403;
  var sc_invisible=1;
  var sc_partition=10;
  var sc_security="bb4d77e9";
  //-->
</script>
<script type="text/javascript"
    src="http://www.statcounter.com/counter/counter_xhtml.js">
</script>
<noscript>
  <div class="statcounter">
    <a class="statcounter" href="http://www.statcounter.com/">
      <img class="statcounter" src="http://c11.statcounter.com
/counter.php?sc_project=1143403&java=0&security=bb4d77e9&invisible
=1" alt="web statistics" />
```

```
      </a>
     </div>
   </noscript>
   <!-- End of StatCounter Code -->
 </body>
</html>
```

There are three unescaped ampersands in there—in the `src` attribute of the `img` element. Replace each of these with the `&amp;` entity, add the code to all of the pages in your web site, and save them all. If you've created a Blogger template, you'll need to update that with the statistics code, too.

Now, try moving around the site, clicking on the links in the navigation, and generally replicating the behavior of a "real" visitor to your site. Also, try refreshing one of the web pages a few times—what we're doing here is building up a bit of dummy traffic to test things out.[6]

Next, log in to the StatCounter web site (using the details you provided at registration). Look for the little icon that looks like a bar chart—this is your way in to the statistics display. Click the icon and you'll see a chart that shows a summary of statistics. Perhaps you'd like to see which are the most popular pages on your web site? Take a look at the navigation options and you'll see a link to "Popular Pages"—that looks like a sensible choice. The resulting display should look something like Figure 10.8.

Figure 10.8. Pages ranked by popularity

		Webpage
Bubble Under (Popular Pages)		**26th January 2006**

dll This stat is based on your log of the last 100 pageloads. Increase your log size today!

TIP ▼ Click the little drill down arrow next to each webpage to show the users that visited

		Webpage
▼	25	/C:/Documents%20and%20Settings/Ian%20Lloyd/My%20Documents/Web/about.html
▼	9	/C:/Documents%20and%20Settings/Ian%20Lloyd/My%20Documents/Web/events.html
▼	9	/C:/Documents%20and%20Settings/Ian%20Lloyd/My%20Documents/Web/gallery.html
▼	6	/C:/Documents%20and%20Settings/Ian%20Lloyd/My%20Documents/Web/contact.html
▼	6	/C:/Documents%20and%20Settings/Ian%20Lloyd/My%20Documents/Web/index.html

You can see from above that the system was able to track popular pages stored on my hard drive (a web site address would be prefixed with http://), and my

---

[6] Note that you must be online for this exercise to work. Although you are only making changes to files on your hard drive at this point, the way this statistics system—and most others of this nature—works is that it requests a file (usually a graphic) from the server, and appends to the filename a bunch of data that links the file to your account. That request is what causes the system to keep a record, so if you don't have an Internet connection, it won't work.

brief clicking around the site has revealed that the "About Us" page was my most popular choice.

There are many other useful statistics here—too many to go into in more detail, in fact. My advice is to sign up, apply the statistics code, and upload your amended pages to your web server. Then, simply leave it for a few days before logging back in to check the statistics. By that time you might have enough data to see some patterns beginning to form.

Getting a Bigger Log File

You can see in Figure 10.8 that the logs created by StatCounter are based on the last 100 page loads. On a popular web site, it won't take long to reach that number. This doesn't mean that, once you reach 100 page loads, the system stops reporting; instead, newer information effectively shunts the older information into oblivion. It is possible to increase the log size, but predictably, this will come at a cost. If you decide that the information you're getting is not rich enough, you might want either to try increasing the log size or trying out one of the other services I mentioned earlier—the process for setting them up will be almost identical to the process I explained here.

What to Look for—a Summary

The most revealing statistics that will be available to you through StatCounter include:

Exit pages: From which pages are people leaving your site to go somewhere else?
If you can see a pattern forming, you can focus on these problem pages and try to work out what it is that's "turning people off." Is the page too wordy? Is it loading too slowly?

Browser and System Stats: What tools do people use to access your web site?
Knowledge is power. If you learn that 99% of your visitors are using one kind of web browser, you might not spend quite so much time worrying about display issues for the other 1% of users. This kind of information helps you prioritize any bugs you might need to fix.

Came From: Through which web pages do visitors arrive at your site?
If another site has linked to your web site, and a user follows that link to your web site, that information will be recorded on the Came From page. It's good to be aware of other web sites that have linked to you (if for no other

reason than to give you an ego boost!), and why they've linked to you—it's easy enough to take a look at the "referring site" from these reports.[7]

A Search Tool for your Site

This one's a cinch! We'll have you set up in minutes. In times gone by, I would have suggested registering for a service such as Atomz,[8] then configuring it precisely to fit your needs. However, now I use Google almost exclusively and find the search results to be very good. If only it were possible to use Google to search just your web site… Hang on—you can! And it's a walk in the park to set up!

Here's the basic markup you'll need to get Google to provide search results based on the content of your web site only:

```
<!-- SiteSearch Google -->
<form method="get" action="http://www.google.com/search">
<label for="q">Search:</label>
<input id="q" name="q" size="20" maxlength="255" value=""
    type="text" />
<input name="domains" value="http://www.bubbleunder.com/"
    type="hidden" />
<input name="sitesearch" value="http://www.bubbleunder.com/"
    checked="checked" id="mysite" type="radio" />
<label for="mysite">Just this site</label>
<input name="sitesearch" value="" id="www" type="radio" />
<label for="www">WWW</label>
<input name="btnG" value="Go" type="submit" />
</form>
<!-- SiteSearch Google -->
```

All you need to do is change the parts in bold so that they match your web site's address. It's so easy!

Here's that same code implemented the Bubble Under web site (at least, on a portion of the events page):

```
<!DOCTYPE html PUBLIC "-//W3C//DTD XHTML 1.0 Strict//EN"
    "http://www.w3.org/TR/xhtml1/DTD/xhtml1-strict.dtd">
<html xmlns="http://www.w3.org/1999/xhtml">
```

---

[7] Sometimes, web site managers talk about "checking their referrer logs." This is what that term means—looking through the lists of sites who have sent traffic to your web site, including search engines (reviewing the search phrases users entered into search engines to find your site).
[8] http://www.atomz.com/

```
<head>
<title>Forthcoming club diving events and trips with Bubble
    Under</title>
<meta http-equiv="Content-Type"
    content="text/html; charset=utf-8" />
<link href="style1.css" rel="stylesheet" type="text/css"
    media="screen" />
</head>
<body>
<div id="header">
  <div id="sitebranding">
    <h1>BubbleUnder.com</h1>
  </div>
  <div id="tagline">
    <p>Diving club for the south-west UK - let's make a
        splash!</p>
  </div>
<!-- SiteSearch Google -->
<form method="get" action="http://www.google.com/search">
<div id="search">
<label for="q">Search:</label>
<input id="q" name="q" size="20" maxlength="255" value=""
    type="text" />
<input name="domains" value="http://www.bubbleunder.com/"
    type="hidden" />
<input name="sitesearch" value="http://www.bubbleunder.com/"
    checked="checked" id="mysite" type="radio" />
<label for="mysite">Just this site</label>
<input name="sitesearch" value="" id="www" type="radio" />
<label for="www">WWW</label>
<input name="btnG" value="Go" type="submit" />
</div>
</form>
<!-- SiteSearch Google -->
</div>
<!-- end of header div -->
...
```

Note that we need to position the search form in an appropriate location, and format the text somewhat. I've used CSS to achieve this, using absolute positioning to place the search box in the top, right-hand corner of the page. To do so, I wrapped a div around the form elements and gave it an id. That way, I have some way of referencing the form in the CSS, as shown below:

```
#search {
  position: absolute;
```

```
top: 77px;
right: 10px;
font-size: x-small;
font-weight: bold;
}
```

Figure 10.9 shows how the search box looks on the page itself.

Figure 10.9. The Bubble Under site with integrated search

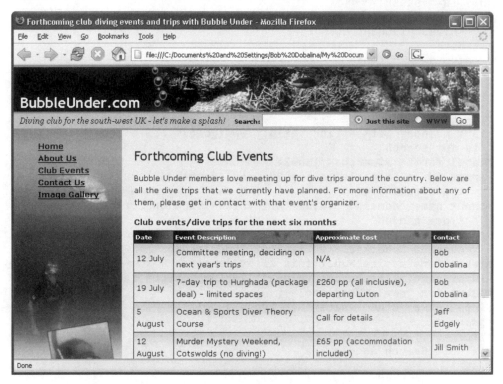

Google Scoped Search Limitations

Using Google's service in this way is certainly easy, but you should be aware of this solution's limitations:

❑ Google will only show search results if it *knows* about your web site—and it will only know about it if you've submitted your web site's address[9] to

---

[9] You can notify Google of your web site's existence at http://www.google.com/addurl/.

Google in the past (and Google has indexed it), or Google has found your web site by following a link from some other site.

❑ The search results may not be completely up-to-date. If you make changes to your site, then upload those changes, Google may not recognize that a change has been made for days or even weeks—it really depends on when the search engine re-indexes your site.

❑ The search results cannot be customized. The results page will look like a standard Google search results page, but the linked search results will all be pages from your web site (aside from sponsored links). However, people are familiar with Google, so this view of the search results also has its benefits.

Searching By Genre

At the time of writing, a new service called Rollyo (a "roll-your-own" search engine) had just been launched. What this service allows you to do is to create a custom search interface—one that lets you pick and choose what web sites you want to search. So, if you're the caring, sharing type, why not try out Rollyo?

Note that these screenshots were taken just after the Beta launch, and as such, they may differ slightly from the final version.

❑ Click on the Register link and complete the scant details requested of you by the registration page shown in Figure 10.10.

Figure 10.10. The Rollyo registration screen

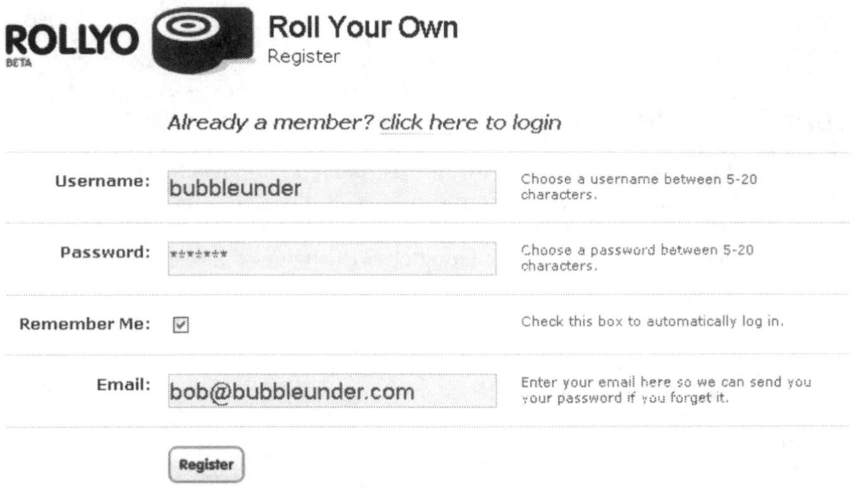

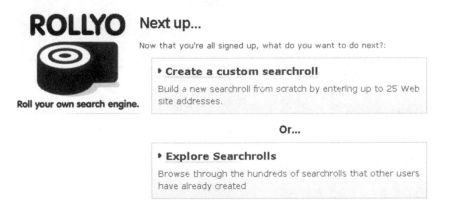

- Next, you'll be asked for profile information, and you'll see a big red arrow with the words, Skip this for now written on it. You know what to do!

- On the following page, select the Create a custom searchroll link, as illustrated in Figure 10.11.

Figure 10.11. Choose Create a custom searchroll

ROLLYO

Roll your own search engine.

Next up...

Now that you're all signed up, what do you want to do next?:

▸ **Create a custom searchroll**

Build a new searchroll from scratch by entering up to 25 Web site addresses.

Or...

▸ **Explore Searchrolls**

Browse through the hundreds of searchrolls that other users have already created

❑ Next, in the page shown in Figure 10.12, you're asked to provide names for your "Searchroll"—a list of web sites that you want to include—and also to identify "tags" (keywords that describe your search facility's purpose) that you'd like to assign to your searchroll.

Figure 10.12. Adding sites that you want to search

Searchroll Name:	BubbleUnder	Choose a name for your searchroll. Be as descriptive as possible. (Limit 25 characters)
Sources:	www.bubbleunder.com www.padi.com www.bsac.co.uk www.subaqua.co.uk www.diveaid.co.uk www.divernet.com	Enter up to 25 Web site address (URLs) - one per line. Rollyo searches entire sites such as **www.cnn.com** or **support.apple.com**, but **not** parts of sites, such as **www.cnn.com/politics/**. Everything after the slash will be ignored. ▶ Need inspiration? Explore searchrolls created by others.
Category: (Optional)	Recreation & Sports	Choose a category where you would like your Searchroll listed in the Rollyo directory.
Tags: (Optional)	dive, diving, scuba	Enter any number of keywords, separated by commas, to help other users find your searchroll.

With that done, you can create your searchroll. At the time of writing, Rollyo had not yet provided a simple method for grabbing the source code required to place the search functionality on your own web site. However, it's possible to view the source of a web page, take what you need, then adapt it slightly. I've done just that to show how Rollyo could be used on any web site. Here's the source code for the Rollyo search I created for Bubble Under:

```
<!-- SiteSearch Rollyo -->
<form id="searchform" name="searchform"
   action="http://www.rollyo.com/search.html" method="get">
  <div id="search">
  <input type="text" name="q" value="" id="search-box" /> in
    <select id="searchmenu" name="sid">
      <option value="6170">Bubble Under</option>
      <option value="web">The web</option>
    </select>
    <input type="submit" value="Search" />
  </div>
```

```
</form>
<!-- SiteSearch Rollyo -->
```

Figure 10.13 shows how the search functionality displays on the web page (I placed everything inside the form in the absolutely positioned `div`, in the same position we gave the Google search box in the earlier example).

Figure 10.13. Adding a Rollyo search to the Bubble Under web site

The next step is to submit your site to Yahoo! for indexing,[10] if you haven't already. As with most search engines, it may take days or weeks before Yahoo! visits your site and adds your pages to its database. Your Rollyo searchroll will still work during this time, it just won't include your site in the results it displays.

Finally, Figure 10.14 depicts the search results displayed on the Rollyo web site.

---

[10] http://search.yahoo.com/info/submit.html

Figure 10.14. Displaying the search results on Rollyo

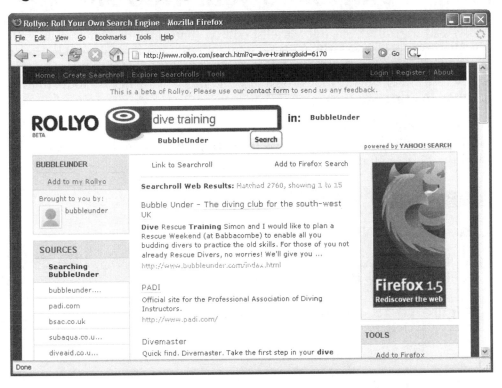

This is a novel way of adding search functionality to your site—but it's one that could potentially send people in another direction! However, if your web site is more of a fun venture, than focused on making cold hard cash, this could be the ethical way to go. Believe me when I say it'll be good for your karma—you'll see!

Caution: Contents May have Shifted in Transit

As I mentioned at the beginning of this section, Rollyo was new at the time of writing (in fact, it was still in "beta" phase—it hadn't been released to the world at large). As such, the service may have changed a little, or even a lot, by the time you read this—heaven forbid, it may even have disappeared altogether! The latter is unlikely (because it's a great service), but please be aware that you may need to adapt some of the steps above if Rollyo's service does change slightly.

Adding a Blogroll to your Web Site

What's a **blogroll**? A blogroll[11] is a list of links that's included on your web site (or blog), and which is easily updated from a central point. A blogroll is often a better option than creating a specific page on your site just for links (which can easily turn stale), and provides you and your visitors with an easy route to fresh content on other web sites.

A range of tools are available for this purpose, but perhaps the simplest one to try is Blogrolling. Here's the process for setting up a Blogroll (once again, I've used the Bubble Under web site as an example).

Signing Up for a Blogroll

❑ Go to the Blogrolling[12] web site.

❑ Follow the link to "Create Account"—you'll be asked for an email address and password, as Figure 10.15 shows.

Figure 10.15. Setting up a Blogrolling account

Once you've submitted the form, Blogrolling will send you an email. Open it and click on the activation link.

❑ Once you've activated your account, you can create a new Blogroll (in fact, you can create several different Blogrolls with just one account).

---

[11] http://en.wikipedia.org/wiki/Blogroll
[12] http://www.blogrolling.com/

Figure 10.16. Creating a new Blogroll

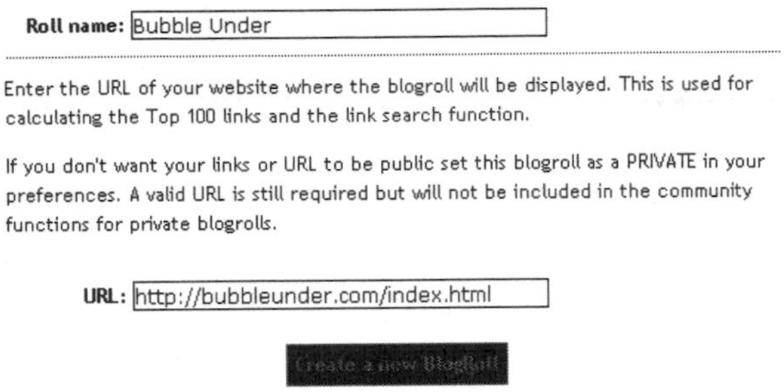

Roll name: Bubble Under

Enter the URL of your website where the blogroll will be displayed. This is used for calculating the Top 100 links and the link search function.

If you don't want your links or URL to be public set this blogroll as a PRIVATE in your preferences. A valid URL is still required but will not be included in the community functions for private blogrolls.

URL: http://bubbleunder.com/index.html

Create a new Blogroll

Simply enter a name and the web address of the page on which you'll be displaying the links, as shown in Figure 10.16.

❏ Most of the tools you'll need to manage your blogroll links are available from the Blogrolling homepage.[13] Figure 10.17 shows the Blogrolling "control panel."

Figure 10.17. All your Blogrolling options are available here

Bubble Under

❷ Preferences   ❷ Add Links
❷ Edit/Delete Links   ❷ Get Code
❷ Sidebar   ❷ Backup
❷ Delete Blogroll   ❷ Empty Blogroll
❷ RecipRoll   ❷ Import OPML
❷ Get A Domain Name For Your Blog
❷ **Total Links:** 0
❷ **Total Displays:** 0
❷ **Public Roll**

❏ Select Add Links. You'll be presented with a small form that looks like the one in Figure 10.18.

---

[13] By "homepage," I mean the page that's linked to by the word Home in the left-hand navigation menu that you see when you're logged in to Blogrolling. I don't mean the Blogrolling web site's main homepage.

Figure 10.18. Adding a link to your Blogroll

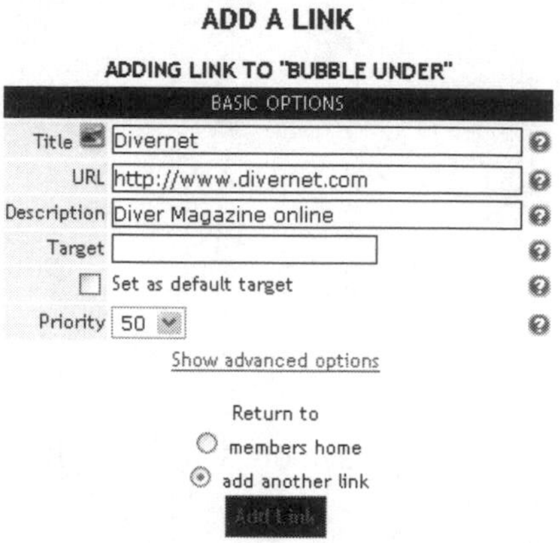

ADD A LINK

ADDING LINK TO "BUBBLE UNDER"

BASIC OPTIONS		
Title ☑	Divernet	❷
URL	http://www.divernet.com	❷
Description	Diver Magazine online	❷
Target		❷
☐ Set as default target		❷
Priority	50 ▾	❷

Show advanced options

Return to

○ members home

◉ add another link

Add Link

You could keep on adding links to this list until you run out of interesting web site addresses, but bear in mind that if you add too many links, your web page is going to start to resemble Yahoo! gone mad.

❏ Once you've added links to your favorite web sites, you need to do just one more thing: determine the order in which you'd like the links to display on your web site. Select Preferences and scroll down to the section that says Sorting your links, as illustrated in Figure 10.19.

Figure 10.19. Setting the order in which your links appear on the page

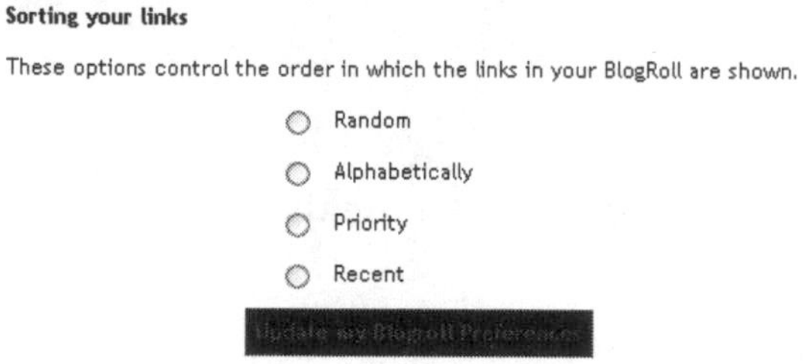

Sorting your links

These options control the order in which the links in your BlogRoll are shown.

○ Random

○ Alphabetically

○ Priority

○ Recent

Update my Blogroll Preferences

❏ Now all you need to do is get the code required for this feature to function on your web site. Go back to the Control Panel's homepage and click on the Get Code link. You should see something like this:

```
<script language="javascript" type="text/javascript"
    src="http://rpc.blogrolling.com/display.php?r=ad7cab20d092c
2ee809d009e26ffcc11"></script>
```

Integrating the Blogroll with your Web Site

Usually, people add blogrolls to their sites' homepages, where it's often tucked away to one side. I'm going to do the same with the Bubble Under blogroll.

As with the other sections on your web site, it's a good idea to wrap the blogroll in a div with an id. This approach will allow you to reference the div in a style sheet, and makes it easy to find the blogroll when you look through the markup at a later date. Here's the markup for the Bubble Under home page (index.html), once the blogroll has been added:

File: **index.html (excerpt)**

```
<div id="navigation">
<ul>
  <li><a href="index.html">Home</a></li>
  <li><a href="about.html">About Us</a></li>
  <li><a href="events.html">Club Events</a></li>
  <li><a href="contact.html">Contact Us</a></li>
  <li><a href="gallery.html">Image Gallery</a></li>
  </ul>
</div>
<div id="bodycontent">
<div id="blogroll">
<h2>Recently updated Diving Sites</h2>
<script language="javascript" type="text/javascript"
    src="http://rpc.blogrolling.com/display.php?r=ad7cab20d092c2
ee809d009e26ffcc11"></script>
</div>
<h2>Welcome to our super-dooper Scuba site</h2>
<p><img src="divers-circle.jpg" alt="A circle of divers practice
    their skills" width="200" height="162" /></p>
<p>Glad you could drop in and share some air with us! You've
    passed your underwater navigation skills and successfully
    found your way to the start point - or in this case, our
    home page. </p>
```

Without any further intervention, your list may look a little on the dull side. Let's suppose you wanted to style your blogroll. This code will do the trick:

```
#blogroll {
  float: right;
  margin-top: 55px;
  margin-left: 10px;
  margin-bottom: 10px;
  margin-right: 10px;
  width: 130px;
  border: 1px solid #006;
  font-size: x-small;
}

#blogroll h2 {
  font-size: x-small;
  background: #006;
  color: #fff;
  padding: 5px;
  margin: 0;
}

#blogroll div {
  padding: 5px;
}
```

Note that I've used contextual selectors (remember them from Chapter 3 and Chapter 4?) to style the heading as well as the links themselves. Although you can't see it from the code extract that Blogrolling provided to us (all that's visible is a link to a JavaScript file), each link that we add is wrapped in a `div`. I've added a little padding to each `div` inside the `blogroll` container, like so:

```
#blogroll div {
  padding: 5px;
}
```

Also note that I've floated the `blogroll div`, and given it a specific width. This will place the list on the right-hand side of the screen (to the right of the previously floated feature image). Figure 10.20 shows how all this fits together on the page.

Figure 10.20. The blogroll in place

We've added a blogroll! Now, any time you add a good web site to your book-marks, if it is related to your own web site's theme, you might consider adding it to your blogroll, too. All you need to do is head over to the Blogrolling site, log in, and add a link as we did above.

Discussion Forums

Arguably one of the best ways to create a virtual community around your web site—and to ensure that people come back time and time again—is to provide a chat forum. There is one small problem with this, though—forums aren't partic-ularly straightforward to set up, and once you start to get regular posts appearing, you'll face the issue of moderating the forum's content. Will you moderate it yourself? Will you just let things take their own course?[14] Will you empower other regular visitors to moderate the forums?

Most of the fully featured (and free) forum software products that you could use have some prerequisites that basically rule out my covering them in this book. For example, many packages require your hosting company to support PHP (a "scripting language") and to make a MySQL database available to you. At this stage, this is probably still something of a foreign language to you.

A simple solution for creating a community is to use Yahoo! Groups.[15] Signing up for the service is as simple as registering for an email account with Yahoo! Then, you can invite people to take part by registering for the discussion group themselves.

The beauty of using Yahoo! Groups is that many people will already be familiar with the mechanics of the Yahoo! services, and they may already have sign-in details that they can use (from their Yahoo! mail accounts). Also, the service is provided by a company that you know and can trust and, as such, it's unlikely to disappear overnight—taking your new virtual community with it.

The downside of using Yahoo! Groups is that this option takes users away from your web site. The best that you can do is to provide a link from your web site to the group that you set up. From that point forward, your community is entirely in the hands of Yahoo! (capable though they are), which could also present problems if you ever wanted to move the forum content to another location.

Summary

In this chapter I've shown that no matter how much work you've put into building your web site, there's always something else that you could do to add a finishing touch or two. I've focused on some add-ons that, I believe, really do improve a web site and encourage you—as well as others visiting the site—to use it more. However, I would like to sound one note of warning at this point, and it is this:

Know when to stop!

---

[14] The short answer to that one is: no! If you give people the option to run wild, they may well do just that, which could even get you into hot water, legally speaking. For example, someone could slander someone else on your forum, or link to copyrighted material for others to download, and you as the web site owner could be responsible for those people's actions. Moderation is a *great* idea.

[15] http://groups.yahoo.com/

There are many web sites still kicking around today that were built in the mid-to-late 90s, when the motto seemed to be "the more flashing/spinning/bouncing widgets on the page, the better the web site." Thankfully, as the art of web design has matured, people have come to realize that "less is more." Please bear this in mind when adding features. Otherwise, before you know it, the "bells and whistles" will have taken over completely!

Don't Be too Reliant on Third-party Services

note

There's one other reason not to go overboard adding to your web site features provided by a third party. If that third party's web server is running slowly for some reason, and your web page is trying to access something from that provider's server, your web page may appear to load slowly. Also, you need to be careful about "putting all your eggs into one basket." If the service you use is free, be prepared for the eventuality that one day, the owners may decide to close the service down, or charge for it. Would your web site be able to function properly if this happened?

At this point, your web site should have all the features that it needs. You've followed the advice I've given in this book, and you have a well-formed, standards-based web site that you can be proud of. If you've enjoyed designing and building your web pages, you might want to improve your skills even further. Instead of me leaving you to fend for yourself at this point, I'm going to make some suggestions about where you can go to get the skills you need, because, frankly, there are an awful lot of bad web sites and books out there, and you could easily pick one up by mistake. The last thing I want is for you to undo any of the good work you've done so far! So, let's continue on to the final chapter, in which we'll explore the possibilities that now lie before you.

11

Where to Now? What you Could Learn Next

In the course of this book I've given you a foundation for building web sites that will set you in good stead for many years to come. The methods described here are not "workarounds"—they don't try to use HTML or CSS to cobble together visual or behavioral effects that were never intended to be created using these technologies. The techniques we've used are based on well-established standards to which any new web browsers should conform. In short, by reading this book and following the advice in its pages, rather than choosing another "beginner's" book that could teach you numerous bad practices, you now have a good footing from which to further develop your skills.[1]

But what exactly can you do from this point forward? What are your options for developing your skills even more, without erring from the path of high quality, standards-based web design? These questions are precisely what this short chapter is all about—it's a roadmap that will ensure that you get to learn from the best of the material out there.

I'm going to break the various options into four areas:

---

[1] Actually, you can afford a little smug smile at this point. Although some of the concepts in this book are, on the face of it, pretty simple (for example, using CSS to control the page layout), there are quite a large number of people out there who would consider them to be "advanced." That's because those people have learned the old (wrong) methods, and know that re-wiring their brains to another way of thinking is not going to be easy. You won't need to do that, though!

❑ XHTML/HTML: looking beyond the basics

❑ CSS: discovering just how far your designs can go with some clever CSS

❑ JavaScript: adding a little interactivity to your web site

❑ Programming: opening up the possibilities with "scripting languages" and databases

Let's start with our web page building blocks: XHTML.

Improving your XHTML

First, let's have another "pat yourself on the back" moment. You've already grabbed a head-start by learning XHTML rather than HTML, and with it, you've been putting into practice such techniques as:

❑ declaring a doctype at the beginning of the document (an essential aspect of XHTML)

❑ ensuring that all attributes are quoted properly (e.g. `<div id="sitebrand-ing">`)

❑ writing your markup entirely in lowercase

❑ closing all tags correctly (e.g. `<p>This is a paragraph</p>`)—and that includes empty elements (e.g. `<input type="input" name="q" value="" id="search-box" />`)

You've learnt some of these techniques by copying, though perhaps you may not always have understood *why* some aspects of XHTML are achieved as they are. To refer this to the car analogy (once again!), when you first learn to drive, you know almost nothing about why you have to do certain things, but you follow the instructor's advice nonetheless. After you've been driving for a while, you stop thinking about *why* you do something a certain way: you just do it and know that's how it should be done. But for some people, driving the car well isn't enough—they want to know how their car works, and to understand how the engine, wheels, gearbox, and electrical system all fit together. If they can understand that, maybe they can get the car to drive more smoothly, and look better—they can really make it their own. And this is the point we're at with XHTML: now's the time to find out more about the nuts and bolts of what you've learned to date.

The Official Documentation

Perhaps that heading should read "recommendations," which is what the World Wide Web Consortium (W3C) likes to call them. If our web site was a car, the W3C recommendations would be the car's technical service manuals, complete with all the electrical wiring diagrams. In short, the recommendations don't make for light reading! However, in the search to truly understand how and why XHTML works the way it does, you can't get a more complete or technically accurate document than the W3C's own XHTML 1.0 recommendation at http://www.w3.org/TR/xhtml1/.

Tip

Making W3C Specs a Little More Understandable

Because your first read of a W3C document will likely be a less-than-fun event (I'm being diplomatic here), it might be an idea to take a look at J. David Eisenberg's article How to Read W3C Specs.[2] This author does a great job of explaining some of the terminology and structures that you'll encounter on the many and varied W3C documents. It won't make reading the documentation as enjoyable as a Dan Brown novel, but you will at least be able to glean the information you need with much less head-scratching.

Other Useful XHTML Resources

If the official documentation is simply too much for you to take on board right now, park it for the time being—you can always go back and check it out when you come across a problem or want clarification on a specific issue. There are other sources of information that you may find a lot easier to take in, some of which I've listed below.

W3Schools

I know of quite a few people who have learned most of what they know from the W3Schools web site's various tutorials. Information is presented in chunks that allow you to undertake a little learning at a time, and each chunk is written in a friendly, accessible way. The W3Schools XHTML tutorial is available at http://www.w3schools.com/xhtml/.

What I particularly like about the W3Schools web site is that you can test your own understanding using a 20-question multiple choice quiz,[3] which covers items

---

[2] http://www.alistapart.com/articles/readspec/
[3] http://www.w3schools.com/xhtml/xhtml_quiz.asp

contained in the various sections of the educational material. The test is timed (so you can re-test yourself at any time to see if your response times have improved), and it really makes you think about your answers; there are no "Who Wants to be a Millionaire"-type, early-round questions that have one obviously correct answer and three equally obvious wrong answers.

HTML Dog

Patrick Griffiths has put together an excellent resource in HTML Dog, at http://www.htmldog.com/guides/htmladvanced/. It breaks HTML[4] and CSS into three neat areas: Beginner, Intermediate, and Advanced. As with W3Schools, the sections are short enough to learn in small bursts, and clearly marked examples illustrate each topic.

With the learning you've gained from this book, you can probably skip straight past the Beginner and Intermediate sections, and head straight to the Advanced information. Here, you'll learn a new set of XHTML elements that we didn't cover in the earlier chapters (though they are included in the appendix to this book).

A List Apart

A List Apart (ALA) is an old favorite among the web design community. Unlike the web sites I mentioned above, this one does not teach in "modules," but takes more of a magazine-like approach—each feature is written as a complete piece that tackles a known problem or explains a creative idea to inspire others. The web site sorts its various articles (of which there are many) into categories, one of which is "HTML and XHTML," at http://alistapart.com/topics/code/htmlxhtml/.

You'll find links to a number of useful articles on that page. Some of the material will cross over into other technologies that you may or may not fully understand at this point (some of the articles on ALA focus on cutting-edge techniques), but you will almost certainly find inspiration from the articles on A List Apart.

Advancing your CSS Knowledge

At this point, I think I'm obliged by web design convention simply to blurt out the following web address for CSS Zen Garden: http://csszengarden.com/.

---

[4] Patrick refers to HTML, but all the examples shown are XHTML-compliant.

More than anything, this web site demonstrates just what CSS can do when it's placed in the right hands. I had intended to structure this section so that the official documentation was referred to first, followed by "other" examples. However, like many thousands of others who have tried to promote greater use of CSS on web sites, I can't help but turn to this site first.

Canadian web designer Dave Shea created CSS Zen Garden because he felt that the examples of CSS-based designs that were available at the time were less than inspiring, and failed to show what the technology made possible. In short, the people who understood the CSS language were technical people first, and designers second (or even third or fourth). Dave approached CSS primarily as a designer, and a coder second. He launched CSS Zen Garden with just a handful of his own designs, then encouraged others to contribute designs they'd based on the same document. Now, the site's archives contain literally hundreds of designs that prove that when you separate the presentation of a document from its structural foundation, you have a very powerful tool at your disposal. Figure 11.1 shows just a few examples of designs from CSS Zen Garden. Dave Shea's first version—which kicked it all off—appears at the top.

Figure 11.1. A selection of styles from CSS Zen Garden

The key point to remember is that all the designs above use *the same underlying document*. All that changes between each design is the linked style sheet (which will refer to a different set of typographic styles, color palettes, and background images).

CSS Zen Garden provides a great source of inspiration. But, if you want to look a little more closely, to learn how some of these designs were achieved, you can look at the CSS for any given style—just look for the link that reads, View This Design's CSS.

The Official Documentation

We're back on track again with the official information! If you've taken a look at some of the work submitted to CSS Zen Garden, you might have spotted some fairly advanced CSS that you're eager to understand. As with XHTML, no source of information is more complete than that maintained by the W3C in its Cascading Style Sheets (CSS) Specification, at http://www.w3.org/TR/CSS21/.[5]

As with the XHTML document I mentioned earlier, the W3C CSS Specification is another highly detailed piece of documentation that's not designed to be read quickly or for kicks. It's very useful as a reference for those moments when you come unstuck with CSS. But where could you go for some information that's a little easier on the old brain-box?

W3Schools/HTML Dog

I won't go into any detail here, as I described above what these sites have to offer. Instead, I'll merely tell you where to look before I move on to highlight other CSS-focused web sites:

❑ HTML Dog's CSS Intermediate page:

   http://www.htmldog.com/guides/cssintermediate/

---

[5] This link refers to CSS level 2, revision 1. There are different versions of the CSS recommendations, as there are versions of other W3C documents. At the time of writing, the CSS2.1 documentation was still labelled a "working draft." However, as version 2 (before the revision) documentation is not linked from the W3C's CSS home page, you can safely infer that this is the version of the specification they want you to use!

You'll know some of the CSS tricks in the intermediate section, but it contains other useful tips that you should pick up before moving on to the advanced section.

❑ W3Schools' CSS Dimension page:

http://www.w3schools.com/css/css_dimension.asp

This link will take you straight to the "advanced" section of the W3Schools CSS tutorial. Of course, you're free to go back a few steps in that tutorial if you wish—this is just my suggestion for a starting point.

CSS Discussion Lists

You can learn a great deal from web sites that carry tutorials like those I've already mentioned, but what happens if you have a question about, or get into difficulty with, something specific? In previous chapters, I've suggested that you raise issues on SitePoint's CSS forum.[6] If you explain that you're a "newbie," you'll find that the forum members will make a real effort to assist you, providing very clear instructions to help solve your problem. You will probably find that this forum (along with the other SitePoint forums) has so many experts "lurking" (and ready to respond to your questions) that you likely won't need to venture much further afield for help.

There are other discussion lists that you could join if you want to further your CSS skills. The two that I'd recommend are:

❑ CSS-Discuss, at http://www.css-discuss.org/

❑ Web Design-L, at http://webdesign-l.com/

These lists tend to get more heavily into the nitty-gritty of CSS issues, and uninitiated observers can, at times, feel as if they've gate-crashed a rocket scientists' convention. These people really do know their stuff, but they're not always so easy-going on the beginners. So my advice is:

❑ Register first, then "lurk" (watch the discussions that come through, and see what goes on) for a while.

❑ When you decide to ask a question, be sure to prefix it with "I'm a newbie."

---

[6] http://www.sitepoint.com/launch/cssforum/

❑ When you reply to comments, take care with your quoting style. The preferred style (which, unfortunately, most email programs don't do for you automatically) is to use top-down quoting.[7]

> **note**
>
> ### Discussion Lists vs Forums
>
> Just what is the difference between a discussion list and a forum? A discussion list is a group that operates via email, and subscribers receive either separate emails for each post that's made by a group member, or a "digest" version of the communications daily, weekly, or monthly. A forum, on the other hand, is a web-based service. That is, you use a web browser to log in to the forum, then pick and choose from the categories to read whichever posts take your fancy.
>
> Which is better? Well, that depends on the way you like to learn. Some people prefer discussion lists because they can store the emails they receive, then search through archived messages to find specific solutions as the need arises. Others prefer to be able to dip in to forums as they please, and avoid having their inboxes clogged up with messages.
>
> The best advice I can give you is to try out a discussion list and see how it goes. If you find the amount of messages you receive too overwhelming, you could try sorting the mail into dedicated folders (check your mail client for "rules" that let you divert mail based on certain criteria). If that doesn't work out, you could try a digest version, or even unsubscribe altogether. But you won't know if discussion lists suit you unless you give them a try, so be sure give them a go!

Other CSS Resources

While most modern browsers do a very good job of understanding CSS and rendering the results on the screen,[8] there are some inconsistencies between browsers. One notable problem relates to Internet Explorer on Windows. Versions prior to IE 6 calculate the widths of block elements incorrectly when a block contains padding or borders. Sometimes, the differences are slight, but at other times (when large padding and border values are used), the different rendering can cause a page layout to break completely on IE, while rendering as expected

---

[7] Matt Haughey has some excellent advice in a piece written for Digital Web magazine called, *How to Write Effective Mailing List Email* [http://www.digital-web.com/articles/how_to_write_effective_mailing_list_email]. Look for point two, "Top Down Formatting."

[8] And also on printouts—it's possible to target different CSS styles to different media types. See W3Schools [http://www.w3schools.com/css/css_mediatypes.asp] for an easy-going introduction to the topic.

on other, more standards-compliant browsers. You can learn more about this specific problem here in the discussion of the Box Model Hack at http://css-discuss.incutio.com/?page=BoxModelHack.

Enter the Hacks

One way that we can work around browser inconsistencies is to use "CSS Hacks." Essentially, these are purposely mangled pieces of CSS code that some browsers are capable of interpreting (technically, this is known as "parsing;" it's as if the browser thinks, "Hang on a minute, you didn't mean *that*, did you? You really meant to type *this*."). Meanwhile, other browsers will not be quite so clever when it comes to parsing that CSS—they'll simply fail to apply that style ("I haven't the slightest idea what you mean by this, so I'm moving on to the next CSS selector instead.").

Designers have discovered many different types of hacks, each of which can be used to target specific browser issues. They generally look quite ugly in your CSS markup (this is actually quite a good thing—it makes them stand out more!), and can be difficult to understand at first.

At Centricle.com,[9] Kevin Smith maintains a thorough chart that lists all the available hacks, and identifies which browsers each hack addresses. The trick is to work backwards on this: identify the issues first, get a clear picture of which aspect of your CSS the browsers are getting confused, then try to identify the hack that addresses those browsers. You can find the CSS Filters (hacks) chart at http://centricle.com/ref/css/filters/.

The thorny topic of CSS hacks is also covered in the Rachel Andrew's book *The CSS Anthology: 101 Essential Tips, Tricks & Hacks*.[10]

A Word of Warning Regarding Hacks

Hacks should never be used as the easy way out. The problem with a hack is that it exploits a browser's shortcomings—its inability to "work it out"—and this is a dangerous thing to rely on, because as new browsers are released, so the CSS programming behind those browsers can be changed or fixed. Indeed, this is the case with IE 7.[11] Here are a few simple rules to follow:

---

[9] http://www.centricle.com
[10] http://www.sitepoint.com/books/cssant1/
[11] See the IEBlog's *Call to action: The demise of CSS hacks and broken pages* [http://blogs.msdn.com/ie/archive/2005/10/12/480242.aspx].

❑ Before resorting to hacks, you *must* verify that your CSS is valid.[12] A problem that appears in just one browser might be the result of a slight typing error that does not cause problems in other browsers. The validator will pick up this kind of fault, removing the need for you to look at using hacks.

❑ You can write CSS in ways that prevent your needing to resort to hacks. Try some of these tips for avoiding hacks[13] before you decide to use them.

❑ If you must admit defeat and use hacks, be very careful about how you apply them. Molly Holzschlag provides a number of useful tips that you should take on board in her article, *Integrated Web Design: Strategies for Long-Term CSS Hack Management.*[14]

Unfortunately, hacks are something of a necessary evil where advanced CSS is concerned. It's an acknowledgement that the browser playing field is not quite as level as it should be.

The CSS Discuss List's Companion Site

The CSS Discuss list has a companion web site that provides an archive of some of the best practices that have been discovered in various email discussions. The information is perhaps not as "ordered" as it is in the tutorials I mentioned previously (at resources such as W3Schools and HTML Dog), but it will make sense once you've had a little more exposure to intermediate and advanced CSS. On the companion site's front page, at http://css-discuss.incutio.com/?page=FrontPage, you'll find links to explanations of a number of good practices, and tips for improving your CSS to expert level.[15]

I recommend you take a closer look at these sections:

Style Switching   all the information and links you need in order to incorporate a "style switcher" into your web site (so that you can have more than one style sheet for users to choose from, according to their specific needs)

Font Size   great advice on how to size fonts consistently across a range of browsers

---

[12] Do so at http://jigsaw.w3.org/css-validator/.
[13] http://css-discuss.incutio.com/?page=AvoidingHacks
[14] http://www.informit.com/articles/article.asp?p=170511
[15] Actually, this page is a "wiki"—a page that can be edited or updated by anyone. Members of that mailing list frequently update the content displayed here.

CSS Layouts	methodologies and examples of various CSS layout techniques, such as two- and three-column layouts, and techniques to position footers that always align correctly
Media Types	more tips on how to make the most of the different media types for which you can hone your CSS

If you make web sites like these your regular haunts, you'll be well on your way to becoming a CSS guru. Perhaps I'll be reading one of your books on the topic one day?

Learning JavaScript

The next logical step after you learn XHTML and CSS must be to take on a client-side scripting language. What's "client-side" all about? Client-side scripts are sets of instructions that are run on the client machine—that's the computer that displays the web page—rather than being processed by the server. The most obvious choice here is a language called JavaScript.[16]

Strangely, I'm going to recommend that you *don't* refer to any official documentation on this language because, frankly, I don't think it's the best way to learn JavaScript (it is the best way to be scared off, though). Once more, I find myself attracted to the modular, step-by-step approach that W3Schools takes in teaching JavaScript, at its Learn JavaScript[17] page. I wish that I'd been able to learn in such a nice way when I began to tinker with this language!

With JavaScript, the possibilities really are limited only by your imagination. If you find yourself thinking, "I'd like that part of the web page to be moveable," or, "I want to be able to hide this part of the web page at the click of a button," JavaScript will let you do it.

Compared with HTML and CSS, though, JavaScript is quite complicated. This is partly because JavaScript is very unforgiving when it comes to typing errors—one missing semi-colon, and your whole script may break—and partly because no one can anticipate what tasks you're going to use JavaScript to achieve on your site. Hence, teaching it can never be as focused or strictly defined as other topics.

To my mind, the budding JavaScripter would be best to do the following:

---

[16] It is possible to run a similar language called VBScript, but it's not widely supported as a client-side language, and I can't recommend it for use on a web site. I mention it here so that you are, at least, aware of its existence.
[17] http://www.w3schools.com/js/js_intro.asp

☐ Run through the W3Schools tutorial, and be sure to try out all the examples to get a feel for what the language can do.

☐ Think about a practical use for JavaScript on your own web site (having run through the tutorial, you should have a feel for a purpose to which you might put this technology). Then, try putting it into action.

☐ Trawl through SitePoint's extensive back catalogue of JavaScript-related articles,[18] beginning with Kevin Yank's JavaScript 101.[19]

☐ Be sure to ask any questions you have about JavaScript at SitePoint's dedicated JavaScript forum.[20]

When you've spent some time playing around with JavaScript, and you're ready for more, look again to SitePoint. The publisher has a book that will take you beyond the intermediate level, and into the realms of the expert! That book is titled *DHTML Utopia: Modern Web Design Using JavaScript & DOM.*[21]

Learning Server-side Programming

The final part of this roadmap to becoming an all-round web designer and developer involves server-side programming (or "server-side scripting"). While JavaScript is downloaded to the client computer and executed there, server-side scripts are executed on the server *before* the resulting web page is sent to the client. We use these types of scripting in different ways, but as a general rule, you can assume the following:

☐ JavaScript is best used to change the display or behavior of elements on the screen in front of you. Depending on what the script does, even if you disconnected your Internet connection, the JavaScript may quite happily continue to function, as it's running locally on your computer within a page that's already downloaded to your hard drive.

☐ Server-side programming is best used to retrieve or update information stored in a database, and to generate a web page based on that information. With server-side programming, a site user's action might be intended to change a record in your database. Thus, a server-side language is essential for tasks such

---

[18] All SitePoint's JavaScript articles are listed at http://www.sitepoint.com/subcat/javascript.
[19] http://www.sitepoint.com/article/javascript-101-1
[20] http://www.sitepoint.com/launch/javascriptforum/
[21] http://www.sitepoint.com/books/dhtml1/

as checking stock levels on an ecommerce site, and adjusting them if an order is placed. JavaScript alone could not achieve this.

Of course you could use both, for example, in a web page that's generated dynamically based on certain search criteria. A search on an ecommerce web site—such as Amazon—that displayed a selection of toasters would use server-side scripting to build the search results page, which would be sent for display on the client computer. JavaScript could then be used on the client computer to manipulate that web page in some way, perhaps allowing the user to drag and drop items into a shopping cart of some kind.[22]

Scripting Languages in Brief

Your options for server-side programming are many. All the languages below could be used to create dynamic web pages, and provide the ability to retrieve information from databases:

❑ PHP

❑ ASP/ASP.NET

❑ ColdFusion

❑ Perl

❑ Python

❑ Ruby/Ruby on Rails

There are many more in addition to this short list, believe me! Which one's right for you, though? This is where we start to veer into dangerous territory! The proponents of each language will swear blind that their language is the best tool for the job. In reality, each has its pros and cons, and some do a better job in certain circumstances than others. I can't list the strengths and weaknesses of all of them here—it would take far too long, and only confuse matters at this stage.

My advice would be to find out which languages your hosting company supports; that will refine your options quite quickly. You can also post questions to Site-

---

[22] There's a great example of this kind of drag-and-drop behavior on Panic's web site [http://www.panic.com/].

Point's Program Your Site forum[23]—explain your requirements and your level of expertise, and you can expect to receive sound advice on which language is best suited to your needs, and why.

Learning PHP

Of those languages listed above, I would recommend that you make PHP your first server-side language, because it's:

❑ intuitive and fairly easy to learn

❑ highly configurable and flexible

❑ a great companion language for MySQL (a free, fully-featured database software)

❑ portable—PHP can be run on Windows, Mac OS, and Linux

Where Can you Learn PHP?

It's beyond the scope of this book for me to teach you how to create a site in PHP—or any other language, for that matter—but thankfully there are many books that do exactly that. Once again, SitePoint has covered this for you: Kevin Yank, an acknowledged PHP expert, is the author of *Build Your Own Database Driven Website Using PHP & MySQL*.[24] If you want to build on the knowledge you've gained in this book to create dynamic web sites, Kevin's book is the logical next step.

If, having done some research, you decide to build your site using Microsoft's .NET Framework,[25] SitePoint can help you with this, too: *Build Your Own ASP.NET Website Using C# & VB.NET*,[26] by Zak Ruvalcaba, will tell you everything you need to know in order to build a dynamic web site using this technology.

---

[23] Actually, this page is a collection of SitePoint's sub-forums [http://www.sitepoint.com/launch/programsiteforum/] that deal with specific languages—it's your best starting point for this kind of query.
[24] http://www.sitepoint.com/books/phpmysql1/
[25] http://en.wikipedia.org/wiki/.NET
[26] http://www.sitepoint.com/books/aspnet1/

Summary

In this chapter, I've provided some pointers as to how you can take your web skills to the next level. I've suggested resources that will help you refine your XHTML and CSS skills to perfection, highlighted JavaScript as a very practical addition to your virtual toolbox, and promoted scripting languages as a means to creating killer web sites. However, the path you choose is entirely up to you. All I hope is that you've enjoyed the steps you've taken to get to this point, and that I've set you up well for the journey ahead.

Appendix A: XHTML Reference

The reference below is not intended as a replacement for the complete XHTML recommendation provided by the W3C.[1] Note that some attributes may not be included here and, unfortunately, it's not possible to demonstrate every possible or likely use for each element.

Common Attributes

In this appendix, specific attributes are highlighted for use with each XHTML element. In addition to these specific cases, the following common attributes may also be applied to any element you use:

id
> This is a unique reference that may be used by CSS for styling purposes, or through scripting (via the Document Object Model, or DOM).

class
> Mostly used in conjunction with CSS, the `class` attribute lets the web page classify elements as being of a certain type. It may be used to set appearance in CSS, or to change behavior in certain circumstances using JavaScript.

style
> This attribute allows CSS styles to be applied to specific elements inline. However, its use is not recommended—it's better to use external style sheets for this purpose.

title
> This attribute allows additional text information to be applied almost to any element. The supplied text usually appears in a hover-help "tooltip."

Internationalization Attributes

These attributes are used to clarify language issues on a web page:

lang
> This attribute allows us to specify the language in which the document is written. It's usually applied to the `html` element, or to a section of a document

---

[1] http://www.w3.org/TR/xhtml1/

that's written in a language that differs from the rest of the document—for instance, the `lang` attribute may be applied to a blockquote element. Examples of its use include `lang="en"` (English), `lang="fr"` (French), and `lang="ja"` (Japanese).

dir

The `dir` attribute allows us to specify the direction of the language (left-to-right is specified using `dir="ltr"`; right-to-left is specified using `dir="rtl"`).

XHTML Elements

XHTML Comments

An XHTML comment (`<!-- -->`) lets you insert into the source code a comment that will be ignored by the browser. It is a useful tool for explaining the practicalities of what you've done within your code (a useful note for yourself or anyone else who might need to edit your web page).

Attributes

Can Contain

anything other than double dashes (which could be misinterpreted by the web browser as the close of the comment)

May be Contained in

any XHTML element, but not inside the tag's opening and closing angle brackets

Examples

Here's an example of the correct usage of this element:

```
<div>
  <p>Here's some blurb about this form. It can include paragraphs
      and can also include</p>
  <!-- Only use list items below -->
  <ul>
    <li>Bullet points</li>
```

```
    <li>Bullet points</li>
    <li>Bullet points</li>
  </ul>
</div>
```

This is incorrect:

```
<div>
  <p>Here's some blurb about this form. It can include paragraphs
     and can also include</p>
  <ul class="funkylist" <!-- Only use list items below --> >
    <li>Bullet points</li>
    <li>Bullet points</li>
    <li>Bullet points</li>
  </ul>
</div>
```

Document Type Declarations

The doctype declaration must be the very first item in your document. It tells the browser which version of HTML or XHTML was used to write the document. HTML and XHTML have three possible doctypes each.

Attributes

no additional attributes; doctype must be typed *exactly* as-is (see below)

Can Contain

nothing

May be Contained in

nothing; must be the document's first item

Examples

HTML Strict DTD

```
<!DOCTYPE HTML PUBLIC "-//W3C//DTD HTML 4.01//EN"
    "http://www.w3.org/TR/html4/strict.dtd">
```

HTML Transitional DTD

```
<!DOCTYPE HTML PUBLIC "-//W3C//DTD HTML 4.01 Transitional//EN"
    "http://www.w3.org/TR/html4/loose.dtd">
```

Frameset DTD

```
<!DOCTYPE HTML PUBLIC "-//W3C//DTD HTML 4.01 Frameset//EN"
    "http://www.w3.org/TR/html4/frameset.dtd">
```

XHTML Strict DTD

```
<!DOCTYPE html PUBLIC "-//W3C//DTD XHTML 1.0 Strict//EN"
    "http://www.w3.org/TR/xhtml1/DTD/xhtml1-strict.dtd">
```

XHTML Transitional DTD

```
<!DOCTYPE html PUBLIC "-//W3C//DTD XHTML 1.0 Transitional//EN"
    "http://www.w3.org/TR/xhtml1/DTD/xhtml1-transitional.dtd">
```

XHTML Frameset DTD

```
<!DOCTYPE html PUBLIC "-//W3C//DTD XHTML 1.0 Frameset//EN"
    "http://www.w3.org/TR/xhtml1/DTD/xhtml1-frameset.dtd">
```

a

The a element (short for "anchor") allows us to create a link to another web page, using the href attribute, or to another location within the same web page.

Type

inline element

Attributes

href, rel, accesskey, tabindex

Can Contain

any inline element (other than a)

May be Contained in

block-level elements, and inline elements except a and button

Example

```
<div id="navigation">
  <ul>
    <li><a href="index.html">Home</a></li>
    <li><a href="about.html">About Us</a></li>
  </ul>
</div>
```

abbr

The abbr element is used to indicate abbreviations of words or phrases. It uses the title attribute to provide the long form of the abbreviation, which usually is seen as a "tooltip" when users hover their cursors over the abbreviation.

Type

inline element

Attributes

title, lang

Can Contain

inline elements

May be Contained in

block-level elements, inline elements

Example

```
<h2><abbr title="PHP Hypertext Preprocessor">PHP</abbr></h2>
<p>This is some block of text containing the odd abbreviation, like
    <abbr title="HyperText Markup Language">HTML</abbr>, for
    example.</p>
```

acronym

Very similar to the `abbr` element, the `acronym` is a special kind of abbreviation—one that can be uttered as if it were a word or phrase in its own right (rather than needing to be spelled out as individual letters). For example, NATO (North Atlantic Treaty Organization), NASA (National Aeronautics and Space Administration), and CAMRA (CAMpaign for Real Ale) are acronyms. As with `abbr`, `acronym` uses the `title` attribute to expand on the abbreviated form.

Type

inline element

Attributes

`title`, `lang`

Can Contain

inline elements

May be Contained in

block-level elements, inline elements

Example

```
<p>We are having discussions with the egg-heads at <acronym
    title="National Aeronautics and Space Administration"
    >NASA</acronym> about the possibility of sending another
    probe to Mars.</p>
```

address

The `address` element is used to provide contact information for a document or a section of a document. This might include the names of the people who maintain the document, email addresses for the provision of feedback, postal addresses, and/or phone numbers. However, it's not to be used simply for the purpose of marking up any old mailing address or email address on the page; use it *only* to mark up addresses that are the contact details for that document itself. By default, most browsers will display the contents of `address` in italics.

Type

block-level element

Attributes

common attributes

Can Contain

inline elements

May be Contained in

block-level elements

Example

```
<address>This document was last updated January 2006 by
    Brenda Smith, Electronic Payments Section (Lower
    Ground C).</address>
```

area

See the discussion of the `map` element for an explanation—and an example—of this element's usage.

Attributes

`shape`, `coords`, `href`, `alt`, common attributes

Can Contain

nothing

May be Contained in

`map` element only

blockquote

If you're quoting a person or publication, use the `blockquote` element, including inside it the usual markup you'd use to format normal text (e.g. paragraphs (`p`), lists (`ul`, `li`), and so on).

Type

block-level element

Attributes

`cite` (URL of the quotation source, if available), common attributes

Can Contain

block-level elements, inline elements

May be Contained in

block-level elements

Example

```
<blockquote cite="http://www.brucelawson.co.uk/index.php/2005/st
upid-stock-photography/">
  <p>It's missing alt text, so it's difficult to determine what
     it's supposed to mean. Presumably "oooh, there's been a
     global ecological catastrophe and we've got the last four
     leaves in the world and we've patented the DNA". Or they're
     rubbing ganja leaves together to extract the resin, but are
     too stupid to recognise Marijuana so are trying it with
     willow or silver birch.</p>
</blockquote>
```

body

This element defines the main body of the web page—everything that will be viewable on the screen.

Attributes

common attributes

Can Contain

block-level elements, inline elements

May be Contained in

html element only

Example

```
<!DOCTYPE html PUBLIC "-//W3C//DTD XHTML 1.0 Strict//EN"
    "http://www.w3.org/TR/xhtml1/DTD/xhtml1-strict.dtd">
<html xmlns="http://www.w3.org/1999/xhtml">
<head>
  <title>A simple web page </title>
  <meta http-equiv="Content-Type"
      content="text/html; charset=utf-8" />
</head>
<body>

  <p>Look at me luvverly body (of the web page, that
      is)</p>
</body>
</html>
```

br

This element forces a line break (or, for those who still remember such devices, a single carriage return on a typewriter). It is a valid element to use in XHTML Strict, but should be avoided where possible (it's presentational to a degree, although in some elements, such as address, we have no other way to create new lines). Wherever possible, use CSS to create visual gaps on a page, instead of relying on the br element.

Type

inline element

Attributes

`style`, common attributes

Can Contain

nothing—empty element

May be Contained in

block-level elements, inline elements

Example

```
<address>This document was last updated January 2006.
    Contact:<br />
    Brenda Smith,<br />
    Electronic Payments Section (Lower Ground C),<br />
    Head Office</address>
```

button

A `button` is used to group a selection of text and/or images into a single, clickable item for use in a form. It's not used often, though, largely because of the poor browser support that, historically, was provided for this element.

Type

inline element

Attributes

`name`, `value`, `type`, `disabled`, `accesskey`, `tabindex`, common attributes

Can Contain

inline elements (except `a`, `input`, `select`, `textarea`, `label`, `button`, and `iframe`), block-level elements (except `form` and `fieldset`)

May be Contained in

block-level elements, inline elements (except `button`)

Example

```
<button type="submit"> Click me, <em>please</em> click me!<br />
    <img src="images/smile.gif" alt="" />
</button>
```

caption

The `caption` element is used to caption the data contained in a table—not for picture captions! By default, the caption usually is centered above the table to which it relates, although you can re-style this default placement using CSS).

Type

block-level element

Attributes

common attributes

Can Contain

inline elements (relating to text formatting)

May be Contained in

`table` element only

Example

```
<table cellspacing="0" summary="Club events/dive trips for the
    next six months">
  <caption>Club events/dive trips for the next six
      months</caption>
  <tr>
    <th scope="col">Date</th>
    <th scope="col">Event Description</th>
```

```
      <th scope="col">Approximate Cost</th>
      <th scope="col">Contact</th>
   </tr>
   ...
</table>
```

cite

The `cite` element should be used to mark up citations, for example, newspaper and magazine titles, theater show titles, references to other sources, and quotation attributions. By default, most browsers will display text marked with `cite` in italic text, though this can be re-styled with CSS.

Type

inline element

Attributes

common attributes

Can Contain

inline elements

May be Contained in

inline elements, block-level elements

Example

```
<p>It was just over a year since I watched a Harry Potter film -
   it was <cite>The Prisoner of Azkaban</cite>, which I caught
   in a cinema in Hobart, Tasmania.</p>
```

code

This element defines computer code of any type. The `code` element is often used in conjunction with the `pre` element (which identifies preformatted text) to retain in source markup the carriage returns and spacing that would otherwise be ignored by a web browser.

Type

inline element

Attributes

common attributes

Can Contain

inline elements

May be Contained in

inline elements, block-level elements

Example

```
<pre><code>/* A CSS example */
p {
  font-family: serif;
  color: red;
}
</code></pre>
```

col

The `col` element allows you to set attributes that are common to a column in a table. It should appear in the `table` element, before the optional `thead` (if present), and may be wrapped inside a `colgroup` element (also optional). The `col` element is useful in that it can save you having to enter CSS class names (and other attributes) many times over in each row—you can set them in the `col` element and the browser works out the rest.

Attributes

`span` (indicates how many columns the attributes should apply to), `char` (sets the character in the column with which the information should be aligned), `charoff` (specifies an "offset" that the aligned information should use—the offset being relative to the character defined by the `char` element)

Can Contain

nothing (empty element)

May be Contained in

colgroup or table only

Example

```
<table border="1">
  <col span="2" class="financial" char="."></col>
  <tr>
    <th>Account Type</th>
    <th>Basic Interest Rate (%)</th>
  </tr>
  <tr>
    <td>SmartInvestor</td>
    <td>2.5</td>
  </tr>
  ...
</table>
```

colgroup

This element is related to the col element mentioned above. It's used to group a number of columns together for formatting purposes.

Attributes

span, char, charoff (see previous entry for col)

Can Contain

col element only

May be Contained in

table element only

Example

```
<table border="1">
  <colgroup span="2" class="financial">
    <col class="unbold"></col>
    <col char="."></col>
  </colgroup>
  <tr>
    <th>Account Type</th>
    <th>Basic Interest Rate (%)</th>
  </tr>
  <tr>
    <td>SmartInvestor</td>
    <td>2.5</td>
  </tr>
  ...
</table>
```

dd

See the entry for dl for a full description.

Type

block-level element

Attributes

common attributes

Can Contain

inline elements, block-level elements

May be Contained in

dl element only

Example

See entry for dl for example.

del

The `del` element signifies a portion of text that has been deleted by the document's author, or the person who maintains the document. It's used to signify changes to the document in a somewhat simpler way than that offered by the likes of Microsoft Word's "Track Changes" facility.

Type

block-level or inline element

Attributes

`cite` (used to provide URL of a web page that explains the reasoning for the change in more detail), `datetime` (date and time that the document was amended), common attributes

Can Contain

inline elements, block-level elements

May be Contained in

inline elements, block-level elements

Example

```
<p>The chemical identified was an alcohol of some kind <del
    cite="/toxicology/reports/20041111/"
    datetime="2004-11-11T12:03:04" title="Cannot be proven at
    this point, awaiting formal results">
    (isopropanol, it is believed)</del></p>
```

dfn

The `dfn` element is used to indicate the defining instance of a term that may be used in several places on a web page or site.

Type

inline element

Attributes

common attributes

Can Contain

inline elements

May be Contained in

inline elements, block-level elements

Example

```
<p>The <dfn>sampler</dfn> records sounds and saves them digitally
    whereby they can be played back, via a keyboard, at a range
    of different pitches. Most recording artists will at some
    time use a sampler for one reason or another (breakbeats,
    strings sounds, vocal stabs).</p>
```

div

The div is a generic block-level element. In the same way that p means paragraph, and blockquote indicates a quotation, div doesn't convey any meaning about its contents, and as such, is easily customized to your own needs. The div element is the most prevalent method for identifying the structural sections of a document, and for laying out a web page using CSS.

Type

block-level element

Attributes

common attributes

Can Contain

inline elements, block-level elements

May be Contained in

`blockquote`, `body`, `button`, `dd`, `del`, `div`, `fieldset`, `form`, `iframe`, `ins`, `li`, `map`, `noframes`, `noscript`, `object`, `td`, `th`

Example

```
<div id="header">
  <div id="sitebranding">
    <h1>BubbleUnder.com</h1>
  </div>
  <div id="tagline">
    <p>Diving club for the south-west UK - let's make a
        splash!</p>
  </div>
</div>
```

dl

If you wanted to list a series of items each of which had a title and a description of some kind (i.e. there were two parts to each item), you'd use the definition list element (`dl`), then mark up each item with a definition term (`dt`) and a definition description element (`dd`). The definition description can contain other block-level text formatting elements, such as `p` elements, which makes it possible for us to use lengthy descriptions in the `dd` without falling foul of XHTML rules. It's possible to nest definition lists by placing a fresh `dl` inside a `dd`.

Type

block-level element

Attributes

common attributes

Can Contain

inline elements, block-level elements

May be Contained in

dl element only

Example

```
<dl>
  <dt>Spam</dt>
  <dd>Unsolicited email sent in the hope of increasing sales of
      some dodgy product that's on offer or simply for the
      purposes of annoying people.
    <dl>
      <dt>Spammer</dt>
      <dd>Someone who sends out spam email and therefore deserves
          to develop a nasty incurable disease of some kind.</dd>
      <dt>Spam Filter</dt>
      <dd>A tool used in email to 'filter out'
          likely spam messages, usually placing them in a
          dedicated junk messages folder or similar.</dd>
    </dl>
  </dd>
  ...
</dl>
```

dt

See the entry for dl for a full description of this element.

Type

block-level element

Attributes

common attributes

Can Contain

inline elements, block-level elements

May be Contained in

dl element only

Example

See the entry for dl for an example of this element.

em

The em element can be used to emphasize any selection of text. Typically, text marked up with em will render in the browser as italic text.

Type

inline element

Attributes

common attributes

Can Contain

inline elements

May be Contained in

inline elements, block-level elements

Example

```
<p>I've told you a <em>million</em> times not to exaggerate!</p>
```

fieldset

A `fieldset` is used to group together a collection of logically related form elements. It works alongside the `legend` element, which is used to provide the descriptive label for the grouped form elements. By default, browsers will render the `fieldset` as a simple border surrounding the grouped form elements. A slight break in the border creates a space in which the legend appears. This display can be restyled using CSS.

Type

block-level element

Attributes

common attributes

Can Contain

a `legend` element followed by zero or more block-level and inline elements

May be Contained in

blockquote, body, dd, del, div, fieldset, form, iframe, ins, li, map, noframes, noscript, object, td, th

Example

```
<form method="post" action="/comments/>
  <fieldset>
  <legend>Your feedback</legend>
  <p><label for="Name">Your name:</label>
    <br />
    <input type="text" name="Name" id="Name" size="45" /></p>
  <p><label for="WebSite">Your web site (optional - just us being
      curious):</label>
    <br />
    <input name="WebSite" type="text" id="WebSite"
        value="http://" size="45" /></p>
    <p><label for="EmailAddress">Your email address:</label>
      <br />
      <input type="text" name="EmailAddress" id="EmailAddress"
```

```
        size="45" /></p>
  <p><label for="Comments">Comments/suggestions/requests:<
      /label>
    <br />
    <textarea name="Comments" id="Comments" rows="7"
      cols="55"></textarea></p>
  <input type="submit" class="button" name="Submit" value="Send
      your feedback &gt;&gt;" />
 </fieldset>
</form>
```

form

The form element defines an interactive form that can include form controls such as input, select, textarea, and button. The form is submitted with an input or button element with a type attribute of submit. The action defines the location to which the form details should be sent for processing.

Type

block-level element

Attributes

method (get or post), action (where the form data is sent for processing), common attributes

Can Contain

one or more script or block-level elements (except form)

May be Contained in

blockquote, body, dd, del, div, fieldset, iframe, ins, li, map, noframes, noscript, object, td, th

Example

```
<form method="get" action="http://search.atomz.com/search/">
  <div id="searcharea">
    <label for="txtSearch">Search</label>
    <input type="text" title="Enter your search phrase here"
```

```
            id="txtSearch" name="sp-q" size="20" />
    <input type="submit" name="search" value="Go &gt;&gt;" />
  </div>
</form>
```

h1 to h6

h1 to h6 are used to define headings on a web page, with h1 being the highest level (and, by default, the largest in terms of font size), and h6 the lowest (and smallest).

Type

block-level element

Attributes

common attributes

Can Contain

inline elements only

May be contained in

block-level elements (except other h1–h6 elements)

Example

```
<h1>Get in touch</h1>
<p>Drop us a line - let us know how we're doing. Please follow
  the instructions below to contact us.</p>
<h2>Account Information</h2>
<p>If you would like to speak to a representative about your
account...
</p>
```

head

The head element contains information about the document, including the title element, meta information (keywords, author details, etc.), and links to any style sheet or script resource files that are required by the document. The `head` is required in all documents, and is followed immediately by the `body` element.

Attributes

`profile`, which is used to provide the URL of a page that contains meta data information about the page (used instead of meta tags)

Can Contain

one `title` element; zero or more `script`, `style`, `meta`, `link`, or `object` elements

May be Contained in

the `html` element only

Example

```
<!DOCTYPE html PUBLIC "-//W3C//DTD XHTML 1.0 Strict//EN"
    "http://www.w3.org/TR/xhtml1/DTD/xhtml1-strict.dtd">
<html xmlns="http://www.w3.org/1999/xhtml">
<head>
  <title>A simple web page</title>
  <meta http-equiv="Content-Type" content="text/html;
      charset=utf-8" />
</head>
<body>
  <p>Look at me luvverly body (of the web page, that is)</p>
</body>
</html>
```

hr

The `hr` element creates a horizontal rule that can be used to section off the content in a document. However, the `hr` element is very "presentational." The preferred method for sectioning off parts of a document is to use a `div` element (wrapping it around the section), and to apply through your CSS a `border-bottom` property, or a custom background image anchored at the section's bottom.

Type

block-level element

Attributes

common attributes

Can Contain

nothing (empty element)

May be Contained in

blockquote, body, button, dd, del, div, fieldset, form, iframe, ins, li, map, noframes, noscript, object, td, th

Example

```
<p>The last few days have been fairly eventful. Actually, scrub
    that - what I mean is busy. Very busy.</p>
<hr / >
<p>Two days ago, things had seemed a lot calmer - it was a whole
    different world, in fact.</p>
```

html

The html is the highest-level element in the document. Every other element is contained within this element.

Type

N/A

Attributes

lang (language), dir (direction of text: left-to-right, right-to-left, etc.), xmlns (XML Name Space)

Can Contain

head, followed by body

May be Contained in

nothing (html is the root—or top-level—element of the document)

Example

```
<!DOCTYPE html PUBLIC "-//W3C//DTD XHTML 1.0 Strict//EN"
    "http://www.w3.org/TR/xhtml1/DTD/xhtml1-strict.dtd">
<html xmlns="http://www.w3.org/1999/xhtml">
<head>
  <title>A simple web page</title>
  <meta http-equiv="Content-Type"
      content="text/html; charset=utf-8" />
</head>
<body>
  <p>Look at me luvverly body (of the web page, that
      is)</p>
</body>
</html>
```

iframe

An iframe is used to embed in a document a new window that contains another entirely different document. This second document is referenced using the src attribute. Often, this element is used to pull into a page content from another location, but to style that content so that it appears to be from the same source (e.g. to display search results).

Type

block-level element

Attributes

src, title, common attributes

Can Contain

block-level elements, inline elements (which are only displayed in browsers that do not understand iframe)

May be Contained in

block-level elements, inline elements (except `button`)

Example

```
<iframe src="tourdates.html" title="Band tour dates ">
  <!-- Alternate content for browsers that do not understand
      iframe -->
  <h1>Tour Dates</h1>
  <h2>UK</h2>
  ...
</iframe>
```

`img`

The `img` element specifies an inline image. The required attribute `src` points to the location of the image on the file system. Common formats of the files used for inline images are `gif`, `jpg`, and `png`. The `alt` attribute is a required attribute that provides a text alternative for the image. This text is used by browsers that do not support images, as well as users who have images disabled, or use assistive technology such as screen readers. The `longdesc` attribute builds on the `alt` attribute (which should be a short text summary) by providing a reference to a file that contains a full-text description for the image—particularly useful for charts or graphs.

Type

inline element

Attributes

`src`, `alt`, `height`, `width`, `longdesc`, `usemap`, common attributes

Can Contain

nothing (empty element)

May be Contained in

inline elements, block-level elements (except `pre`)

Example

```
<img src="peanut-butter.jpg" alt="Vintage label from peanut butter
    jar" longdesc="peanut-butter-label-history.txt" height="300"
    width="240" />
```

input

The input element is used to collect data in a form. It can come in a of a number of different guises that are determined by the type of attribute specified. The different types of input are text, hidden, password, checkbox, radio, submit, reset, file, image, and button.

Type

inline element

Attributes

type, name, value, src, maxlength, size, disabled, readonly, accept, access-key, common attributes

Can Contain

nothing (empty element)

May be Contained in

block-level elements, inline elements (except button)

Example

```
<input type="text" name="txtFirstName" />
<input type="password" name="txtPassword" />
<input type="button" name="cmdChkAvail" value="Check
    Availability" />
<input type="submit" name="cmdBookNow" value="Place
    Booking" />
<input type="radio" name="radMarried" value="Yes" />Yes,
    I am married<br />
<input type="radio" name="radMarried" value="No" /> No,
    I am single
```

```
<input type="checkbox" name="chkSubscribe" value="Subscribe" />
    Subscribe to the newsletter Title<br />
  <select name="ddlTitle">
    <option>Mr</option>
    ...
    </select>
Your comments<br />
<textarea name="txtComments"></textarea>
<button name="cmdBigButton">Go on, click me!</button>
```

ins

Similar to the del element, the ins element is used to mark up a change in the content of a document.

Type

block-level or inline element

Attributes

cite, used to provide the URL of web page that explains the reasoning for the change in more detail; datetime, identifying the date and time that the document was amended; common attributes

Can Contain

inline elements, block-level elements

May be Contained in

inline elements, block-level elements

Example

```
<p>The chemical identified was an alcohol of some kind <del
    cite="/toxicology/reports/20041111/"
    datetime="2004-11-11T12:03:04" title="Cannot be proven at
    this point, awaiting formal results">(isopropanol, it is
    believed)</del> <ins cite="/toxicology/reports/20041112/"
    datetime="2004-11-12T14:13:46" title="Identified by head
```

```
    forensic team">(nothing more harmful than cough mixture, it
    later transpired)</ins>.</p>
```

kbd

The kbd element signifies text that the user needs to enter and is usually rendered by browsers in monospaced text.

Type

inline element

Attributes

common attributes

Can Contain

inline elements

May be Contained in

inline elements, block-level elements

Example

```
<p>If you are unsure of the answer to this question, please type
    <kbd>?</kbd> in the text input.</p>
```

label

A label element is used to link any form field (input, textarea, or select) with its associated descriptive text (e.g. linking a text input for a user's first name with the text "First Name"). It uses the for attribute to point to the id attribute of the related form input.

Type

inline element

Attributes

for, accesskey, common attributes

Can Contain

inline elements (except label)

May be Contained in

block-level elements, inline elements (except button)

Example

```
<label for="txtFirstName">First Name:</label><br />
<input class="input" type="text" title="Enter your first
    name" maxlength="" size="" name="txtFirstName"
    id="txtFirstName" value="">

Age:<br />
<input class="input" type="radio" title="Choose from one of
    the options" name="radAge" id="radAge4_0" value="Under30">
<label for="radAge4_0"> Under 30</label><br />
<input class="input" type="radio" title="Choose from one of the
    options" name="radAge" id="radAge4_1" value="Over30">
<label for="radAge4_1"> Over 30</label>
<br />

What colors do you like:<br />
<input class="input" type="checkbox" title="Select what colors
    you like" name="chk0" id="chk0_0" value="red">
  <label for="chk0_0"> red</label><br />
<input class="input" type="checkbox" title="Select what colors
    you like" name="chk1" id="chk1_1" value="green">
<label for="chk1_1"> green</label><br />
<input class="input" type="checkbox" title="Select what colors
you like" name="chk2" id="chk2_2" value="blue">
<label for="chk2_2"> blue</label><br />
<input class="input" type="checkbox" title="Select what colors
you like" name="chk3" id="chk3_3" value="purple">
<label for="chk3_3"> purple</label><br />

<label for="txtLifeStory">Your life story:</label><br />
<textarea title="Write your life story here" name="txtLifeStory"
```

```
      id="txtLifeStory" rows="5" cols="25" class="input"></textarea>

<label for="ddlTown">Favorite Town:</label><br />
<select title="Please choose your favorite town" name="ddlTown"
    id="ddlTown">
  <option value="">Please Select ... </option>
  <option value="Swindon">Swindon</option>
  <option value="London">London</option>
  <option value="Burkino Faso">Burkino Faso</option>
</select>
```

legend

The legend element defines a title in a fieldset. For its usage and an example, please refer to the entry for fieldset.

Type

inline element

Attributes

common attributes

Can Contain

inline elements

May be Contained in

fieldset only

Example

See the entry for fieldset.

li

The li element defines a list item (or bullet point, to use another term), and can appear either in an unordered list (ul) or an ordered list (ol).

Type

block-level element

Attributes

common attributes

Can Contain

inline elements, block-level elements

May be Contained in

ol and ul only

Example

```
<ul>
  <li><a href="index.html">Home</a></li>
  <li><a href="about.html">About Us</a></li>
  <li><a href="events.html">Club Events</a></li>
  <li><a href="contact.html">Contact Us</a></li>
  <li><a href="gallery.html">Image Gallery</a></li>
</ul>
<p>People attending</p>
<ol>
  <li>Bob James</li>
  <li>Fred Bloggs</li>
  <li>David Dickinson</li>
  <li>Carole Smith</li>
</ol>
```

link

The link element defines relationships between documents, such as which is the previous or next document in a linear series of documents. Many browsers do not support the link element fully (or at all). However, it's used widely for one purpose above all others: linking to stylesheets.

Attributes

rel (the document that's being referred to), rev (the parent document that referred to this document), type, href, charset, media, common attributes

Can Contain

nothing (empty element)

May be Contained in

head only

Example

```
<link rel="prev" href="page1.html" title="setting up your
    development environment" />
<link rel="next" href="page3.html" title="styling your web
    page" />
<link rel="stylesheet" href="style1.css" type="text/css" />
```

map

As well as using an image as a link, you can identify specific areas within an image, called hotspots, that you'll use to link to other web pages. An image is related to the areas that are "clickable" using the map element (the img element requires a usemap attribute to link the two); the area provides the coordinates in that image map (which can be a rectangle, circle, or polygon: rect, circ, poly for short).

Attributes

common attributes

Can Contain

block-level elements, area elements

May be Contained in

inline elements, block-level elements

Example

```
<img src="divers.gif" width="300" height="200" alt="Divers"
    usemap="#divermap" />
<map id="divermap" name="divermap">
  <area shape="rect" coords="0,0,300,100" href="geoff.htm"
      alt="Geoff" />
  <area shape="rect" coords ="0,101,300,200"href="fred.htm"
      alt="Fred" />
</map>
```

meta

The meta element provides metadata, for example keywords, description, and author information. There is no limit to the number of meta elements that can appear in the head. The meta element has two parts: the property name and the content (the corresponding value for that property).

Attributes

name, content, internationalization attributes

Can Contain

nothing (empty element)

May be Contained in

head only

Example

```
<meta name="author" content="Fred Bloggs" />
<meta name="copyright" content="Fred Bloggs, CyberDesign" />
```

noscript

The noscript element is used to provide content for browsers that are unable to interpret JavaScript (either because they are an old browser that doesn't support it, or because JavaScript has been turned off). Such a browser will ignore the

JavaScript code contained in the `script` element, and display the markup contained in the `noscript` element instead.

Attributes

common attributes

Can Contain

block-level elements, inline elements

May be Contained in

blockquote, body, button, dd, del, div, fieldset, form, iframe, ins, li, map, noscript, object, td, th

Example

```
<script type="text/javascript" src="dynamicmenu.js"></script>
<noscript> <!-- basic non-JavaScript menu goes here -->
  <h2>Site Navigation Menu</h2>
  <ul>
    <li><a href="index.html">Home</a></li>
    <li><a href="about.html">About Us</a></li>
    <li><a href="contact.html">Contact Us</a></li>
  </ul>
<noscript>
```

object

Defines an object of any type—an image, video, Java applet, Flash movie or other resource—embedded in a web page.

Type

inline element

Attributes

data, classid, archive, codebase, width, height, name, type, codetype, standby, tabindex, declare, common attributes

Can Contain

any number of param elements followed by block-level elements, inline elements

May be Contained in

head, inline elements, block-level elements (except pre)

Example

```
<object
  type="application/x-shockwave-flash" data="intro.swf"
  width="600" height="400">
  <param name="movie" value="intro.swf" />
</object>
```

ol

See the entry for li for an explanation and examples of this element's usage.

Type

block-level element

Attributes

common attributes

Can Contain

one or more li elements

May be Contained in

block-level elements

optgroup

This element defines a logical grouping of option elements (see option below for a discussion and example of this element's usage).

Attributes

`label`, `disabled`, common attributes

Can Contain

one or more `option` elements

May be Contained in

`select` element only

option

This element defines an option in a drop-down list (the XHTML `select` element). `options` can be grouped using the `optgroup` element, which is identified using the `label` attribute.

Type

N/A

Attributes

`value`, `selected`, `disabled`, `label`, common attributes

Can Contain

text only

May be Contained in

`select` or `optgroup` elements only

Example

```
<select name="favoritefood">
  <optgroup label="Dairy products">
    <option>Cheese</option>
    <option>Egg</option>
  </optgroup>
```

```
  <optgroup label="Vegetables">
    <option>Cabbage</option>
    <option>Lettuce</option>
    <option>Beans</option>
    <option>Onions</option>
    <option>Courgettes</option>
  </optgroup>
  <optgroup label="Fruit">
    <option>Apples</option>
    <option>Grapes</option>
    <option>Pineapples</option>
  </optgroup>
</select>
```

p

One of the most commonly used elements, the p element is used to mark up a paragraph of text. A p element should always be used to create natural breaks in text where a new paragraph begins. Using two br elements at such points should be avoided.

Type

block-level element

Attributes

common attributes

Can Contain

inline elements

May be Contained in

block-level elements (except p)

Example

```
<p>Not only was he slow, but Sebastian hadn't quite mastered
    buoyancy - I regularly heard him inflate his jacket, which
    caused him to rise towards the surface, whereupon he'd dump
```

```
    air and come back down again. Up, down, up, down. This was
    getting frustrating...</p>
<p>Despite the duff dive buddy, I did enjoy it - we got almost
    an hour in the water varying between 12 and 6 meters and even
    got to see an octopus that the dive leader found nestled away.
    It was a good-sized one, too, perhaps two feet long, and
    really enjoyed squirting ink all over the pesky dive leader
    for disturbing his rest.</p>
```

param

The param element is used to provide additional information for a resource that's being pulled into the document by an object or applet element.

Attributes

name, value, type

Can Contain

May be Contained in

object, applet

Example

```
<object data="2litreengine.wav" type="audio/x-wav" title="Sound
    of a 2 liter engine misfiring"> <param name="autostart"
    value="true">
  <param name="hidden" value="true">
</object>
```

pre

The pre element contains "preformatted" text—this means that, no matter how your text appears in the source code, it will be rendered with exactly the same appearance on the web page. Normally, the web browser will ignore line breaks in the source code, and will honor only the first space between words—regardless of whether ten or a hundred spaces actually exist there. However, the pre element ensures that all spaces and carriage returns are rendered. One of the most common uses of `pre` is to preserve the indentation in the display of code examples that are also marked up with the `code` element.

Type

inline element

Attributes

common attributes

Can Contain

inline elements (except `img`, `object`, `sub`, `sup`)

May be Contained in

`blockquote`, `body`, `button`, `dd`, `del`, `div`, `fieldset`, `form`, `iframe`, `ins`, `li`, `map`, `noscript`, `object`, `td`, `th`

Example

```
<pre><code>/* A CSS example */
p {
  font-family: serif;
  color: red;
}
</code></pre>
```

q

The q element is used to mark up short (inline) quotations. While `blockquote` is a block-level element that's used for larger quotations, the q element is useful for partial quotes that may be contained within a paragraph of text. Note that it should be possible to have CSS automatically insert quotation marks around the quoted text using the `content-before` and `content-after` properties, but browser support for these properties is not great at the time of writing. Hence, the example below shows the quotes included in the text.

Type

inline element

Attributes

`cite`, common attributes

Can Contain

inline elements

May be Contained in

block-level elements, inline elements

Example

```
<p>He referred to the man as a <q
    cite="http://somefictionalwebpage.com/">"strange, wily kind of
    character"</q> but kept his juiciest comments for the
    man's business partner:
  <blockquote>"I've never met a slimier creature in the business
      world. He's greased so many palms I'm amazed he was able to
      climb the corporate ladder so easily without slipping.
      Would I trust him with my money? I'd rather bet on the
      horses!"</blockquote>
</p>
```

samp

This element defines sample output, such as the result of a computer program or script.

Type

inline element

Attributes

common attributes

Can Contain

inline elements

May be Contained in

block-level elements, inline elements

Example

```
<p>If you do not configure your server correctly,
    you may receive the following error message:<br />
    <samp>0x0000000B: NO_EXCEPTION_HANDLING_SUPPORT</samp></p>
```

script

The `script` element is used to tell the web browser that a piece of client-side scripting is coming up. The scripted content can appear within the opening `<script>` and closing `</script>` tags; it may also be contained in a separate file, and referred to using the `src` attribute. The most likely use for the `script` element is to mark up JavaScript (although you might also use it to identify VBScript). When it's used to mark up essential features of your page, the `script` element should be followed with a `noscript` element, so that site visitors who have JavaScript disabled, or use browsers that don't understand scripted content, can still access the functionality.

Attributes

`type` (the type of script that's being referred to, e.g. `type="text/javascript"`), `src` (the external script file that the web page refers to, e.g. `src="rollover_ef-fects.js"`)

Can Contain

scripting language content only

May be Contained in

`head` (for functions) and any element in the `body`

Example

```
<!DOCTYPE html PUBLIC "-//W3C//DTD XHTML 1.0 Strict//EN"
    "http://www.w3.org/TR/xhtml1/DTD/xhtml1-strict.dtd">
<html xmlns="http://www.w3.org/1999/xhtml" lang="en">
<head>
  <title>Sydney 2002 - Down Under Part II - arrival at Sydney
      Airport</title>
  <link rel="stylesheet" type="text/css" title="default"
      href="css/style1.css" />
  <link rel="alternate stylesheet" type="text/css"
      title="style2" href="css/style2.css" />
  <link rel="stylesheet" type="text/css" href="css/print.css"
      media="print" />
  <script type="text/javascript"
      src="toggleStyleSheet.js"></script>
</head>
<body>
  <h1>Arrival at the Airport</h1> ...
  <script type="text/javascript">
    // email address obscured using JavaScript to avoid
    // spammers getting hold of it
    document.write('<p><a href="mailto:lloydi' + '@' +
    'lloydi' + '.com">Email me&lt;/a>&lt;/p>')
  </script>
  <noscript>
    <p><a href="email-instructions.html">Find out how to
    email me here</a></p>
  </noscript>
</body>
</html>
```

select

The select element is ideal for use in a form in which you want users to pick a single option from many possible choices. It's sometimes referred to as a "drop-down list" or "pull-down menu." For example, it's often used in registration pages on which users must identify the country in which they live. It's also possible to configure a select to accept multiple selections (with the aid of the multiple and size attributes), but it's not used in this way very often, as it requires the user to know that the **Ctrl** key must be held down while they click.

Type

inline element

Attributes

name, id, size, disabled, tabindex, standard attributes

Can Contain

optgroup and option elements only

May be Contained in

block-level elements, inline-elements (except select element), must be contained in a form element

Example

```
<select name="favoritefood">
  <option>Cheese</option>
  <option>Egg</option>
  <option>Cabbage</option>
  <option>Lettuce</option>
  <option>Beans</option>
  <option>Onions</option>
  <option>Courgettes</option>
  <option>Apples</option>
  <option>Grapes</option>
  <option>Pineapples</option>
</select>
```

span

The span element is really the inline equivalent of the block-level div element—it's an element that conveys no meaning, but is incredibly useful when combined with CSS to mark up the sections of a document. The span can be wrapped around any inline element for purposes of styling it, or as a means to identify it (using the id attribute) so that it can be accessed by a piece of JavaScript.

Type

inline element

Attributes

common attributes

Can Contain

inline elements only (including other span elements)

May be Contained in

block-level elements, inline elements

Example

```
<p>This turtle was spotted swimming around the Great Barrier Reef
   (Queensland, Australia) quite gracefully despite having had a
   large chunk taken out of its right side, presumably in
   a shark attack. <span class="photocredit">[Photographer: Ian
   Lloyd]</span></p>
```

strong

The strong element is used to add strong emphasis to text (i.e., more emphasis than the em element).

Type

inline element

Attributes

common attributes

Can Contain

inline elements

May be Contained in

block-level elements, inline elements

Example

```
<p>I cannot emphasise this enough: if you step out of line once
    more, <strong>you will be punished</strong>.</p>
```

style

The style element appears in the head of the document and is used to contain style declarations for that document. It's also possible to use the style element to link to an external style sheet (using the @import statement).

Attributes

type, media, title, internationalization attributes

Can Contain

embedded style sheet declarations

May be Contained in

head only

Example

```
<!DOCTYPE html PUBLIC "-//W3C//DTD XHTML 1.0 Strict//EN"
    "http://www.w3.org/TR/xhtml1/DTD/xhtml1-strict.dtd">
<html xmlns="http://www.w3.org/1999/xhtml">
<head>
  <title>Hot Air Ballooning in Capadoccia, Central Turkey</title>
  <meta http-equiv="Content-Type"
      content="text/html; charset=utf-8" />
  <style type="text/css">
    @import url(ballooning.css);
    body {
      margin: 0;
      padding: 0;
    }
```

```
    </style>
</head>
...
```

sub

The sub element defines subscript text (that is, text that is dropped below the baseline of the main text slightly—not a footnote). This element doesn't add any real meaning to the text it affects and, as such, is on the presentational side of things. The most likely use for this element is in chemical symbology, for example, the 2 in H_2O. Note, though, that there is a markup language for chemical formulae, called CML.

Type

inline element

Attributes

common attributes

Can Contain

inline elements

May be Contained in

block-level elements, inline elements

Example

```
<p>Sulphuric acid (H<sub>2</sub>SO<sub>4</sub> is quite a nasty
    substance.</p>
```

sup

The sup element is very similar to the sub element in that it's somewhat presentational, and doesn't convey any meaning. The difference is that sup defines superscript (text that's raised above the usual text baseline). This element may be used for mathematical purposes (a number raised to the power of another, for example, 2 squared) and is sometimes used to identify footnotes in a web page.

However, note that there is a markup language that specifically caters for mathematical formulae, called MathML.

Type

inline element

Attributes

common attributes

Can Contain

inline elements

May be Contained in

block-level elements, inline elements

Example

```
<p>2 cubed (meaning 2 * 2 * 2) should be expressed
    as 2<sup>3</sup></p>
```

table

The `table` element is used to present data in a grid-like fashion—in rows and columns. It can be styled effectively using CSS (as demonstrated in Chapter 6), although it's very common to see tables styled using the XHTML attributes listed below. A table should be used only for tabular data; it should not be used (or rather misused) as a page layout mechanism. At its most basic, a table is built using the `table`, `tr`, and `td` elements (with `th` elements used for column or row headings); a slightly more complicated table will see the addition of the `thead`, `tfoot`, and `tbody` elements.

Type

block-level element

Attributes

`summary`, `cellpadding`, `cellspacing`, `width`, `border`, common attributes

Can Contain

`caption` (optional), `col`/`colgroup` elements (optional), `thead` (optional), `tfoot` (optional), `tbody` (optional), `tr`, `th`, `td`

May be Contained in

`blockquote`, `body`, `button`, `dd`, `del`, `div`, `fieldset`, `form`, `iframe`, `ins`, `li`, `map`, `noscript`, `object`, `td`, `th`

Examples

Basic table:

```
<table summary="Interest Rates">
  <tr>
    <th>Account Type</th>
    <th>Interest Rate</th>
  </tr>
  <tr>
    <td>Smart</td>
    <td>From 2%</td>
  </tr>
  <tr>
    <td>Young Saver</td>
    <td>From 1.6%</td>
  </tr>
</table>
```

A more advanced table:

```
<table summary="Interest Rates">
  <caption>Interest Rates</caption>
  <thead>
    <tr>
      <th>Account Type</th>
      <th>Interest Rate</th>
    </tr>
  </thead>
  <tbody>
```

```
    <tr>
      <td>Smart</td>
      <td>From 2%</td>
    </tr>
    <tr>
      <td>Young Saver</td>
      <td>From 1.6%</td>
    </tr>
  </tbody>
</table>
```

tbody

The tbody element is used to group together the rows in a table that make up the main body of the table's data—that is, everything between column header and footer data.

Attributes

common attributes

Can Contain

tr elements

May be Contained in

table element

Example

See the advanced table example shown in the definition for table.

td

The td element defines a table cell (td standing for table data).

Attributes

rowspan, colspan, headers, abbr, common attributes

Can Contain

block-level elements, inline elements

May be Contained in

`tr` element

Example

See the example shown in the definition for `table`.

textarea

The `textarea` element is used within a `form` element to accept multi-line text input. It's often used in webmail applications (such as Yahoo! or Hotmail) for the main text entry area. The `textarea` is a better option than a simple text input because it allows the user to see clearly what they're entering into the form.

Type

inline element

Attributes

`rows` (how many rows of text will be on display), `cols` (how many characters wide should the `textarea` be), `name`, `id`, `disabled`, `accesskey`, `readonly`, common attributes

Can Contain

plain text (either that entered by the user, or default text included in document)

May be Contained in

block-level elements, inline elements (except `button`)

Example

```
<form>
  <label for="txtMessage">Send us your feature
    wish-list:</label><br />
  <textarea id="txtMessage">My wish-list for this web site:
  </textarea>
  ...
</form>
```

tfoot

The tfoot element defines the footer content in table data. Despite the name, the tfoot element does not appear at the foot of the table; instead, the tfoot content should appear between the thead and tbody elements. It's applied in this way so that web browsers are given the footer values up front, and potentially can print the footer values at the foot of any page when the table information spans several pages. In practice, very few browsers are able to re-jig the footer information into the logical order, though, so this element is best avoided unless you know for certain that your site's audience uses browsers that support tfoot properly.

Attributes

common attributes

Can Contain

tr elements

May be Contained in

table element only

Example

```
<table summary="Interest Earned">
  <caption>Interest Earned</caption>
  <thead>
    <tr>
      <th>Account Type</th>
      <th>Interest Rate</th>
```

```
      </tr>
    </thead>
    <tfoot>
      <tr>
        <td>Amount Accrued</td>
        <td>$28.30</td>
      </tr>
    </tfoot>
    <tbody>
      <tr>
        <td>Smart</td>
        <td>$16.05</td>
      </tr>
      <tr>
        <td>Young Saver</td>
        <td>$12.25</td>
      </tr>
    </tbody>
</table>
```

th

The th element is a special kind of table cell (td) that defines the table header. It is most often seen at the top of a table column, though it should also be used for row headings.

Attributes

rowspan, colspan, headers, abbr, common attributes

Can Contain

block-level elements, inline elements

May be Contained in

tr element

Example

See the example shown in the definition for table.

thead

The thead element is used to define the section of the data table that relates to heading content, and usually contains one or more table rows consisting mostly of th elements.

Attributes

common attributes

Can Contain

tr elements

May be Contained in

table element

Example

See the advanced table example shown in the definition for table.

title

The title element is one of the document's most important parts for providing meta information to the user. It's the title that appears along the top of the browser window (styled as per the operating system's defaults). The title is not the same as a heading (h1–h6) set in the body of the web page.

Attributes

Can Contain

plain text only

May be Contained in

head element only

Example

```
<!DOCTYPE html PUBLIC "-//W3C//DTD XHTML 1.0 Strict//EN"
    "http://www.w3.org/TR/xhtml1/DTD/xhtml1-strict.dtd">
<html xmlns="http://www.w3.org/1999/xhtml">
<head>
  <title>Hot Air Ballooning in Capadoccia, Central Turkey</title>
  <meta http-equiv="Content-Type"
      content="text/html; charset=utf-8" />
```

tr

The tr element signifies a new row in a data table.

Attributes

common attributes

Can Contain

th, td elements

May be Contained in

table or, in more advanced tables, thead, tfoot, and tbody elements

Example

See the example shown in the definition for table.

ul

The ul element is used to mark up an unordered list. See the entry for li for an explanation and examples of this element's usage.

Type

block-level element

Attributes

common attributes

Can Contain

one or more `li` elements

May be Contained in

block-level elements

var

The `var` element is used primarily by those in computer programming circles, as it represents a variable or an argument (programming terminology).

Type

inline element

Attributes

common attributes

Can Contain

inline elements

May be Contained in

block-level elements, inline elements

Example

```
<p>The doHover JavaScript function accepts two parameters - a
    <var>name</var> and an <var>action</var></p>
```

Index

JPEG image format, 181, 202–203

K
keyword-based settings, 87–88

L
<label> element, 254, 276, 448
languages
   (*see also* scripting languages)
   internationalization and, 419
layers, image editing, 10
layout
   (*see also* positioning)
   use of tables, 226
<legend> element, 251, 267, 270, 450
legibility (*see* readability)
less-than symbol, 38
letter-spacing property, 106
<li> element, 33, 450
limericks, 66
line feeds, 66
linearizing tables, 227, 233
line-breaks, 273
line-height property, 87, 97
<link> element, 77, 362, 451
link exchange, 333
link states, 101, 103, 136
links
   (*see also* < a> element)
   Bubble Under web site pages, 59
   checking, on uploaded pages, 324
   clickable email links, 45
   images as, 180
   removing underlining, 97
   statistics on inward, 385
   style sheets to web pages, 77
   styling as buttons, 172
links pages, blogroll alternative, 394
Linux operating system, 9
list items (*see* <li> element)
List-O-Matic tool, 173

lists, 33, 171
list-style-type property, 171
LiveJournal service, 336
location.href attribute, 365, 367
logos as backgrounds, 212

M
Mac OS X
   browser checks recommended for,
      315
   file properties in, 311
   Firefox and, 9
   forms appearance in, 264
   FTP clients, 321
   Sites folder, 16
   software tools available, 5, 8, 12
margin property, 142, 148, 193
margins, 150, 272
marketing, 330
markup, xviii
   (*see also* CSS; HTML; XHTML)
   commenting out, 37
   comparing with browser views, 31
   examples, xxv, 22, 33, 43
   generated by Response-O-Matic, 290
   image gallery, 204
   indenting, 53, 64
   site navigation, 60
   validation, 326
   viewing source code, 20, 31, 391
maxlength attribute, <input> element,
      255
measurement units, 140, 165
media types, 410, 413
<meta> element, 27, 453
method attribute, <form> element,
      250, 268
mouseless form submission, 262
Movable Type service, 337
MSN Spaces service, 337
multiple checkbox selections, 260

pseudo-classes, CSS, 102

Q

Quickconnect feature, FileZilla, 320
quirks mode, 143
quotation marks, 50, 83
quotations
    <blockquote> element, 63
    <cite> element, 65
    discussion list replies, 410

R

radio buttons, 257, 283
readability
    backgrounds and, 208
    font style and, 80
    line-height and, 87
    markup, 352
referrer statistics, 375, 385
refreshing pages, 83, 308
relative positioning, 161
reserved characters, 36, 38
resizing images, 202
resizing text, 163, 218
resources, 305
    (*see also* SitePoint forums)
    CSS, 406–413
    image libraries, 206–207
    image resizing tutorials, 204
    XHTML, 404–406
Response-O-Matic service, 288
ridge borders, 126
Rollyo search engine, 389
row and column scopes, 245
rowspan attribute, 243, 246
rules, CSS, 74–75
    grouping, 137
    precedence, 99
    specificity, 108
    syntax, 237

S

Safari browser, 6, 265, 286
sans-serif fonts, 80
scope attribute, 244
screen readers, 178
    <em> and <strong> elements, 94
    summary attribute and, 234
    tables and, 227, 232
scripting languages
    advanced forms processing, 299
    client-side scripting, 413–414
    discussion forums, 400
    server-side scripting, 313, 414–416
search engines
    (*see also* Google; Rollyo; Yahoo!)
    <em> and <strong> elements, 94
    submissions to, 331
search tools, 386, 388–389
"Searchrolls", Rollyo, 391
security, 251, 256
<select> element, 259, 279, 462
selectors, CSS, 74–75
    class and id compared, 107
    class selectors, 105
    contextual selectors, 96, 398
    grouping styles, 98
self-closing elements (*see* empty element
    notation)
semicolons
    CSS declaration separator, 71
    entity terminator, 39
serif fonts, 80
servers
    uploading files to, 316–324
    web hosting and, 302
server-side scripting, 313, 414–416
    client-side and, 414
    discussion forums, 400
    languages, 415
SFTP, 343
shorthand properties, 130, 213

TextWrangler editor, 9
\<th\> element, 228, 236, 238, 472
third-party services, 375, 401
thumbnail images, 205
time zones, 377
\<title\> element, 25–26, 56, 473
tools, software, 1–9
top-down formatting, 410
\<tr\> element, 228, 236, 474
transparent images, 182–185
Turkish Shaving Stories, 162, 165, 169
TV listings example, 233
type attribute, \<input\> element, 253–254
typefaces (*see* font-family property, CSS)
typographic conventions, xxv

U

\<u\> element, 94
\<ul\> element, 33, 474
underlining, 90, 94, 97
units of measurement, 140, 165
unordered lists, 33, 474
uploading to the Internet (*see* web hosting)
uppercase, 92
URLs (Uniform Resource Locators), 23
(*see also* web addresses)
web forwarding services and, 307
user interaction, 247
UTF-8 character set, 28, 30

V

validation
CSS hacks and, 412
CSS of uploaded sites, 329
markup of uploaded pages, 326
value attribute, \<input\> element, 255, 258, 262
vertical background repeats, 211

visited links, 104
visitor counts, 375
(*see also* statistical reports)

W

W3C (World Wide Web Consortium), 23
CSS Specification, 408
CSS Validator, 329
Link Checker, 324
Markup Validator, 327, 365, 368
XHTML recommendations, 405
W3Schools, 405, 408, 413–414
WaSP (Web Standards Project), 20
web addresses, 303, 305–306, 363
web browsers (*see* browsers)
Web Design Group, 329
Web Design-L, 409
web development tools (*see* Dreamweaver)
web forwarding, 306–308
web hosting, 301–333
bandwidth allowance, 312
Blogger and, 341
free services, 304
jargon, 303
paid services, 308
server space, 304, 309
uploading files, 316–324
web page editors, 381
web page essentials, 19–39
web page examples (*see* example web sites; markup)
web server software, 313
web standards, xv, 20, 315, 403
weblogs (*see* blogs)
webmail, 312
width property, 120, 278
"wiki" pages, 412

Books for Web Developers from SitePoint

Visit http://www.sitepoint.com/books/
for sample chapters or to order!

BUILD YOUR OWN

STANDARDS
COMPLIANT
WEBSITE
USING
DREAMWEAVER 8

BY **RACHEL ANDREW**

HTML UTOPIA:
DESIGNING WITHOUT TABLES USING CSS

BY RACHEL ANDREW & DAN SHAFER

THE ULTIMATE BEGINNER'S GUIDE TO CSS

THE CSS ANTHOLOGY

101 ESSENTIAL TIPS, TRICKS & HACKS

BY RACHEL ANDREW

THE MOST COMPLETE QUESTION AND ANSWER BOOK ON CSS

DHTML UTOPIA: MODERN WEB DESIGN USING JAVASCRIPT & DOM

BY STUART LANGRIDGE

THE
JAVASCRIPT
ANTHOLOGY

101 ESSENTIAL TIPS, TRICKS & HACKS

BY **JAMES EDWARDS**
& CAMERON ADAMS

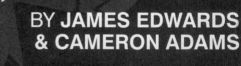

THE MOST COMPLETE QUESTION AND ANSWER BOOK ON JAVASCRIPT